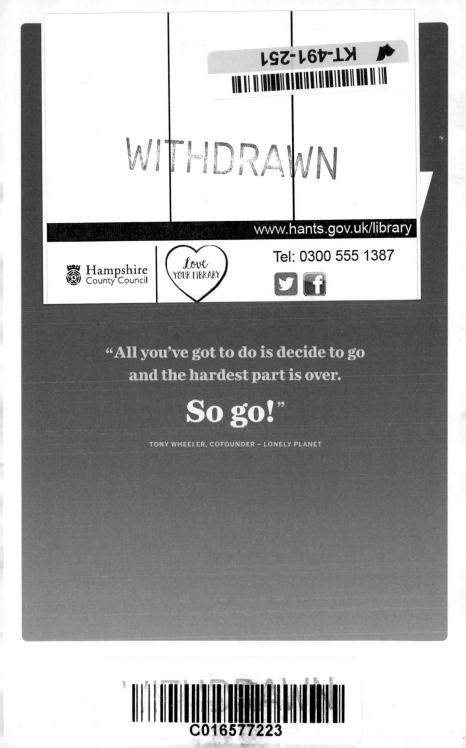

"All you've got to do is decide to go
and the hardest part is over.

So go!"

TONY WHEELER, COFOUNDER – LONELY PLANET

Contents

Plan Your Trip   4

Explore Moscow   54

Understand Moscow   199

Survival Guide   243

Moscow Maps   269

(left) **Cathedral of Christ the Saviour p127** Dancers on Patriarshy footbridge.

(above) **Mayakovskaya station p39** Art deco masterpiece of the Metro.

(right) *Matryoshki* **(nesting dolls)**

Welcome to Moscow

During any season, at any hour of the day, Moscow thrills visitors with its artistry, history and majesty.

Kremlin & Red Square

The very founding site of the city (and arguably, the country), the Kremlin and Red Square are still at the heart of Moscow – historically, geographically and spiritually. Feel the weight of this significance as you wander within the walls of the ancient fortress, marvel at the mind-boggling magnificence of St Basil's Cathedral and pay your respects to the revered leader of a now-defunct state. Moscow will move you. It will tantalise your senses, soothe your spirit and boggle your mind – and it all starts right here at the Kremlin and Red Square.

Communist History

The remains of the Soviet state are scattered all around the city. Monuments remember fallen heroes and victorious battles, while museums attempt to analyse and synthesise the past. See Lenin and Stalin – off their pedestals – at the whimsical Art Muzeon. Step into the socialist-realist fantasy at VDNKh. Descend into the depths of the Soviet system at Bunker-42 Cold War Museum. Ride the museum-like metro and remember the millions who suffered at the Gulag History Museum. Nowadays, retro clubs and cafes give their guests a taste of the Soviet experience. You can even try your hand at Soviet-era arcade games.

Performing Arts

What is more thrilling than watching a ballerina defy gravity, leaping across the stage at the glittering Bolshoi Theatre? Or feeling the force of Tchaikovsky's *1812 Overture,* just a few blocks away from where it premiered more than a century ago? Or oohing and aahing as circus performers soar under the big tent? The classical performing arts in Moscow are still among the best in the world. Nowadays, even the most traditional theatres are experimenting with innovative arrangements, reviving lost favourites and hosting world premieres. Whether you appreciate the classics or prefer the contemporary, the capital's performing arts will impress.

Orthodoxy & Architecture

At nearly every turn in Moscow, you'll see golden domes peeking out over rooftops and hear church bells peeling through the streets, which are dotted with some 600 churches. There are colourful hidden gems, historic fortresses and gargantuan cathedrals. The exteriors are adorned with stone carvings and glittering domes; interiors are packed with ancient icons, swirling incense and faithful worshippers. For more than a millennium, Orthodoxy has helped to define the Russian nation, a significance that is palpable in these atmospheric spiritual places.

Why I Love Moscow

By Mara Vorhees, Writer

Moscow lives and breathes Russian history, from the ancient Kremlin on the city's founding site to the ubiquitous legacy of the Soviet period. Yet the history is not staid: on every visit I witness it unfolding in the here and now. The metro expands in every direction. Old factories and power plants are converted into art centres and nightlife hubs. Bans on imported food inspire an innovative locavore movement. The biggest hotel in the world gives way to a 'wild urbanism' park. Moscow is unstoppable – and it never ceases to inspire me in some unexpected way.

For more about our writers, see p288

Above: St Basil's Cathedral (p76), Red Square

Moscow's
Top 10

Kremlin *(p60)*

1 This ancient fortress is the founding site of Moscow and the ultimate symbol of political power in Russia. Within its ancient walls you can admire the artistry of Russia's greatest icon painters, shed a tear for Russia's great and tragic rulers, peer down the barrel of the gargantuan Tsar Cannon and gawk at the treasure trove that fuelled a revolution. On your way out, admire the bouquets left by newlyweds and scrutinise the perfect synchronicity of the guards at the Tomb of the Unknown Soldier.

⊙ *Kremlin & Kitay Gorod*

Red Square *(p74)*

2 Stepping onto Red Square never ceases to inspire, with the tall towers and imposing walls of the Kremlin, the playful jumble of patterns and colours adorning St Basil's Cathedral, the majestic red bricks of the State History Museum (p78; pictured) and the elaborate edifice of GUM, all encircling a vast stretch of cobblestones. Individually they are impressive, but all together, the ensemble is electrifying. Red Square should be among your first stops in Moscow. Return at night to see the square empty of crowds and the buildings awash in lights.

⊙ *Kremlin & Kitay Gorod*

Ballet at the Bolshoi *(p88)*

3 An evening at the Bolshoi Theatre is the ultimate 'special occasion' in the capital. Ever since its opening in 1856, the neo-classical theatre has offered a magical setting for a spectacle, whether ballet or opera. The main stage still sparkles brightly, with the theatre space draped in rich red velour and glittering with gilded mouldings, but it has also been updated with the latest technologies. The historic theatre is the premier place to see the Bolshoi Ballet – one of the leading ballet companies in the country (and the world).

 Tverskoy

Gorky Park *(p143)*

4 Back in the day, Gorky Park was famous as a setting for a spy novel, but nowadays it is Moscow's hippest, most happening hotspot. From morning (when runners ply the riverside path) to night (when dancers move to sultry music), the hipsters have taken over. In fact, the whole length of the Krymskaya nab – from Red October to Vorobyovy Gory – has been redesigned into a chain of sparkling fountains, sport courts, outdoor art exhibits and summer cafes. From May to September, there's no better place to be.

⊙ *Zamoskvorechie*

Factories Turned Art Centres *(p99)*

5 Nothing exemplifies postindustrial cool such as the art complexes and design centres that have proliferated in the capital's former factories and warehouses. The place that started the trend is Winzavod, (p158; pictured), a former wine-bottling factory that now houses cutting-edge art galleries. Since that initial success, many other factories have followed suit. Flakon (p99) was a crystal production plant, but now it's a centre for design and architecture. A former bread factory, Khlebozavod 9 (p99) bustles with boutiques and trendy cafes. And the list goes on. This is contemporary, creative Moscow at its best.

⊙ *Tverskoy*

Moscow Metro *(p37)*

6 The Moscow metro is at once a history lesson and an art museum (not to mention a pretty efficient form of transportation). Construction started in the 1930s and it continues today. The design of the stations and the direction of the expansion tell a story about Moscow in the 20th and 21st centuries. Even more intriguing is the amazing artwork and architectural design that characterises the stations, many of which are constructed from granite and marble, and are adorned with mosaics, bas-reliefs and other detailing. Belorusskaya station

◉ *Tour of the Metro*

State Tretyakov Gallery *(p141)*

7 The memorable Russian Revival building on Lavrushinsky per is Moscow's largest art museum and the world's premier collection of Russian art, covering the span of Russian art history from ancient icons to avant-garde. (Indeed, the Tretyakov's second building on Krymsky val continues further into the 20th century with supremetism, constructivism and, of course, socialist realism.) The Tretyakov is famed for its impressive collection of wonderful realist paintings by the Peredvizhniki, but the museum also contains show-stopping examples of Russian Revival and art nouveau works.

◉ *Zamoskvorechie*

6

Banya at Sanduny Baths *(p102)*

8 What better way to cope with big-city stress than to have it steamed, sweated, washed and beaten out of you? The *banya* is a uniquely Russian experience that will leave you feeling clean, refreshed and relaxed. In winter, the tension of constant cold is released by the hot, steamy bath, while a beating with birch branches helps to improve circulation. But even in warmer temperatures, the Russian bathhouse experience is refreshing and reinvigorating. Sanduny is Moscow's oldest bathhouse – a luxurious setting in which to indulge in this national pastime.

🏃 *Tverskoy*

Moscow River Boat Tours *(p32)*

9 Avoid traffic jams, feel the breeze on your face and get a new perspective on the city's most famous sights when you see them from one of the ferry boats that ply the Moscow River. The tours provide a wonderful overview of the city, cruising past Novodevichy Convent, Gorky Park, the Cathedral of Christ the Saviour, the Kremlin and Novospassky Monastery. Incidentally, if you purchase a day pass, the ferry can also be a useful form of transport from one sight to another.

🏃 *Guided Tours & Activities*

Russian Cuisine *(p41)*

10 Moscow may not be an obvious choice for culinary travel ('eat up your beets!'). But nowadays, the capital delights visitors with opportunities to sample a rich, diverse and delectable cuisine that's truly come into its own. The temptations are many: old-fashioned *haute-russe* delicacies enjoyed by oligarchs of old; satisfying retro dishes at nostalgic Soviet-themed restaurants, such as fish pie, pictured; and many fresh, modern approaches by innovative chefs emphasising local ingredients. Moscow is also a prime spot to sample the tantalising fare from Central Asia and the Caucasus. *Priatnogo appetita!*

🍴 *Eating*

What's New

Park Zaryadye & Pavilion

Moscow's newest park is so new that it wasn't even open yet at the time of research – except for the pavilion, which gives a glimpse of the park and what will be. Look out for four different microclimates (representing Russia's geographic zones), four museums and (eventually) an outdoor amphitheatre. (p80)

Khlebozavod 9

Once a bread factory, this is now a lively complex of boutiques, cafes and other creative outlets. It's opposite Flakon, making this area the hottest 'converted factory' spot in town. (p99)

Garage Museum of Contemporary Art

Garage is not new, but it does have a new home in the former Vremena Goda restaurant in Gorky Park. The design by Rem Koolhaas preserves the building's mosaics and murals and other dilapidated elements, which serve as a backdrop for the thoroughly modern art on display. (p146)

Museum of Russian Impressionism

This new, private museum showcases a little-known and under-appreciated genre of art, using an impressive collection compiled by a billionaire-turned-art-collector. (p109)

Vladimir I Statue

You can't miss this massive memorial to the founder of the Russian state, just outside Alexander Garden. (p78)

Gulag History Museum

This historical museum has a new location, with nine times more exhibition space, more use of multimedia and expanded research resources. (p92)

Locavore Cuisine

After years of fascination with all things exotic, Muscovites are now discovering the appeal of 'local' when it comes to cooking and eating. Spurred on by a ban on imported foodstuffs, restaurateurs are raising their own cattle, making their own cheese and frequenting the local farmers' markets more than ever before. (p41)

Metro Upgrades

Metro riders are now enjoying free wi-fi and English-language station announcements. The 'I speak English' stickers on the ticket windows were perhaps premature, however. (p245)

Bicycles & Scooters

Muscovites are discovering that bicycles and scooters are an efficient way to get around the city (both are available for rent). And Moscow is gradually becoming a friendlier place for the self-propelled, with wider footpaths and hundreds of kilometres of bike lanes. (p246)

Moscow Central Circle

It's more for commuters than for tourists, but the Moscow Central Circle is a new overground outer ring that circles the city centre. (p245)

For more recommendations and reviews, see **lonelyplanet. com/Moscow**

Need to Know

For more information, see Survival Guide (p243)

Currency
rouble (₽)

Language
Russian

Visas
Required by all; apply at least a month in advance of your trip.

Money
ATMs widely available. Credit cards accepted by most hotels and restaurants.

Mobile Phones
Prepaid SIM cards are readily available. International roaming also works well.

Time
Moscow Time (GMT/UTC plus three hours)

Daily Costs

Budget: Less than ₽1500

➡ Dorm bed: from ₽600

➡ Cheap, filling meal at a cafeteria: less than ₽400

➡ Single ride on the metro: ₽55

➡ Walking tours, parks and churches: free

Midrange: ₽1500–8000

➡ Double room at hostel/mini-hotel: from ₽2500/3500

➡ *Prix-fixe* lunch menu: ₽400–600

➡ Two-course dinner with a glass of wine: ₽800–1000

➡ Museum admission: ₽300–700

Top end: More than ₽8000

➡ Double room at a hotel: from ₽8000

➡ Two-course meal with drinks: from ₽1000

➡ Guided tours: from ₽1500

➡ Travel by taxi: from ₽500

Advance Planning

Two months before Apply for your visa.

One month before Reserve accommodation and tickets for the Bolshoi and other theatres.

One week before Book any guided tours that you intend to take. Purchase online tickets to the Kremlin and the Armoury.

One day before Check the weather forecast to assist with packing. Book a taxi from the airport, if necessary.

Useful Websites

Lonely Planet (www.lonelyplanet.com/moscow) Destination information, hotel bookings, traveller forum and more.

Moscow Times (www.themoscowtimes.com) Leading English-language newspaper in Moscow.

Expat.ru (www.expat.ru) Run by and for English-speaking expats living in Moscow.

Meduza (https://meduza.io) An excellent independent source of news on Russia with an English version.

Calvert Journal (www.calvertjournal.com) A comprehensive site about society, culture and travel in the 'New East', with many Russia-specific articles.

WHEN TO GO

Stand-out seasons to visit are late spring and early autumn. Summer is also pleasant, and long hours of sunlight bring out revellers.

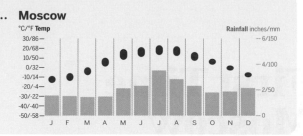

Moscow

Arriving in Moscow

Airports The three main airports (not yet including Zhukovsky; p244) are accessible by the convenient Aeroexpress Train (p244), which takes 35 to 45 minutes from the city centre. If you wish to take a taxi, book an official airport taxi through the dispatcher counter (₽2000 to ₽2500). If you can order a taxi by phone or with a mobile-phone app it will be about 50% cheaper.

Train stations Rail riders will arrive at one of the central train stations. All of the train stations are located in the city centre, with easy access to the metro. Alternatively, most taxi companies offer a fixed rate of ₽400 to ₽600 for a train-station transfer.

For much more on **arrival** see p244

Etiquette

Russians are sticklers for formality. They're also rather superstitious. Follow these tips to avoid faux pas.

➡ **Visiting homes** Shaking hands across the threshold is considered unlucky; wait until you're fully inside. Remove your shoes and coat on entering. Always bring a gift. If you give flowers, make sure they're an odd number – even numbers of blooms are for funerals.

➡ **Religion** Women should cover their heads and bare shoulders when entering a church. In some monasteries and churches it's also required that they wear a skirt – wraps are usually available at the door. Men should remove hats in church and not wear shorts.

➡ **Eating & drinking** Russians eat resting their wrists on the table edge, with fork in left hand and knife in the right. Vodka toasts are common at meals – it's rude to refuse to join in and traditional (and good sense) to eat a little something after each shot.

For much more on **getting around** see p245

Sleeping

Five-star hotels offer fabulous service and amenities, but you will pay for them. Don't expect much value for your money at midrange hotels. Hostels, on the other hand, often offer friendly faces and loads of services for the price of a dorm bed. Advance reservations are highly recommended, especially if you intend to stay at a mini-hotel or hostel, most of which only have a handful of rooms that are often booked out. Weekdays (Sunday to Thursday nights) are especially busy – and more expensive – due to business travellers.

Useful Websites

➡ **Lonely Planet** (www.hotels.lonelyplanet.com) Recommendations and reviews from professional travellers.

➡ **Booking.com** (www.booking.com) Often offers the best deals on rooms, with guest reviews available for reference.

➡ **Moscow Hotels** (www.moscow-hotels.com) Travel agency offering hotel booking, as well as tours, tickets and other information.

For much more on **sleeping** see p188

First Time Moscow

For more information, see Survival Guide (p243)

Checklist

➡ Make sure your passport is valid for at least six months beyond the expiry date of your visa.

➡ Arrange your visa.

➡ Make hotel reservations.

➡ Check airline baggage restrictions.

➡ Check travel advisory websites.

➡ Tell banks and credit-card providers your travel dates.

➡ Organise travel insurance.

➡ Confirm an international plan for your mobile device.

What to Pack

➡ Walking shoes.

➡ Phrasebook or translation app.

➡ A head covering (for women) so you can enter churches respectfully.

➡ Earplugs and eye mask for noisy hotels and bright White Nights.

➡ Supply of painkillers for the morning after.

➡ Sense of humour and a bucketful of patience.

Top Tips for Your Trip

➡ Consider using a specialist travel agency to arrange visas. Be sure to get your visa registered upon arrival if you are staying more than seven days.

➡ Get a local perspective by taking a tour with a Moscow Greeter (p32).

➡ Treat yourself to a stay at a business or luxury hotel at the weekend, when rates drop substantially.

➡ Fixed-prices lunches – common in Moscow – are often a great deal and an ideal way to sample the cuisine at fancier restaurants.

➡ Schedule some time out of the capital at rural or off-the-beaten-track destinations to fully appreciate what is special about Russia.

➡ Avoid driving – or any motorised road transport if possible – as traffic is horrible in and around Moscow.

What to Wear

Muscovites are style mavens. They are not always successful, but most make an effort to look good – not only for the theatre or a posh restaurant, but also for a stroll around town. If you want to go out on the town, plan to 'dress up' – that means dresses and heels for women, collar shirts and leather shoes for men. Sneakers, sandals and jeans are not acceptable. For sightseeing, a comfortable pair of waterproof walking shoes will come in handy, as will an umbrella or rain jacket. In winter, bundle up with several layers and wear a long, windproof coat. Hats and coats are always removed on entering a museum or restaurant and left in the cloakroom.

Bargaining

Prices are fixed in shops; at souvenir markets, such as Izmaylovsky (p161), polite haggling over prices is expected. You'll get 5% off with little effort, but vendors rarely budge past 10%.

Money

➡ Even if prices are listed in US dollars or euros, you will be presented with a final bill in roubles.

➡ ATMs linked to international networks are all over Moscow – look for signs that say bankomat (банкомат).

➡ Credit cards are commonly accepted, but Americans may have some difficulty if they do not have a 'chip and pin' credit card. This is more of a problem at shops than at hotels and restaurants.

Taxes & Refunds

Value-added tax (VAT, in Russian NDS) is 18% (10% for food and children's products). It is usually included in the price listed. Moscow also has a 5% sales tax that is usually only encountered in top hotels.

At the time of research a pilot project was in the process of being set up to allow visitors to recover part of the VAT paid on purchases (other than food) of ₽10,000 or more. The project will involve a limited number of outlets, mainly fashion and luxury brand retailers such as TsUM and the Crocus City Mall.

Tipping

➡ **Guides** Around 10% of their daily rate; a small gift will also be appreciated.

➡ **Hotels** Only in the most luxurious hotels need you tip bellboys etc, and only if service is good.

➡ **Restaurants** Leave small change or 10%, if the service warrants it.

➡ **Taxis** No need to tip as the fare is either agreed to before you get in or metered.

Language

English is becoming more common around Moscow, especially among younger folks. All hotels are likely to have English-speaking staff, while restaurant and museum staff might have more limited skills. In recent years, Moscow has introduced English signs in many metro stations and at major attractions. Most restaurants offer menus in English. Nonetheless, learning Cyrillic and a few key phrases will help you decode street signs, menus and timetables.

 Is this Moscow or local time?
Это московское или местное время?
e·ta ma·skof·ska·ye i·li myes·na·ye vryem·ya

Russia has 11 time zones but the entire country's rail and air networks run on Moscow time. Ask if you're not certain what time zone your transport is running on.

 I live in Moscow, I won't pay that much.
Я живу в Москве, я не буду платить так много.
ya zhih·vu v mask·vye ya nye bu·du pla·tit' tak mno·ga

Taxi drivers and market sellers sometimes try to charge foreigners more, so you may want to bargain in Russian.

 Are you serving?
Вы обслуживаете? vih aps·lu·zhih·va·it·ye

It may be hard to attract the attention of workers in the service industry – if you want to get served, use this polite expression.

 I don't drink alcohol.
Я не пью спиртного.
ya nye pyu spirt·no·va

Refusing a drink from generous locals can be very difficult, so if you're really not in the mood you'll need a firm, clear excuse.

5 **May I have an official receipt, please?**
Дайте мне официальную расписку, пожалуйста.
deyt·ye mnye a·fi·tsi·yal'·nu·yu ras·pis·ku pa·zhal·sta

Russian authorities might expect an unofficial payment to expedite their service, so always ask for an official receipt.

Street Names

We use the transliteration of Russian names of streets and squares to help you when deciphering Cyrillic signs and asking locals the way.

➡ al – alleya (аллея; alley)

➡ bul – bulvar (бульвар; boulevard)

➡ nab – naberezhnaya (набережная; embankment)

➡ per – pereulok (переулок; lane or side street)

➡ pl – ploshchad (площадь; square)

➡ pr – prospekt (проспект; avenue)

➡ sh – shosse (шоссе; highway)

➡ ul – ulitsa (улица; street)

Getting Around

For more information, see Transport (p244)

Metro

The Moscow metro is cheap, efficient, interesting to look at and easy to use. The downside is that it's uncomfortably crowded during peak periods.

Taxi

Well-marked 'official' taxi cabs do not roam the streets looking for fares but you can book a taxi using a mobile phone app or an official agency.

Walking

Distances can be vast, but Moscow is a surprisingly walkable city, especially in the centre. Use the underground crosswalk when crossing busy streets.

Bicycle

Cycling on the streets is dangerous but it's a pleasant way to get around if you stick to the cycling routes along the river and in the city parks. Bikes are available from the bike-share program VeloBike and at various rental stations around town.

Key Phrases

Poezdka (Поездка) Metro ride. When purchasing tickets, ask for 'one ride' (odnu poezdku) or '20 rides' (dvadtsat poezdok) etc.

Vy seychas vykhodite? (Вы сейчас выходите?) Literally 'Are you exiting now?' Used when trying to reach the door to exit the train. (The implication is, 'If not, get out of the way'.)

Perekhod (Переход) Transfer from one line to another.

Vykhod v gorod (Выход в город) Exit to the city.

For much more on the **Russian language** see p253 ➡

How to Book a Taxi

➡ These days, most people use mobile phone apps (such as Yandex.Taxi; p246) to order a cab. This solves the language barrier issue to an extent, given that you know the precise departure and destination address.

➡ If you have the app, try to make sure it's easy to park where you are, otherwise the driver will start calling you and asking questions in Russian.

➡ You can also order an official taxi by phone or book it online, or get a Russian-speaker to do this for you. Normally, the dispatcher will ring you back within a few minutes to provide a description and licence number of the car. Most companies will send a car within 30 minutes of your call.

➡ Some reliable companies offer online scheduling (p246).

TOP TIPS

➡ Moscow traffic can be brutal, especially during peak travel periods. Go metro!

➡ Buy multiride tickets (eg 20 rides) to avoid queuing to purchase tickets every time you ride.

➡ Transfers from one metro line to another require long walks and extra time. Study your metro map before you set out to avoid or minimise changing lines.

➡ If you want to use the Moscow River ferries as transportation, purchase a two-day pass, which allows you to get on and off at any stop along the route.

When to Travel

➡ The metro runs from 5.30am to 1.30am.

➡ On working days (Monday through Friday), street traffic is almost always heavy, and the metro is almost always busy. But during rush hours (8am to 10am, 5pm to 7pm), it's jam-packed.

➡ If you can't avoid travelling during these hours, keep your elbows out and eyes alert. You probably won't encounter any problems, but you will have to queue to ride the escalator and fight for your space on the train.

➡ For more leisurely travel, ride the metro on weekends or during the week after 8pm.

Metro Etiquette

➡ Have your ticket ready before you approach the turnstile.

➡ On the escalator, stand on the right and walk on the left.

➡ When the train pulls up to the platform and the doors open, let riders exit the train before you get on.

➡ Offer your seat to elderly riders, children and pregnant women.

➡ When preparing to exit, position yourself near the door as the train approaches your station. If somebody is in your way, you can ask '*Vy seychas vykhodite?*' (Are you exiting now?) to indicate your intention to get off.

➡ When making transfers between lines, walk on the left side of the *perekhod* (walkway).

Metro Tickets

➡ The Moscow metro is still the capital's best bargain. One ride is ₽55, but you will save time and money if you buy multiride tickets (eg 20 rides for ₽720).

➡ Buy your ticket at the window or at the automated machine.

➡ You will receive a paper card, which you tap on the reader (a circle light) before going through the turnstile.

➡ When you tap your ticket, the reader will turn green to indicate that you should pass. It also displays a number to inform you how many rides you have left.

For much more on **getting around** see p245 ➡

Top Itineraries

Day One

Kremlin & Kitay Gorod (p58)

Arrive at the Kremlin ticket office at 9.30am sharp to reserve your time to enter the **Armoury**. Dedicate your morning to inspecting the ancient icons and gawking at the gold and gems in the Kremlin. Afterwards, stroll through **Alexander Garden** and catch the changing of the guard at the **Tomb of the Unknown Soldier**. Exiting Alexander Garden, jump right into the queue on Red Square for **Lenin's Tomb** before it closes at 1pm.

 Lunch Have lunch at Bosco Cafe (p83) or Stolovaya No 57 (p83).

Kremlin & Kitay Gorod (p58)

Linger over lunch as long as you like, ogling the Kremlin spires and St Basil's domes. If you wish to see the interior of the **cathedral**, you can do so after lunch. Otherwise, stroll through **Kitay Gorod**, discovering the countless **17th-century churches** and checking out **Park Zaryadye**.

Dinner Dine at a restaurant on ul Petrovka, such as Lavka-Lavka (p95).

Tverskoy (p86)

Get tickets in advance to see a show at the world-famous **Bolshoi Theatre**. Afterwards, enjoy a late-evening drink at **3205** in Hermitage Garden.

Day Two

Khamovniki (p118)

A beautiful 17th-century bell tower is the beacon that will guide you to the historic fortress of **Novodevichy Convent**, which contains nearly five centuries of history. After admiring the art and architecture, head next door to the eponymous cemetery, where many famous political and cultural figures are laid to rest.

 Lunch Indulge in a traditional lunch at Golubka (p134) or browse the offerings at Usachevsky Market (p134).

Arbat (p118)

Make your way into the Arbat district for an afternoon of art appreciation. Peruse the collections of the world-famous **Pushkin Museum of Fine Arts**, or investigate one of the smaller niche galleries, such as the whimsical **Burganov House** or the provocative **Multimedia Art Museum**.

Dinner Sample irresistible Russian steaks at Voronezh (p134) or scrumptious Georgian cuisine at Elardzhi (p133).

Arbat (p118)

After dinner you can stroll along Moscow's most famous street – **the Arbat** – enjoying the talents of buskers and the atmosphere of old Moscow. If you prefer a more formal setting for your entertainment, catch a concert at **Rhythm Blues Cafe**.

Day Three

Zamoskvorechie (p139)

 Get an early start to beat the crowds to the **Tretyakov Gallery**. Take your time inspecting the icons, examining the Peredvizhniki, marvelling at the Russian Revival and ogling the avant-garde.

> **Lunch** Grab lunch at Mizandari (p148) at Red October.

Zamoskvorechie (p139)

After lunch, stroll along the **Krymskaya naberezhnaya**, where you can frolic in fountains and explore the outdoor art gallery at **Art Muzeon**. Then head across the street to **Gorky Park** for an afternoon of bicycle riding or boat paddling. Stay into the evening for outdoor cinema, sundowners, and drinking and dancing under the stars.

> **Dinner** Grab a burger at AC/DC in Tbilisi (p148) and wash it down with a cider from Le Boule (p152).

Zamoskvorechie (p139)

It's easy to while away a summer evening in Gorky Park. But if you're up for something more, the former **Red October** factory is now the city's hottest nightlife spot, jam-packed with eating, drinking and entertainment venues. Let yourself wander, stopping here for dessert, there for drinks, and somewhere else for dancing. Explore the galleries. Rock the bar scene. Have fun.

Day Four

Basmanny (p156)

Reserve the morning for shopping at the **Vernisage market**, crammed with souvenir stalls selling everything from silver samovars to Soviet propaganda posters to modern pop-culture *matryoshki* (nesting dolls). The market gets crowded on weekends, so arrive early to beat the crowds and get the best deals.

> **Lunch** Izmaylovsky Market (p161) is famous for its grilled *shashlyk* kebabs).

Basmanny (p156)

On your way back to the centre, make a stop at **Flakon** and **Khlebozavod No 9** or **Winzavod** and nearby **ArtPlay** to see what's happening in Moscow's former industrial spaces. These contemporary art centres now undertake a different kind of production – art, fashion and design. See what Moscow's most creative minds are up to, and perhaps take home a really unique souvenir.

> **Dinner** Reserve your table for a *haute-russe* feast at Cafe Pushkin (p111).

Presnya (p103)

Dinner at the Cafe Pushkin is a multicourse medley of old-fashioned Russian cuisine (accompanied by plenty of vodka shots). If you're still standing afterwards, head to **Jagger** for sunset drinks and dancing the night away.

If You Like...

Architecture

Ascension Church at Kolomenskoe The first building with a tent roof on a brick structure, creating a uniquely Russian style. (p150)

Zaryadye Pavilion An award-winning design that offers a glimpse into the future. (p80)

Hotel Metropol An art nouveau masterpiece, replete with mosaics, stained glass and wrought iron. (p191)

VDNKh Exuberant fountains and socialist-realist architecture galore. (p93)

Narkomfin (p107) and **Melnikov House** (p129) Two quintessential examples of Constructivist architecture.

Ryabushinsky Mansion Shekhtel's whimsical fusion of Russian Revival and art nouveau. (p106)

Church of the Trinity in Nikitniki An exquisite example of Russian baroque, concealed by hulking grey edifices. (p81)

Ostankino TV Tower Still one of the tallest free-standing structures in the world. (p93)

Contemporary History

Garage Museum of Contemporary Art An exciting contemporary-art venue housed in a revamped restaurant at Gorky Park. (p146)

Winzavod A former wine-bottling facility, now containing Moscow's

OLEGDOROSHIN / SHUTTERSTOCK ©

VDNKh (p93)

most prestigious art galleries. (p158)

Multimedia Art Museum
Excellent photography and other multimedia exhibits. (p130)

Art4.ru A private collection of contemporary art that grew into a gallery and museum. (p105)

Red October A former chocolate factory, now home to bars, cafes and a handful of galleries. (p145)

Moscow Museum of Modern Art An eclectic collection of works by artists from the 20th and 21st centuries. (p89)

Soviet History

Lenin's Mausoleum Pay your respects to the founder of the Soviet state. (p75)

Art Muzeon Soviet heroes put out to pasture. (p145)

Bunker-42 Cold War Museum A secret underground Cold War communications centre now open for exploration. (p161)

Moscow metro A monument to socialism and populism. (p37)

VDNKh Aka the USSR Economic Achievements Exhibition. (p93)

Gulag History Museum A memorial to the victims of the harsh Soviet justice system. (p92)

Charming Churches

Ul Varvarka in Kitay Gorod A tiny street lined with 17th-century churches. (p80)

Upper St Peter Monastery Home of the lovely Cathedral of Metropolitan Pyotr. (p90)

Church of the Lesser Ascension A 17th-century beauty with whitewashed walls and carved detailing. (p105)

Church of the Nativity of the Virgin in Putinki An elaborate concoction of tent roofs and onion domes. (p90)

Church of St Nicholas in Khamovniki Colourful church of the weavers' guild, which was also the home church of Leo Tolstoy. (p132)

Church of St John the Warrior An 18th-century example of Moscow baroque. (p146)

Church of the Intercession at Fili A memorial church of mysterious origins, as all records were destroyed in a fire. (p232)

Iconography

Tretyakov Gallery The world's best collection of icons, including the revered *Holy Trinity* by Andrei Rublyov. (p141)

Annunciation Cathedral Iconostasis featuring work by Andrei Rublyov, Theophanes the Greek and Prokhor of Gorodets. (p70)

Museum of the Russian Icon Thousands of examples from the private collection of a ussian businessman. (p161)

Rublyov Museum of Early Russian Culture & Art A small museum on the grounds of the monastery where Rublyov was a monk. (p162)

Parks & Gardens

Gorky Park Moscow's most famous green space, now an ideal spot for riverside strolls and bike rides. (p143)

For more top Moscow spots, see the following:
➡ Eating (p41)
➡ Drinking & Nightlife (p45)
➡ Entertainment (p48)
➡ Shopping (p52)

Zaryadye Pavilion With park coming soon! (p80)

Alexander Garden A flower-filled space just outside the Kremlin walls. (p72)

Hermitage Gardens Summer cafes and outdoor theatres dot this inner-city oasis. (p90)

Aptekarsky Ogorod An urban botanical garden with floral species from three different climate zones. (p159)

Vorobyovy Gory Nature Preserve The wooded hillocks overlooking a picturesque bend in the Moscow River. (p132)

Russian Literature

Tolstoy Estate-Museum The Moscow residence of Russia's greatest realist novelist. (p132)

Mikhail Bulgakov Museum Long an underground pilgrimage site; now a cool cafe and literary hang-out. (p107)

Gogol House The abode where Gogol spent his final tortured months. (p105)

Pushkin House-Museum A short-term residence for the national bard and his new bride. (p128)

Month By Month

January

Though January represents the deepest, darkest days of winter, it is a festive month, kicked off by New Year's celebrations in the grandest tradition.

🎆 Winter Festival

An outdoor fun-fest for two weeks in December and January for those with antifreeze in their veins. Admire the ice sculptures on Red Square, stand in a crowd of snowmen on ul Arbat and ride the troika at Izmailovsky Park.

🎆 Winter Holidays

Locals ring in the New Year with friends, with a city-wide celebration on Red Square. For the faithful, all-night church services take place on Christmas (7 January), while the Epiphany (mid-January) is marked with a plunge into icy water at designated spots around town.

February

Maslenitsa marks the end of winter, but it seems premature. Temperatures are cold, hovering around -10°C for weeks. The city still sparkles with snow, and sledders and skiers are in heaven.

🍴 Maslenitsa

This fete kicks off Orthodox Lent. Besides bingeing on bliny (crepes), the week-long festival features horse-drawn sledges and storytelling clowns. The festival culminates with the burning of an effigy to welcome spring.

March

The spring thaw starts at the end of March, when everything turns to mud and slush. It is Moscow's dreariest month: tourists tend to stay away.

🎆 International Women's Day

Russia's favourite holiday was founded on 8 March to honour the women's movement. On this day men buy champagne, flowers and chocolates for their better halves – and for all the women in their lives.

April

The days are blustery but spring is in the air. Moscow residents flock to sights and museums during this season, since there are not too many tourists.

☆ Golden Mask Festival

The Golden Mask Festival (www.goldenmask.ru) involves two months of performances by Russia's premier drama, opera, dance and musical performers, culminating in a prestigious awards ceremony in April.

May

Spring arrives! Many places have limited hours during the first half of May, due to the public holidays. Nonetheless, flowers are blooming and people are celebrating.

🎆 May Holidays

From May Day (1 May) to Victory Day (9 May), the first half of the month is a nonstop holiday. The city hosts parades on Red Square, as well as fireworks and other events at Park Pobedy.

☆ Chekhov International Theatre Festival

In odd-numbered years, theatre troupes descend on Moscow from all corners of the world for this renowned biannual festival (www.chekhovfest.ru). Drama and musical theatre performances are held at participating venues around town, from mid-May to mid-June.

June

June is the most welcoming month. Temperatures are mild and days long. Markets are filled with wild berries, and girls wear white bows in their hair to celebrate the school year's end.

☆ Moscow International Film Festival

This week-long event (www.moscowfilmfestival.ru) attracts filmmakers from the US and Europe, as well as the most promising Russian artists. Films are shown at theatres around the city.

☕ White Nights

Moscow does not have an official White Nights festival, but the capital still enjoys some 18 hours of daylight in June. Revellers stay out late to stroll in the parks and drink at the many summer terraces and beer gardens.

☆ Outdoor Concerts

June kicks off the summer concert season, which takes place mostly outdoors. Popular events include the Ahmad Tea Music Festival (www.ahmadteafest.ru) at Art Muzeon and the Bosco Fresh Fest (www.boscofreshfest.com) at Tsaritsyno.

July

Many Muscovites retreat to their *dachas* (summer country houses) to escape summer in the city. The weather is hot and humid. Hotel prices are down.

☆ Outdoor Concerts

Though many theatres are closed, the concert calendar is packed. Outdoor music festivals include Park Live (www.parklive.pro) at a local sports stadium, Afisha Picnic (www.picnic.afisha.ru) at Kolomenskoe and Usadba Jazz Festival (www.usadba-jazz.ru) at Arkhangelskoe.

August

The capital is quiet in August, as locals are still at their *dachas* and the cultural calendar is sparse.

☆ Spasskaya Tower Military Music Festival

At the end of August, the capital hosts the Spasskaya Tower Military Music Festival (www.kremlin-military-tattoo.ru). It's a week of military music, equestrian parades, pomp and circumstance in the lead-up to City Day.

September

Early autumn is a standout time to be in the capital. The heat subsides and the foliage brightens the city with splendid oranges, reds and yellows.

☆ City Day

Den goroda – City Day – celebrates Moscow's birthday on the first weekend in September. The day kicks off with a festive parade, followed by live music on Red Square and plenty of food, fireworks and fun.

October

The mild weather and colourful foliage continue in October, though this month usually sees the first snow of the season.

◉ Moscow Biennale of Contemporary Art

This month-long festival (www.moscowbiennale.ru), held in odd-numbered years (and sometimes in different months), aims to establish the capital as an international centre for contemporary art. Venues across the city exhibit works by artists from around the world.

December

Short days and long nights keep people inside for much of the month. But many bundle up to admire Moscow sparkling in the snow and partake of one of the city's premier cultural events.

☆ December Nights Festival

One of Moscow's most prestigious music events, this annual festival (www.arts-museum.ru) is hosted by the Pushkin Museum of Fine Arts, with a month of performances by musicians and accompanying art exhibits.

With Kids

Filled with icons and onion domes, the Russian capital might not seem like an appealing destination for kids, but you'd be surprised. In Moscow, little people will find museums, parks, theatres and even restaurants that cater especially to them.

Kid-Friendly Museums

Most sights and museums offer reduced-rate tickets for children up to 12 or 18 years of age. Kids younger than five are often free of charge. Look out for family tickets.

Art Museums

The Pushkin Museum of Fine Arts (p123) and the Museum of Decorative & Folk Art (p92) both have educational centres that allow kids aged five to 13 years to create their own art. Garage Museum of Contemporary Art (p146) also has programs for kids.

Moscow Planetarium

The planetarium (p106) has interactive exhibits that allow kids to perform science experiments, taste freeze-dried space food and run around on the surface of the moon.

Central Museum of the Armed Forces

You might not let your children play with guns, but how about tanks, trucks and missiles at this museum (p92)?

Experimentanium

A place (p94) for children to discover for themselves the answer to the endless 'Why?'

Museum of Soviet Arcade Machines

Find out what it was like to be a kid in the Soviet Union (p89).

VDNKh

This Soviet relic (p93) contains countless kid-friendly exhibits, including special sites dedicated to sea creatures, space travel and robots.

MARIAKRAYNOVA / SHUTTERSTOCK ©

Moscow Planetarium (p106)

Outdoor Fun

Even in winter, there are plenty of chances to get outside for fresh air and exercise.

Parks

With more than 100 parks and gardens, Moscow has plenty of space for kids to let off steam – many parks include playgrounds. Larger spaces such as Gorky Park (p143) and Vorobyovy Gory Nature Preserve (p132) rent bicycles, paddle boats and such. The new Park Zaryadye (p82) will have plenty of interactive exhibits to capture kids' attention.

River Cruises

Most little ones love a boat ride (p33). It's the perfect way for kids to see the historic sights, as there's no need to fight the crowds or linger too long in one place.

Moscow Zoo

Even toddlers will get a kick out of the Moscow Zoo (p109), with close-up encounters with their favourite animals.

Eating Out

Many restaurants host 'children's parties' on Saturday and Sunday afternoons, offering toys, games, entertainment and supervision for kids while their parents eat.

Cafeterias

Self-service places such as Grably (p151) are family favourites, as children can see and choose what looks good to them. The dessert selection is also a draw.

Pizza

Pizza guarantees good reception, but several outlets of Akademiya (p135) also offer children's programming on weekends.

NEED TO KNOW

The metro might be fun for young ones, but be careful during rush hour, when trains and platforms are packed. Both Lingo Taxi (p246) and Detskoe Taxi (p246) will look out for your children, offering smoke-free cars and child seats upon request.

Play Areas

Restaurants such as Anderson for Pop (p113) and Professor Puf (p134) have dedicated play areas for children. At Elardzhi (p133), kids frolic in the courtyard with playground and petting zoo.

Children's Theatre

Little ones have never had such a range of entertainment choices.

Musical Theatre

Local legend Natalya Sats founded the Moscow Children's Musical Theatre (p137) to entertain and educate kids with song and dance.

Puppet Theatre

Kids will see hundreds of puppets at the Obraztsov Puppet Museum (p101), then see them come to life at the attached theatre.

Animal Theatre

Kuklachev's cats (p136) and Durov's animals (p102) put on a good show for kids of all ages.

Circus

The acrobatics will astound and amaze, while clowns and animal tricks will leave them laughing. Choose between two acclaimed circuses: Bolshoi Circus on Vernadskogo (p136) and Nikulin Circus on Tsvetnoy Bulvar (p101).

For Free

The good news is that Moscow is no longer the most expensive city in the world; the bad news is that it's still pretty darn close. However, budget-minded travellers can find a few bargains if they know where to look.

Art Centres

Most of Moscow's postindustrial art centres – such as Winzavod (p158) – are free to enter (though you may pay for individual galleries or special exhibits). Spend an afternoon browsing the galleries and admiring the architectural repurposing.

Churches

Many of Moscow's churches contain amazing iconography and eye-popping frescoes. The Cathedral of Christ the Saviour (p127) in particular feels more like a museum than a church. By the way, some churches are museums, such as St Basil's Cathedral, which is not free.

Estates

At Kolomenskoe Museum-Reserve (p150) and Tsaritsyno Palace (p147) you pay to enter the museums, but seeing the beautiful grounds and churches costs nothing.

Lenin's Tomb

Don't pay money, just pay your respects at Lenin's Mausoleum (p75). This is one of Moscow's most wacky and wonderful (and free) things to do.

Moscow Metro

So it's not quite free. But it only costs ₽55 to ride the metro, which is an amazing amalgamation of art museum, history lesson and mass-transit system (p37).

EFESENKO / SHUTTERSTOCK ©

Christmas toys, Izmaylovsky Market (p161)

Free Museums

All state museums are free on the third Sunday of the month. Some private museums are always free:

Art4.ru

Part gallery and part museum (p105), this private museum offers a chance to check out some contemporary Russian art for free (unless you choose to buy something).

Museum of the Russian Icon

This is the private collection (p161) of a Russian businessman, who has put it on display – for free – in hopes of reigniting interest in this under-appreciated art form.

Sakharov Centre

Free political and artistic exhibits, as well as information about the life and times of the dissident (p160).

Free Tours

Moscow Free Tour

This highly rated outfit (p32) offers a free daily walking tour, led by knowledge-able and extremely enthusiastic guides.

Moscow Greeter

Volunteer 'greeters' (p32) – local residents – show visitors their favourite places in the city. Donations accepted.

Parks

Maybe it's no surprise that a park does not charge an admission fee: the surprise is what you'll find inside. Gorky Park (p143) has an open-air cinema and an observatory, both of which are free of charge. Hermitage Gardens (p90) has yoga classes and dance lessons – all free. Zaryadye Pavilion (p80) was also free during the construction of the park, although that may change once the park is open.

VDNKh

Replete with fountains and socialist-realist splendour, this vast complex (p93) is a curious vestige of communist paradise gone awry. Capitalism has taken hold here, but it's still free to enter.

Izmaylovsky Market

Perhaps it goes without saying that you don't have to pay to shop, but this souvenir market (p161) is still a fun, practically free way to spend a day.

Wi-Fi

At hotels, restaurants and cafes all over Moscow, wi-fi is almost always free. There's also free wi-fi on the metro and at hotspots around the city.

Visas

Save for a handful of exceptions, everyone needs a visa to visit Russia. Arranging one is straightforward but time-consuming, bureaucratic and sometimes costly. Start the application process at least a month before your trip.

Tourists in front of St Basil's Cathedral (p76), Red Square

Types of Visas

For most travellers a tourist visa (single- or double-entry, valid for a maximum of 30 days) will be sufficient. If you plan to stay longer than a month, you can apply for a business visa or – if you are a US citizen – a three-year multi-entry visa.

Tourist Visa

These are the most straightforward Russian visas available, but they are also the most inflexible. They allow a stay of up to 30 days in the country, with one or two entries within that time period. It is not possible to extend a tourist visa. In addition to the standard documents required for all Russian visas, you'll need a voucher issued by the hotel or travel agency that provided your invitation.

Note that Russian consulates also reserve the right to see your return ticket or some other proof of onward travel, but this is rarely requested.

Business Visa

Available for three months, six months or one year (or three years in the US), and as single-entry, double-entry or multiple-entry visas, business visas are valid for up to 90 days of travel within any 180-day period. You don't actually need to be on business to apply for these visas. In fact, they're great for independent tourists with longer travel itineraries and flexible schedules. But you must have a letter of invitation from a registered Russian company or organisation (available from specialist visa agencies) and a covering letter stating the purpose of your trip. Some applicants are also asked to provide proof of sufficient funds to cover their visit.

Transit Visa

For transit by air, a transit visa is usually valid for up to three days. For a nonstop Trans-Siberian Railway journey, it's valid for 10 days, giving westbound passengers a few days in Moscow; those heading east, however, are not allowed to linger in Moscow.

Note that transit visas for train journeys are tricky to secure and are usually exactly the same price as a single-entry tourist visa (in the UK £70 for either, plus a service charge of £38.40).

ANDREY ARUSHA / SHUTTERSTOCK ©

Application Process

Invitation

To obtain a visa, everyone needs an invitation, also known as 'visa support'. Hotels and hostels will usually issue anyone staying with them an invitation voucher for free or for a small fee (typically around €20 to €40). If you are not staying in a hotel or hostel, you will need to buy an invitation – this can be done through most travel agents or via specialist visa agencies. Prices may vary depending on how quickly you need your invitation.

Application

Invitation voucher in hand, you can then apply for a visa. Wherever in the world you are applying you can start by entering details in the online form of the Consular Department of the Russian Ministry of Foreign Affairs (https://visa.kdmid.ru/PetitionChoice.aspx). Keep a note of the unique identity number provided for your submitted form – if you have to make changes later, you will need this to access it without having to fill the form in from scratch again.

Russian embassies in many countries, including the UK, US, France and Germany, have contracted separate agencies to process the submission of visa applications and check everything is in order; these companies use online interfaces that direct the relevant information into the standard visa application form:

➡ **VFS.Global** (http://ru.vfsglobal.co.uk) Offices in London and Edinburgh.

➡ **Invisa Logistic Services** (http://ils-usa.com) Offices in Washington, DC, New York, San Francisco, Houston and Seattle.

Consular offices apply different fees and slightly different application rules country by country. Avoid potential hassles by checking well in advance what these rules might be. The charge for the visa will depend on the type of visa applied for and how quickly you need it.

Registration

Every visitor to Russia is obligated to have their visa registered within seven business days of arrival. If you are in Moscow for less than seven business days, you are exempt. If you leave Moscow, you must register again in any city where you stay seven days or longer. The obligation to register is with the accommodating party – your hotel or hostel, or landlord, friend or family if you're staying in a private residence.

When you check in at a hotel or hostel, you surrender your passport and visa so the hotel can register you with the local visa office. You'll get your documents back the next day. If you are staying in a homestay or rental apartment, your landlord can register your visa through the local post office. But this is a big hassle that most landlords don't care to undertake. An easier alternative is to get registered through the agency that issued your invitation (though you'll probably pay an extra fee).

It is unlikely but possible that police officers may request to see your proof of registration, so keep all documentation and transportation tickets. This is perhaps more of a concern for those who are travelling extensively outside of Moscow. In any case, you will not have to show proof of registration upon departure.

Visa Extensions

Any extensions or changes to your visa will be handled by Russia's Federal Migration Service (Federalnoy Migratsionnoy Slyzhby), often shortened to FMS. It's possible you'll hear the old acronyms PVU and OVIR used for this office.

Extensions are time consuming and difficult; tourist visas can't be extended at all. Avoid the need for an extension by arranging a longer visa than you might need. Note that many trains out of St Petersburg and Moscow to Eastern Europe cross the border after midnight, so make sure your visa is valid up to and including this day.

NEED TO KNOW

➡ **Passport** Valid for at least six months beyond your return date.

➡ **Photos** One or two passport-sized photos.

➡ **Completed application form** Allow some time for this: it's a doozy.

➡ **Handling fee** Usually in the form of a money order; amount varies.

➡ **Visa-support letter** Provided by hotel, travel agent or online service.

Guided Tours & Activities

Moscow is a big, overwhelming city with a strange alphabet. Letting the locals show you around is a good way to get your bearings and learn something new. It also gives you a chance to chat with a real, live Muscovite and perhaps make a friend.

Radisson boat cruise on Moscow River

PELIKH ALEXEY / SHUTTERSTOCK ©

Walking Tours

Moscow Free Tour

These enthusiastic **guides** (☎495-222 3466; www.moscowfreetour.com; Nikolskaya ul 4/5; guided walk free, paid tours from €31) offer an informative, inspired 2½-hour guided walk around Red Square and Kitay Gorod daily – and it's completely free. It's so good that (they think) you'll sign up for one of their excellent paid tours, covering the Kremlin, the Arbat and the metro, or thematic tours such as communist Moscow.

Moscow Greeter

Let a local **volunteer** (www.moscowgreeter.ru) **FREE** show you what they love about their city! Every tour is different, as the volunteer decides (perhaps with your input) where to go. Donations are accepted, but the tour is entirely free.

Moscow 360

Paul is a private **guide** (☎8-985-447 8688; www.moscow360.org; tours per group from ₽2000) who offers excellent and entertaining walking tours in the centre, including the standards like a metro tour and a communist history tour. His speciality, however, is the AK-47 tour, which takes you to a shooting range to learn all about the infamous AK weapons and take a few shots yourself.

Moscow ArchiGeek

These architectural **tours** (Москва Глазами Инженера; ☎499-322 2325; www.archigeek.ru; tours from ₽1200) around Moscow hit some unusual destinations indeed (such as the modernist Chaika swimming pool or the clock tower of Kievsky vokzal). Most are in Russian, but there are English-language tours to VDNKh, Narkomfin and St Basil's Cathedral.

Moscow Mania

This team of historians (with PhDs) are passionate about their city and their subject. They have designed 50-plus **tours** (www.mosmania.com; 2hr walk from ₽3500) on specialised topics – or they will customise one for you. Private tours for up to eight people.

Patriarshy Dom Tours

Provides a changing schedule of specialised **tours** (☑495-795 0927; www.toursinrussia.com; Moscow School No 1239, Vspolny per 6; Moscow tours from US$22, day trips from US$65; Ⓜ Barrikadnaya) of local museums, specific neighbourhoods and unusual themes, as well as out-of-town trips to the Golden Ring towns and other day-trip destinations. Occasionally takes groups inside the Great Kremlin Palace, which is otherwise closed to the public. Pick up the monthly schedule at upscale hotels or view it online.

Bicycle Tours

Cover more ground and see more sights, while getting fresh air and a bit of exercise: that's a win-win-win!

Moscow Bike Tours

On these recommended bike **tours** (☑8-916-970 1419; www.moscowbiketours.com; 2½hr tour US$40-60), you'll enjoy magnificent views of Moscow from Krymskaya embankment, riding through Gorky Park and all the way down to Sparrow Hills, before crossing into Khamovniki. Day and evening rides offered, with an extended tour available on weekends.

Kruty Pedaly

This bike rental **company** (Круты Педали; www.kruti-pedali.ru; Bldg 1, Universitetsky pr 6; per hr/day from ₽150/600; ☉open 1-11.30pm Mon-Fri, 11am-11.30pm Sat & Sun; Ⓜ Universitet) offers weekly tours (in Russian), seeing sights from the Kremlin to Novodevichy in about 3½ hours.

Boat Tours

Two boat-tour companies offer a few different routes, usually from Kievsky vokzal (or the Radisson Royal) in Dorogomilovo to Novospassky Monastery in Taganka, or some variation on that. Highlights of the trip are Novodevichy Convent, MGU, Gorky Park, the Cathedral of Christ the Saviour and the Kremlin.

Capital Shipping Co

Originally, these **ferries** (ССК, Столичная Судоходная Компания; ☑495-225 6070; www.cck-ship.ru; adult/child 60min cruise ₽900/700, 2-day pass ₽2400/2000) were simply a form of transport, but visitors realised that riding the entire route was a great way to see the city, and CCK eventually developed fixed routes with higher prices. Nowadays, ferries ply the Moscow River from May to September; board at one of six docks for a cruise ranging from one to two hours. Alternatively, buy a two-day pass, which allows you to get on and off at will.

Radisson River Cruises

The Radisson operates big **river boats** (www.radisson-cruise.ru; adult/child from ₽750/550; Ⓜ Kievskaya) that cart 140 people up and down the Moscow River from the dock in front of the hotel and from the dock in Gorky Park. In summer, there are five or six daily departures from each location. Boats are enclosed (and equipped with ice cutters), so the cruises run year-round, albeit less frequently in winter.

Bus Tours

Hop On Hop Off

This colourful **bus** (www.hoponhopoff.ru; adult/child ₽1300/900; ☉10am-5pm) circulates around the city centre, following one of two routes, with 18 to 25 designated stops on each. As the name implies, you can hop on and off wherever you want within a one-day period. Buses are supposed to run every 20 to 40 minutes, but Moscow's horrible traffic means that this is very unreliable.

NEED TO KNOW

➡ **Getting Around** Heavy traffic in Moscow means that travelling by car or bus can be an excruciating experience. Keep this in mind when choosing your tour.

➡ **Reservations** Most tours need advance booking, even the free ones.

➡ **Tipping** Tipping your guide (₽300 to ₽500) is an accepted (but not expected) practice. Small gifts from home are also appropriate and appreciated.

Travelling to St Petersburg

Travel between Moscow and St Petersburg has never been easier. If you plan to include the second capital in your itinerary, you're sure to find a transportation option to fit your mood and budget.

Train

All trains to St Petersburg depart from Leningradsky vokzal (p245). Book your tickets at any train station or through your hotel. Alternatively, buy tickets online at the official site of the Russian railroad (www.rzd.ru).

Overnight

There are about a dozen overnight trains travelling between Moscow and St Petersburg. Most depart between 10pm and 1am, arriving the following morning between 6am and 8am. On the more comfortable *firmeny* trains, a 1st-class *lyuks* ticket (two-person cabin) costs ₽5500 to ₽7000, while a 2nd-class *kupe* (four-person cabin) is ₽3000 to ₽4000.

Sample departure times and fares:

➡ **2 Krasnaya Strela** 1st/2nd class ₽7000/3600, eight hours, 11.55pm

➡ **4 Ekspress** 1st/2nd class ₽5300/3400, nine hours, 11.30pm

➡ **20 Megapolis** 1st/2nd class ₽6300/3800, 8½ hours, 12.20am

➡ **54 Grand Express** 1st/2nd class ₽6600/3840, nine hours, 11.40pm

Sapsan

These high-speed trains travel at speeds of 200km/h to reach their destination in about four hours or less. Trains depart throughout the day. Comfortable seats are ₽3500 to ₽4500.

Sample departure times:

➡ **752 Sapsan** 5.40am

➡ **754 Sapsan** 7.40am

➡ **766 Sapsan** 1.30pm

➡ **774 Sapsan** 5.30pm

➡ **778 Sapsan** 7.30pm

Air

All airlines fly into **Pulkovo International Airport** (LED; ☑812-337 3822; www.pulkovo airport.ru; Pulkovskoye sh) in St Petersburg (75 to 90 minutes). Book flights through the airline websites in advance and you can get tickets as cheap as ₽2500 one way, although normally prices are between ₽3500 and ₽5900.

Aeroflot (www.aeroflot.ru) Flies out of Sheremetyevo (p244) more than a dozen times a day.

Rossiya Airlines (www.rossiya-airlines.com) Based in St Petersburg, this airline flies out of Vnukovo (p244) eight to 10 times a day.

S7 Airlines (www.s7.ru) This Siberian airline offers 10 daily flights out of Domodedovo (p244) to St Petersburg.

Boat

There are numerous cruise boats plying the routes between Moscow and St Petersburg, most stopping at Uglich, Yaroslavl, Goritsky Monastery, Kizhi and Mondrogy (near Lake Ladoga). Ships are similar in quality and size, carrying about 250 passengers.

Mosturflot (www.mosturflot.ru) Cruises from seven to 10 days.

Orthodox Cruise Company (www.cruise.ru) The *Anton Chekhov* spends 11 days cruising between the cities.

Rechturflot (www.rtflot.ru, in Russian) Ships spend 12 to 14 days going to St Petersburg and back.

Vodohod (www.bestrussiancruises.com) This 12-day cruise departs three times a month, in summer.

IMAGE COURTESY OF THE JEWISH MUSEUM & CENTRE OF TOLERANCE ©

Jewish Museum & Centre of Tolerance (p90)

◉ Museums & Galleries

Moscow's rich history and dynamic culture are highlights of this cosmopolitan capital, as showcased by the ever-expanding array of museums and galleries. Once a cornerstone of conservatism, these venues are now experimenting with new technologies and subject matter, in an attempt to entertain and educate.

Museums

Moscow is packed with museums. History museums remember every era of Russia's past; countless country estates are now architectural museums; military museums commemorate the nation's wartime heroics; and anybody who was anybody has a 'house-museum' in their honour. There are two space museums, two Jewish museums, a chocolate museum and a video-game museum. Whatever you're into, Moscow has a museum for you.

Galleries

Moscow is home to two world-class art museums: the State Tretyakov Gallery (p141), exhibiting Russian art, and the Pushkin Museum of Fine Arts (p123), a showcase mainly for European art. They are both spectacular venues – well worth a day (or more) to admire their wide-ranging collections. In addition to these standard bearers, the capital contains countless smaller niche galleries dedicated to particular artists or genres.

NEED TO KNOW

Opening Hours

Most museums are open from about 10am to 6pm, though hours often fluctuate from day to day. Be aware that most museums are completely closed at least one day a week – often Monday. Look for late evening hours on at least one day a week (usually Thursday).

Sanitary Day

Many museums close for cleaning one day per month, usually during the last week of the month.

Admission Prices

Many museums still maintain a dual pricing system, whereby foreign visitors must pay a higher admission fee than Russian residents. Even student prices are often reserved for students of local universities, though this is not a uniform practice so it's worth enquiring.

Lonely Planet's Top Choices

Armoury (p72) Russia's storehouse of priceless treasures and historic artefacts.

State Tretyakov Gallery (p141) The crème de la crème of Russian art, from ancient icons to exquisite modernism.

Jewish Museum & Centre of Tolerance (p90) Genii and outcasts, dissidents and revolutionaries – the history of Jews in Russia at a glance.

Garage Museum of Contemporary Art (p146) Moscow's most cutting-edge museum.

Best History Museums

Moscow Kremlin (p60) Recounting nearly 1000 years of history, starting from the founding of Moscow.

Bunker-42 Cold War Museum (p161) Descend to the underground – literally – to see this secret Cold War bunker.

Gulag History Museum (p92) Stalin's slaughterhouse – the history of one of the world's cruellest prison systems.

Jewish Museum & Centre of Tolerance (p90) Explores a history that was long overlooked.

State History Museum (p78) A massive collection covering Russian history from the Stone Age to Soviets.

Best Art Galleries

State Tretyakov Gallery (p141) First stop for art lovers: the world's premier venue for Russian art.

19th & 20th Century Art Gallery (p124) The Pushkin's collection of Impressionist and post-Impressionist paintings is unparalleled.

New Tretyakov Gallery (p146) All of the 20th century: socialist realism versus avant-garde and nonconformist art.

Museum of Russian Impressionism (p109) A new museum to educate and inform about a specific genre.

Best Offbeat Museums

Museum of Soviet Arcade Machines (p89) Arcade games as history lesson and sociological study.

Zaryadye Pavilion (p80) Decode the QR-coded exhibits, or just admire the unusual decor.

Lumiere Brothers Photography Centre (p145) A favourite for photographers.

Glinka Museum of Musical Culture (p92) An amazing collection of musical instruments from through the years and around the world.

Moscow Design Museum (www.moscowdesignmuseum. ru) Catch an exhibit in the big, bold, black-and-white bus (or at some other venue around town).

Best Literary Museums

Mikhail Bulgakov Museum (p107) The censored writer's former flat offers a calendar of lively cultural events.

Tolstoy Estate-Museum (p132) See where Russia's most celebrated novelist lived and worked.

Ryabushinsky Mansion (p106) This architectural landmark was also the home of Soviet writer Maxim Gorky.

Gogol House (p105) Gaze into the fireplace where Gogol famously tossed his *Dead Souls* manuscript.

Best Contemporary Art

Garage Museum of Contemporary Art (p146) Unusual, thought-provoking art in a ruined restaurant in Gorky Park.

Moscow Museum of Modern Art (p89) Hosts compelling rotating exhibits, especially at the branch outlets.

Winzavod (p158) A former wine-bottling facility now filled with art.

Multimedia Art Museum (p130) Rotating exhibits featuring photography and all manner of media.

Komsomolskaya station (p38)

Tour of the Metro

Every day, as many as seven million people ride the Moscow metro. What's more, this transport system marries function and form: many of the stations are marble-faced, frescoed, gilded works of art. Take this tour for an overview of Moscow's most interesting and impressive metro stations.

Komsomolskaya

At Komsomolskaya, the red line 1 (Sokolnicheskaya liniya) intersects with line 5, also known as the Ring line (Koltsevaya liniya). Both stations are named for the youth workers who helped with early construction. In the line 1 station, look for the Komsomol emblem at the top of the limestone pillars and the majolica-tile panel showing the volunteers hard at work. The Ring-line station has a huge stuccoed hall, the ceiling featuring mosaics of past Russian military heroes.

From Komsomolskaya, proceed anticlockwise around the Ring line, getting off at each stop along the way.

Prospekt Mira

Originally named for the nearby MGU Botanical Garden, Prospekt Mira features elegant, white-porcelain depictions of

Tour of the Metro

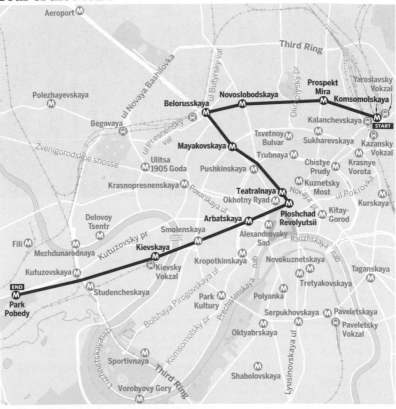

figures planting trees, bringing in the harvest and generally living in harmony.

Novoslobodskaya

Thirty-two stained-glass panels envelop this station in art nouveau artistry. Six windows depict the so-called intellectual professions: architect, geographer, agronomist, engineer, artist and musician. At one end of the central hall is the mosaic *Peace in the Whole World*. The pair of white doves was a later addition to the mosaic, replacing a portrait of Stalin.

Belorusskaya

The ceiling mosaics celebrate the culture, economy and history of Russia's neighbour to the west. The 12 ceiling panels illustrate different aspects of their culture, while the floor pattern reproduces traditional Belarusian ornamentation.

Switch here to line 2 (the green Zamoskvoretskaya line), where the Belarusian theme continues, and travel south.

Mayakovskaya

This is the pièce de résistance of the Moscow metro. The grand-prize winner at the 1938 World's Fair in New York has an art deco central hall that's all pink rhodonite, with slender, steel columns. The inspiring, upward-looking mosaics on the ceiling depict *24 Hours in the Land of the Soviets*. This is also one of the deepest stations (33m), which allowed it to serve as an air-raid shelter during WWII.

Teatralnaya

This station was formerly called Ploshchad Sverdlova in honour of Lenin's right-hand man (whose bust was in the hall). Nonetheless, the station's decor follows a theatrical theme. The porcelain figures represent seven of the Soviet republics by wearing national dress and playing musical instruments from their homeland.

Change here to Ploshchad Revolyutsii station on line 3 (the dark blue Arbatsko-Pokrovskaya line).

Kievskaya station (p40)

HISTORY OF THE MOSCOW METRO

When Stalin announced plans for *Metrostroy* (construction of the metro) in the 1930s, loyal communists turned out in droves to lend a hand. Thousands of people toiled around the clock in dire conditions, using pickaxes and spades and hand-pulled trolleys. Some 10,000 members of the Moscow Komsomol (Soviet youth league) contributed their time to building the communist dream.

The first metro line opened on 16 May 1935 at 7am. Thousands of people spent the night at the doors of the station so they might ride the first train on the red line (between Park Kultury in the south and Sokolniki in the north). Two additional lines opened in 1938.

Construction continued during the Great Patriotic War, with the opening of two additional lines. Several stations actually served as air-raid shelters during the Siege of Moscow in 1941. The Ring line (Koltsevaya line) opened in the early 1950s.

Khrushchev's tastes were not as extravagant as Stalin's, so later stations employ a uniform, utilitarian design. But the metro continued to expand, and still continues today (as does Moscow itself).

Ploshchad Revolyutsii

This dramatic station is basically an underground sculpture gallery. The life-sized bronze statues represent the roles played by the people during the revolution and in the 'new world' that comes after. Heading up the escalators, the themes are: revolution, industry, agriculture, hunting, education, sport and child rearing. Touch the nose of the border guard's dog for good luck on exams. Take line 3 heading west.

Arbatskaya

This shallow station was damaged by a German bomb in 1941. The station was closed (supposedly permanently) and a parallel line was built much deeper. Service was restored on this shallow line in the following decade, which explains the existence of two Arbatskaya stations (and two Smolenskaya stations, for that matter) on two different lines.

At 250m, Arbatskaya is one of the longest stations. A braided moulding emphasises the arched ceiling, while red marble and detailed ornamentation give the whole station a baroque atmosphere.

Kievskaya

This elegant white-marble hall is adorned with a Kyivan-style ornamental frieze, while the frescoed panels depict farmers in folk costume, giant vegetables and other aspects of the idyllic Ukrainian existence. The fresco at the end of the hall celebrates 300 years of Russian–Ukrainian cooperation. Ironic.

Park Pobedy

This newer station opened after the complex at Poklonnaya Gora, which commemorated the 50th anniversary of the victory in the Great Patriotic War. It is the deepest Moscow metro station, and it has the longest escalators in the world. The enamel panels at either end of the hall (created by Zurab Tsereteli) depict the victories of 1812 and 1945.

From here you can return to the centre by retracing your ride on line three.

ARKONT / GETTY IMAGES ©

Shchi (traditional cabbage soup)

Eating

In recent years Moscow has blossomed into a culinary capital. Foodies will be thrilled by the dining options, from old-fashioned haute-russe to contemporary 'author cuisine'. The ban on imported foodstuffs means that chefs are finding innovative ways to utilise local ingredients, rediscovering ancient cooking techniques and inventing new ones in the process. And Moscow diners are eating it up. Literally.

Local Specialities

Russian cuisine is strongly influenced by climate and class. Long winters and short growing seasons mean the cuisine is dependent on root vegetables such as potatoes and beets. Fresh produce has always been a rarity, so vegetables are often served pickled; fruit is frequently served in the form of compote. According to an old Russian proverb, *'shchi* (cabbage soup) and *kasha* (porridge) is our nourishment'. This saying emphasises the important role played by soups and grains in sustaining generations of peasants through cold, dark winters.

BREAKFAST

Russians rarely skip breakfast, or *zavtruk*. Russian cuisine includes half a dozen kinds of *kasha*, or porridge, including buckwheat, millet, oat and semolina. Bliny are thin, crepe-like pancakes with sweet or savoury fillings. At the very least, you'll get bread *(khleb)* with butter and jam, alongside your tea.

APPETISERS & SALADS

Whether as the preamble to a meal, or something to snack on between vodka shots, *zakuski* (appetisers) are an important part of Russian cuisine. Back in the day, a good host always had a spread of *zakuski* on the table to welcome unexpected guests.

NEED TO KNOW

Opening Hours

Many eateries are open noon to midnight daily, sometimes with later hours on Friday and Saturday.

Price Ranges

Price ranges refer to a main course.

€   less than ₽500

€€   ₽500–1000

€€€ more than ₽1000

Business Lunch

Discounts of up to 25% are sometimes available for dining before 4pm. Many places also offer a fixed-price 'business lunch' during this time, which is a great time to sample some of the pricier restaurants around town.

Reservations

Most of the top-end restaurants require booking in advance for dinner, as well as for lunch or brunch on weekends.

Tipping

The standard for tipping in Moscow is 10%, while a slightly smaller percentage is acceptable at more casual restaurants. The service charge is occasionally included in the bill, in which case an additional tip isn't necessary. If you pay by credit card, you will not have an opportunity to add the tip onto the charge, so leave the tip in cash.

Useful Websites

➡ **Moscow Times** (https://themoscow times.com/places) Reviews for hundreds of restaurants in the capital.

➡ **Menu.ru** (www.menu.ru) Listings (in Russian) of menus, maps and other logistical info for hundreds of restaurants, bars and clubs.

ost famously, *ikra* (caviar) is the snack of tsars and New Russians. The best caviar is black caviar, from *osetra* or beluga sturgeon. Due to overfishing, sturgeon populations have declined drastically in recent years, driving up prices and threatening the fish with extinction. The much cheaper and saltier option is red salmon caviar. Russians spread it on buttered bread and wash it down with a slug of vodka or a toast of champagne.

Most traditional menus offer a multitude of salads, many with names that will leave you scratching your head. The universal favourite is *salat olivye* (Olivier salad), which is chopped chicken or ham, mixed with potatoes, eggs, peas and mayonnaise. Another classic is *seld pod shuby,* or 'herring in a fur coat' – a colourful conglomeration of herring, beets and potatoes.

SOUPS

Soups are perhaps the pinnacle of Russian cooking, with both hot and cold varieties turning up on menus and in local kitchens. The most famous is borsch, or beetroot soup, but other favourites include *solyanka,* a meat broth with salty vegetables and a hint of lemon, and *okroshka,* a cold soup made from *kvas* (fermented rye-bread water).

Soups are served as the first course of a Russian meal. As such, they often appear on the menu under the heading *Pervaya,* or 'first'.

MAIN COURSES

Traditional Russian main courses are usually heavy, meat-based dishes. Fried cutlets *(kotlet)* and grilled kebabs (shashlyk) are popular preparations that often show up on the menu, listed under *Glavnaya* (main) or *Vtoraya* (second). Especially satisfying in winter, look for *zharkoye* (hot pot), an appropriately named meat stew served piping hot in a single-serving ceramic pot.

Pelmeni (dumplings) are the ultimate Russian comfort food. Traditionally from Siberia but now served everywhere, these bite-size dumplings are usually stuffed with pork or beef, then topped with sour cream. Variations such as salmon or mushroom *pelmeni* are also on the menus of modern Moscow restaurants.

Moscow Trends

FOREIGN CUISINES

A decade ago, Moscow was mad for sushi. You'll still see it on many menus, but the raw-fish craze is finally starting to tap out. What is not going anywhere is the more general interest in international flavours. When you tire of beetroot soup and beef stroganoff, you'll be able to find excellent French, Italian and American restaurants, not to mention Chinese, Lebanese, Thai, Turkish and more.

Also popular – and perhaps more interesting for visitors to Moscow – are the rich cuisines from former Soviet republics of Central Asia and the Caucasus. The capital is littered with restaurants representing

GEORGIAN CUISINE

In *The Georgian Feast*, writer Darra Goldstein describes the former Soviet republic of Georgia as 'a land blessed by Heaven's table scraps', and Moscow is the best place outside the Caucasus to sample this rich, spicy cuisine at one of the scores of Georgian restaurants in the capital, across all price ranges.

Georgian cooking shows glimpses of Mediterranean and Middle Eastern flavours, but the differences are what make this cuisine so delectable. Most meat and vegetable dishes use ground walnuts or walnut oil as an integral ingredient, yielding a distinctive, nutty flavour. Also characteristic is the spice mixture *khmeli-suneli*, which combines coriander, garlic, chillies and pepper with a saffron substitute made from dried marigold petals.

Georgian chefs love to prepare food over an open flame, and grilled meats are among the tastiest items on any Georgian menu. Herbs such as coriander, dill and parsley are often served fresh, with no preparation or sauce, as a palate-cleansing counterpoint to rich dishes. Grapes and pomegranates show up not only as desserts, but also as tart complements to roasted meats. The most beloved item on the Georgian menu is undoubtedly *khachapuri*, a rich, cheesy bread that is made with circles of fresh dough cooked with sour, salty *suluguni* cheese. Sometimes it is topped with a raw egg in the crater.

the best of Armenian, Azeri, Georgian and Uzbek cuisines – usually with natives manning the kitchen.

CREATIVE CUISINE

Nowadays, the most exciting trend in Moscow cuisine is the emergence of *avtorskaya kukhnya,* or 'author cuisine'. As the name implies, young chefs are creating their own brands of cooking, incorporating the best of local and international elements. Seasonal menus highlight local ingredients – a trend that has become more urgent and more creative since the sanctions have been levied on imported food products. Still, cooking techniques, food preparations and flavours are adapted from all over the world, resulting in menus that are innovative, unique – and delightfully delicious.

This fresh take on cooking is on full display at the annual Omnivore Festival (www.omnivoremoscow.ru), which is held over several days in March or April, with master classes, taste testing, eating and drinking, culminating with a giant dinner party.

VEGETARIANS

The culinary revolution has opened up some new options for vegetarians and vegans. Most restaurants now offer at least one vegetarian choice. Additionally, there is no shortage of Indian and Italian restaurants offering meat-free options. During the 40 days before Orthodox Easter (Пасха in Russian), many restaurants offer a Lenten menu that is happily animal-free.

Cook Like a Local

If you love Russian food, you can learn to make it yourself. **Taste of Russia** (📞8-929-694 3797; www.tasterussia.ru; bldg 4, Kazarmenny per 3; 3hr course ₽3500, market tour ₽1500; Ⓜ Kurskaya) offers courses in English, as well as market tours, wine tastings and special children's classes. Cooking courses take place in the evening, when you prepare the meal, then eat it together.

Eating By Neighbourhood

➡ **Kremlin & Kitay Gorod** (p83) There are a few restaurants inside GUM, with more options at the northeastern end of Nikolskaya ul.

➡ **Tverskoy** (p94) Dozens of restaurants along Tverskaya ul and ul Petrovka, as well as the smaller side streets, especially inside the Boulevard Ring.

➡ **Presnya** (p109) The area around Patriarch's Ponds is a dining hub, as is Bolshaya Nikitskaya ul.

➡ **Arbat & Khamovniki** (p133) Excellent eating options around ul Arbat, ul Volkhonka and ul Lva Tolstogo.

➡ **Zamoskvorechie** (p148) Red October is a dining hotspot, but there are also loads of restaurants between Tretyakovskaya and Kovokuznetskaya metros.

➡ **Meshchansky & Basmanny** (p163) Ul Maroseyka and ul Pokrovka are lined with eateries.

Lonely Planet's Top Choices

Delicatessen (p95) Eat, drink and chat at Moscow's smartest and friendliest gastropub.

Café Pushkin (p111) Moscow's long-standing favourite for traditional Russian food delights in an aristocratic mansion.

Khachapuri (p110) A casual, contemporary place for the eponymous Georgian speciality.

Kitayskaya Gramota (p163) A very serious take on Cantonese cooking in a playful, ironic environment.

Lavka-Lavka (p95) Delicacies straight from local farms cooked by a creative chef.

Twins (p110) Two contrasting perspectives create a singular dining experience.

Best By Budget

€

Varenichnaya No 1 (p133) A friendly, family place for dumplings and other old-fashioned Russian cooking.

Dukhan Chito-Ra (p164) Possibly the best *khinkali* (dumplings) this side of the Caucasus range.

Zupperia (p94) Casual lunchtime eatery run by a celebrity chef; it's just about soup.

Stolle (p112) A friendly cafe serving fresh-baked pies with your favourite fillings.

€€

Elardzhi (p133) Delicious Georgian cuisine in a delightful courtyard.

AQ Kitchen (p113) An Argentinian chef shows off Mediterranean flavours at this Moscow kitchen.

Khachapuri (p110) Georgian favourites in a casual but cosmopolitan setting.

Twins (p110) Simple, local and delicious – all at an affordable price.

€€€

Café Pushkin (p111) Still the best splurge in Moscow.

Voronezh (p134) A carnivore's delight, featuring Russian beef.

Brasserie Most (p97) A luxury gastro tour from Bretagne to Alsace and down to Corsica.

Nedalny Vostok (p111) A taste of the Near East.

Pinch (p111) A delightfully trendy stop for small plates.

Best By Neighbourhood

Ryby Net (p83) A butcher, a burger joint and a steakhouse (but no fish!).

Delicatessen (p95) A hidden spot that's worth finding for modern foodies.

Café Pushkin (p111) Offers a wonderfully extravagant Russian dining experience.

Elardzhi (p133) A tasty and tasteful place to indulge in a Georgian feast.

Mizandari (p148) Classy but congenial setting for Georgian fare.

Kitayskaya Gramota (p163) Outstanding Cantonese fare in an opulent setting.

Best By Cuisine

Russian

Café Pushkin (p111) Dine in *haute-russe* style, just like the aristocrats of old.

Chemodan (p134) Get a taste of the wilds of Siberia.

Twins (p110) Sample the brothers' *new* Russian cuisine.

Caucasian

Khachapuri (p110) Refreshingly affordable, but still delicious Georgian fare.

Elardzhi (p133) Traditional Georgian fare, served in a comfortable but cool courtyard setting.

Darbazi (p166) This Georgian place goes beyond the standards.

Levon's Highland Cuisine (p164) Armenia's answer to street food.

Mizandari (p148) A classy, inexpensive place in Red October.

Ukrainian

Odessa-Mama (p165) Comfortable, casual and delicious Ukrainian fare.

Shinok (p113) Delicious dining on a Ukrainian farm.

Vegetarian

Fresh (p96) Not only fresh, but diverse, nutritious and delicious.

Receptor (p110) Fresh, healthy and veg-heavy choices.

Bardeli (p151) A hip spot for Indian delights.

Scramble (p110) Eggs, waffles and other veg-friendly breakfast items.

Best Chefs

Delicatessen (p95) Ivan Shishkin can claim responsibility for the capital's first food-centric gastropub.

Lavka-Lavka (p95) Boris Akimov launched the farm-to-table movement in Moscow.

Twins (p110) Sergey and Ivan Berezutskiy will woo you with their cooperative take on Russian cooking.

Uilliam's (p111) Chef Uilliam Lamberti's flagship restaurant, where he 'cooks from the heart'.

Drinking alfresco

Drinking & Nightlife

Back in the day, the local pub was the ryumochnaya, *which comes from the word* ryumka, *or 'shot'. This was a grim place, serving up 100g, but nothing else. Moscow's drinking possibilities have expanded exponentially (although there are still a few old-school* ryumochnye *around). Now, drinkers can choose from wine bars, whisky bars, cocktail bars, sports bars, microbreweries and more.*

What to Drink

VODKA

The word 'vodka' is the diminutive of the Russian word for water, *voda*, so it means something like 'a wee drop'. Most often vodka is tipped down in swift shots, often followed by a pickle. In recent years, drinking cocktails has become more fashionable, meaning that women at least can get away with mixing their vodka.

BEER

Many visitors to Moscow are surprised to learn that *pivo* (beer) is the city's most popular alcoholic drink. The market leader is Baltika, which makes no fewer than 12 excellent brews. Craft beer has also become popular in recent years, and there's no shortage of microbreweries and speciality beer bars offering a fine selection.

SPARKLING WINE

Russians traditionally drink sparkling wine, or *Sovietskoe shampanskoe*, to toast special occasions and to sip during intermission at the theatre. It tends to be sickeningly sweet: look for the label that says *sukhoe* (dry), or at least *polsukhoe* (semidry). Nowadays, the capital has a few classy wine bars, where Muscovites drink fine vintages, mostly from Europe.

NEED TO KNOW

Opening Hours

Most bars and pubs are open from noon to midnight. Some hotspots stay open for drinking until 5am or 6am, especially on Friday and Saturday nights.

How Much?

Prices for alcohol vary widely, depending on where you are drinking. Expect to pay anywhere from ₽200 to ₽600 for a pint of beer or for 50g of vodka. At upscale clubs, cocktails can cost ₽500 and up.

How to Get Past Face Control

➡ Dress sharp. No shorts, sneakers or sportswear.

➡ Smile. Show the bouncer that you are going to enhance the atmosphere inside.

➡ Book a table (sometimes requires a table deposit).

➡ Speak English. Foreigners are not as special as they used to be, but they're still sort of special.

KVAS

Kvas is a mildly alcoholic, fermented, rye-bread water. Cool, refreshing and slightly sweet, it is a popular summer drink that tastes something like ginger beer. In the olden days it was dispensed on the street from big, wheeled tanks. Nowadays, the kegs are smaller, but they still set up in parks and outside metro stations to serve thirsty passers-by. This cool, tasty treat is also sometimes served in restaurants.

Where to Drink

Drinking is a favourite national pastime in Russia, and modern Moscow offers venues for every occasion, mood and season. Former factories have been converted into nightclubs; leafy courtyards contain beer gardens; and communal apartments now serve as cosy cafes. Pedestrian streets such as ul Arbat and Kamergersky per are hotspots for strollers and drinkers. The former Red October chocolate factory in Zamoskvorechie is packed with diverse drinking establishments.

SUMMER CAFES

Summer doesn't last very long in Moscow, so locals know they need to take advantage of the warm weather. That's why every restaurant worth going to opens a *letnoe kafe,* or summer cafe. They take over the courtyard, or the footpath, or the rooftop – because people want to be outside.

NIGHTCLUBS

In recent years, Moscow nightclubs became notorious for their fast pace and over-the-top excesses. Each new wild club outdid the last with glitz and glamour. Several outlandish clubs are still alive and well. To ensure the clientele enhances the atmosphere, many such clubs still exercise 'face control', allowing in only select patrons.

Fortunately for the rest of us, the night scene has changed dramatically, becoming more 'democratic' and more laid-back. Nowadays, there's a slew of less discriminating clubs that also have great music and cool vibes. It's still recommended to dress sharp and look cool though.

Most clubs start hopping after midnight and keep going until dawn.

PUB CRAWLS

Solo traveller looking for drinking buddies? Freaked out by face control? An organised pub crawl is a guaranteed way to meet fine folks from around the world, get into some cool clubs and discover Moscow's nightlife. The **City Pub Crawl** (www.citypubcrawl.ru; ₽1500) includes four clubs, four drinks and one band of very merry Moscow travellers. Dancing on the bar is also included.

Drinking & Nightlife By Neighbourhood

➡ **Kremlin & Kitay Gorod** (p84) It's not exactly a nightlife hotspot but there are a few places to drink on Nikolskaya ul.

➡ **Tverskoy** (p98) No shortage of pubs and cafes all around these districts, especially inside the Garden Ring and near Flakon.

➡ **Presnya** (p113) The neighbourhood is peppered with bars and clubs, with pockets of extreme cool around Patriarch's Ponds and Tryokhgornaya Manufaktura.

➡ **Arbat & Khamovniki** (p135) There are drinking establishments clustered along ul Arbat and Novy Arbat.

➡ **Zamoskvorechie** (p152) This neighobourhood is packed with cafes and clubs and pubs, especially between Tretyakovskaya and Novokuznetskaya metro stations.

➡ **Meshchansky & Basmanny** (p166) Ul Maroseyka is buzzing after dark.

Lonely Planet's Top Choices

Enthusiast (p98) A hidden bar disguised as a scooter repair shop.

32.05 (p98) An extensive and innovative bar menu, served in a delightful garden setting.

Noor (p98) A little hippie, a little hipster, totally cool.

Time-Out Rooftop Bar (p115) Cool cocktails and fabulous views.

Jagger (p115) A hot club in the Tryokhgornaya Manufaktura complex.

Best By Drink

Beer

Zoo Beer & Grill (p115) A great selection of beers with some animal accompaniment.

Jawsspot Msk (p84) A Yekaterinburg favourite with views of Lubyanskaya pl.

Kolkovna (p84) Cosy basement quarters to drink Czech pilsner.

Wine

Dom 12 (p136) Warm up with a glass of vino in these cosy surrounds.

32.05 (p98) The garden setting is begging for a glass of Bordeaux.

Jean-Jacques (p111) Moscow's original wine bar now has outlets all over town.

Cocktails

Time-Out Rooftop Bar (p115) Speciality cocktails for every hour of the day.

Delicatessen (p95) The 'pub' part of this gastropub mixes a killer cocktail.

Bar Klava (p114) An understated but unrivalled place for cocktails and whisky.

Coffee

OMG! Coffee (p167) An encyclopaedia of coffee brewing in one long menu.

Coffee Bean (p166) It was the first coffee chain in Moscow – it's still one of the best.

Art Lebedev Cafe Studio (p113) An art-filled nook for stylish coffee drinkers.

Conversation (p115) This Brooklyn-style coffee place encourages lingering.

Best Summer Cafes

Le Boule (p152) Proof that alcohol and sports are compatible – cider and pétanque at Gorky Park.

32.05 (p98) A perfectly lovely place in the Hermitage Gardens.

Zhurfak Cafe (p135) The shady garden is a lovely place for a drink.

Cafe Mart (p98) A top spot for drinks in the open air.

Best for LGBTIQ

Secret (p167) Against the political odds, people keep sharing the Secret.

Propaganda (p168) Long-running and much-loved gay disco on Sunday night.

Best for Dancing

Gipsy (p152) Modern nomads' gathering on the roof of a former chocolate factory.

Disco Rooms (p115) Dance to the hits from the 1970s and 1980s.

Mandarin Combustible (p84) Drinking and dancing all night long.

Best for Watching Sport

Zhiguli Beer Hall (p136) Locally brewed beer and big-screen sports – amen.

Underdog (p152) Everybody wins at this craft beer bar.

Radio City (p115) A huge place with dozens of TVs – one of which is sure to show your team.

Performance at the Tchaikovsky Concert Hall (p116)

☆ Entertainment

Moscow's performing arts are a major drawcard: classical ballet, music and theatre are at the heart of Russian culture. For so long, that's all there was. Happily, times have changed, as directors, conductors and choreographers unleash their creative spirits. If your heart's set on Tchaikovsky, you won't be disappointed, but if you're yearning for something experimental, you'll find that too.

Performing Arts

The classical performing arts are one of Moscow's biggest attractions. Highly acclaimed, professional artists stage productions in elegant theatres around the city, most of which have been recently revamped and look marvellous.

OPERA & BALLET

Nobody has ever complained about a shortage of Russian classics at the opera and ballet. Take your pick from Tchaikovsky, Prokofiev, Rimsky-Korsakov or one of the other great Russian composers, and you are guaranteed to find them on the playbill at one of the major theatres. The choreography and staging of these classics is usually pretty traditional (some might even say uninventive), but then again, that's why they're classics. If you tire of the traditional, keep your eye out for more modern productions and premieres that are also staged by some local companies.

The largest opera and ballet company in the city – and the most celebrated – is the Bolshoi (p88). The repertoire of this world-famous company is mostly classical, with choreography in the style of Balanchine and Petipa. In recent years, the Bolshoi has premiered many new works.

A sort of rival to the Bolshoi is the Stanislavsky & Nemirovich-Danchenko Musical Theatre (p101), which is approaching its centennial in 2019. In addition to its classical repertoire, this prominent company has staged ground-breaking ballets and avant-garde operas in recent years.

There is a slew of younger opera and ballet companies around the city. For experimental, contemporary fare, check out the ground-breaking New Ballet (p168), performing in a small theatre in Basmanny.

CLASSICAL MUSIC

It's not unusual to see highly talented musicians working the crowds inside the metro stations, often violinists single-handedly performing Vivaldi's *Four Seasons* and flautists whistling away at Mozart or Bach. While it's possible to hear a good show in the metro station, a visit to one of the local orchestra halls is highly recommended.

Founded in 1922, the city's oldest and most prestigious symphony orchestra is Moscow Philharmonic Society, which performs at the Tchaikovsky Concert Hall (p116), as well as the Great Hall of the Moscow Conservatory. Giving hundreds of concerts a year, the orchestra is still the standard bearer for orchestral music in the capital, if not the country.

Across town at the International House of Music (p154), the National Philharmonic of Russia was the country's first private symphony orchestra when it was founded in 1990. Also around that time, the feisty Levine sisters founded the Moscow Symphony Orchestra (MSO), an upstart assemblage that still operates on a relatively small budget, under the direction of the young Vladimir Ziva. The MSO performs at the Moscow Tchaikovsky Conservatory (p116).

CONTEMPORARY MUSIC

Live bands and DJs travel from other parts of Russia and all over Europe to perform in Moscow's many clubs and theatres. Summer is an especially busy concert season, with several big outdoor music festivals. Check the schedules of local clubs or look for signs advertising the biggest names.

THEATRE

Due to the language barrier, drama and comedy are less alluring prospects for

non-Russian speakers than are music and dance. Nonetheless, Moscow has a long theatre tradition, which remains vibrant today. The capital has around 40 professional theatres and countless amateur theatres, staging a wide range of plays.

Recognising the lack of options for non-Russian speakers, English actor Jonathan Bex founded the Moscow English Theatre (MET; p116), which performs contemporary American and British plays for English-speaking audiences. The MET performs at the Mayakovsky Theatre.

CIRCUS

The circus has long been a favourite form of entertainment for Russians young and old. There are two highly lauded, permanent circuses in Moscow, putting on glittering shows for Muscovites of all ages. Near the centre of town, Tsvetnoy bul has been the site of the Moscow circus since 1880. This so-called 'Old' Circus – now named Nikulin Circus (p101) for the famous clown Yury Nikulin – had always set the standard by which all other circuses were measured. Until 1971, that is, when the new Bolshoi Circus on Vernadskogo (p136) was built. This state-of-the-art facility was bigger and better, with five replaceable arenas (water, ice, equestrian etc) and room for 3500 spectators.

NEED TO KNOW

Tickets

Nowadays, most theatres sell tickets online. Or, you can do it the old-fashioned way and buy tickets directly from the theatre box office or from a *teatralnaya kassa* (theatre kiosk), several of which are scattered about the city.

Prices

The classical performing arts remain an incredible bargain in Moscow, especially if you go anywhere other than the Bolshoi Theatre. Tickets start at around ₽500, with prices for the best seats ranging from ₽1500 to ₽4000. Happily, Moscow venues do not charge higher prices for foreigners.

Theatre Seasons

Unfortunately for summer visitors, many venues are closed between late June and early September.

SUMMER MUSIC FESTIVALS

Some of the best things about summer in Moscow:

➜ **Afisha Picnic** (www.picnic.afisha.ru) Indie-rock at Kolomenskoe (p150).

➜ **Ahmad Tea Music Festival** (www.ahmadteafest.ru) Alt-rock festival at Art Muzeon (p145).

➜ **Bosco Fresh Fest** (www.boscofreshfest.com) Mostly Russian bands at Tsaritsyno (p147).

➜ **Park Live** (www.parklive.pro) Modern-rock big names at CSKA Arena.

➜ **Usadba Jazz Festival** (www.usadba-jazz.ru) Jazz at Arkhangelskoe.

The shows performed by both companies feature acrobatics and animals, as well as dance, cabaret and clowns. The displays of daring-do are truly amazing, especially the aerial arts. Only the Nikulin Circus features big cats in its performances, but both venues have monkeys, bears and sea lions. The animals are apparently not mistreated – though their very involvement in the show might make you cringe.

Spectator Sports

Russia's international reputation in sport is well founded, with athletes earning international fame and glory for their success in ice hockey, gymnastics and figure skating.

FOOTBALL

The most popular spectator sport in Russia is football (soccer), and five Moscow teams play in Russia's premier league (Vysshaya Liga). Currently, football is enjoying a boom, with several state-of-the-art stadiums recently built for the World Cup in 2018.

Moscow's most successful team is FC Spartak (www.spartak.com). The team's nickname is Myaso, or 'Meat', because it was sponsored by the collective farm association during the Soviet era. Nowadays, Spartak plays at the new Spartak Stadium (also known as Otkrytie Arena; p116), north of the centre near Tushino Airfield.

Meanwhile, their rivals, FC Dynamo (www.fcdynamo.ru), will soon be playing at the new ultramodern VTB Arena.

Additionally, six-time winner Central Sports Club of the Army (CSKA; www.pfc-cska.com) plays at CSKA Arena, part of the CSKA Stadiums complex. Two-time winner FC Lokomotiv (www.fclm.ru) plays at the eponymous stadium east of the centre.

ICE HOCKEY

Moscow's main entrant in the Continental Hockey League (KHL) is HC CSKA (www.cska-hockey.ru), or the Red Army team. HC CSKA has won more Soviet championships and European cups than any other team in history. They play at the CSKA Ice Palace, which is part of the CSKA Stadiums complex.

BASKETBALL

Men's basketball has dropped in popularity since its days of Olympic glory in the 1980s, but Moscow's top basketball team, CSKA (www.cskabasket.com), still does well in the European league. They play at USH CSKA, which is part of the CSKA Stadiums complex.

Banya

Nothing beats winter like the *banya*. Less hot but more humid than a sauna, the Russian bath sweats out all impurity.

Enter the steam room *(parilka)* naked (yes, the *banya* is normally segregated by gender). Bathers can control the temperature – or at least increase it – by ladling water onto the hot rocks. You might add a few drops of eucalyptus to infuse the steam with scent. Then sit back and watch the mercury rise. To eliminate toxins and improve circulation, bathers beat each other with a bundle of birch branches, known as *veniki* (or you might have a professional do this for you).

When you can't take the heat, retreat. A public *banya* allows access to a plunge pool, usually filled with ice-cold water. The contrast in temperature is invigorating, energising and purifying.

A *banya* is not complete without a table spread with snacks, or at least a thermos of tea. And just when you think you have recovered, it's time to repeat the process. As they say in Russia, *'s lyokum parom'* (easy steaming).

Lonely Planet's Top Choices

Bolshoi Theatre (p88) Russia's ultimate theatre experience and one of the world's most opulent and sophisticated theatre venues.

Gazgolder (p168) An atmospheric postindustrial space with an eclectic live-music line-up.

Moscow Tchaikovsky Conservatory (p116) Hear a concert by the Moscow Symphony Orchestra in the Great Hall.

Best Opera & Ballet

Bolshoi Theatre (p88) Watch the dancers glide across the stage in Moscow's most famous and most historic theatre.

Stanislavsky & Nemirovich-Danchenko Musical Theatre (p101) A long-standing opera and ballet company with a tendency towards innovation.

New Ballet (p168) Breaking down barriers (physically and culturally) in dance.

Novaya Opera (p100) Re-creating the classics in a beautiful setting in the Hermitage Gardens.

Best Classical Music

Tchaikovsky Concert Hall (p116) A huge auditorium that is home to the city's oldest philharmonic.

Moscow International House of Music (p154) An impressive venue for the National Philharmonic of Russia.

Moscow Tchaikovsky Conservatory (p116) Hosts several different professional orchestras, as well as student recitals.

Best Contemporary Music

Gazgolder (p168) Hottest spot for live indie and rock.

Sixteen Tons (p116) A long-standing venue for local acts and national names.

Rhythm Blues Cafe (p137) Good old-fashioned jazz and blues music in a casual setting.

Svoboda (p100) Skater daters and music-lovers unite at this hipster hang-out.

Spectator Sports

Spartak Stadium (p116) A state-of-the-art facility for Moscow's most successful football team.

Luzhniki Stadium (p136) Coming off a major upgrade, but still the capital's largest and most storied stadium.

CSKA Stadiums An expansive complex that is home to the football, basketball and hockey teams.

Best Banyas

Sanduny Baths (p102) The tsar of Russian *bani* – a historic and opulently decorated bathhouse.

Krasnopresnkiye Bany (p117) A popular, public *banya* with excellent, clean facilities.

Shopping

News flash: Moscow is an expensive city, so don't come looking for bargains. Do come looking for creative and classy clothing and jewellery by local designers; an innovative art scene; high-quality handicrafts, linens, glassware and folk art; and unusual souvenirs that you won't find anywhere else.

Fashion

Beware of sticker shock when you check out the up-and-coming fashion industry in Moscow. A few local designers have blazed a trail, inventing sophisticated and stylish fashions, which you can try on at boutiques around town.

EVENTS

Mercedes-Benz Fashion Week (www.mercedesbenzfashionweek.ru) attracts top-name Russian and international fashion designers to unveil their new collections on Moscow runways. The event takes place at Manege Exhibition Centre (p78) in March or April and again in October or November.

FUR

Winter brings out the best or the worst of Russian style (depending on your perspective). Muscovites still see fur as the most effective and fashionable way to stay warm. The idea that fur constitutes animal cruelty is foreign and, frankly, incomprehensible to most Russians. As local fashion connoisseurs advise, don't come in winter if this offends you. If you think you might want to do as the Muscovites do when in Moscow, stop by **Yekaterina** (Екатерина; www.mexa-ekaterina.ru; ul Bolshaya Dmitrovka 11; ⊘11am-9pm; ⓂTeatralnaya) and pick out a fur hat.

Arts & Crafts

Moscow's prolific craftspeople display their knick-knacks and bric-a-brac at souvenir shops around town, as well as at the market at the kremlin in Izmaylovo (p161). Feel free to haggle, but don't expect prices to decrease more than 5% or 10%.

The speciality of Russian craftspeople is painted wooden knick-knacks. Traditional wooden nesting dolls, dishes and utensils are painted in decorative floral patterns, known as *khokhloma*. Painted lacquer boxes – or *palekh* boxes – are usually black with a colourful, detailed scene.

Gzhel, a village about 50km southeast of Moscow, has been known for its pottery since the 14th century, and nobody will leave Russia without forming a decisive opinion about *gzhel* porcelain, those curly white pieces with cobalt blue floral design.

Textiles

Welcome to Calico Moscow. Once famed for its textile industry, the capital still offers bargains on soft, rich linens and woollens. Russia's cool, moist summers and fertile soil are ideal for producing flax, the fibre used to manufacture linen. This elegant, durable fabric is respectfully known in Russia as 'His Majesty Linen'.

High-quality linen products such as tablecloths, napkins, bed covers and even clothing are still manufactured in Russia – and prices are lower than their Western counterparts.

Lonely Planet's Top Choices

Flakon (p99) Browse the output of contemporary creatives.

Izmaylovsky Market (p161) A sprawling souvenir market in fancy 'kremlin' digs.

Khokhlovka Original (p168) Unusual and controversial clothes from a co-op of young Russian designers.

Podarki vMeste s Vorovski (p102) Designer gifts – from felt boots to stylish ceramics inspired by folklore.

Association of Artists of the Decorative Arts (p138) Who knows what you might find in this crowded collection of shops?

Best for Art

Winzavod (p158) The city's first postindustrial contemporary art centre is now home to its highest-profile art galleries.

Artefact Gallery Centre (p138) A cluster of high-end galleries with a wide variety of paintings and artwork.

New Tretyakov Gallery (p146) The on-site Central House of Artists (TsDKh) houses galleries and exhibition space.

Best for Handicrafts

Izmaylovsky Market (p161) Moscow's biggest selection of traditional handmade items.

Podarki vMeste s Vorovski (p102) New forms for Russian folklore – great for gifts and souvenirs.

Association of Artists of the Decorative Arts (p138) A trove of tiny shops, packed with handcrafted treasures.

Russian Embroidery & Lace (p137) Handmade sweaters, dresses, linens and other beauties.

Best for Fashion

Khokhlovka Original (p168) See the best and boldest new Russian designers at this hidden showroom.

Flakon (p99) A redeveloped factory occupied by shops selling all kinds of designer items and clothing.

Lnyanaya Lavka (p85) Sensual, stylish clothing made from linen.

Alena Akhmadullina Boutique (p85) This romantic designer showcases her designs on one of Moscow's best shopping streets.

Vassa & Co (p138) Elena Vassa brings New York sensibilities to Russian fashion.

NEED TO KNOW

Opening Hours

Most shops are open from 10am until 8pm. Large shopping centres stay open until 10pm or later. Hours are shorter on Sunday, from about noon to 8pm.

Customs Regulations

Items more than 100 years old cannot be taken out of the country. Art, musical instruments, antiques or antiquarian books (published before 1975) must be assessed by the Expert Collegium (p248). Bring two photographs of your item, your receipt and your passport.

Katya Dobryakova (p117) Fanciful designs on a seasonal theme.

Best for Homewares

ArtPlay (p159) A postindustrial space largely dedicated to interior design, with many shops in the premises.

Russian Embroidery & Lace (p137) Handmade linens and lovelies.

Tryokhgornaya Manufaktura Factory Outlet (p117) High quality fabrics from one of the country's oldest textile factories.

PLAN YOUR TRIP SHOPPING

Explore Moscow

MOSCOW'S
TOP SIGHTS

GUM department store,
Red Square (p74)

Neighbourhoods at a Glance

❶ Kremlin & Kitay Gorod p58

Red Square and the Kremlin are the historical, geographic and spiritual heart of Moscow, as they have been for nearly 900 years. The mighty fortress, the iconic onion domes of St Basil's Cathedral and the granite mausoleum of Vladimir Ilych Lenin are among the city's most important historical sights. The surrounding streets of Kitay Gorod are crammed with churches and old architecture. This is the starting point for any visit to Moscow.

❷ Tverskoy p86

Tverskoy is Moscow's busiest, swankiest and most commercialised district. Few people can afford to live here, but millions pour in daily to work, hunt for garments at shopping

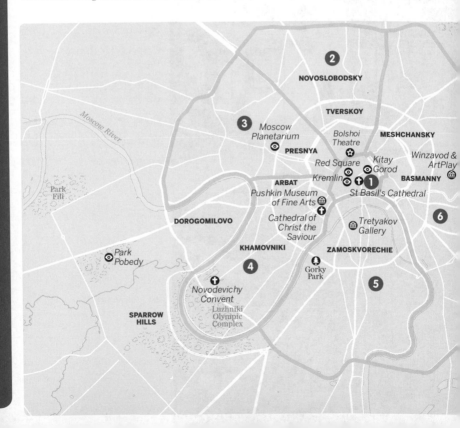

arcades or dine out. It is also home to 20-plus theatres and concert halls, including the world-famous Bolshoi Theatre, several renowned galleries and – last but not least – the opulent Sanduny Baths.

Beyond the Garden Ring, Tverskoy blends into the more relaxed Novoslobodsky district, home of the Jewish Museum and a cluster of bustling bars and restaurants around Mendeleyevskaya metro station.

③ Presnya p103

The vast, diverse Presnya district spans the centuries, with a remarkable blend of building styles from the last three. The district's ample attractions include its impressive and varied architecture, several noteworthy literary sites, and more traditional venues such as the zoo and planetarium. Presnya is also home to many of Moscow's top restaurants, including the highly lauded Cafe Pushkin. The former textile factory

at Tryokhgornaya is fast becoming a centre for nightlife and dining.

④ Arbat & Khamovniki p118

The side-by-side districts of Arbat and Khamovniki are rich with culture. Moscow's most famous street, ul Arbat, is something of an art market, complete with portrait painters and soapbox poets, while the nearby streets are lined with museums and galleries, including the world-class Pushkin Museum of Fine Arts. Khamovniki is home to the ancient Novodevichy Convent and Cemetery, as well as several unique newer museums. It's worth a trip to the south side of the Moscow River for certain key destinations, such as triumphant Park Pobedy.

⑤ Zamoskvorechie p139

With its low-rise buildings, quaint courtyards and multitude of onion domes, Zamoskvorechie is like a provincial Russian town that somehow ended up in central Moscow. The people responsible for the lingering old-world ambience are *kuptsy* (merchants) who populated the area until the 19th century and had completely different lifestyles and habits to the nobility living across the river. But modernity is very much present thanks to the ever-expanding gentrification belt that stretches along the river, showcasing beautifully renovated parks, art spaces and hipster clusters filled with restaurants and bars.

⑥ Meshchansky & Basmanny p156

Covering a large swathe of central Moscow, Meshchansky is markedly laid-back compared with its neighbouring districts. Here you'll find fewer offices, dominated as it is by prerevolutionary residential buildings. Beyond the Garden Ring, Basmanny is an area of 19th-century red-brick factories, now taken over by innovative postmodern galleries, cool cafes and digital startups. South of the Yauza, Taganskaya pl is a monster intersection that can be difficult to navigate, but the area is home to a few unusual sights, including Bunker-42 and the Museum of the Russian Icon.

Kremlin & Kitay Gorod

Neighbourhood Top Five

1 **Kremlin** (p60)
Wandering around the grounds and exploring 500 years of artistic mastery, political power and spiritual devotion; and gawking at the royal treasures in the Armoury.

2 **St Basil's Cathedral** (p76) Marvelling at the multicoloured, multidomed spectacle that is the icon of Russia.

3 **Lenin's Mausoleum** (p75) Paying your respects to embalmed Vladimir Ilych and other communist heavy hitters.

4 **Kitay Gorod** (p80)
Discovering the ancient churches hidden among the narrow streets of this 13th-century neighbourhood.

5 **Alexander Garden** (p72) Visiting the Tomb of the Unknown Soldier and catching the changing of the guard.

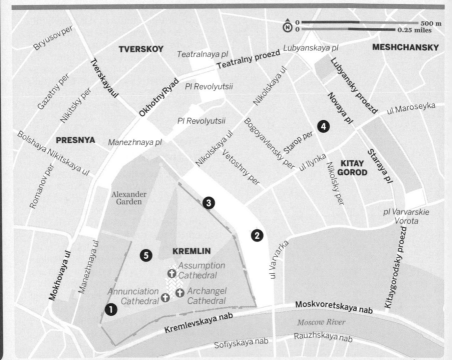

For more detail of this area see Map p271 ➡

Explore Kremlin & Kitay Gorod

If you have only one day in Moscow, you will probably spend it here. With more time, you might spend more than a day here, exploring the churches and museums, and viewing the trappings of power.

The neighbourhood's key attractions are clustered around Red Square and within the walls of the Kremlin. It doesn't matter which of these two you take in first, but try to leave time for both. Your visit to the Kremlin should be planned around admission to the Armoury: it requires advance purchase of tickets, which specify the admission times.

Besides being a major tourist attraction, Red Square hosts concerts, festivals, parades and other official events. As a result, the place is sometimes closed to the public and it's almost always packed with people. Come early in the morning or late in the evening to catch a glimpse of the square when it is sparsely populated, vast and majestic. Travellers with some extra time will enjoy wandering the medieval streets of Kitay Gorod, discovering ancient hidden churches and popping into shops and cafes. It is a welcome change from the hustle and bustle that characterises the Kremlin and Red Square.

Local Life

➜**Parks** Muscovites don't often hang out on Red Square, but they do enjoy Alexander Garden, where they stroll among the flower beds, snap photos and (gasp) lounge on the grass.

➜**Wedding Parties** The Tomb of the Unknown Soldier is Moscow's top destination for wedding parties, who snap photos and drink champagne while the bride and groom pay their respects by laying flowers on the grave site.

➜**Shopping Malls** It may be too expensive for most Muscovites to shop at the stores in GUM, but it's affordable to eat at the mall's Stolovaya No 57 – as evidenced by the lines of locals out the door at lunchtime.

Getting There & Away

➜**Red Square** Three metro lines converge at Red Square. Okhotny Ryad station is on line 1 (red); Teatralnaya station is on line 2 (dark green); and Ploshchad Revolyutsii is on line 3 (dark blue).

➜**Kitay Gorod** Lines 6 and 7 (orange and purple) intersect in Kitay Gorod, with both stations sharing the name of the neighbourhood. Line 1 (red) has an eponymous station at Lubyanka, which is also useful for Kitay Gorod.

Lonely Planet's Top Tip

If you think Red Square is impressive by day, come back at night, when the crowds are gone and the lights cast a magical glow on the historic buildings.

✕ Best Places to Eat

➜ Stolovaya No 57 (p83)
➜ Grand Coffee Mania (p83)
➜ Bosco Cafe (p83)
➜ Ryby Net (p83)

For reviews, see p83.➡

⬤ Best Places to Drink

➜ Ciderella (p84)
➜ Mandarin Combustible (p84)
➜ Jawsspot Msk (p84)

For reviews, see p84.➡

🔒 Best for Fashion

➜ GUM (p74)
➜ Lnyanaya Lavka (p85)
➜ Alena Akhmadullina Boutique (p85)

For reviews, see p85.➡

TOP SIGHT
KREMLIN

The apex of Russian political power and once the centre of the Orthodox Church, the Kremlin is not only the kernel of Moscow but of the whole country. From here, autocratic tsars, communist dictators and modern-day presidents have done their best – and worst – for Russia. These red-brick walls and tent-roof towers enclose 800 years of artistic accomplishment, religious ceremony and political clout.

Entrance Towers

Kutafya Tower

The Kutafya Tower (Кутафья башня), which forms the main visitors' entrance today, stands apart from the Kremlin's west wall, at the end of a ramp over the Alexander Garden. The ramp was once a bridge over the Neglinnaya River and used to be part of the Kremlin's defences; this river has been diverted underground, beneath the Alexander Garden, since the early 19th century. The Kutafya Tower is the last of a number of outer bridge towers that once stood on this side of the Kremlin.

Trinity Gate Tower

From the Kutafya Tower, walk up the ramp and pass through the Kremlin walls beneath the 1495 Trinity Gate Tower (Троицкая башня). At 80m it's the tallest of the Kremlin's towers. Right below your feet were the cells for prisoners in the 16th century.

Government Buildings

Poteshny Palace & State Kremlin Palace

Immediately inside the Trinity Gate Tower, the lane to the right (south) passes the 17th-century Poteshny Palace (Потешный дворец), where Stalin lived. The yellow palace was built by Tsar Alexey Mikhailovich and housed the first Russian theatre. Here, Tsar Alexey

DON'T MISS
➔ Assumption Cathedral
➔ Archangel Cathedral
➔ Annunciation Cathedral
➔ The Armoury

PRACTICALITIES
➔ Кремль
➔ Map p271, C3
➔ ☎495-695 4146
➔ www.kreml.ru
➔ ₽500
➔ ⊙10am-5pm Fri-Wed, ticket office 9.30am-4.30pm Fri-Wed
➔ Ⓜ Aleksandrovsky Sad

enjoyed various comedic performances. In keeping with conservative Russian Orthodox tradition, however, after the shows he would go to the *banya* (Russian bathhouse), then attend a church service to repent his sins.

The bombastic marble, glass and concrete **State Kremlin Palace** (Государственный Кремлёвский дворец; Map p271; ☑495-620 7846; www.kremlinpalace.org/en), built between 1960 and 1961 for Communist Party congresses, is now home to the Kremlin Ballet (p84).

Arsenal

North of the State Kremlin Palace is the 18th-century Arsenal (Арсенал), commissioned by Peter the Great to house workshops and depots for guns and weaponry. An unrealised plan at the end of the 19th century was to open a museum of the Napoleonic Wars in the Arsenal. Now housing the Kremlin Guard, the building is ringed with 800 captured Napoleonic cannons.

Senate

The offices of the president of Russia, the ultimate seat of power in the modern Kremlin, are in the yellow, triangular former Senate (Сенат) building, a fine 18th-century neoclassical edifice, east of the Arsenal. Built in 1785 by architect Matvei Kazakov, it was noted for its huge cupola. In the 16th and 17th centuries this area was where the boyars (high ranking Russian nobles) lived. Next to the Senate is the 1930s Supreme Soviet (Верховный Совет) building.

Patriarch's Palace

Patriarch's Palace (Патриарший дворец) was mostly built in the mid-17th century for Patriarch Nikon, whose reforms sparked the break with the Old Believers. In its heyday, the palace was a busy place. Apart from the Patriarch's living quarters, it had huge kitchens, warehouses and cellars stocked with food, workshops, a school for high-born children, offices for scribes, dormitories for those waiting to be baptised, stables and carriage houses.

The palace now contains an exhibit of 17th-century household items, including jewellery, hunting equipment and furniture. It often holds special temporary exhibits, which can be visited individually, without access to the other buildings on Sobornaya pl.

Church of the Twelve Apostles

From inside the Patriarch's Palace, you can access the five-domed Church of the Twelve Apostles (Церковь двенадцати апостолов). The pretty little chapel contains a gilded wooden iconostasis and a collection of icons by leading 17th-century icon painters.

PLANNING

Visiting the Kremlin and the Armoury is at least a half-day affair. If you intend to visit the Diamond Fund or other special exhibits, plan on spending most of the day here. If you are short on time, skip the Armoury and the Diamond Fund and dedicate an hour to admiring the historic buildings around Sobornaya pl (Cathedral Sq), the central square within the Kremlin walls.

The first stone structures in the Kremlin were built in the 1330s at the behest of Ivan 'Moneybags' Kalita. Only the Church of the Saviour's Transfiguration survived into the 20th century, but it was demolished by Stalin approximately 600 years after it was built.

CHECK YOUR BAGS

Before entering the Kremlin, deposit large bags at the **left-luggage office** (Map p271; Alexander Garden; ☺9am-6.30pm Fri-Wed).

The Kremlin

A DAY AT THE KREMLIN

Only at the Kremlin can you see 800 years of Russian history and artistry in one day. Enter the ancient fortress through the Trinity Gate Tower and walk past the impressive Arsenal, ringed with cannons. Past the Patriarch's Palace, you'll find yourself surrounded by white-washed walls and golden domes. Your first stop is ❶ **Assumption Cathedral** with the solemn fresco over the doorway. As the most important church in prerevolutionary Russia, this 15th-century beauty was the burial site of the patriarchs. The ❷ **Ivan the Great Bell Tower** now contains a nifty multimedia exhibit on the architectural history of the Kremlin. The view from the top is worth the price of admission. The tower is flanked by the massive ❸ **Tsar Cannon & Bell**.

In the southeast corner, ❹ **Archangel Cathedral** has an elaborate interior, where three centuries of tsars and tsarinas are laid to rest. Your final stop on Sobornaya pl is ❺ **Annunciation Cathedral**, rich with frescoes and iconography.

Walk along the Great Kremlin Palace and enter the ❻ **Armoury** at the time designated on your ticket. After gawking at the goods, exit the Kremlin through Borovitsky Gate and stroll through the Alexander Garden to the ❼ **Tomb of the Unknown Soldier**.

Assumption Cathedral

Once your eyes adjust to the colourful frescoes, the gilded fixtures and the iconography, try to locate *Saviour with the Angry Eye*, a 14th-century icon that is one of the oldest in the Kremlin.

Arsenal

BOROVITSKY TOWER

Use the entrance at Borovitsky Tower if you intend to skip the churches and visit only the Armoury or Diamond Fund.

Borovitsky Tower

Trinity Gate Tower

Alexander Garden

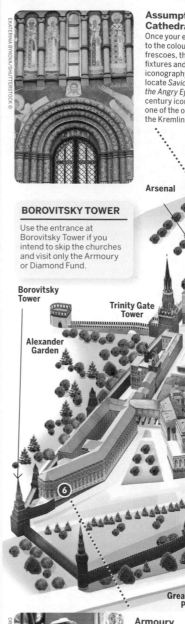

Great Kremlin Palace

Armoury

Take advantage of the free audio guide to direct you to the most intriguing treasures of the Armoury, which is chock-full of precious metalworks and jewellery, armour and weapons, gowns and crowns, carriages and sledges.

Tomb of the Unknown Soldier

Visit the Tomb of the Unknown Soldier honouring the heroes of the Great Patriotic War. Come at the top of the hour to see the solemn synchronicity of the changing of the guard.

ANDREW KOTURANOV/SHUTTERSTOCK ©

Patriarch's Palace

Ivan the Great Bell Tower

Check out the artistic electronic renderings of the Kremlin's history, then climb 137 steps to the belfry's upper gallery, where you will be rewarded with super, sweeping vistas of Sobornaya pl and beyond.

Moscow River

Tsar Cannon & Bell

Peer down the barrel of the monstrous Tsar Cannon and pose for a picture beside the oversized Tsar Bell, both of which are too big to serve their intended purpose.

Sobornaya pl

Annunciation Cathedral

Admire the artistic mastery of Russia's greatest icon painters – Theophanes the Greek and Andrei Rublyov – who are responsible for many of the icons in the deesis and festival rows of the iconostasis.

Archangel Cathedral

See the final resting place of princes and emperors who ruled Russia for more than 300 years, including the visionary Ivan the Great, the tortured Ivan the Terrible and the tragic Tsarevitch Dmitry.

EKATERINA BYKOVA/SHUTTERSTOCK ©

KREMLIN & RED SQUARE

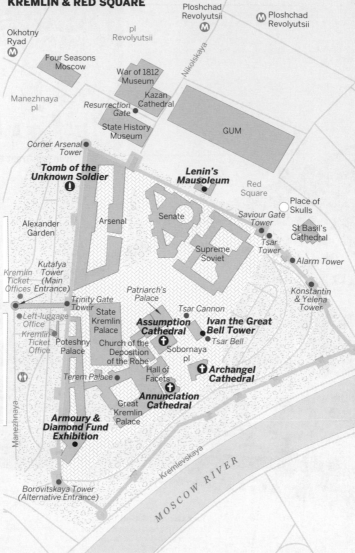

Ploshchad Revolyutsii Ⓜ

Ⓜ Ploshchad Revolyutsii

Okhotny Ryad Ⓜ

pl Revolyutsii

Four Seasons Moscow

War of 1812 Museum

Nikolskaya

Manezhnaya pl

Resurrection Gate

Kazan Cathedral

State History Museum

GUM

Corner Arsenal Tower

Tomb of the Unknown Soldier ❶

Lenin's Mausoleum

Red Square

Place of Skulls

Alexander Garden

Arsenal

Senate

Saviour Gate Tower

St Basil's Cathedral

Tsar Tower

Supreme Soviet

Alarm Tower

Kutafya Tower (Main Entrance)

Kremlin Ticket Offices

Patriarch's Palace

Konstantin & Yelena Tower

Trinity Gate Tower

Tsar Cannon

Left-luggage Office

State Kremlin Palace

Assumption Cathedral

Ivan the Great Bell Tower ❶

Kremlin Ticket Office

Poteshny Palace

Church of the Deposition of the Robe

Tsar Bell

Sobornaya pl

Terem Palace

Hall of Facets

Archangel Cathedral ❶

Annunciation Cathedral

Great Kremlin Palace

Maneznaya

Armoury & Diamond Fund Exhibition

Borovitskaya Tower (Alternative Entrance)

Kremlevskaya

MOSCOW RIVER

Cross Hall

The highlight of the Patriarch's Palace is perhaps the ceremonial Cross Hall (Крестовая палата), where feasts for the tsars and ambassadors were held. From the 18th century the room was used to produce *miro* (a holy oil used during church services, which contains over 30 herbal components); the oven and huge pans from the production process are on display.

Assumption Cathedral

TICKETS

Full-price Armoury tickets are available for advance online purchase. Otherwise, tickets go on sale 45 minutes prior to each session. Be at the ticket window when sales begin, as ticket numbers are limited.

The director of the Kremlin museums is Elena Gagarina, the daughter of pilot and cosmonaut Yury Gagarin.

ENTRY TIMES

Visitors are allowed to enter the Armoury only at specified times (10am, noon, 2.30pm and 4.30pm). Visitors are also allowed to enter Ivan the Great Bell Tower only at specified times (10.15am, 11.15am, 1pm, 2pm, 3pm and 4pm).

Assumption Cathedral

On the northern side of Sobornaya pl, with five golden helmet domes and four semicircular gables facing the square, the Assumption Cathedral (Успенский собор) is the focal church of prerevolutionary Russia and the burial place of most of the heads of the Russian Orthodox Church from the 1320s to 1700. A striking 1660s fresco of the Virgin Mary faces Sobornaya pl, above the door once used for royal processions. If you have limited time in the Kremlin, come straight here. The visitors' entrance is at the western end.

Construction & History

In 1470 Russian architects Krivtsov and Myshkin were commissioned by Ivan the Great to replace the old dilapidated cathedral, which dated from 1326. As soon as the ceiling was put up, one of the walls collapsed. During Soviet times, history books said this calamity was the result of bad handiwork, but today revisionist history indicates that an earthquake caused the collapse. Either way, Krivtsov and Myshkin lost their jobs, and Italian architect Aristotle Fioravanti was given a crack at it. After the foundation was completed, Fioravanti toured Novgorod, Suzdal and Vladimir to acquaint himself with Russian architecture. His design is a more spacious version of the Assumption Cathedral at Vladimir, with a Renaissance twist.

The church closed in 1918. According to some accounts, in 1941, when the Nazis were on the outskirts

HISTORY OF THE KREMLIN

A 'kremlin' – or fortified stronghold – has existed on this site since Moscow's earliest years. In 1147 Yury Dolgoruky summoned his allies to this spot, which would have been occupied by a wooden fort. When the city became the capital of medieval Rus in the 1320s, the Kremlin served as the headquarters of the Russian Orthodox Church and the seat of the prince.

The ambition of Ivan III (the Great) was to build a capital that would equal the fallen Constantinople in grandeur, power, achievements and architecture. In an effort to build the 'Third Rome', Ivan brought from Italy stonemasons and architects, who built new walls, three great cathedrals and other structures. Most of the present-day buildings date from this period.

Although Peter I (the Great) shifted the capital to St Petersburg, the tsars still showed up here for coronations and other celebrations. The fortress was captured by Napoleon, who inflicted serious damage before making his retreat in 1812. But still the ancient symbol endured. The citadel wouldn't be breached again until the Bolsheviks stormed the place in November 1917.

The Kremlin has been open to tourists since 1955.

of Moscow, Stalin secretly ordered a service in the cathedral to protect the city from the enemy. The cathedral was officially returned to the Church in 1989, but it now operates as a museum.

Frescoes & Murals

The interior of the Assumption Cathedral is unusually bright and spacious, full of frescoes painted in warm golds, reds and blues. The west wall features a scene of the Apocalypse, a favourite theme of the Russian Church in the Middle Ages. The pillars have pictures of martyrs, considered to be the pillars of faith. Above the southern gates there are frescoes of Yelena and Constantine, who brought Christianity to Greece and the south of Russia. The space above the northern gate depicts Olga and Vladimir, who brought Christianity to the north.

Most of the existing images on the cathedral walls were painted on a gilt base in the 1640s, with the exception of three grouped together on the south wall: *The Apocalypse* (Апокалипсис), *The Life of Metropolitan Pyotr* (Житие Митрополита Петра) and *All Creatures Rejoice in Thee* (О тебе радуется). These are attributed to Dionysius and his followers, the cathedral's original 15th-century mural painters.

Patriarchs' Tombs

The tombs of many leaders of the Russian Church (metropolitans up to 1590, patriarchs from 1590 to 1700) are against the north, west and south walls of Assumption Cathedral. Near the west wall is a shrine with holy relics of Patriarch Hermogen, who instigated an uprising during the Time of Troubles in 1612. Also a supporter of Minin and Pozharsky's revolt against the Polish occupation, the martyr was later arrested, beaten and starved to death.

Throne of Monomakh

Near the south wall, the tent-roofed wooden throne is known as the Throne of Monomakh. It was made in 1551 for Ivan the Terrible. Its carved scenes highlight the career of 12th-century Grand Prince Vladimir Monomakh of Kiev – considered to be Ivan's direct predecessor.

Iconostasis

Assumption Cathedral's iconostasis dates from 1652, but its lowest level contains some older icons. The 1340s *Saviour with the Angry Eye* (Спас Ярое око) is second from the right. On the left of the central door is the *Virgin of*

Vladimir (Владимирская Богоматерь), an early-15th-century Rublyov-school copy of Russia's most revered image, the *Vladimir Icon of the Mother of God* (Владимирская икона Богоматери). The 12th-century original, now in Moscow's Tretyakov Gallery, stood in the Assumption Cathedral from the 1480s to 1930. One of the oldest Russian icons, the 12th-century red-clothed *St George* (Святой Георгий) from Novgorod, is by the north wall.

The original icons of the lower, local tier are symbols of victory brought from Vladimir, Smolensk, Veliky Ustyug and other places. The south door was brought from the Nativity of the Virgin Cathedral in Suzdal.

Church of the Deposition of the Robe

The delicate single-domed Church of the Deposition of the Robe (Церковь Ризоположения), beside the west door of the Assumption Cathedral, was built between 1484 and 1486 in exclusively Russian style. It was the private chapel of the heads of the Church, who tended to be highly suspicious of such people as Italian architects.

Originally an open gallery or porch surrounded the church; it was later removed and the church was connected with the palace for the convenience of the tsars. The interior walls, ceilings and pillars are covered with 17th-century frescoes. It houses an exhibition of 15th- to 19th-century woodcarvings.

Ivan the Great Bell Tower

With its two golden domes rising above the eastern side of Sobornaya pl, the **Ivan the Great Bell Tower** (Колокольня Ивана Великого; Map p271; ₽250; ⊙10am-5pm Apr-Oct) is the Kremlin's tallest structure – a landmark visible from 30km away. Before the 20th century it was forbidden to build any higher than this tower in Moscow. Purchase a ticket for a specifically timed admission to climb the 137 steps to the top for sweeping views.

The bell tower's history dates back to the Church of Ioann Lestvichnik Under the Bells, built on this site in 1329 by Ivan I (and later destroyed). In 1505, Italian Marco Bono designed a new belfry, originally with only two octagonal tiers beneath a drum and a dome. In 1600 Boris Godunov raised it to 81m.

The building's central section, with a gilded single dome and a 65-tonne bell, dates from between 1532 and 1542. The tent-roofed annexe, next to the belfry, was commissioned by Patriarch Filaret about 100 years later.

Architectural Exhibition

Ivan the Great houses a multimedia presentation of the architectural history of the Kremlin complex. Using architectural fragments and electronic

STAND ON CEREMONY

Every Saturday at noon from April to October, the Presidential Regiment shows up on Sobornaya pl for a ceremonial procession, featuring some very official-looking prancing and dancing, both on foot and on horseback. The price of admission to the Kremlin allows access to the demonstration.

In 1812 French troops used the Assumption Cathedral as a stable; they also looted 295kg of gold and over 5 tonnes of silver from here, but much of it was recovered.

CAMERA SHY

Photography is not permitted inside the Armoury or in any of the buildings on Sobornaya pl (Cathedral Sq).

projections, the exhibition illustrates how the Kremlin has changed since the 12th century. Special attention is given to individual churches within the complex, including several churches that no longer exist. The 45-minute audio tour ends with a 137-step climb to the top of the tall tower, yielding an amazing (and unique!) view of Sobornaya pl, with the Church of Christ the Saviour and the Moskva-City skyscrapers in the distance.

The bell tower is only open when weather allows. Purchase your ticket (for a specific admission time) at the ticket office in Alexander Garden before you enter the Kremlin grounds. The number of people admitted for each time slot is extremely limited, so it may require some flexibility.

Tsar Cannon

North of the Ivan the Great Bell Tower is the 40-tonne Tsar Cannon (Царь-пушка). It was cast in 1586 by the blacksmith Ivan Chokhov for Fyodor I, whose portrait is on the barrel. Shot has never sullied its 89cm bore and certainly not the cannonballs beside it, which are too big even for this elephantine firearm.

Tsar Bell

Beside (not inside) the Ivan the Great Bell Tower stands the world's biggest bell (Царь-колокол), a 202-tonne monster that has never rung. An earlier version, weighing 130 tonnes, fell from its belfry during a fire in 1701 and shattered. Using these remains, the current Tsar Bell was cast in the 1730s for Empress Anna Ivanovna. The bell was cooling off in the foundry casting pit in 1737 when it came into contact with water, causing an 11-tonne chunk to break off. One hundred years later, the architect Montferrand took the damaged bell out of the pit and put it on a pedestal. Bas-reliefs of Empress Anna and Tsar Alexey, as well as some icons, were etched on its sides.

Archangel Cathedral

The Archangel Cathedral (Архангельский собор), at the southeastern corner of Sobornaya pl, was for centuries the coronation, wedding and burial church of tsars. It was built by Ivan Kalita in 1333 to commemorate the end of the great famine, and dedicated to Archangel Michael, guardian of the Moscow princes. By the turn of the 16th century it had fallen into disrepair and was rebuilt between 1505 and 1508 by the Italian architect Alevisio Novi. Like the Assumption Cathedral, it has five domes and is essentially Byzantine-Russian in style. However, the exterior has many Venetian Renaissance features, notably the distinctive scallop-shell gables and porticoes.

Tsarist Tombs

The tombs of almost all Muscovy's rulers from the 1320s to the 1690s are here. The only absentee is Boris Godunov, whose body was taken out of the grave on

---

KREMLIN TICKET OFFICE

The **main ticket office** (Кассы музеев Кремля; Map p271; ◷9am-5pm Fri-Wed May-Sep, 9.30am-4.30pm Fri-Wed Oct-Apr; Ⓜ Aleksandrovsky Sad) is in Alexander Garden, next to the Kremlin wall. The ticket to the 'Architectural Ensemble of Sobornaya pl' covers entry to all five church-museums, as well as Patriarch's Palace. It does not include the Armoury, the Diamond Fund Exhibition or Ivan the Great Bell Tower, but you can and should buy those tickets here too. You can also order full-price tickets (not children's tickets) for the Kremlin churches and the Armoury on the Kremlin website, but you still have to pick them up at the ticket office in Alexander Garden.

Tsar Cannon

In 1600 Boris Godunov increased the height of the Ivan the Great Bell Tower from 60m to 81m. Local legend says that this was a public works project designed to employ the thousands of people who had come to Moscow during a famine, but historical documents contradict the story, as the construction apparently did not coincide with a famine. The height was probably increased so that the belfry could also serve as a watch tower.

the order of a 'False Dmitry' and buried at Sergiev Posad in 1606. The bodies are buried underground, beneath the 17th-century sarcophagi and 19th-century copper covers. Tsarevitch Dmitry (a son of Ivan the Terrible), who died mysteriously in 1591, lies beneath a painted stone canopy. It was Dmitry's death that sparked the appearance of a string of impersonators, known as False Dmitrys, during the Time of Troubles. Ivan's own tomb is out of sight behind the iconostasis, along with those of his other sons, Ivan (whom he killed) and Fyodor I (who succeeded him). From Peter the Great onwards, emperors and empresses were buried in St Petersburg, the exception being Peter II, who died in Moscow and is here.

Murals

Some 17th-century murals were uncovered during restorations of the Archangel Cathedral in the 1950s. The south wall depicts many of the rulers buried here; on the pillars are some of their predecessors, including Andrei Bogolyubsky, Prince Daniil and Alexander Nevsky.

Hall of Facets & Terem Palace

Hall of Facets

Named for its Italian Renaissance stone facing, the Hall of Facets (Грановитая палата) was designed and built by Marco Ruffo and Pietro Solario between 1487 and 1491, during the reign of Ivan the Great. Its upper floor housed the tsars' throne room,

KREMLIN TOURS

➔ **Kremlin Excursion Office** (Map p271; ☑495-697 0349; www.kremlin.museum.ru; Alexander Garden; 90min tour ₽4000; Ⓜ Aleksandrovsky Sad)

➔ **Moscow Free Tour** (Map p271; ☑495-222 3466 ; www.moscowfreetour.com; Nikolskaya ul 4/5; guided walk free, paid tours from €31)

➔ **Kremlin Tour with Diana** (☑8-965-150 0071; www.kremlintour.com)

the scene of banquets and ceremonies. The hall is 500 sq metres, with a supporting pillar in the centre. The walls are decorated with gorgeous murals of biblical and historical themes, although none are original. Alas, the building is closed to the public.

Access to the Hall of Facets was via an outside staircase from the square below. During the Streltsy Rebellion of 1682, several of Peter the Great's relatives were tossed down the exterior Red Staircase, so called because it ran red with their blood. (It's no wonder that Peter hated Moscow and decided to start afresh with a new capital in St Petersburg.) Stalin destroyed the staircase, but it was rebuilt in 1994.

Terem Palace

The 16th- and 17th-century Terem Palace (Теремной дворец) is the most splendid of the Kremlin palaces. Made of stone and built by Vasily III, the palace's living quarters include a dining room, living room, study, bedroom and small chapel. Unfortunately, the palace is closed to the public, but you can glimpse its cluster of 11 golden domes and chequered roof behind and above the Church of the Deposition of the Robe.

Annunciation Cathedral

The Annunciation Cathedral (Благовещенский собор), at the southwest corner of Sobornaya pl, contains impressive murals in the gallery and an archaeology exhibit in the basement. The central chapel features the celebrated icons of master painters Theophanes the Greek and Andrei Rublyov.

TOWERS OF POWER

The present Kremlin walls were built between 1485 and 1495, replacing the limestone walls from the 14th century. The walls are 6m to 17m tall, depending on the landscape, and 2m to 5m thick. They stretch for 2235m. Originally, a 32m-wide moat encircled the northern end of the Kremlin, connecting the Moscow and Neglinnaya Rivers.

The 20 distinctive towers were built between 1485 and 1500, with tent roofs added in the 17th century. Originally, the towers had lookout posts and were equipped for heavy fighting. Most were designed by Italian masons.

The most prominent tower is the Saviour Gate Tower (p75), the clock tower soaring above Red Square. Right next to it is the Tsar Tower (Царская башня), a later addition (1680), which sits on top of the Kremlin wall. Legend has it that Ivan the Terrible watched executions and other Red Square activities from the old wooden tower that previously stood on this site. Next along is the Alarm Tower (Набатная башня), which used to house the Spassky Alarm Bell, used to warn of enemy attacks and to spur popular uprisings. After quashing one such uprising, Catherine the Great was so outraged that she had the clapper removed from the bell, so it could sound no more.

The two towers anchoring the northern and southern ends of this eastern wall played important roles in the Kremlin's defences. At the corner of Alexander Garden, St Nicholas Tower (Никольская башня) was previously a gated defensive tower on the northeastern flank. Through this gate, Dmitry Pozharsky and Kuzma Minin (as depicted in the statue in front of St Basil's Cathedral) led a civilian army and drove out the Polish occupiers. At the southern end of Red Square, Konstantin & Yelena Tower (Константино-Еленинская башня) was built to protect the settlements outside the city. It is complete with firing platforms and a drawbridge over the moat.

Vasily I built the first wooden church on this site in 1397. Between 1484 and 1489, Ivan the Great had the Annunciation Cathedral rebuilt to serve as the royal family's private chapel. Originally the cathedral had just three domes and an open gallery around three sides. Ivan the Terrible, whose tastes were more elaborate, added six more domes and chapels at each corner, enclosed the gallery and gilded the roof.

Frescoes

Many murals in the Annunciation Cathedral's gallery date from the 1560s. Among them are *Capture of Jericho* in the northern porch, *Jonah and the Whale* in the northern arm of the gallery and the *Tree of Jesus* on its ceiling. Other frescoes feature ancient philosophers such as Aristotle, Plutarch, Plato and Socrates holding scrolls inscribed with their own wise words. Socrates' scroll reads: 'No harm will ever come to a good man. Our soul is immortal. After death the good shall be rewarded and the evil punished.' Plato's says: 'We must hope God shall send us a heavenly Teacher and a Guide'. The small central part of the cathedral has a lovely jasper floor. The 16th-century frescoes include Russian princes on the north pillar and Byzantine emperors on the south, both with Apocalypse scenes above them.

Iconostasis

The real treasure of the Annunciation Cathedral is the iconostasis, where in the 1920s restorers uncovered early-15th-century icons by three of the greatest medieval Russian artists. It was most likely Theophanes who painted the six icons at the right-hand end of the biggest row of the six tiers of the iconostasis. From left to right, these are the *Virgin Mary, Christ Enthroned, St John the Baptist,* the *Archangel Gabriel,* the *Apostle Paul* and *St John Chrysostom.* Theophanes was a master of portraying pathos in the facial expressions of his subjects, setting these icons apart from most others.

The third icon from the left, *Archangel Michael,* is ascribed to Andrei Rublyov, who may also have painted the adjacent *St Peter.* Rublyov is also reckoned to be the artist of the first, second, sixth and seventh (and probably the third and fifth) icons from the left end of the festival row, above the *deesis* (biggest) row. The seven icons at the right-hand end are attributed to Prokhor of Gorodets.

Archaeological Exhibition

The basement of the Annunciation Cathedral holds a permanent exhibition on the archaeology of the Kremlin – an appropriate place, as this is actually a remnant of the 14th-century church that previously occupied this site. On display are hundreds of

GET INSIDE THE GREAT KREMLIN PALACE

The Great Kremlin Palace is not open to the public, but Patriarshy Dom Tours (p33) sometimes arranges tours inside this grandiose building.

Under Orthodox law, the fourth marriage of Ivan the Terrible disqualified him from entering the church proper, so he had the southern gallery of the Annunciation Cathedral converted into the Archangel Gabriel Chapel, from where he could watch services through a grille.

DIAMOND FUND

The Diamond Fund is managed by the Ministry of Finance, which retains a monopoly on the mining and sale of precious stones. As such, the collection includes many magnificent raw diamonds, some in excess of 300 carats.

artefacts – glassware, ceramics, tools and woodwork – that were excavated from Borovitsky Hill in the 1960s and 1970s. Archaeologists found around 30 'treasure troves', which included silver jewellery and coins dating to medieval times.

Great Kremlin Palace

Housing the Armoury and much more, the 700-room Great Kremlin Palace (Большой Кремлёвский дворец) was built between 1838 and 1849 by architect Konstantin Thon as an imperial residence for Nicholas I. It is now an official residence of the Russian president, used for state visits and receptions. However, unlike the Russian tsars, the president doesn't have living quarters here.

The huge palace incorporates some earlier buildings such as the Hall of Facets, Terem Palace and several chapels. Although vast, the building has never received great praise, being criticised as 'barrack-like' and 'pretentious'. Several ceremonial halls are named after saints, including St George, St Vladimir, St Andrew, St Catherine and St Alexander. St George's Hall is mainly used for state awards ceremonies, while major international treaties are signed in St Vladimir's Hall.

The majority of the Great Kremlin Palace is not open to the public, but Patriarshy Dom Tours (p33) sometimes arranges tours.

Armoury

The **Armoury** (Оружейная палата; Map p271; adult/child ₽700/free; ⊘ tours at 10am, noon, 2.30pm & 4.30pm Fri-Wed; M Aleksandrovsky Sad) dates back to 1511, when it was founded under Vasily III to manufacture and store weapons, imperial arms and regalia for the royal court. Later it also produced jewellery, icon frames and embroidery. During the reign of Peter the Great all craftspeople, goldsmiths and silversmiths were sent to St Petersburg, and the Armoury became a mere museum storing the royal treasures. To this day, the Armoury still contains plenty of treasures for ogling, and remains a highlight of any visit to the Kremlin.

If possible, buy your ticket to the Armoury when you buy your ticket to the Kremlin. Your ticket will specify a time of entry. A one-hour audio guide is available to point out some of the highlights of the collection.

Diamond Fund of Russia

If the Armoury hasn't sated your lust for diamonds, there are more in the separate **Diamond Fund Exhibition** (Алмазный фонд России; Map p271; ☑ 495-629 2036; www.gokhran.ru; ₽500; ⊘ 10am-1pm & 2-5pm Fri-Wed). The fund dates back to 1719, when Peter the Great established the Russian Crown treasury. The bulk of the exhibit is gemstones and jewellery garnered by tsars and empresses, including the 190-carat diamond given to Catherine the Great by her lover Grigory Orlov. The Great Imperial Crown, encrusted with 4936 diamonds, was the coronation crown of Catherine the Great and successive rulers. Security is super tight and you are not allowed to bring cameras, phones or bags of any sort.

Alexander Garden

The first public park in Moscow, **Alexander Garden** (Александровский сад; Map p271) sits along the Kremlin's western wall. Colourful flower beds and impressive Kremlin views make it a favourite strolling spot for Muscovites and tourists alike. Back in the 17th century, the Neglinnaya River ran through the present gardens, with dams and mills along its banks. When the river was diverted underground, the garden was founded by architect Osip Bove, in 1821.

At the north end of Alexander Garden, the Tomb of the Unknown Soldier (Могила неизвестного солдата) contains the remains of one soldier who died in December 1941 at km41 of Leningradskoe sh – the nearest the Nazis came to Moscow. It is a kind of national pilgrimage spot, where newlyweds bring flowers and have their pictures taken.

ARMOURY

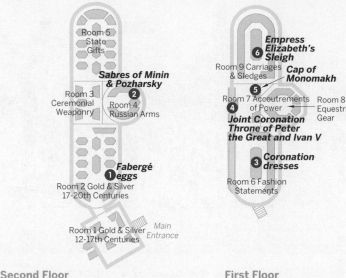

Second Floor   **First Floor**

🏃 Museum Tour
Armoury

START ARMOURY
LENGTH ONE HOUR

Your tour starts upstairs, where the first two rooms house gold and silver from the 12th to 20th centuries, many pieces crafted in the Kremlin workshops. In Room 2, you'll find the renowned ❶**Easter eggs** made by St Petersburg jeweller Fabergé. The tsar and tsarina traditionally exchanged these gifts each year at Easter. Most famous is the Grand Siberian Railway egg, with gold train, platinum locomotive and ruby headlamp, created to commemorate the Moscow–Vladivostok line.

The following rooms display armour, weapons and more armour and more weapons. Don't miss the helmet of Prince Yaroslav, the chainmail of Boris Godunov, and the ❷**sabres of Minin and Pozharsky**.

Downstairs in Room 6, you can see the ❸**coronation dresses** of 18th-century empresses (Empress Elizabeth, we're told, had 15,000 other dresses). Look for Catherine the Great's wedding gown, which is covered with silver brocade (note the 43cm waist size!). Other 'secular' clothing is also on display, including an impressive pair of boots that belonged to Peter the Great.

The following room contains some impressive furniture, including the 800-diamond throne of Tsar Alexey. The most unusual item is the ❹**joint coronation throne** of boy tsars Peter the Great and his half-brother Ivan V (with a secret compartment from which Regent Sofia prompted them). In the same room, you'll see the glittering and fur-lined crowns of the emperors through the ages. The gold ❺**Cap of Monomakh,** jewel-studded and sable-trimmed, was used for two centuries at coronations.

End your tour in Room 9, which houses centuries' worth of royal carriages and sledges. Look also for the ❻**sleigh** in which Elizabeth rode from St Petersburg to Moscow for her coronation, pulled by 23 horses at a time.

TOP SIGHT
RED SQUARE

One's first time setting foot on Red Square is a guaranteed awe-striker. The vast rectangular stretch of cobblestones is surrounded by architectural marvels, including St Basil's Cathedral. This panorama never fails to send the heart aflutter, especially at night. It evokes an incredible sense of import to stroll across the place where so much of Russian history has unfolded.

Resurrection Gate

At the northwestern corner of Red Square, Resurrection Gate (Воскресенские ворота) provides a great vantage point for your first glimpse of the square. With its twin red towers topped by green tent spires, the original 1680 gateway was destroyed because Stalin thought it an impediment to the parades and demonstrations held in Red Square. This exact replica was built in 1995. Just outside the gateway is the bright Chapel of the Iverian Virgin, originally built in the late 18th century to house the icon of the same name.

Kazan Cathedral

The little church occupying this site is a 1993 replica of the original 17th-century beauty, which was built in thanks for the 1612 expulsion of Polish invaders. The original **Kazan Cathedral** (Казанский собор; Map p271; Nikolskaya ul 3; ☺8am-7pm; MOkhotny Ryad) **FREE** was founded on this site at the northern end of Red Square in 1636. For two centuries it housed the Virgin of Kazan icon, which supposedly helped to rout the Poles. Three hundred years after it was built, the cathedral was completely demolished, allegedly because it impeded the flow of celebrating workers during holiday parades.

GUM

Behind its elaborate 240m-long facade on the northeastern side of Red Square, **GUM** (ГУМ; Map p271; www.gum.ru; ☺10am-10pm) is a bright, bustling shopping mall with hundreds of fancy stores and restaurants. With a skylight roof and three-level arcades, the

DON'T MISS

➡ Lenin's Mausoleum
➡ Saviour Gate Tower
➡ Resurrection Gate

PRACTICALITIES

➡ Красная площадь
➡ Map p271, D3
➡ Krasnaya pl
➡ MPloshchad Revolyutsii

spectacular interior was a revolutionary design when it was built in the 1890s, replacing the Upper Trading Rows that previously occupied this site.

Pronounced *goom,* the initials GUM originally stood for the Russian words for 'State Department Store'. When it was privatised in 2005, the name was officially changed to 'Main Department Store'. Fortunately, the words for 'state' and 'main' both start with a Russian 'G'.

Lenin's Mausoleum

Although Vladimir Ilych requested that he be buried beside his mum in St Petersburg, he still lies in state at the foot of the Kremlin wall, receiving visitors who come to pay their respects to the founder of the Soviet Union. Line up at the western corner of the square (near the entrance to Alexander Garden) to see the **embalmed leader** (Мавзолей Ленина; Map p271; www.lenin.ru; ⊙10am-1pm Tue-Thu, Sat & Sun) FREE, who has been here since 1924. Photography is not allowed; and stern guards ensure visitors remain respectful and silent.

Don't forget to inspect the Kremlin wall where other communist heavy hitters are buried, including:

➡ **Josef Stalin** Second general secretary, successor to Lenin.

➡ **Leonid Brezhnev** Fourth general secretary, successor to Khrushchev.

➡ **Felix Dzerzhinsky** Founder of the Cheka (forerunner of the KGB).

➡ **Yakov Sverdlov** A key organiser of the revolution and first official head of the Soviet state.

➡ **Andrei Zhdanov** Stalin's cultural chief and second most powerful person in the USSR immediately after WWII.

➡ **Mikhail Frunze** Red Army leader who secured Central Asia for the Soviet Union in the 1920s.

➡ **Inessa Armand** Lenin's rumoured lover. The director of Zhenotdel, an organisation fighting for equality for women within the Communist Party.

➡ **John Reed** American author of *Ten Days that Shook the World,* a first-hand account of the revolution.

Saviour Gate Tower

The Kremlin's 'official' exit onto Red Square is the red-brick **Saviour Gate Tower** (Спасская башня; Map p271). This gate – considered sacred – has been used for processions since tsarist times. The two white-stone plaques above the gate commemorate the tower's construction in 1491. The current clock was installed in the gate tower in the 1850s. Hauling 3m-long hands and weighing 25 tonnes, the clock takes up three of the tower's 10 levels. Its melodic chime sounds every 15 minutes across Red Square.

PHOTO OP

For an excellent photo op with good selfie potential, go around to the south side of St Basil's Cathedral, where there are unimpeded views and fewer people.

From 1953 to 1961, Lenin shared his mausoleum with Stalin. During the 22nd Party Congress, the esteemed and ancient Bolshevik Madame Spiridonova announced that Vladimir Ilych had appeared to her in a dream, insisting that he did not like spending eternity with his successor. With that, Stalin was removed and given a place of honour immediately behind the mausoleum.

PLACE OF SKULLS

The 13m circular stone platform in front of St Basil's Cathedral is known as the **Place of Skulls** (Лобное место; Map p271; Krasnaya pl). Legend has it that it was the site of executions; in reality, it was a stage for tsarist decrees and religious ceremonies.

TOP SIGHT
ST BASIL'S CATHEDRAL

At the southern end of Red Square stands the icon of Russia: St Basil's Cathedral. This crazy confusion of colours, patterns and shapes is the culmination of a style that is unique to Russian architecture. In 1552 Ivan the Terrible captured the Tatar stronghold of Kazan on the Feast of Intercession. He commissioned this landmark church, officially the Intercession Cathedral, to commemorate the victory.

Exterior

The cathedral's apparent anarchy of shapes hides a comprehensible plan of nine main chapels. The tall, tent-roofed tower in the centre houses the namesake Church of the Intercession of the Mother of God. The four biggest domes top four large octagonal-towered chapels; and there are four smaller chapels in between, each consecrated in honour of an event or battle in the struggle against Kazan.

The onion domes were originally green, most likely acquiring their characteristic colours and patterns during an 18th-century restoration. But the church has always been a spectacle. Dutch tiles and gilded rings embellish the tent roof. Approximately 300 multicoloured, semicircular gables adorn the upper tiers of the churches, while pink and white columns and coffers decorate the lower tiers.

Church of St Vasily the Blessed

The Church of St Vasily the Blessed, the northeastern chapel on the ground floor, contains the canopy-covered crypt of its namesake saint, one of the most revered in Moscow.

DON'T MISS

➡ Church of St Vasily the Blessed

➡ Portals from the vestry to the central church

➡ Icon of the Old Testament Trinity

➡ Icon of the Life of St Alexander Nevsky

PRACTICALITIES

➡ Покровский собор, Храм Василия Блаженного

➡ Map p271, D3

➡ adult/student ₽350/150

➡ ⊙ticket office 11am-5pm Nov-Apr, to 6pm May-Oct

➡ Ⓜ Ploshchad Revolyutsii

Vasily (Basil) the Blessed was known as a 'holy fool', sometimes going naked and purposefully humiliating himself for the greater glory of God. He was believed to be a seer and miracle maker, and even Ivan the Terrible revered and feared him. This 10th chapel – the only one at ground level – was added in 1588, after the saint's death. Look for the icon depicting St Vasily himself, with Red Square and the Kremlin in the background.

Church of the Intercession of the Holy Mother of God

The tall, tent-roofed tower in the centre of the cathedral houses the Church of the Intercession of the Holy Mother of God. The ceiling soars to nearly 47m. Some of the walls have been restored to their original appearance (a painted red-brick pattern), while others show off fragments of oil murals that were painted later. From the vestry, the doorways into this central chapel are among the most elaborate architectural elements in the cathedral, gorgeously embellished with tile and brickwork.

Church of the Holy Trinity

With whitewashed walls and a spiralling symbol of eternity painted in the vault, the light-filled Church of the Holy Trinity is a favourite. A gorgeous 16th-century chandelier is suspended from the 20m ceiling. But the gem of the room is the unusual iconostasis. The 16th-century *Icon of the Old Testament Trinity* in the third tier is among the oldest and most esteemed pieces of artwork in the cathedral.

Church of St Cyprian & St Justina

The colourful Church of Sts Cyprian & Justina is adorned with oil paintings depicting the lives of the 4th-century saints, as well as Biblical stories. At 20m, the vault in the dome depicts the *Mother of God of the Burning Bush*. The paintings and the iconostasis date to the end of the 18th century.

Church of the Entry of the Lord into Jerusalem

This chapel is dedicated to the Entry of the Lord into Jerusalem, also known in Orthodoxy as Willow Sunday. At 23m, this is one of the tallest towers in the cathedral. Whitewashed walls (as originally painted) show off the architectural elements. Above the northern entrance, you can see the scar left by a shell that hit the wall in October 1917. The iconostasis was moved from the Cathedral of St Alexander Nevsky in the Kremlin in 1770. One of the most sacred and revered pieces in the cathedral is the 17th-century icon of the *Life of St Alexander Nevsky*, which depicts 33 scenes from the saint's life.

AUDIO GUIDE

An audio guide to the history and architecture of St Basil's is available for ₽200.

Out front of St Basil's is a statue of Kuzma Minin and Dmitry Pozharsky, one a butcher and the other a prince, who raised and led the army that ejected occupying Poles from the Kremlin in 1612.

INTERCESSION CATHEDRAL

The official name of St Basil's Cathedral is the Intercession Cathedral. The misnomer 'St Basil's' refers to the extra northeastern chapel, which was built over the grave of Vasily (Basil) the Blessed.

⊙ SIGHTS

The neighbourhood of Red Square and Kitay Gorod is only about 1 sq km, but it is densely packed with sights. Most of them are clustered right around the square itself (and in the Kremlin). East of the square, the streets of Moscow's oldest neighbourhood are lined with churches and interesting architecture, and Park Zaryadye will soon occupy the plot of land next to the river.

KREMLIN   MUSEUM
See p60.

RED SQUARE   HISTORIC SITE
See p74.

ST BASIL'S CATHEDRAL   CHURCH
See p76.

VLADIMIR I STATUE   MONUMENT
Map p271 (Памятник Владимиру Великому; Borovitskaya pl) In 2016 Vladimir Putin unveiled a new monument dedicated to his namesake Vladimir I, ruler of Kyivan Rus from 980 to 1015. At 17m high, the massive statue towers over the surrounding Borovitskaya pl. Vladimir is credited with uniting the fledgling Russian state and establishing the Orthodox Church.

With the ongoing tensions between Russia and Ukraine, the statue was controversial, as Vladimir is also considered the founder of the Ukrainian nation.

MANEGE EXHIBITION CENTRE   GALLERY
Map p271 (Выставочный центр Манеж; http://moscowmanege.ru; Manezhnaya pl; exhibits ₽200-300; ⊗11am-8pm Tue-Sun; ⓂBiblioteka im Lenina) The long, low neoclassical building is Moscow Manege, a vast space that is used for art exhibitions and other events. In the works is a permanent exhibit dedicated to the iconic Soviet sculpture *Worker & Kolkhoz Woman,* on display at VDNKh (p93). Other events are wide-ranging, including exhibitions, concerts, poetry readings, film screenings and more.

STATE HISTORY MUSEUM   MUSEUM
Map p271 (Государственный исторический музей; www.shm.ru; Krasnaya pl 1; adult/student ₽350/100, audio guide ₽300; ⊗ticket office 10am-5pm Wed, Thu, Sun & Mon, to 9pm Fri & Sat; ⓂOkhotny Ryad) At the northern end of Red Square, the State History Museum has an enormous collection covering Russian

🏃 Neighbourhood Walk
Red Square & Kitay Gorod

START LUBYANSKAYA PL
END STARAYA PL
LENGTH 3KM; THREE HOURS

Start your tour at Lubyanskaya pl, dominated by the forbidding facade of the (former) Lubyanka Prison, a once notorious place. Nearby, the modest ❶ **Memorial to the Victims of Totalitarianism** (p83) remembers the individuals who suffered within these walls.

Leave behind the institutional buildings and heavy traffic when you enter Kitay Gorod, strolling down Nikolskaya ul. This was the main road to Vladimir and used to be the centre of a busy icon trade. Today it is a pleasant pedestrian street, lined with shops, churches and cafes. You'll pass the elaborate gated walkway at ❷ **Tretyakovsky Proezd** (p82), now home to Moscow's fanciest designer boutiques. Look also for the decorated, Gothic facade of the ❸ **Synod Printing House** (p82) – easily identified by the lion and the unicorn – and the gold-domed steeples of the ❹ **Zaikonospassky Monastery** (p81), peeking out over the rooftops.

In Kitay Gorod it seems like there are churches and monasteries on every corner and in every courtyard. Duck down Bogoyavlensky per to get a look at another one – the ❺ **Monastery of the Epiphany** (p82). This 13th-century monastery is the second oldest in Moscow, though the pink baroque church that stands here now was built later.

Cut through the courtyard and out to pl Revolyutsii. This busy square displays its own impressive array of architecture. The ❻ **Hotel Metropol** (p84) is a stunning example of art nouveau architecture, featuring spectacular tilework by the painter Mikhail Vrubel.

Further west, the unusual ❼ **Four Seasons Moscow** (p191) exhibits two contrasting architectural styles, thanks to a funny fluke of history. The story goes that Stalin was shown two possible designs for the Hotel Moskva on Manezhnaya pl. Not realising they were

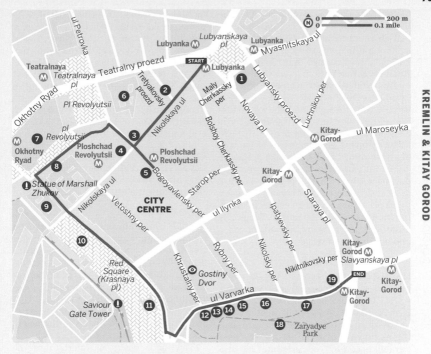

alternatives, he approved both. The builders did not dare point out his error, and so built half the hotel in constructivist style and half in Stalinist style. On the south side of the square, you'll notice the impressive red-brick facade of the **8 War of 1812 Museum** (p80) and the **9 State History Museum** (p78), both exhibiting Russian Revival and neo-Renaissance grandeur. A statue of the WWII general (and hero) Georgy Zhukov stands stoically in front.

Turn south and walk between the two museums – through Resurrection Gate – and feast your eyes on the glorious display in front of you: the stunning expanse of **10 Red Square** (p74). On the south side, the mighty Kremlin wall is punctuated by tall towers, most notably the Saviour Gate Tower. Beneath the wall, Lenin's Mausoleum still receives visitors, paying their respects. On the north side, the pretty little Kazan Cathedral complements the ornate facade of GUM. And at the far end, with its electrifying assemblage of shapes, colours and textures, stands Russia's most famous landmark, **11 St Basil's Cathedral** (p76). Walk across the expanse of cobblestones to see amazing architecture.

At the southern end of Red Square, turn left on ul Varvarka, a small street filled with ancient buildings. Walking from west to east, you'll pass the pink-and-white **12 St Barbara's Church**, dating to 1804; the peak-roofed **13 Old English Court** (p81), dating to the 16th century; the 17th-century **14 Church of St Maxim the Blessed**; the monks' building and golden-domed cathedral of the **15 Monastery of the Sign**; the ancient **16 Chambers of the Romanov Boyars** (p81); and the 1658 **17 St George's Church**. On the opposite side of the street are the trading arcades of Gostinny Dvor.

South of ul Varvarka and running down to the river, the 14th-century Zaryadye district was once home to Moscow's garment industry, as well as a large Jewish population. The district was razed in the 1940s to make way for a gargantuan hotel. In the 21st century, the area is transformed once again, as the site of the highly anticipated **18 Park Zaryadye** (p82).

Continue east and emerge onto Staraya pl. In the underground passage on the corner, look out for the **19 remains of the old city wall**. This *perekhod* walkway is also the entrance to the Kitay-Gorod metro station.

history from the time of the Stone Age. The building, dating from the late 19th century, is itself an attraction – each room is in the style of a different period or region, some with highly decorated walls echoing old Russian churches.

The exhibits about medieval Rus are excellent, with several rooms covering the Mongol invasions and the consolidation of the Russian state. The 2nd floor is dedicated to the Imperial period, with exhibits featuring personal items of the royals, furnishings and decoration from the palace interiors, and various artworks and documents from the era. Specific rooms are dedicated to the rules of various tsars. An unexpected highlight is an exhibit addressing the expansion of the Russian Empire by examining the growing network of roads and how people travelled.

ARCHAEOLOGICAL MUSEUM   MUSEUM
Map p271 (Музей археологии Москвы; www.mosmuseum.ru; Manezhnaya pl 1; adult/child ₽300/150; ⊙10am-8pm Tue, Wed & Fri-Sun, 11am-9pm Thu; ⓂOkhotny Ryad) An excavation of Voskresensky Bridge (which used to span the Neglinnaya River at the foot of Tverskaya ul) uncovered coins, clothing and other artefacts from old Moscow. The museum displaying these treasures is situated in a 7m-deep underground pavilion that was formed during the excavation itself. The entrance is at the base of the Four Seasons Moscow hotel.

GEORGY ZHUKOV STATUE   STATUE
Map p271 (Manezhnaya pl) Georgy Zhukov was Chief of Staff of the Red Army during the Great Patriotic War. He oversaw the defence of both Leningrad and Stalingrad, as well as the Battle of Moscow. The centrepiece of Manezhnaya pl, he is depicted riding his upon his steed.

WAR OF 1812 MUSEUM   MUSEUM
Map p271 (Музей отечественной войны 1812 года; www.shm.ru; pl Revolyutsii 2; adult/child ₽350/150; ⊙10am-6pm Sun-Thu, to 9pm Fri & Sat, closed Mon Sep-May; ⓂPloshchad Revolyutsii) Part Russian Revival, part neo-Renaissance, this red-brick beauty was built in the 1890s as the Moscow City Hall and later served as the Central Lenin Museum. It was converted into the War of 1812 Museum in honour of the war's 200-year anniversary. Artwork, documents, weapons and uniforms are all on display, with good

multimedia exhibits offering a detailed depiction of the events and effects of the war.

Exhibits provide detailed, chronological coverage of all phases of the war, with good signage in English. There are also film depictions of various battles and interactive maps to enhance your understanding of events. Highlights include a series of paintings by Vasily Verechshagin entitled *1812*, old film footage of Nicholas II at Borodino and Napoleon's getaway sleigh.

KARL MARX STATUE   STATUE
Map p271 (Памятник Карлу Марксу; pl Revolyutsii) Since 1961, Karl Marx has occupied this prominent position on pl Revolyutsii.

KITAY GOROD   AREA
Map p271 This 13th-century neighbourhood was the first in Moscow to grow up outside the Kremlin walls. While its name means 'China Town' in modern Russian, do not expect anything Chinese – the name derives from an old Russian word meaning 'wattle', for the supports used for the walls that protected the suburb. This is the heart of medieval Moscow and parts of the neighbourhood's walls are visible.

The main places of interest are the collection of churches, especially along ul Varvarka, and the new Park Zaryadye (p82).

PARK ZARYADYE PAVILION   MUSEUM
Map p271 (Павильон парка "Зарядье"; Moskvoretskaya ul) FREE This glass-dome pavilion was the first element of Park Zaryadye (p82) to open to the public. A creation of Sergei Kuznetsov, the pavilion was designed as an 'observation deck' for the ongoing work on the park. Construction was not actually visible from the pavilion; rather, the central chamber is wallpapered in QR codes – a surprisingly appealing look – that contain maps, designs, photographs and other information about the new park. At the entrance, visitors receive tablets which they can use to decode the electronic exhibits.

Kuznetsov's design first appeared in 2012 at the Venice Biennale of Architecture, where it received high praise. Although it was originally meant to be a temporary structure, the current plan is to keep the pavilion in place as an information centre about the park. The QR-code decor will remain, but the subjects of the electronic exhibits may change. And eventually, this so-called observation deck will also offer an actual view of the park, not just a virtual one.

OLD ENGLISH COURT
MUSEUM

Map p271 (Палаты старого Английского двора; www.mosmuseum.ru; ul Varvarka 4a; adult/child ₽200/100; ☺10am-6pm Tue, Wed & Fri-Sun, 11am-9pm Thu; Ⓜ Kitay-Gorod) This reconstructed 16th-century house, white with wooden roofs, was the residence of England's first emissaries to Russia (sent by Elizabeth I to Ivan the Terrible).

It also served as the base for English merchants, who were allowed to trade duty-free in exchange for providing military supplies to Ivan. Today, it houses a small exhibit dedicated to this early international exchange.

CHAMBERS OF THE ROMANOV BOYARS
MUSEUM

Map p271 (Палаты бояр Романовых; www.shm.ru; ul Varvarka 10; Ⓜ Kitay-Gorod) This small but interesting museum is devoted to the lives of the Romanov family, who were mere boyars (nobles) before they became tsars. The house was built by Nikita Romanov, whose grandson Mikhail later became the first tsar of the 300-year Romanov dynasty. Exhibits show the house as it might have been when the Romanovs lived here in the 16th century. Enter from

was closed for renovation at the time of research.

CHURCH OF THE TRINITY IN NIKITNIKI
CHURCH

Map p271 (Церковь Троицы в Никитниках; Ipatyevsky per; Ⓜ Kitay-Gorod) Hidden between big government blocks, this little gem of a church is an exquisite example of Russian baroque. Built in the 1630s, its onion domes and tiers of red-and-white spade gables rise from a square tower. Its interior is covered with 1650s gospel frescoes by Simon Ushakov and others. A carved doorway leads into St Nikita the Martyr's Chapel, above the vault of the Nikitnikov merchant family, who were among the patrons who financed the church's construction.

ZAIKONOSPASSKY MONASTERY
MONASTERY

Map p271 (Заиконоспасский монастырь; Nikolskaya ul 7-9; Ⓜ Ploshchad Revolyutsii) This monastery was founded by Boris Godunov in 1600, although the church was built in 1660. The name means 'Behind the Icon Stall', a reference to the busy icon trade that once took place here. The now-functioning, multitiered Saviour Church is tucked into the courtyard away from the street.

On the orders of Tsar Alexey, the Likhud brothers – scholars of Greek – opened the

Park Zaryadye Pavilion

monastery premises in 1687. (Mikhail Lomonosov was a student here.) The academy later became a divinity school and was transferred to the Trinity Monastery of St Sergius in 1814.

MONASTERY OF
THE EPIPHANY
MONASTERY

Map p271 (Богоявленский монастырь; Bogoyavlensky per 2; ⓂPloshchad Revolyutsii) This monastery is the second-oldest in Moscow, founded in 1296 by Prince Daniil, son of Alexander Nevsky. The current Epiphany Cathedral – with its tall, pink, gold-domed cupola – was constructed in the 1690s in the Moscow baroque style. If you're lucky, you may hear the bells ringing forth from the old wooden belfry nearby.

SYNOD PRINTING
HOUSE
HISTORIC BUILDING

Map p271 (Печатный двор Синод; Nikolskaya ul 15; ⓂPloshchad Revolyutsii) Now housing the Russian State University for the Humanities, this elaborately decorated edifice is where Ivan Fyodorov reputedly produced Russia's first printed book, *The Apostle,* in 1563. You can see a statue of the man himself nearby. Spiralling Solomonic columns and Gothic windows frame the lion and unicorn, who are facing off in the centre of the facade.

Up until the early 19th century, Kitay Gorod was something of a printing centre, home to 26 of Moscow's 31 bookshops.

TRETYAKOVSKY PROEZD
STREET

Map p271 (Третьяковский проезд; ⓂTeatralnaya) The gated walkway of Tretyakovsky proezd (originally built in the 1870s) leads from Teatralny proezd into Kitay Gorod. Nearby, you can see where archaeologists uncovered the 16th-century fortified wall that used to surround Kitay Gorod, as well as the foundations of the 1493 Trinity Church. There is also a statue of Ivan Fyodorov, the 16th-century printer responsible for Russia's first book.

PARK ZARYADYE

For the first time in 50 years, Moscow is getting a major new park, and it's happening in the heart of the historic centre – just a few steps from Red Square.

Park Zaryadye will occupy a prominent site along the Moscow River, wedged into historic Kitay Gorod. It is designed by the New York firm Diller Scofidio & Renfro (DS&R), which is renowned for its use of 'wild urbanism', a technique that merges the historic city streets with wild natural habitats. The 13ha site will include four different areas representing Russia's geographic zones – tundra, steppe, forest and wetlands – flowing seamlessly into each other. The most anticipated feature, perhaps, is a sort of bridge to nowhere, which stretches out across Moskvoretskaya nab and over the Moscow River, then loops back to Zaryadye.

In addition to the parkland, Zaryadye will contain a vast outdoor amphitheatre and several new museums, built into the hillsides and showcasing Russia's natural resources and richness.

The centrepiece is the Media Centre, where visitors can watch aerial-view films such as Soaring over Russia on a 39m movie screen. In the Time Machine Room, the history of Russia unfolds on a 360-degree screen that surrounds the viewers. Other exhibits and videos show off various national parks and promote travel within Russia.

The Zapavednaya Posolstvo (Conservation Embassy) will be a state-of-the-art museum featuring a large terrarium and laboratory space, offering many educational programs. A separate ice cave – kept below freezing year-round – will feature the creations of Arctic ice artist Alexander Ponomarev.

The smaller Podzemniy Museum (Underground Museum) is an archaeological exhibition, showing off a piece of the old Kitay Gorod wall that was uncovered during excavation.

Finally, the Park Zaryadye Pavilion (p80) serves as a museum of Park Zaryadye, providing an overview of the park and its development. The building was introduced by architect Sergei Kuznetsov at the Venice Biennale of Architecture in 2012.

Park Zaryadye was inaugurated in September 2017, while the museums and other features are likely to roll out over the course of the following year.

Back in the day, the archway was financed by the Tretyakov brothers (founders of the namesake art gallery). Apparently the construction of the medieval-style gate and the opening of the passageway were an attempt to relieve traffic on Nikolskaya ul. It was reopened in 2000 and is now lined with exclusive shops.

MEMORIAL TO THE VICTIMS OF TOTALITARIANISM
MEMORIAL

Map p271 (Мемориал жертвам тоталитаризма; Lubyanskaya pl) This humble memorial stands in the little garden south of the notorious Lubyanka Prison (p160). The single stone slab comes from an infamous 1930s labour camp situated on the Solovetsky Islands in the White Sea.

EATING

Considering the number of tourists who pass through Red Square every day, there's a surprising dearth of good places to eat. There are plenty of options inside the GUM and Okhotny Ryad malls: most are unappealing chain restaurants and fast-food joints, but there are a few gems. Otherwise, stroll down to the northern end of Nikolskaya ul for some excellent choices.

STOLOVAYA NO 57
CAFETERIA €

Map p271 (Столовая 57; ☑495-620 3129; https://gumrussia.com/shops/stolovaya-57; 3rd fl, GUM, Krasnaya pl 3; mains ₽200-300; ⊗10am-10pm; 🚇; ⓂOkhotny Ryad) Newly minted, this old-style cafeteria offers a nostalgic recreation of dining in post-Stalinist Russia. The food is good – and cheap for such a fancy store. Meat cutlets and cold salads come highly recommended. This is a great place to try 'herring in a fur coat' (herring, beetroots, carrots and potatoes).

FARSH
BURGERS €

Map p271 (Farш; ☑495-258 4205; www.farshburger.ru; Nikolskaya ul 12; burgers ₽250-580; ⊗10am-midnight; ⓂLubyanka) Burger mania is sweeping the capital and Farsh is at the forefront, serving gourmet burgers and amazing French fries, as well as chicken wings, barbecue ribs and grilled steaks. This is the equally tasty fast-food counterpart to neighbouring Ryby Net (except it's not always that fast during busy times).

GRAND COFFEE MANIA
CAFE €€

Map p271 (Кофе мания; ☑495-960 2295; www.coffeemania.ru; Mal Cherkassky per 2; breakfast ₽300-500, mains ₽500-1200; ⊗8am-midnight Mon-Thu, to 2am Fri, 10am-2am Sat, 10am-midnight Sun; 🌬🛜🚭🚇; ⓂLubyanka) This place has the same overpriced but appetising fare as other outlets of the ubiquitous chain, but the fabulous 'grand cafe' interior makes this one a special experience. Marble floors, art deco chandeliers and elaborate latticework evoke another era. Efficient service and excellent atmosphere.

BON APP CAFE
EUROPEAN €€

Map p271 (www.facebook.com/bonappcafe; 1st fl, Nikolskaya ul 25; pizza & pasta ₽420-480, mains ₽480-840; ⊗9am-midnight Mon-Fri, from 11am Sat & Sun; 🛜🚇; ⓂLubyanka) On the 1st floor of the Nautilus shopping centre, this is a popular lunch spot for workers, shoppers and tourists recovering from Red Square. The interior is cool and contemporary, but still comfortable. The wide-ranging menu includes pizza, pasta and other Russian and European fare, so there is something for everyone.

RYBY NET
STEAK €€€

Map p271 (Рыбы Нет; ☑495-258 4206; www.novikovgroup.ru; Nikolskaya ul 12; mains ₽800-2000; ⊗noon-midnight; ⓂLubyanka) If you don't get the name, which means 'No Fish', the sides of beef hanging in the window should give you a clue. This is where you come to get your carnivore on. Steaks are prepared from top-quality marbled meat and served with a fresh-baked baguette. There's a good wine list and custom cocktails to accompany.

If the steaks are going to bust your budget, go next door for burgers at Farsh.

BOSCO CAFE
ITALIAN €€€

Map p271 (☑495-620 3182; https://gumrussia.com/cafe/bosco-cafe; GUM, Krasnaya pl 3; pasta ₽500-1000, mains ₽1200-2000; ⊗10am-10pm; 🚇; ⓂPloshchad Revolyutsii) Sip a cappuccino in view of the Kremlin. Munch on lunch while the crowds line up at Lenin's Mausoleum. Enjoy an afternoon aperitif while admiring St Basil's domes. Service is lacking and the menu is overpriced, but this cafe on the 1st floor of the GUM mall is the only place to sit right on Red Square and marvel at its magnificence.

HOTEL METROPOL

The Hotel Metropol (p191) is among Moscow's finest examples of art nouveau architecture. The decorative panel on the hotel's central facade, facing Teatralny proezd, is based on a sketch by the artist Mikhail Vrubel. It depicts the legend of the Princess of Dreams, in which a troubadour falls in love with a kind and beautiful princess and travels across the seas to find her. He falls ill during the voyage and is near death when he finds his love. The princess embraces him, but he dies in her arms. Naturally, the princess reacts to his death by renouncing her worldly life. The ceramic panels were made at the pottery workshop at Savva Mamontov's estate in Abramtsevo (p174).

The ceramic work on the side of the hotel facing Teatralnaya pl is by the artist Alexander Golovin. The script was originally a quote from Nietzsche: 'Again the same story: when you build a house you notice that you have learned something'. During the Soviet era, these wise words were replaced with something more appropriate for the time: 'Only the dictatorship of the proletariat can liberate mankind from the oppression of capitalism'. Lenin, of course.

The menu is wide-ranging, so you don't have to spend a fortune. Reservations recommended for dinner.

🍷 DRINKING & NIGHTLIFE

There are only a few places to drink in Kitay Gorod – all clustered around the northern end of Nikolskaya ul. The neighbourhood is mostly quiet at night.

MANDARIN COMBUSTIBLE   LOUNGE

Map p271 (☑495-745 0700; Mal Cherkassky per 2; ☺noon-6am; ☎; Ⓜ Lubyanka) Dining, drinking and dancing are all on offer in this sexy space. There is a long menu of Pan Asian cuisine – as well as sushi, pasta, tapas and more – served all night long for Moscow's nonstop party people. Drinks are forgettable and service is slack, but everything (and everyone) looks fine – and sometimes that's what matters.

CIDERELLA   BAR

Map p271 (www.facebook.com/ciderellatapas; Nikolskaya ul 11; ☺9am-11pm; ☎; Ⓜ Ploshchad Revolyutsii) If you're getting tired of craft beer and gourmet burgers, here is something different: cider and tapas. Choose from 90 different types of cider and a smaller selection of snacks. High stools, exposed brick and the hipster clientele create an atmosphere of convivial bohemia.

JAWSSPOT MSK   CRAFT BEER

Map p271 (http://tinyurl.com/yc9wcakx; 6th fl, Nautilus, Nikolskaya ul 25; ☺noon-midnight Sun-Thu, to 2am Fri & Sat; ☎; Ⓜ Lubyanka) On the top floor of the Nautilus shopping centre, you'll find this small surfer beer bar. An even smaller terrace gives a fantastic view of Lubyanskaya pl. Jawsspot hails from the Urals, where they've been brewing beer in a former laundry since 2008. Now they're serving their great-tasting, cleverly named brews in the capital.

KOLKOVNA   BAR

Map p271 (Колковна; www.kolkovna.su; Lubyansky proezd 15; ☺11am-midnight; ☎; Ⓜ Kitay-Gorod) This cool and cosy basement – with exposed brick walls and arcade ceiling – is the perfect setting to sip a refreshing Czech beer. There are sausages and other traditional Czech food to accompany the freshly drawn lagers and ales.

⭐ ENTERTAINMENT

KREMLIN BALLET   BALLET

Map p271 (Кремлевский балет; ☑495-620 7846; www.kremlinpalace.org; ☺box office noon-8pm; Ⓜ Aleksandrovsky Sad) The Bolshoi Theatre doesn't have a monopoly on ballet in Moscow. Leading dancers also appear with the Kremlin Ballet, which performs in the State Kremlin Palace (p61). The Bolshoi is magical, but seeing a show inside the Kremlin is something special too. The repertoire is unapologetically classical. The box office is near the entrance to the Biblioteka im Lenina metro station.

🔒 SHOPPING

With hundreds of fancy stores and restaurants, GUM (p74) is a bright, bustling shopping mall that's worth a browse when you visit Red Square. There are a few other boutiques and souvenir stores along Nikolskaya ul.

LNYANAYA LAVKA   CLOTHING

Map p271 (☑8-925-597 8167; Nikolskaya ul 8/1; ⊙11am-6pm; ⓂPloshchad Revolyutsii) Russian fashion designers are doing wonderful things with linen, crafting this potentially drab material into modern, playful clothing. Styles are interesting, attractive and – in some cases – subtly sexy. Reasonable prices.

ALENA AKHMADULLINA
BOUTIQUE   FASHION & ACCESSORIES

Map p271 (Бутик Алёны Ахмадуллиной; www.alenaakhmadullina.ru; Nikolskaya ul 25; ⊙11am-10pm; ⓂLubyanka) Alena Akhmadullina's romantic, flowing fashions have been wowing trendsetters since 2005, when the St Petersburg designer first showed her stuff in Paris. She has received loads of international attention ever since (including an invitation to provide an outfit for Angelina Jolie in the film *Wanted*). The subtly seductive designs are known for offering a new perspective on Russian themes.

OKHOTNY RYAD   MALL

Map p271 (ТЦ Охотный ряд; www.ox-r.ru; Manezhnaya pl; ⊙10am-10pm; ⓂOkhotny Ryad) The best part of this underground mall is the fanciful troika fountain that splashes the shoppers as they enter and exit from Alexander Garden. Aside from the clothing and electronic stores, there is a big, crowded food court.

Tverskoy

Neighbourhood Top Five

1 Bolshoi Theatre (p88) Spending an evening at one of the world's grandest opera and ballet venues.

2 Hermitage Gardens (p90) Eating, drinking, dancing and otherwise frolicking at one of Moscow's liveliest parks, where art,

culinary or musical festivals take place almost weekly.

3 Jewish Museum & Centre of Tolerance (p90) Learning about daily life for Jews in Russia from the partition of Poland to the late USSR times at this ultramodern museum.

4 Sanduny Baths (p102) Sweating away your city stresses amid ultimate architectural opulence.

5 Delicatessen (p95) Enjoying delicious food and award-winning cocktails at a gastrobar that regularly makes it into world's best lists.

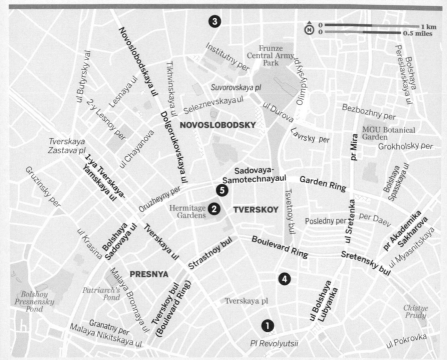

For more detail of this area see Map p274 ➡

Explore Tverskoy

Start your exploration at the majestic Teatralnaya pl (Theatre Sq), home to the world-famous Bolshoi Theatre. This glittering jewel of a theatre is a sight to behold.

Several commercial streets, most filled with boutiques and cafes, radiate from Teatralnaya pl towards the Boulevard Ring. Car-free Kamergersky per connects to Tverskaya ul, Moscow's main thoroughfare, lined with stately pre-Soviet and Stalin-era buildings. This is the best area in Moscow for people-watching, where government officials and business people mingle with domestic tourists and Moscow hipsters. Many cafes accommodate this activity, some with sidewalk seating.

Further up, trendy Stoleshnikov per connects ul Bolshaya Dmitrovka with quaint ul Petrovka, which leads past the Moscow Museum of Modern Art to the charming Hermitage Gardens. Outside the Garden Ring, Novoslobodsky is a pleasant part of town with several important museums scattered around a fairly large area. Two metro stops away, Flakon and Khlebozavod 9 form a single area of former factories converted into attractive shopping and entertainment spaces.

Local Life

→**Parks** Hermitage Gardens is one of the city's liveliest places, with fresh air, greenery and cocktails at 32.05.

→**Gathering point** The Pushkin monument in the centre of Pushkinskaya pl (Pushkin Sq) is the city's most popular meeting point and political protest venue.

→**Student life** The proximity of a major university makes the cluster of bars around Mendeleyevskaya station especially lively.

Getting There & Away

→**Teatralnaya pl** Take the green Zamoskvoretskaya metro line to Teatralnaya metro station.

→**Tverskaya ul** Manezhnaya pl, at the bottom of Tverskaya ul, is accessible from the Okhotny Ryad metro station on the red Sokolnicheskaya line. The green Zamoskvoretskaya metro line provides easy access to Pushkinskaya pl (at Tverskaya station), Triumfalnaya pl (at Mayakovskaya station) and pl Tverskaya Zastava (at Belorusskaya station).

→**Beyond the Garden Ring** The green Zamoskvoretskaya metro line follows Tverskaya ul (which becomes 1-ya Tverskaya-Yamskaya ul, then Leningradsky pr and eventually Leningradskoe sh) almost all the way to the MKAD ring road, terminating at Rechnoy Vokzal. Novoslobodsky district is accessible via the connecting metro stations at Novoslobodskaya or Mendeleyevskaya.

Lonely Planet's Top Tip

While the Bolshoi is Russia's most famous theatre, it is not the only one. Several other opera and ballet theatres in Moscow offer the same level of professionalism and panache in their performances at a fraction of the price. If you have your heart set on going to the opera, consider the Novaya Opera (p100) – a gorgeous theatre set in charming gardens.

TVERSKOY

⊙ **Best Soviet History**

→ Contemporary History Museum (p90)

→ Gulag History Museum (p92)

→ Central Museum of the Armed Forces (p92)

For reviews, see p89.➡

✗ **Best Places to Eat**

→ Delicatessen (p95)

→ Brasserie Most (p97)

→ Lavka-Lavka (p95)

→ Seven (p96)

→ Golodny-Zloy (p95)

For reviews, see p94.➡

☐ **Best Places to Drink**

→ Noor / Electro (p98)

→ Enthusiast (p98)

→ Cafe Mart (p98)

→ 32.05 (p98)

→ Svoboda (p100)

For reviews, see p98.➡

DIMBAR76 / SHUTTERSTOCK ©

TOP SIGHT
BOLSHOI THEATRE

The Bolshoi is still one of Moscow's most romantic and entertaining options for a night on the town. The glittering six-tier auditorium has an electric atmosphere, evoking over 240 years of premier music and dance. Both ballet and opera are on offer.

The present pink-and-white beauty was built in 1824, and saw the premiers of Tchaikovsky's *Swan Lake* in 1877 and *The Nutcracker* in 1919. The facade is famed for the bronze troika that is seemingly about to fly off the front. Gracing Teatralnaya Sq, the fountain by Vitali, which features bronze sculptures of the three muses, is Moscow's oldest. A welcome supplement, Bolshoi's new stage was opened next door in 2002.

Opera and ballet directors come and go, leaving their imprint on the repertoire and generating controversy. But classic gems, such as the iconic *Swan Lake* and *Boris Godunov,* remain. There have been successful experiments with 20th-century and modern music in recent years, but they don't tend to linger for long.

Juicy stories about the Bolshoi's singers and ballerinas regularly appear in tabloids. In the last two decades, the Bolshoi has been marred by politics, scandal and even outright crime. Yet the show must go on – and it will.

A few tips for a fabulous night at the Bolshoi:

➡Purchase tickets online at www.bolshoi.ru/en/timetable before you set off on your trip to Moscow.

➡Dress to the nines so you can blend into the jet-set crowd.

➡Come early to explore the richly decorated building.

➡Have a ritual glass of bubbly in the buffet, a great place for people-watching.

DON'T MISS
➡ Fountain by Vitali
➡ Bronze troika
➡ Your performance!

PRACTICALITIES
➡ Большой театр
➡ Map p274, E8
➡ ☏495-455 5555
➡ www.bolshoi.ru
➡ Teatralnaya pl 1
➡ tickets ₽100-12,000
➡ ⊙closed late Jul–mid-Sep
➡ Ⓜ Teatralnaya

⊙ SIGHTS

Although mostly a commercial district, Tverskoy is dotted with museums and boasts the excellent Hermitage Gardens – a much-needed escape from the city madness. Beyond the Garden Ring, several major attractions are found in the quieter Novoslobodsky district and around VDNKh metro (orange line).

⊙ Tverskoy

DETSKY MIR HISTORIC BUILDING

Map p274 (☑ 495-777 8077; www.detmir.ru; Tea-tralny pr 5/1; ⊙10am-10pm; 🛗) FREE Dominated by the infamous KGB compound, Lubyanskaya pl made adults shiver in Soviet times, but children dreamed of coming here, because another stately edifice in the square was filled with toys and goods intended entirely for them. Although the 1950s interior was lost in a 2008 reconstruction, it's worth visiting this children's department store to check out Soviet toy fashions at the Museum of Childhood and admire sweeping views of central Moscow from a rooftop observation point above it.

Access to the museum and the roof is from the food court on the top floor of the department store, which is now primarily occupied by Western brands.

HOUSE OF UNIONS NOTABLE BUILDING

Map p274 (Дом союзов; Okhotny ryad 2/1; Ⓜ Te-atralnaya) The green-columned House of Unions dates from the 1780s. Its ballroom, called the Hall of Columns, is famous as the location of one of Stalin's most grotesque show trials: that of Nikolai Bukharin, a leading Communist Party theorist who had been a close associate of Lenin.

The House of Unions can only be accessed when they stage one of the infrequent concerts.

STATE DUMA NOTABLE BUILDING

Map p274 (www.duma.gov.ru; Okhotny ryad 1; Ⓜ Okhotny Ryad) The glowering State Duma was erected in the 1930s for Gosplan (Soviet State Planning Department), source of the USSR's Five-Year Plans. It is now the seat of the Russian parliament, and is closed to public.

TVERSKAYA PLOSHCHAD HISTORIC SITE

Map p274 (Тверская площадь) A statue of the founder of Moscow, Yury Dolgoruky, presides over this prominent square near the bottom of Tverskaya ul. So does Mayor Sergei Sobyanin, as the buffed-up five-storey building opposite is the Moscow mayor's office.

Many ancient churches are hidden in the surrounding backstreets, including the 17th-century Church of Sts Kosma and Damian.

MUSEUM OF SOVIET ARCADE MACHINES MUSEUM

Map p274 (☑ 495-628 4515; http://15kop.ru; ul Kuznetsky most 12; admission incl tour ₽450; ⊙11am-9pm; Ⓜ Kuznetsky Most) Growing up in the 1980s USSR was a peculiar, but not necessarily entirely bleak experience. Here is an example – a collection containing dozens of mostly functional Soviet arcade machines. At the entrance, visitors get a paper bag full of 15-kopek Soviet coins, which fire up these recreational dinosaurs that would look at home in the oldest episodes of *Star Trek*.

Most of the games test your shooting or driving skills. Times and attitudes were different, so don't be surprised by having to target fluffy squirrels and rabbits in Winter Hunt. You can also measure your force by pulling out a rather defiant turnip, or try to beat your friend in table ice hockey. If the effort makes you sweat, get some fruit-flavoured fizzy water from an authentic machine – it's only 3 kopeks! The admission ticket includes a tour, during which you get to play 15 machines.

MOSCOW MUSEUM OF MODERN ART MUSEUM

Map p274 (Московский музей современного искусства; MMOMA; www.mmoma.ru; ul Petrovka 25; adult/student ₽450/250, joint ticket for three venues ₽500/300; ⊙noon-8pm Tue, Wed & Fri-Sun, 1-9pm Thu; Ⓜ Chekhovskaya) A pet project of the ubiquitous artist Zurab Tsereteli, this museum is housed in a classical 18th-century merchant's home, originally designed by Matvei Kazakov (architect of the Kremlin Senate). It is the perfect light-filled setting for an impressive collection of 20th-century paintings, sculptures and graphics, which include both Russian and foreign artists. The highlight is the collection of avant-garde art, with works by Chagall, Kandinsky and Malevich.

Unique to this museum is its exhibit of 'nonconformist' artists from the 1950s and '60s – those whose work was not acceptable to the Soviet regime. The gallery also hosts temporary exhibits that often feature contemporary artists. Be sure not to bypass the whimsical sculpture garden in the courtyard, where Tsereteli's own strange and kitschy works are on display. There are four additional MMOMA outlets, used primarily for temporary exhibits, including those on Tverskoy bul (p105) and Yermolayevsky per (p107).

UPPER ST PETER
MONASTERY
MONASTERY

Map p274 (Петровский монастырь; cnr ul Petrovka & Petrovsky bul; ⊘8am-8pm; MChekhovskaya) The Upper St Peter Monastery was founded in the 1380s as part of an early defensive ring around Moscow. The main, onion-domed Virgin of Bogolyubovo Church dates from the late 17th century. The loveliest structure is the brick Cathedral of Metropolitan Pyotr, restored with a shingle roof. When Peter the Great ousted the Regent Sofia in 1690, his mother was so pleased she built him this church.

CHURCH OF THE
NATIVITY OF THE
VIRGIN IN PUTINKI
CHURCH

Map p274 (Церковь Рождества Богородицы в Путинках; ul Malaya Dmitrovka 4; MPushkinskaya) When this church was completed in 1652, Patriarch Nikon responded by banning tent roofs like those featured here. Apparently, he considered such architecture too Russian, too secular and too far removed from the Church's Byzantine roots. Fortunately, the Church of the Nativity has survived to grace this corner near Pushkinskaya pl.

CONTEMPORARY
HISTORY MUSEUM
MUSEUM

Map p274 (Музей современной истории России; ☏495-699 6724; www.sovr.ru; Tverskaya ul 21; adult/student ₽250/100; ⊘10am-6pm Tue-Sun; MPushkinskaya) Complete with stone lions, this opulent mansion was built to host the English Club – a venue favoured by Anglophile gentlemen and native Brits in tsarist times. After a stint as the Revolution Museum in the Soviet era, it now houses exhibitions that trace Russian history from the 1905 and 1917 revolutions up to present days.

Reflecting the government's penchant for rewriting history, a popular joke goes that Russia is a country with an unpredictable past. That attitude manifested itself when the main section of the museum, dedicated to the 20th century, was closed for renovation in 2017, the year of the October Revolution's 100th anniversary – a date President Vladimir Putin is very uncomfortable with. Temporary exhibitions, including those dedicated to Putin's reign, were open at the time of writing.

★HERMITAGE GARDENS
PARK

Map p274 (Сады Эрмитажа; www.mosgorsad.ru; ul Karetny Ryad 3; ⊘24hr; MPushkinskaya) **FREE** All the things that have improved Moscow parks no end in recent years fill this small, charming garden to the brim. Today, it is possibly the most happening place in Moscow, where art, food and crafts festivals, and concerts, occur almost weekly, especially in summer. Apart from the welcoming lawns and benches, it boasts a large children's playground, a summer cinema and a cluster of food and crafts kiosks. Come here to unwind and mingle with the coolest Muscovites.

The garden was created in 1894 around a theatre that saw the screening of the Lumière brothers' first film in 1896, as well as the 1898 Moscow premiere of Chekhov's *Seagull* – performed by the troupe that had just been scrambled together by Stanislavsky and Nemirovich-Danchenko.

M'ARS CONTEMPORARY
ART CENTRE
GALLERY

Map p274 (Центр Современного Искусства М'АРС; www.marsgallery.ru; Pushkarev per 5; ₽950-1300; ⊘2-8pm Tue-Fri, noon-10pm Sat & Sun; MTsvetnoy Bulvar, Sukharevskaya) Founded by artists who were banned during the Soviet era, this gallery space includes 10 exhibit halls showing the work of top contemporary artists, as well as a cool cafe in the basement. The target audience here is people who invest in art – hence the high admission prices.

◉ Novoslobodsky

JEWISH MUSEUM &
CENTRE OF TOLERANCE
MUSEUM

(Еврейский музей и Центр толерантности; ☏495-645 0550; www.jewish-museum.ru; ul Obraztsova 11 str 1a; adult/student ₽400/200;

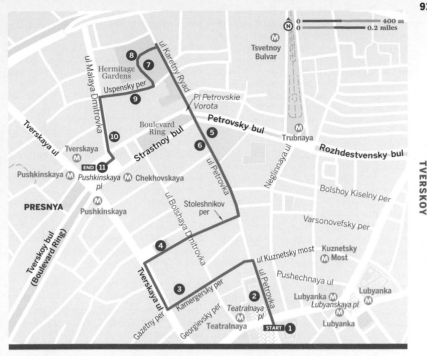

🏃 Neighbourhood Walk Tverskoy

START TEATRALNAYA PL
END PUSHKIN MONUMENT
LENGTH 3KM; 3½ HOURS

Start your tour at the stately Teatralnaya pl, ringed with eye-catching architecture. The magnificent **❶ Hotel Metropol** (p191) is an art nouveau masterpiece. Across the street, the **❷ Bolshoi Theatre** (p88) is the centrepiece of the square. The Maly Theatre and the National Youth Theatre frame it on either side.

Head up ul Petrovka and turn left onto Kamergersky per, Moscow's prime people-watching spot. Look out for the **❸ Moscow Art Theatre** (p101), founded by Konstantin Stanislavsky in 1898.

From here walk up Tverskaya ul to **❹ Tverskaya ploshchad** (p89), home to two Moscow heroes: the centre statue is Yury Dolgoruky, founder of Moscow; across in city hall sits Sergei Sobyanin, mayor of Moscow. East of here, Stoleshnikov per is another quaint cobblestone strip, lined with fancy boutiques and trendy cafes.

From Stoleshnikov per turn left into ul Petrovka and walk north towards pl Petrovskie Vorota, named for the gates that used to guard the city. In this area, you can wander around the ancient **❺ Upper St Peter Monastery** and the courtyard of the **❻ Moscow Museum of Modern Art** (p89), which contains a collection of weird and oversized sculptures by controversial Georgian artist Zurab Tsereteli.

Cross the Boulevard Ring and walk up ul Karenty Ryad to continue your tour amid the shady greenery of **❼ Hermitage Gardens**. Get a drink at **❽ 32.05** (p98) and, in summer, give yourself a rest in a lounge chair while watching children play on the green lawn.

Exit the gardens through the back door into Uspensky per, which features the pretty **❾ Uspenskaya Church**. Turn left into ul Malaya Dmitrovka and walk past the Lenkom Theatre towards the magnificent **❿ Church of the Nativity of the Virgin in Putinki**. Nearby, in the middle of Pushkin Sq, is the **⓫ Alexander Pushkin monument** is a favourite meeting point.

⊘noon-10pm Sun-Thu, 10am-3pm Fri; Ⓜ︎Novo-slobodskaya) Occupying a heritage garage, purpose-built to house a fleet of Leyland double-deckers that plied Moscow's streets in the 1920s, this vast museum, filled with cutting-edge multimedia technology, tackles the uneasy subject of relations between Jews and the Russian state over the centuries. The exhibition relates the stories of pogroms, Jewish revolutionaries, the Holocaust and Soviet anti-Semitism in a calm and balanced manner. The somewhat limited collection of material exhibits is compensated for by the abundance of interactive video displays.

We especially like those that encourage visitors to search for answers to dilemmas faced by early-20th-century Jews – to stand up and fight, to emigrate or to assimilate and keep a low profile.

Russia's Jewish population was quite small until the 18th century, when the empire incorporated a vast chunk of Poland then inhabited by millions of Yiddish-speaking Jews. They were not allowed to move into Russia proper until the early 20th century – a policy that became known as the Pale of Settlement. This led to the perception of Jews as an ethnic, rather than religious group, which still lingers today.

CENTRAL MUSEUM OF THE ARMED FORCES
MUSEUM

Map p274 (Центральный музей Вооружённых Сил; ☑495-681 6303; www.cmaf.ru; ul Sovetskoy Armii 2; adult/student ₽200/100; ⊘10am-4.30pm Wed-Fri & Sun, to 6.30pm Sat; Ⓜ︎Dostoyevskaya) Covering the history of the Soviet and Russian military since 1917, this massive museum occupies 24 halls plus open-air exhibits. Over 800,000 military items, including uniforms, medals and weapons, are on display. Among the highlights are remainders of the American U2 spy plane brought down in the Ural Mountains in 1960 and the victory flag raised over Berlin's Reichstag in 1945.

MUSEUM OF DECORATIVE & FOLK ART
MUSEUM

Map p274 (Всероссийский музей декоративно-прикладного и народного искусства; ☑495-609 0146; www.vmdpni.ru; Delegatskaya ul 3 & 5; adult/student ₽250/130; ⊘10am-6pm Sun, Mon, Wed & Fri, to 9pm Thu, noon-8pm Sat; Ⓜ︎Tsvetnoy Bulvar) Just beyond the Garden Ring, this museum showcases centuries-old arts-and-crafts traditions

from around Russia and the former Soviet republics. Of the 40,000 pieces in the collection, you might see *khokhloma* (lacquered) woodwork from Nizhny Novgorod, including wooden toys and *matryoshki* (nested) dolls; baskets and other household items made from birch bark, a traditional Siberian technique; intricate embroidery and lacework from the north, as well as the ubiquitous Pavlov scarves; and playful Dymkovo pottery and Gzhel porcelain.

Look also for the so-called 'propaganda porcelain' – fine china decorated with revolutionary themes. The museum is known for its impressive collection of *palekh* – black lacquer boxes and trays painted with detailed scenes from Russian fairy tales. The collection fills two rooms. It features, among others, pieces by Ivan Golikov and Ivan Markichev, often considered the originators of the *palekh* style.

GLINKA MUSEUM OF MUSICAL CULTURE
MUSEUM

Map p274 (Музей музыкальной культуры Глинки; ☑495-739 6226; www.glinka.museum; ul Fadeeva 4; ₽200; ⊘noon-7pm Tue-Sun; Ⓜ︎Mayakovskaya) This musicologist's paradise boasts over 3000 instruments – handcrafted works of art – from the Caucasus and the Far East. Russia is very well represented – a 13th-century *gusli* (traditional instrument similar to a dulcimer) from Novgorod, skin drums from Yakutia, a *balalaika* (triangular instrument) by the master Semyon Nalimov – but you can also see such classic pieces as a violin made by Antonio Stradivari. Recordings accompany many of the rarer instruments, allowing visitors to experience their sound.

This incredible collection started with a few instruments that were donated by the Moscow Tchaikovsky Conservatory at the end of the 19th century. The collection grew exponentially during the Soviet period. It was named after Mikhail Glinka in 1945, in honour of the composer's 150th birthday.

GULAG HISTORY MUSEUM
MUSEUM

Map p274 (Музей истории ГУЛАГа; ☑495-621 7310; www.gmig.ru; 1-y Samotechny per 9 str 1; adult/student ₽300/150; ⊘11am-6pm Tue, Wed & Fri, noon-8pm Thu; Ⓜ︎Dostoyevskaya) Stalin's genocide is a subject many Russians prefer to forget rather than reflect on, but this modern multimedia space serves as both a learning centre and a memorial to

VDNKH & OSTANKINO

Palaces for workers! There is no better place to see this Soviet slogan put into practice than at **VDNKh** (ⓂVDNKh), which stands for Exhibition of Achievements of the National Economy. The place feels like a Stalinesque theme park, with palatial pavilions, each designed in its own unique style to represent all the Soviet republics and various industries, from geology to space exploration. A thorough reconstruction, under way at the time of writing, is expected to breathe new life into the area.

Built in 1939, VDNKh was designed as the main showcase of the socialist economy and lifestyle. The highlights are two opulently decorated fountains. Positioned in the second square from the main gate, People's Friendship Fountain is surrounded by 16 gilded female figures dressed in ethnic costumes representing Soviet republics (the mysterious 16th figure stands for the Karelo-Finnish republic disbanded in 1956). Further on, the jaw-dropping Stone Flower Fountain, themed around Ural Mountains miners' mythology, is covered in semiprecious stones from the area.

Only a handful of the grandiose pavilions were open at the time of writing, and these were mostly used for commercial purposes, but the Space Pavilion has become a temporary shelter for the Polytechnical Museum and a venue for insightful natural science and technology exhibitions. Two recently added features are the giant Mosquarium, dubbed the largest oceanarium in Europe, and the My History Park compound, which contains vast multimedia exhibitions designed to support rather controversial views on history held by Vladimir Putin's entourage.

Approaching VDNKh from the metro, the soaring 100m titanium obelisk is a monument 'To the Conquerors of Space', built in 1964 to commemorate the launch of Sputnik. In its base is the **Cosmonautics Museum** (www.kosmo-museum.ru; ₽250; ◷11am-7pm Tue, Wed & Fri-Sun, to 9pm Thu), featuring cool space paraphernalia such as the first Soviet rocket engine and the moon rover Lunokhod. An inspiring collection of space-themed propaganda posters evokes the era of the space race.

If you reach the far end of VDNKh, you have the choice of either pressing on towards the extensive grounds of **Moscow Main Botanical Gardens** (www.gbsad.ru; ⓂBotanichesky Sad) **FREE**, or turning left towards the quaint Ostankino Park, surrounding a namesake palace.

Nearby Sights

When the **Ostankino TV Tower** (Останкинская башня; ☏8-800-100 5553; https://tv tower.ru; adult/child ₽1000/500; ◷10am-10pm Mon-Thu, to 11pm Fri-Sun; ⓂVDNKh) was built in 1967, it was the tallest free-standing structure in the world (surpassing the Empire State Building). At 540m, it is now fourth on the list. The 337m-high observation deck is open for visitors. A super-speedy lift whisks passengers up in less than 60 seconds. From the top, there are 360-degree views and – horror! – a bit of glass floor.

Admission is by guided tour only. Tours take place hourly and must be booked in advance; bring your passport. There's a 40% discount on 10am and 11am weekday tours.

About the holiest of Soviet icons, **Worker & Kolkhoz Woman** (☏495-683 5640; http://moscowmanege.ru; ₽200; ◷noon-9pm Tue-Sun), a powerful monument designed by Vera Mukhina, depicts a fierce-looking couple raising the hammer and sickle and symbolising the union of peasants and the working class. Initially, the sculpture crowned the striking Soviet pavilion at Paris Expo in 1937, but it came back to Moscow in 1939. After a recent reconstruction, the monument now stands on top of an exhibition hall that resembles the Paris pavilion. Exhibitions rotate every year.

Eating

A typical white colonnaded VDNKh pavilion contains **Moskovskoye Nebo** (☏499-650 0031; pr Mira 119, str 422; mains ₽500-700; ◷noon-11pm), a restaurant that draws inspiration from the Stalinist utopia that surrounds it without overdoing the Soviet nostalgia. Like VDNKh itself, the menu represents the USSR's republics, most notably Ukraine. The borsch with smoked pork and chicken kiev are superb and indeed much better than they were in Soviet times.

the millions who perished in concentration camps for 'enemies of the people'. The centrepiece display of objects handmade by prisoners is especially moving.

DOSTOEVSKY HOUSE-MUSEUM
MUSEUM

Map p274 (Дом-музей Достоевского; ☑495-681 1085; ul Dostoevskogo 2; adult/student ₽150/50; ⊙11am-5.30pm Tue & Fri-Sun, to 6.30pm Wed & Thu; ⓂDostoyevskaya) Though this renowned Russian author is more closely associated with St Petersburg, Fyodor Dostoevsky was actually born in Moscow, where his family lived in a tiny apartment on the grounds of Mariinsky Hospital. He lived here until the age of 16, when he went to St Petersburg to enter a military academy. The family's Moscow flat has been recreated according to descriptions written by Fyodor's brother.

Visitors can see the family's library, toys and many other personal items, including Fyodor's quill pen, an original autograph and a wooden chest with vaulted cover he slept on during his childhood, which clearly contributed to the writer's view of the world as a place full of pain. Shedding further light on the author's psyche, the house stood next to a morgue and an asylum that received lunatics from all over the city.

EXPERIMENTANIUM
SCIENCE CENTRE

(Эксперименториум; ☑495-789 3658; www.experimentanium.ru; ul Butyrskaya 46/2; adult/child ₽650/550; ⊙9.30am-7pm Mon-Fri, 10am-8pm Sat & Sun; ⑭; ⓂSavyolovskaya) Travelling with children who ask too many questions about life, the universe and everything? Here is a place that provides answers for them to ponder for a while. Experimentanium is an exciting place where children learn physics, chemistry, mechanics, acoustics, anatomy and whatnot by playing, and indeed experimenting, with a vast number of interactive exhibits.

VASNETSOV HOUSE MUSEUM
MUSEUM

Map p274 (Дом-музей Васнецова; ☑495-681 1329; www.tretyakovgallery.ru; per Vasnetsova 13; adult/student ₽300/150; ⊙10am-5pm Wed-Sun; ⓂSukharevskaya) Viktor Vasnetsov was a Russian-revivalist painter, who drew inspiration from fairy tales and village mysticism. In 1894 he designed his own house in Moscow, which is now a museum. Fronted by a colourful gate, it is a charming home

in neo-Russian style filled with the original wooden furniture, a tiled stove and many of the artist's paintings. The attic studio, where he once worked, is now adorned with paintings depicting Baba Yaga and other characters from Russian fairy tales.

Early on, Vasnetsov was scorned for his fantastical style, as it was such a startling contrast to the realism of the Peredvizhniki (Wanderers, 19th-century art movement). Even Pavel Tretyakov, the most prominent patron of the arts at the time, refused to buy his paintings. However, by the turn of the century, he found a source of support in Savva Mamontov, whose financing drove the Russian-revivalist movement.

✖ EATING

The inner part of Tverskoy up to the Boulevard Ring is swarming with restaurants. The area between Novoslobodskaya and Mendeleyevskaya metro stations is also growing into a major restaurant row.

✖ Tverskoy

LEPIM I VARIM
RUSSIAN €

Map p274 (Лепим и варим; ☑8-985-688 9606; www.lepimivarim.ru; Stoleshnikov per 9, str 1; mains ₽220-350; ⊙10am-11pm) This cosy place touts itself as 'the most visited boutique' in the flashy Stoleshnikov per, but instead of Armani clothes it celebrates arguably the most vital item on any Russian menu – *pelmeni* (dumplings), as well as their relatives from all around the world. Perfectly shaped, the dumplings seem fit for a catwalk display in Milan and taste even better. The place is tucked away in a courtyard, accessed through an archway.

ZUPPERIA
INTERNATIONAL €

Map p274 (☑8-915-391 8309; www.facebook.com/Zupperia; Sadovaya-Samotechnaya ul 20; soups & salads ₽300-400; ⊙8am-11pm; ⓐⓓ; ⓂTsvetnoy Bulvar) Designed to look like a transplant from some old-worldish European city, this unpretentious eatery is run by local celebrity chef Uilliam Lamberti. The minimalist menu includes soups, bruschettas and salads. At first glance, the place seems to consist of one long table, but there is more seating downstairs. Takeaway is available.

TSVETNOY FOOD
COURT   INTERNATIONAL €

Map p274 (📱495-737 7773; www.tsvetnoy.com; Tsvetnoy bul 15, str 1; tapas ₽100-400; ⏾noon-10pm; Ⓜ Tsvetnoy Bulvar) The two upper floors of Tsvetnoy Central Market shopping mall are filled with refined delis and cafes, some of them outstandingly good. Little snacks hailing from Basque Country in Spain have generated a bit of a cult following for Tapas & Pintxos, on the 5th floor. The Dagestani dumpling shop on the 6th floor makes for equally exciting culinary travel.

ANDERSON   DELI €

Map p274 (Андерсон; www.cafe-anderson.ru; Strastnoy bul 4; mains ₽360-540; ⏾9am-11pm; 📶📱; Ⓜ Pushkinskaya) This sweet, child-friendly deli serves salads, soups, and cakes styled as Cornish pasties, as well as smoothies and lemonade. The honey latte might be a little too experimental, but the tea with raspberry purée and sage is quite exceptional.

BUTTERBOARD   AMERICAN €

Map p274 (📱499 990 0272; www.facebook.com/Burgernaya; Tverskaya ul 27, str 2; burgers ₽280; ⏾noon-11.45pm; Ⓜ Mayakovskaya) This semi-secret place draws a crowd of windsurfers, among whom it still goes by the owner's name – Slavik's. A refuge for California dreamers washed onto the shore of Tverskaya, it serves delicious burgers and a good selection of beers. To enter, look for an unmarked door next to a Korean cafe.

SELENGE   MONGOLIAN €

Map p274 (Сэлэнгэ; www.selenge.ru; ul Malaya Dmitrovka 23/15; mains ₽230-450; ⏾noon-midnight; Ⓜ Mayakovskaya) If you want a foretaste of your future Trans-Eurasian adventure, come here to sample food hailing from all cultures affiliated with Mongolia – Buryat, Kalmyk, Tyvan and Tibetan. For a safe introduction, try Buryat *buuzy* dumplings. Brave diners tuck into Kalmyk lamb giblet soups and main courses, watering them down with *kumiss* – fermented mare's milk.

JAGANNATH   VEGETARIAN €

Map p274 (Джаганнат; www.jagannath.ru; Kuznetsky most 11; mains ₽120-140; ⏾10am-midnight; 📱; Ⓜ Kuznetsky Most) If you are in need of

vitamins, this is a funky vegetarian cafe, restaurant and shop. Its Indian-themed decor is more New Agey than ethnic. Service is slow but sublime, and the food is worth the wait.

★ DELICATESSEN   INTERNATIONAL €€

Map p274 (Деликатесы; www.newdeli.ru; Sadovaya-Karetnaya ul 20; mains ₽500-800; ⏾noon-midnight Tue-Sun; 📶📱; Ⓜ Tsvetnoy Bulvar) The affable and chatty owners of this place travel the world and experiment with the menu a lot, turning burgers, pizzas and pasta into artfully constructed objects of modern culinary art. The other source of joy is a cabinet filled with bottles of ripening fruity liquors, which may destroy your budget if consumed uncontrollably (a pointless warning, we know).

The latter asset brought Delicatessen into the World's Top 50 Bars list – entering at number 50 and climbing to number 41 in 2016. Go through the archway next to Shokoladnitsa cafe, turn left and look for a green door on your right. The sign above it reads: 'Thank you for finding us'.

★ LAVKA-LAVKA   INTERNATIONAL €€

Map p274 (Лавка-Лавка; 📱8-903-115 5033; www.restoran.lavkalavka.com; ul Petrovka 21, str 2; mains ₽500-950; ⏾noon-midnight Tue-Thu & Sun, to 1am Fri & Sat; 📶📱; Ⓜ Teatralnaya) 🍃 Welcome to the Russian Portlandia – all the food here is organic and hails from little farms where you may rest assured all the lambs and chickens lived a very happy life before being served to you on a plate. Irony aside, this is a great place to sample local food cooked in a funky improvisational style.

Each item on the menu is attributed to an individual farmer. Geography spans from central Russia to Sakhalin. Of special note are the ales and different kinds of *kvas* (fermented rye-bread drink) produced on farms near Moscow. The restaurant comes with a great (if expensive) shop selling farm produce.

GOLODNY-ZLOY   FUSION €€

Map p274 (Голодный-Злой; Hangry; 📱495-792 7105; http://perelmanpeople.com/restoran/golodnyy-zloy; Tsvetnoy bul 2; mains ₽500-700; ⏾noon-midnight Sun-Thu, to 2am Fri & Sat; 📱; Ⓜ Trubnaya) Filling up with white collars from the business centre above it, this trendsetting establishment combines unlikely ingredients and cooking methods with unfailingly excellent results – just try their smoked-mussel soup or dorado cooked with sorrel. Visual art is also involved, with each dish designed to entertain the eye as much as to please the stomach.

SEVEN
EUROPEAN €€

Map p274 (☑495-205 0277; Dmitrovsky per 7; mains ₽500-900; ☺8am-11pm; MTeatralnaya) You'll find a pleasant mix of post-industrial and theatrical in this dimly lit space, where low-hanging chandeliers and comfortable chairs make for a long and enjoyable evening. The menu mirrors the city outside – inventively cosmopolitan with a sprinkle of Soviet nostalgia and a strong bias towards domestic meat and vegetable producers.

The ministerial schnitzel – a hint at menus of Brezhnev-era restaurants for the party elite – is outstanding, even though it has very little in common with the prototype.

TECHNICUM
EUROPEAN €€

Map p274 (☑495-230 0605; www.tehnikum bistro.ru; ul Bolshaya Dmitrovka 7/5, str 2; mains ₽480-650; ☺9am-midnight; MTeatralnaya) Casual, friendly and focused on taste, rather than trying to impress with shocking exoticism, Technicum is one of the places that shape the modern outlook of Moscow's culinary scene. The laconic menu contains a short list of fish and meat dishes (note the outstanding mutton with aubergine) as well as soups, including an exemplary borsch served with Borodinsky rye bread.

SHELL, YES! SEAFOOD BAR
SEAFOOD €€

Map p274 (☑495-621 2735; www.facebook.com/shellseafoodbar; Rozhdestvensky bul 10/7; mains ₽600-1300; ☺6pm-midnight; MTrubnaya) Not a gas station, this small place defies geography by teleporting guests from Boulevard Ring to an oceanfront tavern. Displayed at the entrance, fish and oysters come from as far away as Sri Lanka and New Zealand, but it feels like the schooner that brought them is moored right outside. The cooking and wine list don't fail to impress either.

CAFE TAJINE
MOROCCAN €€

Map p274 (☑8-919-764 4440; http://cafe tagine.ru; Trubnaya ul 15; mains ₽570-1100; ☺9am-11pm Sun-Thu, to 12.30am Fri & Sat; MTrubnaya) With a reputation as a bohemian hang-out, this place specialises in modern Moroccan cuisine. Prominently on the menu are four types of *tajine* (slow-cooked stew with meat and vegetables) and numerous meze snacks. Worth a special note is the long (and stellar) list of desserts, such as date pudding with caramel, tahini ice cream and pomegranate granita.

VORONEZH
INTERNATIONAL €€

Map p274 (Воронеж; www.voronej.com; ul Bolshaya Dmitrovka 12/1, str 1; mains ₽300-720; ☺9am-9pm; MTeatralnaya) Its darkened, scarlet-coloured interior makes this bistro look a bit like an oriental opium den, but it is in fact a carnivore temple, where patrons seem to fall into a deeply meditative state while munching on their burgers and excellent pastrami sandwiches. One of the best places for lunch in the city centre.

FRESH
VEGETARIAN €€

Map p274 (Свежий; ☑8-965-278 9089; www.freshrestaurant.ru; ul Bolshaya Dmitrovka 11; mains ₽500-650; ☺11am-11pm; ☎⊕; MTeatralnaya) Fresh out of Canada, this is the kind of vegetarian restaurant that people pour into not for lifestyle reasons, but because the modern, postethnic food and the escapist ambience are great. Definitely go for the smoothies. Vegans and rawists will not feel neglected.

BARASHKA
AZERBAIJANI €€

Map p274 (Барашка; ☑495-625 2895; www.novikovgroup.ru; ul Petrovka 20/1; mains ₽500-950; ☺11am-midnight; MTeatralnaya) Yes, it's expensive – but it's also a sophisticated setting, done up as an understated Baku courtyard, adorned with jars of pickled lemons and blooming plants. Barashka offers a menu full of fresh tasty salads, grilled meats and slow-cooked stews, many of which feature the little lamb, for which the restaurant is named.

UZBEKISTAN
UZBEK €€

Map p274 (Узбекистан; ☑495-623 0585; www.uzbek-rest.ru; Neglinnaya ul 29; mains ₽350-1000; ☺noon-3am; ❄⊕; MTrubnaya) This place opened in 1951 by order of the Ministry of Trade of the Uzbek Soviet Socialist Republic. Six decades later, the place has expanded its menu to include Chinese, Arabic and Azeri food, in addition to the Uzbek standards. Make yourself comfortable on the plush cushions and order some spicy *plov* (pilaf-like meat and rice) or delicious fried kebabs.

Now brace yourself for a belly-dancing show.

DZHONDZHOLI
GEORGIAN €€

Map p274 (Джонджоли; ☑495-650 5567; www. ginzaproject.ru; Tverskaya ul 20/1; mains ₽380-690; ☺11am-midnight; ☎🔢; MPushkinskaya) Exposed brick walls, wood and wicker furniture and muted tones ensure that the focus of the Dzhondzholi dining room is the open kitchen, where the chefs are busy preparing delicious *dolma* (stuffed vine leaves), *khachapuri* (cheese bread), *kharcho* (rice with beef or lamb soup) and other authentic favourites.

Fun fact: food connoisseur and cookbook author Darra Goldstein explains in her book *A Georgian Feast* that *dzhondzholi* is 'a garlicky long-stemmed green, usually eaten pickled', which is common in Georgian cuisine. Try it for ₽280.

TRATTORIA VENEZIA
ITALIAN €€

Map p274 (www.trattoria-venezia.ru; Strastnoy bul 4/3; meals ₽400-800; ☺11am-midnight; MChekhovskaya) Pretend that the Boulevard Ring is the Grand Canal. Imagine the cars ensconced in traffic are really gondolas, and the billboard-plastered facade of the Pushkinsky Cinema is actually the Ducal Palace. If you're still reading, then the Trattoria Venezia is for you. The long menu includes more than 25 pasta plates, as well as pizza, risotto, lasagne and Italian-style meat and fish dishes.

COURVOISIER CAFE
EUROPEAN €€

Map p274 (☑495-632 9995; www.courvoisier-cafe.ru; Malaya Sukharevskaya pl 8; mains ₽380-650; ☺24hr; 🚲🔢; MSukharevskaya) This informal, French-themed cafe is furnished with picnic tables and park benches, evoking an idyllic outdoor setting. (There is outdoor seating too, but fronting the Garden Ring, it is not so peaceful.) Serving breakfast, soups, pasta and grills, it's a popular spot for breakfast, happy hour (4pm to 7pm) or a late-night snack.

SCANDINAVIA
SWEDISH €€

Map p274 (☑495-937 5630; www.scandinavia. ru; Maly Palashevsky per 7; mains ₽600-1000; ☎🔢♿; MPushkinskaya) In most parts of the world, Swedish cuisine is not really celebrated; in Moscow, it is. Much beloved of Moscow expats, Scandi offers an enticing interpretation of what happens 'when Sweden meets Russia'. A delightful summer cafe, it features sandwiches, salads and treats from the grill (including the best burgers in Moscow, by some accounts).

★ BRASSERIE MOST
FRENCH €€€

Map p274 (☑495-660 0706; www.brasserie most.ru; ul Kuznetsky most 6/3; mains ₽1000-3000; ☺8am-midnight Mon-Fri, from 9am Sat & Sun; MTeatralnaya) Moscow's most venerated and erudite restaurateur Alexander Rappoport shares his love for regional French cuisine in this classy and expensive place on Kuznetsky most. The menu is a grand gastrotour taking in seemingly every major area of France from Brittany to Alsace. Authenticity is religion here. If they say bouillabaisse, you can be sure it will taste exactly like Marseilles' best.

✗ Novoslobodsky

BATONI
GEORGIAN €

Map p274 (☑499-653 6530; www.batoni-kafe. ru; Novoslobodskaya ul 18; mains ₽300-600; ☺11.30am-midnight; MMendeleyevskaya) Among myriad Georgian places in Moscow, Batoni is about the loveliest and the most scrupulous at sourcing all the right ingredients for century-old recipes. *Pkhali* (walnut paste) snacks, *khachapuri* and lamb shashlyk kebabs are all up to Mt Kazbek–high standards. For a proper taste of Georgia, order a bottle of Mukuzani or Kindzmarauli – the country's best reds.

RYNOK &
OBSHCHEPIT SHOUK
ISRAELI €

Map p274 (Рынок и Общепит Шук; ☑495-966 2501; www.facebook.com/rynokshuk; Veskovsky per 7; sandwiches ₽250-320; ☺8am-11pm; MNovoslobodskaya) This quirky place, a cross between a corner shop and a hip falafel joint, also makes top-quality *shawarma* (grilled meat and salad wrapped in flat bread) in the fashionably open kitchen. The shop section has a good selection of Israeli vegetable preserves, fruit and wine.

GOKOS
GREEK €

Map p274 (Гокос; ☑499-670 9298; Sushhevskaya ul 19/4; lunch meals ₽290; ☺10am-10pm; MMendeleyevskaya) The gyros craze is gradually spreading around Moscow, with Greek eateries opening here and there, but this place is outstanding. Simple as it is – meat slices in a pita – gyros has never been served with so much style, not in Moscow anyway. Owners hailing from the fashion industry must be the explanation. Excellent Greek frappé, too!

MADAME WONG
CHINESE €€

Map p274 (☑495-280 1566; www.madamewong.ru; ul Lesnaya 7; mains ₽540-980; ☺noon-midnight; MBelorusskaya) Suit-and-tie corporates from nearby business centres throng to this classy Hong Kong restaurant that celebrates Cantonese cuisine while also flirting with Japan. The menu includes numerous kinds of super-tender dim sum, the classic crispy duck and more unusual items, such as Hainan black curry. Note the Japanese section – the crab cakes and octopus are delicious!

DRUZHBA
CHINESE €€€

Map p274 (Дружба; ☑499-973 1212; Novoslobodskaya ul 4; mains ₽700-1200; ☺11am-11pm; ☑; MNovoslobodskaya) Druzhba earns high marks for authenticity, and as far as Sichuan cuisine goes that means spicy. Chinese restaurants in Moscow are notorious for turning down their seasoning to appeal to Russian taste buds, but Druzhba is the exception, which explains why this place is often packed with Chinese patrons. The chicken with peppers gets red-hot reviews.

🍷 DRINKING & NIGHTLIFE

There are plenty of bars in the inner part of the district, inside the Garden Ring. Outside it, Mendeleyevskaya metro area and Flakon are two growing pub-crawling scenes.

🍸 Tverskoy

★NOOR / ELECTRO
BAR

Map p274 (☑8-903-136 7686; www.noorbar.com; ul Tverskaya 23/12; ☺8pm-3am Mon-Wed, to 6am Thu-Sun; MPushkinskaya) There is little to say about this misleadingly unassuming bar, apart from the fact that everything in it is close to perfection. It has it all – prime location, convivial atmosphere, eclectic DJ music, friendly bartenders and superb drinks. Though declared 'the best' by various magazines on several occasions, it doesn't feel like they care.

32.05
CAFE

Map p274 (☑8-905-703 3205; www.veranda3205.ru; ul Karetny Ryad 3; ☺11am-3am; MPushkinskaya) The biggest drinking and eating establishment in Hermitage Gardens, this verandah positioned at the back of the park's main building looks a bit like a greenhouse. In summer, tables (and patrons) spill out into the park, making it one of the city's best places for outdoor drinking. With its long bar and joyful atmosphere, the place also heaves in winter.

ENTHUSIAST
BAR

Map p274 (Энтузиаст; Stoleshnikov per 7, str 5; ☺noon-11pm Sun-Thu, to 2am Fri & Sat; MTeatralnaya) Scooter enthusiast, that is. But you don't have to be one in order to enjoy this superbly laid-back bar hidden at the far end of a fancifully shaped courtyard and disguised as a spare-parts shop. On a warm day, grab a beer or cider, settle into a beach chair and let harmony descend on you.

GLAVPIVMAG
CRAFT BEER

Map p274 (Главпивмаг; ☑8-965-223 4492; http://glavpivmag.com; Tverskaya ul 18; ☺10am-3am; MTverskaya) Strategically located on the city's busiest square, this place has nothing but a long bar and lots of taps pumping from barrels, representing dozens of microbreweries from all over Russia and its near vicinity. This is Moscow's craft-beer central. The brew can be consumed on the spot or poured into takeaway bottles.

TAP & BARREL
IRISH PUB

Map p274 (☑495-636 2904; http://tbpub.ru; ul Bolshaya Dmitrovka 13; ☺noon-midnight Sun-Thu, to 6am Fri & Sat; MTeatralnaya) Amid the craft-beer mayhem, a good old – and not-so-fake – Irish pub feels like a welcome refuge. Occupying a vast cellar space with vaulting bare brick walls, it is the place to befriend English-speaking veteran expats over a pint of Guinness, or to watch football on a large screen.

CAFE MART
CAFE

Map p274 (Кафе Март; www.cafemart.ru; ul Petrovka 25; ☺11am-midnight Sun-Wed, 11am-6am Thu-Sat, jazz concert 9pm Thu; MChekhovskaya) It looks like just another cellar bar, but if you walk all the way through the underground maze you'll find yourself in the huge overground 'orangerie' hall with mosaic-covered walls, warm lighting and possibly a jazz concert. When the weather is fine, Mart spills into the sculpture-filled courtyard of the adjacent Moscow Museum of Contemporary Art.

WORTH A DETOUR

FLAKON & KHLEBOZAVOD 9

Like the Bolsheviks a hundred years ago, Moscow hipsters are capturing one factory after another and redeveloping them, according to their tastes. **Flakon** (www.flacon.ru; ul Bolshaya Novodmitrovskaya 36; ⓂDmitrovskaya) is arguably the most visually attractive of all the redeveloped industrial areas around town, its mixture of brightly painted buildings and bare red brick resembling Portobello Rd in London. Once a glassware plant that produced bottles for the perfume industry, it is now home to dozens of funky shops and other businesses. Shopping for designer clothes and unusual souvenirs is the main reason for coming here.

The main shopping area covers three floors of the factory's central building. Climb to the top to find **Zaporozhets Heritage** (☑925-465 3410; http://zaporojec.ru; ul Bolshaya Novodmitrovskaya 36; ⓉLlam-9pm; ⓂDmitrovskaya) – a shop representing a brand that produces clothes themed on classic Soviet children's cartoons. Weekends are the best time to visit as this is when you are most likely to encounter a festival or craft fair. You'll also find several cool cafes, a cinema and even a summertime swimming pool in the area.

Khlebozavod 9 fills the gap between Flakon and Dmitrovskaya metro station. Exiting the latter, walk about 100m away from the busy avenue and you'll find the back entrance to this new space. The front entrance is across the road from Flakon.

A former bread factory (a giant Soviet-era bakery designed to cater to millions), Khlebozavod 9 was filling up with tenants at the time of writing, one of the early comers being Svoboda (p100) bar, a craft-beer and music venue. The other notable resident is Moscow ArchiGeek (p32), which runs guided tours of the city's architectural landmarks.

GOGOL CLUB

Map p274 (Гоголь; www.gogolclub.ru; Stoleshnikov per 11; ⓉLnoon-5am; ⓂTeatralnaya) Fun, informal and affordable (so surprising on swanky Stoleshnikov), Gogol is great for food, drinks and music. The underground club takes its bunker theme seriously, notifying customers that their food is ready with an air-raid siren. In summer the action moves out to the courtyard, where the gigantic tent is styled like an old-fashioned street scene.

HEROES PUB

Map p274 (Герои; www.facebook.com/the heroesbar; Trubnaya ul 23; ⓉL2pm-midnight; ⓂTsvetnoy Bulvar) Giant murals depicting Russian countercultural icons – Vladimir Vysotsky, Shnur and Sergei Bodrov Jr – observe a merry crowd of hipsters ticking off new items on the endless list of local and foreign craft beers. It is unambitiously local with occasionally sloppy service, but full of loyal regulars and great for a quiet conversation over a pint or two.

KAMCHATKA BAR

Map p274 (Камчатка; www.novikovgroup.ru; ul Kuznetsky most 7; ⓉL10am-1am Sun-Thu, noon-3am Fri & Sat; ⓂTeatralnaya) Kamchatka is a generic term for all things fringe, and this cavernous pub seems to have been designed to prove that beer can go for ₽80 even in a prime location in front of the TsUM department store. But make sure you ask for their trademark Kamchatka beer, or you'll get an expensive one.

Kamchatka is best in summer, when you and your friend the pint can walk out into the street to enjoy the sunshine with fellow lumpen intellectuals.

SIMACHYOV BAR

Map p274 (Симачёв; Stoleshnikov per 12/2; ⓉL11am-last guest; ⓂChekhovskaya) By day it's a boutique and cafe, owned and operated by the famed fashion designer of the same name; by night, this place becomes a hip-hop-happening nightclub that combines glamour and humour. The eclectic decor includes leopard-skin rugs tossed over tile floors, toilet stools pulled up to a washbasin bar, Catholic confessionals for private dining, and more.

You still have to look sharp to get in here, but at least you can be bohemian about it.

🍷 Novoslobodsky

FCKING CRAFT PUB   BAR

Map p274 (☑️8-929-989 7864; www.facebook. com/pg/fcpub; Novoslobodskaya ul 16a; ⊘6pm-10am; Ⓜ️Mendeleyevskaya) The scale of the craft beer craze is so terrifying for some folks in Moscow, they've decided it's time for a backlash. This large pub has no Russian beer on principle – only British and other international brands, most of which you probably know. A separate team operating on the same premises serves excellent grilled meat.

The more inquisitive of you may find an unassuming little door leading to a popular clandestine speakeasy bar on the same premises, but that's as many clues as we can give!

SVOBODA   BAR

(Novodmitrovskaya ul 1, str 9; ⊘noon-11.30pm; Ⓜ️Dmitrovskaya) A flagship of the new converted factory space, Khlebozavod 9, this is a relatively large two-level bar specialising in craft beer. At the end of the week, local bands play live gigs on the stage shaped like a rollerblading ramp. Food is served, too.

CAFE BROCARD   BAR

(☑️495-646 7843; www.facebook.com/ CAFEBROCARD; Bolshaya Novodmitrovskaya 36, str 1; ⊘noon-late; Ⓜ️Dmitrovskaya) Cool cats from Flakon, notably journalists from Dozhd, Russia's only independent TV channel, congregate here after work to sip cocktails and chat. As often happens in places that become local institutions, there is nothing special about this one except a really cool crowd (and good cocktails). There's an open-air verandah in summer.

⭐ ENTERTAINMENT

BOLSHOI THEATRE   BALLET, OPERA

See p88.

STANISLAVSKY ELECTROTHEATRE   ARTS CENTRE

Map p274 (☑️495-699 7224; http://electro theatre.ru; ul Tverskaya 23; Ⓜ️Pushkinskaya) Renowned performance artist Boris Yukhananov has revived this old theatre as Moscow's hottest venue for experimental performance and visual art. Dance, music, cinema and theatre form a sparkling cocktail of genres and there is not a day without something new, strange and exciting going on.

NOVAYA OPERA   OPERA

Map p274 (Новая опера; ☑️495-694 0868; www.novayaopera.ru; ul Karetny Ryad 3; ⊘box office noon-7.30pm; Ⓜ️Tsvetnoy Bulvar) This theatre company was founded in 1991 by then-mayor Luzhkov and artistic director

---

STANISLAVSKY'S METHODS

In 1898, over an 18-hour restaurant lunch, actor-director Konstantin Stanislavsky and playwright-director Vladimir Nemirovich-Danchenko founded the Moscow Art Theatre as the forum for method acting. The theatre is known by its Russian initials, MKhT, short for Moskovsky Khudozhestvenny Teatr.

More than just providing another stage, the Art Theatre adopted a 'realist' approach, which stressed truthful portrayal of characters and society, teamwork by the cast (not relying on stars) and respect for the writer. 'We declared war on all the conventionalities of the theatre... in the acting, the properties, the scenery, or the interpretation of the play', Stanislavsky later wrote.

This treatment of *The Seagull* rescued playwright Anton Chekhov from despair after the play had flopped in St Petersburg. *Uncle Vanya, Three Sisters* and *The Cherry Orchard* all premiered in the MKhT. Gorky's *The Lower Depths* was another success.

In short, the theatre revolutionised Russian drama, while method acting's influence in Western theatre has been enormous. In the USA Stanislavsky's theories are, and have been, the primary source of study for many actors, including such greats as Stella Adler, Marlon Brando, Sanford Meisner, Lee Strasberg, Harold Clurman and Gregory Peck.

MKhT, now technically called the Chekhov Moscow Art Theatre (see opposite for more), still stages regular performances of Chekhov's work, among other plays.

Evgeny Kolobov. Maestro Kolobov stated, 'We do not pretend to be innovators in this beautiful and complicated genre of opera'. As such, the 'New Opera' stages the old classics, and does it well. The gorgeous, modern opera house is set amid the Hermitage Gardens.

NIKULIN CIRCUS ON TSVETNOY BULVAR
CIRCUS

Map p274 (Цирк Никулина на Цветном бульваре; ☑495-625 8970; www.circusnikulin.ru; Tsvetnoy bul 13; tickets ₽400-2500; ☺box office 11am-2pm & 3-7pm; Ⓜ Tsvetnoy Bulvar) Founded in 1880, this circus is now named after beloved actor and clown Yury Nikulin (1921–97), who performed at the studio here for many years. Nikulin's shows centre on a given theme, which serves to add some cohesion to the productions. There are lots of trapeze artists, tightrope walkers and performing animals.

MOSCOW ART THEATRE (MKHT)
THEATRE

Map p274 (Московский художественный театр (МХАТ); www.mxat.ru; Kamergersky per 3; ☺box office noon-7pm; Ⓜ Teatralnaya) Often called the most influential theatre in Europe, this is where method acting was founded over 100 years ago, by Stanislavsky and Nemirovich-Danchenko. Besides the theatre itself and an acting studio-school, a small museum about the theatre's history is also on-site.

STANISLAVSKY & NEMIROVICH-DANCHENKO MUSICAL THEATRE
OPERA, BALLET

Map p274 (Музыкальный театр Станиславского и Немирович-Данченко; ☑495-723 7325; https://stanmus.ru; ul Bolshaya Dmitrovka 17; ☺box office 11.30am-7pm; Ⓜ Chekhovskaya) This historic company was founded when two legends of the Moscow theatre scene – Konstantin Stanislavsky and Vladimir Nemirovich-Danchenko – joined forces in 1941. Their newly created theatre became a workshop for applying the innovative dramatic methods of the Moscow Art Theatre to opera and ballet.

BB KING
LIVE MUSIC

Map p274 (☑495-699 8206; www.bbkingclub.ru; Sadovaya-Samotechnaya ul 4/2; ☺noon-midnight, music from 8.30pm; Ⓜ Tsvetnoy Bulvar) This old-style blues club hosts an open jam

session on Wednesday night, acoustic blues on Sunday and live performances other nights. The restaurant is open for lunch and dinner, when you can listen to jazz and blues on the old-fashioned jukebox. Enter from the courtyard.

MALY THEATRE
THEATRE

Map p274 (Малый театр; ☑495-624 4046; www.maly.ru; Teatralnaya pl 1/6; ☺box office 11am-8pm; Ⓜ Teatralnaya) 'Maly' means small, meaning smaller than the Bolshoi across the street. Actually, the name dates back to the time when there were only two theatres in town: the opera theatre was always called the 'Bolshoi', while the drama theatre was the 'Maly'. Founded in 1824, it mainly features performances of 19th-century works by Ostrovsky and his fellow classic playwrights.

SATIRIKON THEATRE
THEATRE

(Театр Сатирикон; ☑495-602 6583; www.satirikon.ru; Sheremetyevskaya ul 8; ☺box office 11am-8pm; Ⓜ Marina Roshcha) Boasting one of Moscow's most talented theatre producers, Konstantin Raikin, as well as a host of big-name directors, the Satirikon earned a reputation in the early 1990s with its outrageously expensive production of the *Three penny Opera*. It has since broken its own record for expenditure with *Chantecler*, which featured ducks, cockerels and hens dancing on stage.

LENKOM THEATRE
THEATRE

Map p274 (Ленком театр; ☑495-699 9668, box office 495-699 0708; www.lenkom.ru; ul Malaya Dmitrovka 6; tickets ₽200-2000; ☺box office noon-3pm & 4-7pm; Ⓜ Pushkinskaya) The Lenkom isn't the most glamorous theatre, but it's widely considered to have the strongest acting troupe in the country. The flashy productions and musicals performed here keep non-Russian speakers entertained.

OBRAZTSOV PUPPET THEATRE & MUSEUM
PUPPETRY

Map p274 (Театр и музей кукол Образцова; ☑495-699 5373; www.puppet.ru; Sadovaya-Samotechnaya ul 3; ☺box office 11am-2.30pm & 3.30-7pm; Ⓜ Tsvetnoy Bulvar) The country's largest puppet theatre performs colourful Russian folk tales and adapted classical plays. Kids can get up close and personal with the incredible puppets at the museum, which holds a collection of more than 3000.

TVERSKOY ENTERTAINMENT

RUSSIAN BALL AT YAR   LIVE PERFORMANCE

(Яр; ☑495-960 2004; www.rusball.com; Leningradsky pr 32/2, Sovietsky Hotel; tickets ₽1000, dinner ₽800-1200; ⓂDinamo) Everything about Yar is over the top, including the vast, gilded interior, the traditional Russian menu and the Moulin Rouge–style dancing girls. The thematic show is famous for its elaborate costumes, and the old-fashioned Russian food is pretty elaborate, too. Buy tickets in advance. To find it, walk 1km southeast from Dinamo metro station.

DUROV ANIMAL THEATRE   THEATRE

Map p274 (Театр животных Дурова; ☑495-631 3047; www.ugolokdurova.ru; ul Durova 4; tickets ₽150-600; ⊙11am-5pm Wed-Sun, show times vary; 🚼; ⓂProspekt Mira) Dedushka Durov (Grandpa Durov) founded this zany theatre for kids as a humane alternative to the horrible treatment of animals he saw at the circus. His shows feature mostly domestic animals, including cats and dogs, farm animals and the occasional bear. His most popular show is Railway for Mice. Guided tours of the museum give kids a closer look at the railway. Take tram 7 from Prospekt Mira metro station, or walk 1.5km west on ul Durova.

🛍 SHOPPING

PODARKI VMESTE S VOROVSKI   GIFTS & SOUVENIRS

Map p274 (Подарки вМесте с Воровски; www.facebook.com/svorovskim; Kuznetsky most 21/5; ⊙10am-9pm; ⓂLubyanka) This sweet little boutique houses a cooperative of four designer gift producers. The rather cramped space is filled with hundreds of useful and useless (but pretty) items, including Galereyka's felt slippers and hats (some shaped as Soviet tanks) and Ptitsa Sinitsa's stylish ceramics with Eastern European folklore motifs.

🏃 SPORTS & ACTIVITIES

★SANDUNY BATHS   BATHHOUSE

Map p274 (☑495-782 1808; www.sanduny.ru; ul Neglinnaya 14; ₽1800-2800; ⊙8am-10pm Wed-Mon, second male top class 10am-midnight Tue-Fri, 8am-10pm Sat & Sun; ⓂKuznetsky Most) Sanduny is the oldest and most luxurious *banya* (hot bath) in the city. The Gothic Room is a work of art with its rich wood-carving, while the main shower room has an aristocratic Roman feel to it. There are several classes, as on trains; regulars say that second male top class is actually better than the premium class.

No matter which class you choose, it will be a costly experience, especially if you rent the essential items – a sheet to wrap yourself (₽250), a felt hat to avoid burning your hair and a pair of slippers.

Presnya

Neighbourhood Top Five

❶ Mikhail Bulgakov Museum (p107) Retracing the footsteps and flight patterns of the characters of the Russian literary classic *The Master and Margarita,* following up with a visit to the author's home.

❷ Cafe Pushkin (p111) Dining in *haute-russe* style and experiencing the cuisine of the tsars in a lovely 19th-century building.

❸ Time-Out Rooftop Bar (p115) Hitting this trendy top-floor bar for top-shelf cocktails and top-notch city views.

❹ Moscow Tchaikovsky Conservatory (p116) Listening to a world-class concert by the up-and-coming Moscow Symphony Orchestra in the conservatory's grandiose Great Hall.

❺ Ryabushinsky Mansion (p106) Admiring the unique collection of architecture along Bolshaya Nikitskaya ul, including this 1906 art nouveau visual fantasy.

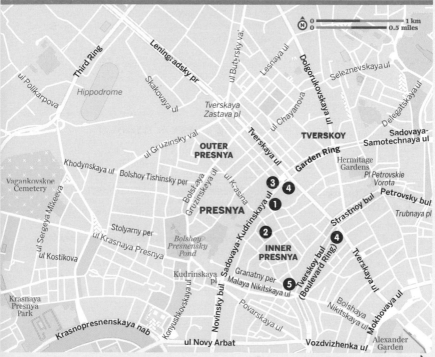

For more detail of this area see Map p278 ➡

Lonely Planet's Top Tip

In the backstreets around Bolshaya Nikitskaya ul, many old mansions have survived – some renovated, others dilapidated. Most of those on the streets closest to the Kremlin were built by the 18th-century aristocracy, while those further away were built by rising 19th-century industrialists. Nowadays many of these buildings are occupied by embassies and cultural institutions. With little traffic, Bolshaya Nikitskaya ul is excellent for a quiet ramble.

☉ Best Kids' Outings

➡ Moscow Planetarium (p106)

➡ Moscow Zoo (p109)

➡ Patriarch's Ponds (p106)

➡ Tsereteli Studio-Museum (p109)

For reviews, see p105. ➡

✕ Best Places to Eat

➡ Cafe Pushkin (p111)

➡ Volkonsky (p110)

➡ Khachapuri (p110)

➡ AQ Kitchen (p113)

➡ Twins (p110)

For reviews, see p109. ➡

☐ Best Places to Drink

➡ Time-Out Rooftop Bar (p115)

➡ Jagger (p115)

➡ Art Lebedev Cafe Studio (p113)

➡ Bar Klava (p114)

➡ Nikuda ne edem (p115)

For reviews, see p113. ➡

Explore Presnya

Presnya encompasses some of the capital's oldest neighbourhoods as well as its newest developments. Start by exploring the lovely residential areas of Inner Presnya, chock-full of evocative architecture, historic parks and fantastic drinking and dining spots. The whole neighbourhood is a wonderful place for a wander, especially with a copy of Mikhail Bulgakov's Presnya-set novel *The Master and Margarita* in hand. Come in the late afternoon, then stay for dinner – the area around Patriarch's Ponds has emerged as a dining hotspot, with restaurants lined up along Spiridonovsky per.

The more traditional sights – the state-of-the-art planetarium and the newly renovated zoo – are set on the busy Garden Ring (ring road 3km from the Kremlin). Further out, the metallic spires of the Moscow International Business Centre are the symbol of the 21st-century capital.

In Outer Presnya, the wide roads, heavy traffic and ongoing construction mean this part of the district is not particularly user-friendly. Make the trip only if you have your heart set on a particular destination.

Local Life

➡**Parks** Packs of teens, grandmothers with wee ones and starry-eyed couples all congregate at Patriarch's Ponds to sit on the shady benches and feed the ducks.

➡**Bakery** The queue often runs out the door as loyal patrons wait their turn for the city's best freshly baked breads, pastries and pies at Volkonsky.

➡**Brunch** Weekends at Scramble are an expat institution.

Getting There & Away

➡**Inner Presnya** Inner Presnya is most easily accessed from Mayakovskaya station on line 2 (green) or Pushkinskaya station on line 7 (purple).

➡**Outer Presnya** For the more western parts of the district, the most useful metro stations are at Kudrinskaya pl: Barrikadnaya on line 7 and Krasnopresnenskaya on line 5 (Ring line).

➡**International Business Centre** The new development around the International Business Centre has its own mini metro spur branching off from Kievskaya station, with convenient stops at Vystavochnaya and Mezhdunarodnaya.

PRESNYA

◉ SIGHTS

The pleasant, walkable streets of Inner Presnya are home to some of the district's smaller sights – parks, churches and noteworthy homes. But the biggest draws are located on the Garden Ring and even further out.

◉ Inner Presnya

CHURCH OF THE RESURRECTION
CHURCH

Map p278 (Храм Воскресения Словущего на Успенском вражке; www.vslov.ru; Bryusov per 15/2; Ⓜ Pushkinskaya) Through the arch from Tverskaya ul, the rosy-pink, gold-domed Church of the Resurrection was one of the few churches to remain open throughout the Soviet period and so attracted artists and performers from the surrounding theatre district. Even acclaimed actor and director Konstantin Stanislavsky was apparently sighted here.

CHURCH OF THE LESSER ASCENSION
CHURCH

Map p278 (Храм Малое Вознесение; http://mvoznesenie.ru; Bolshaya Nikitskaya ul) Built in the early 17th century, the festive Church of the Lesser Ascension features whitewashed walls and primitively carved stone embellishments.

ART4.RU
GALLERY

Map p278 (☑499-136 5656; www.art4.ru; Khlynovsky tupik 4; ⊙11am-7pm Mon-Fri; Ⓜ Okhotny Ryad) FREE Anyone can be a museum director, as demonstrated by Moscow businessman-turned-art-collector Igor Markin. His 700-plus-piece collection had outgrown his private properties, so he decided to start a museum where he could display his art and share it with the public. And so art4.ru ('Art for Russia') was born. Nowadays it operates as more of a gallery, as much of the artwork is also for sale.

MOSCOW MUSEUM OF MODERN ART TVERSKOY
MUSEUM

Map p278 (MMOMA; www.mmoma.ru; Tverskoy bul 9; ₽150; ⊙noon-8pm; Ⓜ Pushkinskaya) This small exhibition space, known as the 'Zurab Gallery', was formerly the studio of sculptor Zurab Tsereteli. As such, the space has seen many talented artists, musicians and writers among its guests. Nowadays it is an offshoot of the main MMOMA outlet on ul Petrovka (p89), and continues to host exhibitions, performances and cultural events. Be sure to check the website to see what's on, as the museum often closes between shows.

MUSEUM OF ORIENTAL ART
MUSEUM

Map p278 (Музей искусства народов востока; ☑495-691 0212; www.orientmuseum.ru; Nikitsky bul 12a; ₽400; ⊙11am-8pm Tue-Sun; Ⓜ Arbatskaya) This impressive museum on the Boulevard Ring holds three floors of exhibits spanning the Asian continent. Of particular interest is the 1st floor, dedicated mostly to the Caucasus, Central Asia and North Asia (meaning the Russian republics of Cukotka, Yakutia and Priamurie). Several rooms on the 2nd floor are dedicated to Nikolai Rerikh, the Russian artist and explorer who spent several years travelling and painting in Asia.

The entire continent is pretty well represented here, including the countries that were not part of the Russian or Soviet empires. The collection covers an equally vast time period, from ancient times through to the 20th century, including painting, sculpture and folk art.

GOGOL HOUSE
MUSEUM

Map p278 (Дом Гоголя; www.domgogolya.ru; Nikitsky bul 7; ₽150; ⊙noon-7pm Tue, Wed & Fri, 2-9pm Thu, noon 5pm Sat & Sun; Ⓜ Arbatskaya) The 19th-century writer Nikolai Gogol spent his final tortured months here. The rooms – now a small but captivating museum – are arranged as they were when Gogol lived in them. You can even see the fireplace where he famously threw his manuscript of *Dead Souls*.

An additional reading room contains a library of Gogol's work and other reference materials about the author. The quiet courtyard contains a statue of the emaciated, sad author surrounded by some of his better-known characters in bas-relief.

CHURCH OF THE GRAND ASCENSION
CHURCH

Map p278 (Храм Большое Вознесение у Никитских Ворот; http://bolshoevoznesenie.ru; pl Nikitskie Vorota; ⊙8am-6pm) In 1831 poet Alexander Pushkin married artist Natalia Goncharova in the elegant Church of the Grand Ascension, on the western side of pl Nikitskie Vorota. Six years later he died in St Petersburg, defending her honour in a

TOP SIGHT
MOSCOW PLANETARIUM

The Moscow Planetarium (Московский планетарий) has become one of the biggest and brightest stars on the capital's museum circuit, now incorporating all kinds of high-tech gadgetry, interactive exhibits and educational programs.

The centrepiece is the Large Star Hall, with its 25m silver dome roof, a landmark which is visible from the Garden Ring. With the starry sky projected across the dome, the shows take viewers on a journey around the world and around the universe. Your ticket includes access to the old-school exhibits in the Urania Museum (think meteorite collection). From May to October, you can also explore the rooftop Sky Park sprinkled with astronomical instruments from sun dials to solar panels.

In addition to the traditional planetary attractions, the facility includes the innovative interactive Lunarium, where visitors can perform experiments. Fun hands-on activities include generating electrical energy, riding a cosmic bicycle and determining your weight on another planet.

Another favourite attraction is the four-dimensional cinema, which features 3D images plus other special sensual effects such as sounds, smells and movement.

DON'T MISS

➡ 'Universarium' show in the Large Star Hall

➡ 'Lunarium' museum

➡ Sky Park

PRACTICALITIES

➡ Map p278, D5

➡ www.planetarium-moscow.ru

➡ Sadovaya-Kudrinskaya ul 5

➡ Large Star Hall ₽550-750, Small Star Hall ₽100-200

➡ ⊙10am-10pm Wed-Mon

➡ Ⓜ Barrikadnaya

---

duel. Such passion, such romance... The celebrated couple is featured in the Rotunda Fountain, erected in 1999 to commemorate the poet's 100th birthday.

RYABUSHINSKY MANSION · MUSEUM

Map p278 (Особняк Рябушинского; Malaya Nikitskaya ul 6/2; adult/student ₽400/150; ⊙11am-5.30pm Wed-Sun; ⓂPushkinskaya) Also known as the Gorky House-Museum, this fascinating 1906 art nouveau mansion was designed by architect Fyodor Shekhtel and gifted to celebrated author Maxim Gorky in 1931. The house is a visual fantasy with sculpted doorways, ceiling murals, stained glass, a carved stone staircase and exterior tilework. Besides the fantastic decor it contains many of Gorky's personal items, including his extensive library.

SYNAGOGUE ON BOLSHAYA BRONNAYA · SYNAGOGUE

Map p278 (Синагога на Большой Бронной; Bolshaya Bronnaya ul 6; ⓂPushkinskaya) Built in 1883, the Synagogue on Bolshaya Bronnaya was the private place of worship of a prerevolutionary millionaire. Closed in the 1930s, the building was still used for informal gatherings by the Jewish community throughout the Soviet period. Today it is a working synagogue, as well as a social centre for the small but growing Jewish community in Moscow.

PATRIARCH'S PONDS · PARK

Map p278 (Патриаршие пруды; Bolshoy Patriarshy per; ⓂMayakovskaya) Patriarch's Ponds hark back to Soviet days, when the parks were populated with children and *babushky*. Today you'll see grandmothers pushing strollers and lovers kissing on park benches. In summer, children romp on the swings, while winter sees them ice skating on the pond. The small park has a huge statue of 19th-century Russian writer Ivan Krylov, known to Russian children for his didactic tales.

Patriarch's Ponds were immortalised by writer Mikhail Bulgakov, who had the devil appear here in *The Master and Margarita*. The initial paragraph of the novel describes the area to the north of the pond, where the devil enters the scene and predicts the rapid death of Berlioz. Contrary to Bulgakov's tale, a tram line never ran along the pond. Bulgakov's flat (now a museum, opposite), where he wrote the novel and lived up until his death, is around the corner on the Garden Ring.

MOSCOW MUSEUM OF MODERN ART YERMOLAYEVSKY
MUSEUM

Map p278 (MMOMA; www.mmoma.ru; Yermolayevsky per 17; adult/student ₽250/100; ⊙noon-8pm; MMayakovskaya) This handsome neoclassical building houses a branch of the main MMOMA on ul Petrovka (p89). Formerly the Moscow Union of Artists, it is now utilised for temporary exhibits of paintings, sculpture, photography and multimedia pieces. Be sure to check the website to see what's on, as the museum often closes between shows.

★MIKHAIL BULGAKOV MUSEUM
MUSEUM

Map p278 (Музей Михаила Булгакова; www.bulgakovmuseum.ru; Bolshaya Sadovaya ul 10; adult/child ₽150/50; ⊙noon-7pm Tue-Sun, 2-9pm Thu; MMayakovskaya) Author of *The Master and Margarita* and *Heart of a Dog*, Mikhail Bulgakov was a Soviet-era novelist who was labelled a counter-revolutionary and censored throughout his life. His most celebrated novels were published posthumously, earning him a sort of cult following in the late Soviet period. Bulgakov lived with his wife, Tatyana Lappa, in a flat in this block, which now houses an arts centre and theatre (p116) on the ground floor, and a small museum in their actual flat.

Back in the 1990s the empty Bulgakov flat was a hang-out for dissidents and hooligans, who painted graffiti and wrote poetry on the walls. Nowadays, this tradition continues and you can add your own contribution to the historic scrawlings. Inside the flat, you'll find some of the author's personal items, as well as posters and illustrations of his works. More interesting are the readings and concerts that are held here, as well as the offbeat tours on offer. A black cat hangs out in the courtyard.

CENTRAL HOUSE OF WRITERS (CDL)
NOTABLE BUILDING

Map p278 (Центральный дом литераторов (ЦДЛ); www.moscowwriters.ru; Povarskaya ul 50; MBarrikadnaya) The Central House of Writers is an elaborate art nouveau mansion dating to 1889. The historic mansion housed the administrative offices of the writers' union for most of the Soviet period. As such, it

was featured in Mikhail Bulgakov's famous novel *The Master and Margarita*.

The on-site restaurant is worth a peek for its ornate interior. Otherwise, the building is not open to the public.

CHEKHOV HOUSE-MUSEUM
MUSEUM

Map p278 (Дом-музей Чехова; www.goslitmuz.ru; Sadovaya-Kudrinskaya ul 6; ₽150; ⊙11am-6pm Tue-Sun, to 9pm Wed & Thu; MBarrikadnaya) 'The colour of the house is liberal, ie red', playwright Anton Chekhov wrote of his house on the Garden Ring, where he lived from 1886 to 1890. The red house now contains the Chekhov House-Museum, with bedrooms, drawing room and study all intact.

The overall impression of Chekhov's home is one of a peaceful and cultured family life. The walls are decorated with paintings that were given to Chekhov by painter Isaac Levitan and art nouveau architect Fyodor Shekhtel, who often visited him here. Photographs depict the playwright with literary greats Leo Tolstoy and Maxim Gorky. One room is dedicated to Chekhov's time in Melikhovo, showing photographs and manuscripts from his country estate.

◉ Outer Presnya

KUDRINSKAYA APARTMENT BLOCK
NOTABLE BUILDING

Map p278 (Высотка на Кудринской площади; Kudrinskaya pl 1; MBarrikadnaya) The 160m, 22-storey Stalinist skyscraper at Kudrinskaya pl contains elite apartments, mostly occupied by pre-eminent cultural figures during Soviet times.

NARKOMFIN
NOTABLE BUILDING

Map p278 (Наркомфин; Novinsky bul 25; MBarrikadnaya) The model for Le Corbusier's Unité d'Habitation design principle, this architectural landmark was an early experiment in semicommunal living. Designed and built in the 1920s by Moisei Ginzburg and Ignatii Milinis, Narkomfin offered housing for members of the Commissariat of Finances. In line with constructivist ideals, communal space is maximised and individual space is minimised. Apartments have minute kitchens (or none at all) to encourage residents to eat in the communal dining room. Tours are available through Moscow ArchiGeek (p32).

Having been in a semiruinous state for many years, Narkomfin is finally slated for

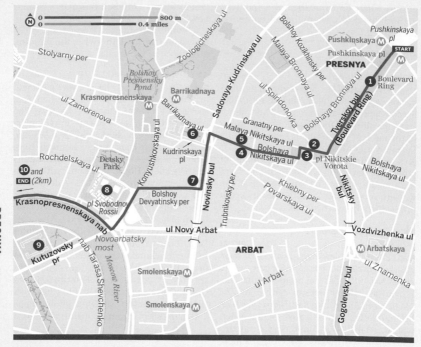

Neighbourhood Walk
Presnya

START PUSHKINSKAYA PL
END KRASNOPRESNENSKAYA NAB
LENGTH 4KM; TWO HOURS

Walk from the previous century into the present (and beyond). From Pushkinskaya pl, stroll south along ❶**Tverskoy bulvar**. This is the loveliest stretch of the Boulevard Ring, lined with grand architecture, colourful blooms and a statue of poet Sergei Yesenin. At the end, sneak a peek at ❷**Ryabushinsky Mansion** (p106), an art nouveau beauty where celebrated author Maxim Gorky lived.

Looming over the busy intersection, the ❸**Church of the Grand Ascension** (p105) hosted the wedding of poet Alexander Pushkin and artist Natalia Goncharova, and a sculpture of the lovebirds graces the fountain out front. Turn right and walk west on Bolshaya Nikitskaya ul, which is studded with mansions. Some of the most striking include the elaborate facade at ❹**No 51** and the tiled edifice of ❺**Lopatina Building** at No 54.

At the end of Bolshaya Nikitskaya ul, use the underground crosswalk to reach ❻**Kudrinskaya pl**, dominated by a massive skyscraper (one of Stalin's 'Seven Sisters'). Just south is one of Moscow's last and best examples of modernist architecture, ❼**Narkomfin** (p107).

Turn right onto Bolshoy Devyatinsky per, then left onto Konyushkovskaya ul, continuing south to Krasnopresnenskaya nab. On the banks of the Moscow River is the massive facade of the ❽**White House**, home of the Russian parliament and site of several decisive historic events in the 1990s. The ❾**Radisson Royal** (p195), another of the 'Seven Sisters', stands on the opposite side of the river. In the distance, the ❿ **International Business Centre** sprouts up along the Moscow River. Note the double-pronged City of Capitals building, representing Moscow and St Petersburg. The eastern spire of the Federation Tower, looms some 374m. Turn right on Nikolaeva ul and duck into the **Tryokhgornaya Manufaktura** (p114) complex and finish at one of its many restaurants, bars and cafes.

restoration – a three-year project that began in late 2017. The architect overseeing the project is Alexey Ginzburg, grandson of the original architect, who intends to preserve and restore as much of the constructivist detail as possible. The apartments are likely to remain in private hands but the communal block is expected to house a cultural centre and museum that will hopefully be open to the public.

MOSCOW ZOO
ZOO

Map p278 (Московский зоопарк; www.moscow zoo.ru; Bolshaya Gruzinskaya ul 1; ₽500; ⊙10am-8pm Tue-Sun Apr-Sep, to 5pm Oct-Mar; ⊕; Ⓜ Barrikadnaya) Renovations in honour of the zoo's 150th anniversary are ongoing, but the place should be in great shape in coming years. Huge flocks of feathered friends populate the central ponds, making for a pleasant stroll for birdwatchers. For a new perspective on Moscow's nightlife, check out the nocturnal animal exhibit. Other highlights include the big cats (featuring Siberian tigers) and the polar bears. For more four-legged fun, follow the footbridge to see exhibits featuring animals from each continent.

TSERETELI STUDIO-MUSEUM
MUSEUM

Map p278 (Музей-мастерская Зураба Церетели; www.mmoma.ru; Bolshaya Gruzinskaya ul 15; adult/child ₽250/150; ⊙noon-8pm Fri-Wed, 1-9pm Thu; ⊕; Ⓜ Belorusskaya) Moscow's most prolific artist has opened up his 'studio' as a space to exhibit his many masterpieces. You can't miss this place – whimsical characters adorn the front lawn. They give just a tiny hint of what's inside: a courtyard crammed with bigger-than-life bronze beauties and elaborate enamelwork.

The highlight work is undoubtedly Putin in his judo costume, although the huge tile Moscow cityscapes are impressive. You'll also recognise some smaller-scale models of monuments that appear around town. Indoors, there are three floors of the master's sketches, paintings and enamel arts.

MUSEUM OF RUSSIAN IMPRESSIONISM
MUSEUM

(www.rusimp.su; Bldg 11, Leningradsky pr 15; ₽250; ⊙11am-8pm Fri-Tue, noon-9pm Wed-Thu; Ⓜ Belorusskaya) Few Russian artists embraced the Impressionist moniker, but many were influenced by the movement's style and techniques. At Moscow's newest art museum, billionaire art collector Boris Mint aims to educate and impress Muscovites (and visitors) about this important niche, at the same time showcasing his own collection, which includes works by the likes of Valentin Serov, Boris Kustodiev and Konstantin Korovin. The museum occupies part of the former Bolshevik chocolate factory – the sugar silo, to be exact. Sweet!

WHITE HOUSE
NOTABLE BUILDING

Map p278 (Белый дом; Krasnopresnenskaya nab 2; Ⓜ Krasnopresnenskaya) The White House – officially the House of Government of the Russian Federation – fronts a stately bend in the Moscow River, just north of the Novoarbatsky most.

It was here that Boris Yeltsin rallied the opposition that confounded the 1991 hardline coup, then two years later sent in tanks and troops to blast out conservative rivals. The images of Yeltsin climbing on a tank in front of the White House in 1991, and of the same building ablaze after the 1993 assault, are among the most unforgettable from those tumultuous years.

MOSCOW INTERNATIONAL BUSINESS CENTRE
AREA

(Москва-сити; Ⓜ Delovoi Tsentr) This strip along the Moscow River is the site of one of the capital's largest ongoing urban projects, also known as 'Moscow City'. Here, skyscrapers of glass and steel tower 20 storeys over the rest of the city, shining like beacons to Moscow's wheeler-dealers and fortune-seekers. The 93-storey Tower East (Vostok) of the Federation complex is the tallest building in both Russia and Europe.

🍴 EATING

Presnya is home to some of Moscow's most exciting and enticing eateries. In particular, the streets around Patriarch's Ponds (p106) are crowded with trendy cafes and sophisticated restaurants, many showing off truly creative cooking by internationally renowned chefs. Other noteworthy dining destinations include Bolshaya Nikitskaya ul (inside the Boulevard Ring) and Bolshaya Gruzinskaya ul (near Tverskaya ul). Tryokhgornaya Manufaktura (p114) is fast becoming a centre for dining and drinking, adding to the existing venues along ul 1905 goda.

✖ Inner Presnya

VOLKONSKY
BAKERY €

Map p278 (Волконский; www.wolkonsky.com; Bolshaya Sadovaya ul 2/46; mains ₽250-400, sweets from ₽100; ⊘ bakery 8am-11pm, cafe 24hr; 🔊 🖉 👬; Ⓜ Mayakovskaya) The queue often runs out the door, as loyal patrons wait their turn for the city's best freshly baked breads, pastries and pies. It's worth the wait, especially if you decide on a fruit-filled croissant or to-die-for olive bread. Next door there are big wooden tables where you can get large bowls of coffee or tea.

SCRAMBLE
BREAKFAST €

Map p278 (🖉 495-691 1850; www.friends-forever.ru; ul Spiridonovka 24/1; mains ₽390-450; ⊘ 8am-11pm; Ⓜ Mayakovskaya) This Brooklyn-styled local has emerged as a breakfast alternative for the well-off residents of the affluent Patriarshy neighbourhood, who are not bothered to cook at home. Perhaps the best omelettes in town.

RECEPTOR
CAFE €

Map p278 (Рецептор; www.cafereceptor.ru; Bolshoy Kozikhinsky per 10; mains ₽350-650; ⊘ noon-midnight; Ⓜ Tverskaya) Your body will love the fresh, healthy foods on offer at Receptor, including many vegetarian options. And your soul will love the bright interior, where leafy greenery grows in window boxes and artwork is everywhere – even on the ceiling. There is another outlet on Bolshaya Nikitskaya ul.

COOL KULINARIYA
RUSSIAN €

Map p278 (Cool Кулинария; Bldg 6, Bolshaya Nikitskaya ul 24/1; mains ₽200-400; ⊘ 8am-11pm Mon-Fri, from 10am Sat & Sun; 🔊 🖉; Ⓜ Okhotny Ryad) Tucked into a cosy basement crowded with comfy tables, this inviting little hovel makes it easy to sample fresh Russian soups and salads, as well as more exotic fare from the wok. Just take a peek inside the glass case and see what looks good. The only hard part is saving room for one of the tempting pastries.

RECEPTOR
FUSION €

Map p278 (Рецептор; www.cafereceptor.ru; Bolshaya Nikitskaya ul 22/2; mains ₽350-650; ⊘ noon-midnight; 🔊 🖉 👬; Ⓜ Okhotny Ryad) 🖉 Colourful graffiti, amateur artwork and old photographs adorn the walls of this quirky basement cafe. The decor creates an arty setting for healthy, veg-heavy meals, fresh juices and fancy teas. There is another outlet on Bolshoy Kozikhinsky per.

★ TWINS
RUSSIAN €€

Map p278 (🖉 495-695 4510; www.twinsmoscow.ru; Malaya Bronnaya ul 13; mains ₽650-1750; 🔊 🖉 🗐; Ⓜ Tverskaya) Swoon-worthy identical-twin chefs Sergei and Ivan Berezutskiy bring their contrasting tastes and creative talents to this delightful restaurant. The brothers take a thoroughly modern approach to Russian cooking, with ingredients procured from all corners of the country. Seating is on the pleasant terrace or in the classy, kitschy dining room.

★ KHACHAPURI
GEORGIAN €€

Map p278 (Хачапури; 🖉 8-985-764 3118; www.hacha.ru; Bolshoy Gnezdnikovsky per 10; khachapuri ₽220-420, mains ₽430-690; ✳ 🔊 🗐; Ⓜ Pushkinskaya) Unassuming, affordable and appetising, this urban cafe exemplifies what people love about Georgian culture: the warm hospitality and the freshly baked *khachapuri* (cheese bread). Aside from eight types of delicious *khachapuri,* there's also an array of soups, shashlyk (kebabs), *khinkali* (dumplings) and other Georgian favourites.

GRAN CAFE DR ZHIVAGO
RUSSIAN €€

Map p278 (Гранд Кафе Dr Живаго; 🖉 499-922 0100; www.drzhivago.ru; Mokhovaya ul 15/1; mains ₽540-1200; ⊘ 24hr; Ⓜ Okhotny Ryad) An excellent breakfast choice before visiting the Kremlin, this round-the-clock place mixes Soviet nostalgia with a great deal of mischievous irony in both design and food. The chef has upgraded the menu of a standard pioneer camp's canteen to near-haute-cuisine level, with masterfully cooked porridge, pancakes, *vareniki* (boiled dumplings, like ravioli) and cottage-cheese pies.

Dr Zhivago occupies the premises of the historic Cafe Berlin inside the Hotel National (p194).

MARI VANNA
RUSSIAN €€

Map p278 (Мари Ванна; 🖉 495-650 6500; www.marivanna.ru; Spiridonyevsky per 10; mains ₽600-900; ⊘ 9am-midnight; 🖉 🗐 👬; Ⓜ Pushkinskaya) Ring the doorbell at No 10 and you'll be ushered into the homey environs. Inside, the shelves are stuffed with books, photographs and mismatched tea sets, and old Soviet programs are showing on the black-and-white TV. Here you'll be served delicious Russian home cooking on little plates. You may even get a visit from the friendly resident *kiska* (pussy cat).

PUSHKIN KONDITERSKAYA DESSERTS €€

Map p278 (Кондитерская "Кафе Пушкинъ"; www.sweetpushkin.ru; Tverskoy bul 26; candies ₽75-175, desserts from ₽400; ☺10am-11pm; ⓘ; ⓂPushkinskaya) If you want to impress your date, but you can't afford the Cafe Pushkin (p111) for dinner, head next door to the *konditerskaya* (confectioner) for dessert. It's every bit as opulent as the restaurant, from the crystal chandeliers down to the marble floors, with plenty of embellishments in between (not the least of which is the glass case displaying the sweets).

UILLIAM'S EUROPEAN €€

Map p278 (Вилльям'с; ☑8-925-206 9046; www.ginzaproject.ru; Malaya Bronnaya ul 20a; mains ₽700-1350; ☺10.30am-11.30pm; ☑ⓘ; ⓂMayakovskaya) This tiny little spot is always packed with patrons who come to watch the action in the open kitchen, which is basically the centrepiece of the restaurant. Chef Uilliam Lamberti prides himself on using only the highest-quality ingredients and offering his heart and soul in the preparation.

UGOLYOK EUROPEAN €€

Map p278 (Уголёк; ☑495-629 0504; Bolshaya Nikitskaya ul 12; mains ₽600-1100; ☺noon-1am; ☎☑; ⓂOKhotny Ryad) Everything at Ugolyok is perfectly pleasing to the eye, from the slick postindustrial interior, to the funky but fine tableware, to the tantalising food and drinks laid before you. Fortunately, it tastes good too, as deliciously fresh ingredients are mixed up in unusual ways. A+ for brunch. The restaurant is attached to the Nikitskaya Hotel (p194).

AQ CHICKEN INTERNATIONAL €€

Map p278 (☑495-699 5313; www.aqchicken.ru; Tryokhprudny per 11/13; mains ₽490-990; ☺noon-11pm; ☎ⓘ; ⓂMayakovskaya) After making a name for himself at AQ Kitchen (p113), chef Adrian Quetglas decided to mix things up at AQ Chicken. At once quirky and classy, the new place offers an innovative approach to the chef's favourite poultry, with sophisticated salads, soups, cutlets, casseroles and more. The results are surprisingly diverse and delightful.

You're in the right place when you spot the giant eggs on the pavement.

DOLKABAR INTERNATIONAL €€

Map p278 (Долькабар; www.dolkabar.ru; ul Krasina 7; mains ₽450-950; ☺noon-11pm; ☎☑; ⓂMayakovskaya) Dolkabar is the culinary creation of traveller and blogger Sergei Kolya, who wanted to make a place where folks could come to share their adventures and get inspired for their next trip. Maps on the tables and photos on the walls create the perfect setting for a menu of international favourites.

JEAN-JACQUES FRENCH €€

Map p278 (Жан-Жак; www.facebook.com/JanJak.Cafe; Nikitsky bul 12; mains ₽400-800; ☺8am-6am; ☎; ⓂArbatskaya) In a prime location on the Boulevard Ring, this friendly wine bar welcomes everybody wanting a glass of wine, a bite to eat, some music and a few smiles. The basement setting is cosy but not dark, making it an ideal spot to share a bottle of Bordeaux and nibble on brie.

★CAFE PUSHKIN RUSSIAN €€€

Map p278 (Кафе Пушкинь; ☑495-739 0033; www.cafe-pushkin.ru; Tverskoy bul 26a; business lunch ₽620-930, mains ₽1000-2500; ☺24hr; ❄☎ⓘ; ⓂPushkinskaya) The tsarina of *haute-russe* dining, offering an exquisite blend of Russian and French cuisines. Service and food are done to perfection. The lovely 19th-century building has a different atmosphere on each floor, including a richly decorated library and a rooftop cafe.

PINCH FUSION €€€

Map p278 (☑495-691 9988; http://pinch.moscow; Bolshoy Palashyovsky per 2; small plates ₽550-1200, mains ₽800-1600; ☺8.30am-midnight; ☎☑) Chef Luigi Magni lends his creative flare and Italian accent to this casual, cosmopolitan joint. The menu combines fresh ingredients with true innovation, paying close attention to the food presentation on each and every plate. Favourites include chicken pâté with figs, different kinds of ceviche and a delectable house-made ricotta ravioli.

NEDALNY VOSTOK ASIAN €€€

Map p278 (Недальний Восток; ☑495-694 0641; www.novikovgroup.ru; Tverskoy bul 15; mains ₽900-1900; ☑ⓘ; ⓂPushkinskaya) Seafood is the star of the show at this classy pan-Asian restaurant. Oysters, lobsters – and especially Kamchatka crab – are prepared in the wok, on the grill or in the oven, all in plain sight of the diners. The Japanese-designed interior also has style mavens drooling over the juxtaposition of dark woods, granite and glass. Here's one for a splurge.

TURANDOT
CHINESE €€€

Map p278 (☑495-739 0011; www.turandot-palace.ru; Tverskoy bul 26/5; meals ₽1500-2000; ⓂPushkinskaya) If you wanted to go to Disney World, but somehow ended up in Moscow, Turandot should top your dining list. Musicians costumed in wigs and gowns play chamber music while servers scuttle to and fro. Turandot is named for a Puccini opera set in old Peking, which is as good a reason as any to serve Chinese and Japanese food. The baroque interior is unbelievably extravagant, with hand-painted furniture, gilded light fixtures and a frescoed cupola ceiling.

✕ Outer Presnya

★STOLLE
CAFE €

Map p278 (Штолле; www.stolle.ru; Bldg 1, Bolshaya Sadovaya ul 3; mains ₽200-400; ⓒ8am-11pm; ✷❄❖♿; ⓂMayakovskaya) The entire menu at Stolle is excellent, but the *pirozhki* (savoury pies) are irresistible. A 'stolle' is a traditional Saxon Christmas cake: the selection of sweets and savouries sits on the counter, fresh from the oven. It may be difficult to decide (mushroom or meat, apricot or apple?), but you really can't go wrong.

BULKA
BAKERY €

Map p278 (Булка пекарня; www.bulkabakery.ru; Bolshaya Gruzinskaya ul 69; pastries ₽100-200; ⓒ7.30am-11pm; ❖♿; ⓂBelorusskaya) The coffee is good but the pastries are even better. Whether you're hankering for something savoury or sweet, you're sure to find it in the big glass display case. Late in the day, everything goes on sale so the bakers can start afresh the following morning.

DOBAVKA
RUSSIAN €

Map p278 (Добавка; Bldg 1, Rochdelskaya ul 15; mains ₽200-500; ⓒ8am-10pm; ✎) Tucked into the corner of the Tryokhgornaya complex (p117), this Soviet-style throwback is a popular spot for breakfast and lunch for local workers. Smiling, kerchief-clad *devushki* serve up hearty portions of Russian food, with plenty of concessions to modern tastes.

SOUP CAFE
RUSSIAN €

Map p278 (Суп кафе; ☑499-251 1383; www.cafesoup.ru; 1-ya Brestskaya ul 62; soups ₽125-300; ⓒ5am-11pm Mon-Fri, to 2pm Sat & Sun; ❖✎; ⓂBelorusskaya) This aptly named restaurant takes the most appetising element of Russian food to new heights, offering some 44 varieties of soup, including meat- and fish-based, as well as vegetarian. If you're really into it, you can also get a soup for dessert. The atmosphere is urban-casual, with exposed brick walls and pillow-strewn couches.

COOK'KAREKU
INTERNATIONAL €

Map p278 (☑495-660 5339; http://cookkareku.ru; Bldg 4, Sadovaya-Kudrinskaya ul 9; breakfast ₽460; ⓒ24hr; ⓂMayakovskaya) Here is your reliable round-the-clock breakfast option. Each selection on the breakfast menu represents one of the world's 24 time zones – from Magadan in far-eastern Russia to California. You get a 30% discount if you opt for the zone where the sun is rising at the time of your visit. The service can be grumpy.

CORNER BURGER
BURGERS €

Map p278 (Корнер Бургер; www.cornerburger.ru; Bolshaya Gruzinskaya ul 76; burgers ₽370-520; ⓒnoon-midnight, to 2am Fri & Sat; ❖▯; ⓂBelorusskaya) Nowadays, there are burger joints on every block in Moscow. But this place was one of the first, and it's still one of the best. These babies feature high-quality ground beef, grilled the way you like it and served with a variety of intriguing toppings. Despite the restaurant's name, there's also pizza and other options on the menu.

UDC CAFE
BAKERY €

Map p278 (udc Кафе; www.upsidedowncake.ru; Bolshaya Gruzinskaya ul 76; desserts ₽200-400, mains ₽350-650; ⓒ9am-11pm Mon-Fri, from 10am Sat & Sun; ❖✎▯; ⓂBelorusskaya) ✐ We hope you saved room for dessert. Also known as Upside Down Cake, this bakery features lots of cupcakes and pastries, delicious sorbet and herbal teas by the pot.

BOTANICA
FUSION €

Map p278 (Ботаника; ☑495-251 9760; www.cafe-botanica.ru; Bolshaya Gruzinskaya ul 61; mains ₽300-600; ⓒ9am-midnight Mon-Fri, from 11am Sat, from 1pm Sun; ❖▯; ⓂBelorusskaya) Both fashionable and affordable, Botanica offers light, modern fare, with plenty of soups, salads and grills (as well as sushi, spring rolls and noodle dishes). Wood furniture and subtle floral prints complement the garden-themed decor, all of which makes for an enjoyable, all-natural eating experience.

★AQ KITCHEN
MEDITERRANEAN €€

Map p278 (☑499-393 3224; http://aq.kitchen; Bolshaya Gruzinskaya ul 69; mains ₽700-1200; ☺noon-midnight; 🛜; Ⓜ️Belorusskaya) AQ stands for Adrian Quetglas, the Argentinian chef who is the brains behind this creative endeavour. With huge windows and stressed-wood details, the shabby-chic interior is a perfect setting for the eclectic menu. Look for Moroccan chicken with couscous, grilled squid with romesco sauce and other unexpected delicacies.

SHINOK
UKRAINIAN €€

Map p278 (Шинок; ☑495-651 8101; www.shinok.ru; ul 1905 goda 2; mains ₽500-1200; ☺noon-midnight; 🖉🚼; Ⓜ️Ulitsa 1905 Goda) If you feel the need to get back to nature, this restaurant has recreated a Ukrainian peasant farm in central Moscow. The house speciality is *vareniki* (boiled dumplings), which are superb, as are other Ukrainian specialities such as borscht and *salo* (lard). The place has been redone in a pared-down, contemporary style, which is an odd contrast with the farm.

BARASHKA
AZERBAIJANI €€

Map p278 (Барашка; ☑495-653 8303; www.novikovgroup.ru; ul 1905 goda 2; mains ₽450-950; 🖉; Ⓜ️Ulitsa 1905 Goda) Step off a busy Moscow street and into a charming Azeri courtyard, where you can dine on delectable salads, grilled meats and hearty stews.

MOLON LAVE
GREEK €€

Map p278 (Молон Лаве; ☑495-272 0047; www.molonlaverestaurant.com; Bolshaya Gruzinskaya ul 39; mains ₽530-1150; ☺11am-midnight; 🗐; Ⓜ️Belorusskaya) Given Moscow's climate and intensity, emulating the super-relaxed ambience of a genuine Greek taverna is out of the question. So, thankfully, the owners of this restaurant never tried that, but instead they created a very modern Greek-themed place that serves taverna staples – tzatziki, fava, grilled octopus – transformed by 21st-century culinary wizards. Greek expats abound – a sure sign of success!

CORREA'S
EUROPEAN €€

Map p278 (☑495-933 4684; www.correas.ru; Bolshaya Gruzinskaya ul 32; sandwiches ₽290-550, mains ₽400-700; ☺8am-11pm Mon-Fri, from 9am Sat & Sun; 🛜🖉🗐; Ⓜ️Belorusskaya) The original Correa's occupies a tiny space and there are only a handful of tables. But the large windows and open kitchen guarantee it does not feel cramped, just cosy. The menu – salads, sandwiches, pizza and grills – features nothing too fancy, but everything is prepared with the freshest ingredients and the utmost care. A popular lunch spot.

ANDERSON FOR POP
INTERNATIONAL €€

Map p278 (Андерсон для Пап; ☑499-753 1601; www.cafe-anderson.ru; Malaya Gruzinskaya ul 15/1; mains ₽390-620; ☺9am-11pm Mon-Fri, 10am-11pm Sat & Sun; 🚼; Ⓜ️Barrikadnaya) The ultimate in family-friendly, this place is designed for dads and kids (and mums, too). The play area is well equipped with air hockey, a ball pit and even a drumming room – plenty for kids to do while parents enjoy some downtime. The food and drinks are nothing extraordinary, but reliably good, with the right mix of kids' and grown-up fare.

🍷 DRINKING & NIGHTLIFE

Presnya is more about dining than drinking; but of course, you can't have one without the other, which means there are plenty of cool places to drink coffee, sip cocktails or quaff a cold beer. Hotspots are clustered around Patriarch's Ponds (p106) and around Tryokhgornaya Manufaktura (p114).

🍷 Inner Presnya

ART LEBEDEV CAFE STUDIO
CAFE

Map p278 (Кафе Студия Артемия Лебедева; www.artlebedev.ru; Bolshaya Nikitskaya ul 35b; ☺8am-11pm Mon-Fri, from 10am Sat & Sun; 🛜; Ⓜ️Arbatskaya) Owned by design guru Artemy Lebedev, this tiny space invites an attractive arty crowd to sip fancy coffee drinks and exotic teas. Regulars love the house-made *kasha* (porridge) for breakfast and the shady terrace in summer months. Don't miss the shop downstairs.

BAR KLAVA
BAR

Map p278 (Бар Клава; http://semifreddo-group.com; Malaya Bronnaya ul 26; ☺noon-6am; 🛜; Ⓜ️Mayakovskaya) The chic interior and

TRYOKHGORNAYA MANUFAKTURA

Tryokhgornaya Manufaktura (Трёхгорная Мануфактура) is one of the oldest textile factories in Russia, founded in 1799 on the banks of the Moscow River. The factory played a key role in the development of the Presnya district. Over the years, it has employed hundreds of thousands of mill workers, weavers and designers. The company survived both Wars of the Fatherland (War of 1812 and WWII), as well as the uprisings of 1905, which took place at its doorstep. It has survived both nationalisation and privatisation – and is now learning to survive capitalism.

Although the company continues to design and produce fabrics, the level of production has dropped dramatically since its peak in the early 1980s. Meanwhile, the administration of Moscow has been actively moving industry out of the historic city centre. (Never mind that Tryokhgornaya is part of the history of this city centre; it too must go.)

Most of the company's production has already moved to Yaroslavl, but the design centre and administrative offices continue to operate in the original location. In that vein, many of its warehouses have been converted into studios and showrooms, especially for interior design. You can also check out the Tryokhgornaya product line at the on-site Factory Outlet (p117).

Like other repurposed industrial zones, Tryokhgornaya has become a hotspot for nightlife, as restaurants and clubs such as Jagger (p115) and Nikuda ne edem (p115) take advantage of the prime location and vast postindustrial spaces.

intimate atmosphere make for a sophisticated little bar that's trendy but not pretentious. The menu features a full page of whiskies and some enticing house cocktails. It's an expensive place to drink, if that's your activity for the evening, but a perfectly pleasant place to pop in for a sip before or after your night out.

TOLSTOY PUB
CRAFT BEER

Map p278 (Толстой Паб; www.facebook.com/tolstoy.pub; Bldg 3, Povarskaya ul 52/55; ⊙noon-11pm Sun-Thu, to 3am Fri & Sat; Ⓜ Barrikadnaya) Occupying a historic building on one of Moscow's loveliest streets, this beer bar is about as welcoming as they come. This cosy spot offers an intimate interior and a leafy summer terrace – both ideal places to sample the nice selection of draughts.

COFFEE MANIA
CAFE

Map p278 (Кофемания; www.coffeemania.ru; Bolshaya Nikitskaya ul 13, Moscow Conservatory; ⊙24hr; 🖥; Ⓜ Okhotny Ryad) A longtime popular place for the rich and beautiful to congregate, this friendly, informal cafe is beloved for its homemade soups, freshly squeezed juices and steaming (if overpriced) cappuccinos, not to mention its summer terrace overlooking the leafy courtyard of the Moscow Conservatory.

KVARTIRA 44
BAR

Map p278 (Квартира 44; www.kv44.ru; Bolshaya Nikitskaya ul 22/2; ⊙noon to midnight; 🖥;

Ⓜ Okhotny Ryad) Somebody had the brilliant idea to convert an old Moscow apartment into a crowded, cosy bar, with tables and chairs tucked into every nook and cranny, and jazz and piano music on Friday and Saturday nights.

MAYAK
BAR

Map p278 (Маяк; www.clubmayak.ru; Bolshaya Nikitskaya ul 19; business lunch ₽270, mains ₽300-350; ⊙noon-6am; 🖥; Ⓜ Okhotny Ryad) Named for the Mayakovsky Theatre downstairs, this is a remake of a much-beloved club that operated in this spot throughout the 1990s. The reincarnated version is more pub than club, exuding the air of a welcoming, old-fashioned inn. But it still attracts actors, artists and writers, who come to let loose in the wee hours.

RYUMOCHNAYA
BAR

Map p278 (Рюмочная; Bolshaya Nikitskaya ul 22/2; meals ₽200-400; ⊙11am-11pm; Ⓜ Okhotny Ryad) A holdover (or a comeback?) from the days when a drinking establishment needed no special name. The *ryumochnaya* was the generic place where comrades stopped on their way to or from work to toss back a shot or two before continuing on their way. This version also offers some tasty food to accompany your *sto grammov* (100 grams).

CRAFT NOIR
CRAFT BEER

Map p278 (Крафт Нуар; www.facebook.com/craftnoirpub; Bldg 2, Sadovaya-Kudrinskaya ul

32; ☺2pm-midnight Sun-Thu, to 2am Fri & Sat; 🛜; Ⓜ Mayakovskaya) Enter from the back courtyard, and climb the graffiti-scrawled staircase to the 2nd floor to find this hole-in-the-wall craft-beer paradise. There's not much to this place, except for 20 different craft beers (mostly Russian) on tap and 100 more in the bottle. The place is pretty unassuming, though you can't get away from the TV screens.

CONVERSATION
CAFE

Map p278 (www.friends-forever.ru; Bolshaya Nikitskaya ul 23/14/9; ☺8am-midnight; 🛜; Ⓜ Arbatskaya) The 'conversation' at this inviting, contemporary cafe is sure to revolve around the elaborate display of cakes and pies which is its centrepiece. Soups and sandwiches are also on the menu, but it's the decadent desserts and wake-me-up coffee drinks that keep the seats filled.

📍 Outer Presnya

★ TIME-OUT ROOFTOP BAR
COCKTAIL BAR

Map p278 (http://hotelpeking.ru/timeout-rooftop-bar; 12th fl, Bolshaya Sadovaya ul 5; ☺noon-2am Sun-Thu, to 6am Fri & Sat; Ⓜ Mayakovskaya) On the upper floors of the throwback Peking Hotel (p194), this trendy bar is nothing but 'now'. That includes the bartenders sporting plaid and their delicious concoctions, specially created for different times of the day. The decor is pretty impressive – particularly the spectacular city skyline view. A perfect place for sundowners (or sun-ups, if you last that long).

JAGGER
BAR

Map p278 (www.jaggercity.ru; Bldg 30, Rochdelskaya ul 15; ☺noon-midnight Mon-Wed, to 6am Thu-Sat, 2pm-midnight Sun, Ⓜ Ulitsa 1905 Goda) Tucked into the courtyard in the old Tryokhgornaya (p117) manufacturing complex, Jagger is a super-hot bar with a super-cool vibe. Excellent cocktails, sharp clientele and laid-back atmosphere are characteristic of a new Moscow nightlife that is cosmopolitan and cultured, not over-the-top outrageous. Still, you have to know where to look for this place. And you have to look good.

Enter from ul 1905 goda and head to the inner courtyard. Reservations (and table deposit) are essential on weekends.

ZOO BEER & GRILL
CRAFT BEER

Map p278 (www.novikovgroup.ru; Konyushkovskaya ul 4; ☺noon-3am; Ⓜ Krasnopresnenskaya) Here's a place for animal-lovers and beer-lovers. Ten craft beers on tap (including one house brew) and dozens more in bottles accompany an excellent, meat-heavy menu. The slick, postindustrial decor gives a few artistic nods to the animal friends from across the street. If you're hoping to sneak a peek, there's a view into the zoo (p109) from the rooftop terrace.

NIKUDA NE EDEM
COCKTAIL BAR

Map p278 (Никуда не едем; ☎495-926 2322; www.nikudaneedem.ru; Bldg 8, Rochdelskaya ul 15; ☺11am-midnight Sun-Thu, to 3am Fri & Sat; Ⓜ Ulitsa 1905 Goda) This split-level gastropub also has a sort of split personality, with cosy living-room decor in one area and a slick back-lit bar in another. The overall effect is one that is cool but casual, sophisticated but sympathetic. There is an eclectic menu of food to complement the very creative cocktails.

The place is disguised as an innocuous office, staffed by a pleasant receptionist who will ask *My kudo-to edem?* (Are we going somewhere?) when you enter. If you answer correctly, the shelves and bookcases will magically open, inviting you into the enticing interior. In case you haven't guessed already, the correct answer is *Nikuda ne edem* (We go nowhere).

DISCO ROOMS
CLUB

Map p278 (www.discoroom.ru; Bolshaya Gruzinskaya ul 4/6; ☺restaurant from 8pm, club from 10pm; Ⓜ Barrikadnaya) 'Retro' has become very popular in Moscow, but this is the first place hearkening back to the boogie nights of the 1970s. Out front is an old-fashioned diner where you can fuel up on burgers and breakfast food. Slip through the curtains to the dance floor, illuminated by sparkling disco ball and crowded with dancers doing the Hustle (or not).

RADIO CITY
BAR

Map p278 (Радио-Сити; www.radiocitybar.ru; Bolshaya Sadovaya ul 5; ☺24hr; Ⓜ Mayakovskaya) On the ground floor of the Peking Hotel (p194), this is not the most interesting or original bar in Moscow but it has a few things going for it. Twenty-six, to be exact. That's the number of TV screens strewn about the bar (22 plasmas, four big screens), all of which are usually tuned into one sporting match or another.

Other than that, the place has 10 kinds of beer on tap and a menu of munchies that gets mixed reviews. There's also live entertainment starting at 8pm from Wednesday to Sunday.

⭐ ENTERTAINMENT

MOSCOW TCHAIKOVSKY
CONSERVATORY   CLASSICAL MUSIC
Map p278 (Московская консерватория имени Чайковского; ☑box office 495-629 9401; www.mosconsv.ru; Bolshaya Nikitskaya ul 13; Ⓜ Okhotny Ryad) The country's largest music school, named for Tchaikovsky of course, has two venues, both of which host concerts, recitals and competitions. The Great Hall of the Conservatory is home to the Moscow Symphony Orchestra (MSO; www.moscow symphony.ru), a low-budget but highly lauded orchestra under the direction of Vladimir Ziva.

The Conservatory is also known for the prestigious International Tchaikovsky Competition (www.tchaikovsky-competition.net), which takes place every four years, awarding titles of top pianist, singer, cellist and violinist.

TCHAIKOVSKY
CONCERT HALL   CLASSICAL MUSIC
Map p278 (Концертный зал имени Чайковского; ☑495-232 0400; www.meloman.ru; Triumfalnaya pl 4/31; tickets ₽800-3000; ⊘concerts 7pm, closed Aug; Ⓜ Mayakovskaya) Home to the famous Moscow State Philharmonic (Moskovskaya Filharmonia), the capital's oldest symphony orchestra, Tchaikovsky Concert Hall was established in 1921. It's a huge auditorium, with seating for 1600 people. Expect to hear the Russian classics, such as Stravinsky, Rachmaninov and Shostakovich, as well as other European favourites. Look out for children's concerts, jazz ensembles and other special performances.

SPARTAK STADIUM
(OTKRYTIE ARENA)   SPECTATOR SPORT
(Стадион Спартак (Открытие Арена); ☑495-411 5200; www.otkritiearena.ru; Volokolamskoe sh 67; Ⓜ Tushinskaya) Home to professional football club FC Spartak, this bizarre-looking arena – easy to recognise by the Spartak red-and-white on the exterior – was built for the 2018 World Cup (and expected to host the opening game). In addition to the 42,000-capacity stadium, the complex includes an indoor arena and extensive facilities for other sports.

GELIKON OPERA   OPERA
Map p278 (Геликон опера; ☑box office 495-250 2222, call centre 495-250 1111; www.helikon.ru; Bolshaya Nikitskaya ul 19/16; tickets ₽500-10,000; ⊘box office noon-10pm; Ⓜ Arbatskaya) Named after famous Mt Helicon, home to the muses and inspiration for musicians, this opera company is unique in Moscow for its innovative, even experimental, opera performances. Director Dmitry Bertman is known for 'combining musical excellence with artistic risk', according to one local dramaturge.

MOSCOW ENGLISH THEATRE   THEATRE
Map p278 (MET; ☑495-690 4658; www.moscowenglishtheatre.com; Bolshaya Nikitskaya ul 19/13; Ⓜ Arbatskaya) Founded by English actor Jonathan Bex, the MET performs contemporary American and British plays for English-speaking audiences. The company's original production – the comedy *Educating Rita*, by Willy Russell – sold out five straight seasons. The repertoire has expanded to include drama and mystery. The MET performs at the Mayakovsky Theatre.

SIXTEEN TONS   LIVE MUSIC
Map p278 (Шестнадцать тонн; ☑495-253 1550; www.16tons.ru; ul Presnensky val 6; cover ₽600-1200; ⊘11am-6am; ☎; Ⓜ Ulitsa 1905 Goda) Downstairs, the brassy English pub-restaurant has an excellent house-brewed bitter. Upstairs, the club gets some of the best Russian bands that play in Moscow and occasional first-rate or semi-obscure Western groups. Show times are subject to change so check the website for details.

BULGAKOV HOUSE
& THEATRE   ARTS CENTRE
Map p278 (Булгаковский Дом и Театр; www.dombulgakova.ru; 1st fl, Bolshaya Sadovaya ul 10; ⊘1-11pm, to 1am Fri & Sat) This little cultural centre occupies the ground floor of the building where novelist Mikhail Bulgakov resided. The author lived in a communal flat, no 50, which now houses the Mikhail Bulgakov Museum (p107). After your museum visit, it's worth stopping by here to see the atmospheric cafe and check out the cultural offerings and a few exhibits.

🛍 SHOPPING

Presnya is not exactly a shopping destination. But if you are in the neighbourhood, there are a few shops that are worth popping into, especially if you're into fashion or chocolate (and who isn't?).

CHOCOLATE SALON   FOOD & DRINKS

Map p278 (Шоколадный салон; Povarskaya ul 29/36; ☺9am-9pm; ⓜBarrikadnaya) This bustling store is the factory outlet for several local candy makers, including the most famous, Krasny Oktyabr (Red October). The display case is brimming with tempting filled candies and chocolate sculptures in all forms. We can't resist the old-fashioned Alyonka candy bar.

TRYOKHGORNAYA MANUFAKTURA FACTORY OUTLET   TEXTILES

Map p278 (Трёхгорная Мануфактура фирменный магазин; www.trekhgorka.ru; Rochdelskaya ul 15; ☺9.30am-8.30pm Mon-Sat, 10am-6pm Sun; ⓜBarrikadnaya) Tryokhgornaya Manufaktura is one of the oldest textile factories in Moscow, founded in 1799 on the banks of the Moscow River. The factory played a key role in the development of the Presnya district. While production no longer takes place here, the design centre and administrative offices still operate in the original location, as does this on-site factory outlet.

PONAROSHKU   TOYS

Map p278 (Понарошку; www.ponaroshku.ru; Maly Palashevsky per 2/8; ☺10.30am-8.30pm; ⓜPushkinskaya) This tiny store is packed with books, games, plush animals and beautiful painted wooden toys. This is the place to find some souvenirs for the little people in your life.

VALENTIN YUDASHKIN BOUTIQUE   FASHION & ACCESSORIES

Map p278 (www.yudashkin.com; Bldg 1, Voznesenskiy per 6/3; ☺10am-7pm; ⓜKievskaya) The best-known Russian fashion designer is Valentin Yudashkin, whose classy clothes are on display at the Louvre and the Met, as well as the State History Museum in Moscow (look but don't touch!). If you wish to try something on, head to this swanky boutique, which seems like a museum but has many things that you can, in fact, buy.

KATYA DOBRYAKOVA   CLOTHING

Map p278 (www.katyadobryakova.com; Bolshoy Palashev per 1; ☺11am-10pm; ⓜTverskaya) Katya makes dresses, blouses, sweatshirts and more with brightly coloured applications – all around a single theme. It was 'Tropical Dreams' when we visited, so think jaguars and monkeys.

ARMIYA ROSSII   CLOTHING

Map p278 (Армия России; www.armrus.ru; Bolshaya Sadovaya ul 14; ☺10am-9pm; ⓜMayakovskaya) In case you hadn't noticed the increasing militarisation of Russian society, here's an example: the Russian Army now has its own fashion line. There's plenty of camouflage here (for men and women) but much of the clothing is surprisingly tasteful.

ADRESS   CLOTHING

Map p278 (Адресс; www.adresscollection.ru; Bolshoy Kislovskiy per 4; ☺10am-9pm Mon-Sat, to 8pm Sun; ⓜArbatskaya) Specialising in 'unusual clothing', this sweet boutique carries a range of dresses, tops and accessories. The creative designers represent the whole continent, including Russia, such as the sophisticated styles of Feodora.Moscow and whimsical pieces by Masha Velikanova.

DOM FARFORA   HOMEWARES

Map p278 (Дом Фарфора; www.domfarfora.ru; 1-ya Tverskaya-Yamskaya ul 17; ☺10am-9pm; ⓜBelorusskaya) The 'house of china' sells the world's most famous brands of fine china, including Russia's own *Imperatorsky farforovy zavod* (imperial china factory). Designs are tasteful, traditional, whimsical and wonderful, and sometimes all of the above.

🏃 SPORTS & ACTIVITIES

KRASNOPRESNKIYE BANY   BATHHOUSE

Map p278 (Краснопресненские бани; ☑men's banya 495-255 5306, women's banya 495-253 8690; www.baninapresne.ru; Stolyarny per 7; ₽1400-1900; ☺8am-11pm; ⓜUlitsa 1905 Goda) Lacking an old-fashioned, decadent atmosphere, this modern, clean, efficient place nonetheless provides a first-rate *banya* (hot-bath) experience. The facility has a Russian steam room, a Finnish sauna, a plunge pool and massage services.

Arbat & Khamovniki

Neighbourhood Top Five

1 **Pushkin Museum of Fine Arts** (p123) Perusing the collections of the museum's three branches, especially the incredible array of Impressionist and post-Impressionist art in the 19th and 20th Century Art Gallery.

2 **Novodevichy Convent** (p120) Soaking up five

centuries of artistry and history and paying respects to Russian cultural greats at the adjacent cemetery.

3 **Varenichnaya No 1** (p133) Eating the Soviet-throwback way (dumplings at Cold War–era prices) after strolling and shopping on ul Arbat.

4 **Cathedral of Christ the Saviour** (p127) Marvelling at the ostentation and sheer size of the capital's largest church.

5 **Park Pobedy** (p125) Recalling WWII, Russia's greatest tragedy and triumph of the 20th century, at this huge memorial complex.

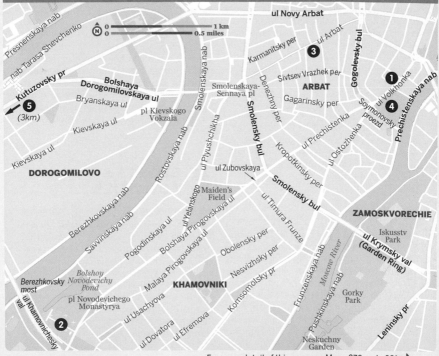

For more detail of this area see Map p276 and p281 ➡

Explore Arbat & Khamovniki

These two adjacent districts are an art-lover's dream. The Arbat district is packed with world-class art museums and smaller artist-dedicated galleries, not to mention the elaborate Cathedral of Christ the Saviour. One might spend an entire day wandering the area, starting at the top-notch Pushkin Museum of Fine Arts, then strolling up ul Prechistenka in the afternoon and dropping into various sights along the way.

Evening is also a wonderful time to wander the storied cobblestone streets around the old Arbat, the historic haunt of artists, musicians and street performers. Though Arbat today has been taken over by souvenir stands and is often packed with tourists, it still evokes the free-thinking artistic spirit of yesteryear.

In Khamovniki, the Unesco-recognised Novodevichy Convent and Cemetery is a worthwhile half-day destination. Further away from the city centre, the roads become wider, the traffic faster and the distances greater. As such, Dorogomilovo and Sparrow Hills are not great for wandering. But it's worth making a special trip for a few choice destinations, such as Park Pobedy and the forested hillsides of Vorobyovy Gory Nature Preserve.

Local Life

→**Yandexification** In Khamovniki, ul Lva Tolstogo is home to the headquarters of Yandex (the Google of Russia, by some accounts), which has transformed this old industrial area. Hipsters and computer nerds buzz around on scooters and hang out at lcoal cafes.

→**Student City** The area southwest of Moscow State University (known as Yugozapadnaya, or 'southwest') is the city's academic area, populated by students and other energetic young people.

→**River Walk** Vorobyovy Gory attracts students, families and other active people who walk, run, skate and cycle along the riverside path.

Getting There & Away

→**Arbat** Lines 3 and 4 (dark blue and light blue respectively) run in parallel across the Arbat district. They both have stations called Arbatskaya, with the entrance near Arbatskaya pl; and they both have stations called Smolenskaya, with the entrance near Smolenskaya pl. Make sure you know which line you are getting on.

→**Khamovniki** Line 1 (red) traverses the Khamovniki district, from Kropotkinskaya station at pl Prechistenskie Vorota (near the Cathedral of Christ the Saviour); to Park Kultury station along the Garden Ring; and to Sportivnaya station.

Lonely Planet's Top Tip

All of the neighbourhood art museums stay open late on Thursdays (till 9pm), but beware that ticket sales often stop 30 minutes or even one hour before closing.

⊙ Best Art Galleries

→ 19th and 20th Century Art Gallery (p124)

→ Pushkin Museum of Fine Arts main building (p123)

→ Multimedia Art Museum (p130)

→ Burganov House (p129)

For reviews, see p128.➡

✖ Best Places to Eat

→ Elardzhi (p133)

→ Chemodan (p134)

→ Varenichnaya No 1 (p133)

→ Voronezh (p134)

For reviews, see p133.➡

☕ Best Places to Drink

→ Dom 12 (p136)

→ Balalaechnaya (p136)

→ Rhythm Blues Cafe (p137)

→ Zhiguli Beer Hall (p136)

→ Arbat 13 (p137)

For reviews, see p135.➡

ARBAT & KHAMOVNIKI

 TOP SIGHT
NOVODEVICHY CONVENT & CEMETERY

In 1524 Grand Prince Vasily III founded the Novodevichy Convent to celebrate the taking of Smolensk from Lithuania. From early on, the 'New Maidens' Convent' was a place for women from noble families to retire – some more willingly than others.

Walls & Towers

Enter the convent through the red-and-white Moscow-baroque Transfiguration Gate-Church (Преображенская надвратная церковь), built in the north wall between 1687 and 1689. All of these striking walls and towers, along with many other buildings on the grounds, were rebuilt around this time, under the direction of Sofia Alexeyevna. The elaborate bell tower (Колокольня) against the east wall soars 72m over the rest of the monastery. When it was built in 1690 it was one of the tallest towers in Moscow.

Smolensk Cathedral

The centrepiece of the monastery is the white Smolensk Cathedral (Смоленский собор; 1524–25), built to house the precious *Our Lady of Smolensk* icon. The sumptuous interior is covered in 16th-century frescoes, considered to be among the finest in the city. The gilded iconostasis includes icons that date from the time of Boris Godunov. The icons on the 5th tier are attributed to 17th-century artists Simon Ushakov and Feodor Zubov. The tombs of Sofia Alexeyevna and Eudoxia Lopukhina are in the south nave.

DON'T MISS

➜ Smolensk Cathedral frescoes & iconostasis

➜ 72m bell tower

➜ Graves of Nikita Khrushchev and Boris Yeltsin

PRACTICALITIES

➜ Новодевичий монастырь

➜ Map p281, A3

➜ Novodevichy pr 1

➜ adult/student ₽500/250, photos ₽300

➜ ⓖ grounds 8am-8pm, museums 9am-5pm Wed-Mon

➜ Ⓜ Sportivnaya

Chambers of Sofia Alexeyevna

Sofia Alexeyevna used the Novodevichy Convent as a residence when she ruled Russia as regent in the 1680s. During her rule, she rebuilt the convent to her liking – which was fortunate, as she was later confined here when her half-brother, Peter the Great, came of age. After being implicated in the Streltsy rebellion, she was imprisoned here for life, primarily inhabiting the Pond Tower (Напрудная башня).

Chambers of Eudoxia Lopukina

Eudoxia Lopukhina, the first wife of Peter the Great, stayed in the Chambers of Eudoxia Lopukhina (Лопухинские Палаты). Although she bore him a son, Peter detested her conservative, demanding personality, and soon rejected her for the beautiful daughter of a Dutch wine merchant. Eudoxia retired to a monastery in Suzdal, where she further estranged herself by taking her own lover and founding an opposition movement within the church. The tsar responded by executing the bishops involved and banishing his former wife. Upon Peter's death, he was succeeded by Peter II, who recalled his grandmother Eudoxia back to Moscow.

Other Buildings

Other churches include the red-and-white Assumption Church (Успенская церковь), dating from 1685 to 1687, and the 16th-century St Ambrose's Church (Амвросиевская церковь). Boris Godunov's sister, Irina, lived in the building adjoining the latter. Today, Irina's Chambers (Палаты Ирины Годуновой) hold exhibits of religious artwork.

Novodevichy Cemetery

The **Novodevichy Cemetery** (Новодевичье кладбище; Map p281; Luzhnetsky pr 2; ⊙9am-5pm; MSportivnaya) FREE is one of Moscow's most prestigious resting places – a veritable who's who of Russian politics and culture. Here you will find the tombs of Rostrovpovich, Bulgakov, Chekhov, Gogol, Mayakovsky, Prokofiev, Stanislavsky and Eisenstein, among many other Russian and Soviet cultural luminaries. The most recent notable addition to the cemetery is former president Boris Yeltsin, who died in 2007. His tomb is marked by an enormous sculpture of a Russian flag. In Soviet times Novodevichy Cemetery was used for eminent people the authorities judged unsuitable for the Kremlin wall, most notably Nikita Khrushchev, with intertwined white-and-black blocks around his bust.

The tombstone of Nadezhda Alliluyeva, Stalin's second wife, is covered by unbreakable glass to prevent vandalism.

DISCRETION ADVISED

Novodevichy is a functioning monastery. Women are advised to cover their heads and shoulders when entering the churches; men should wear long pants.

The Soviets shut down Novodevichy in 1922 and – always ironic – converted it into a Museum of Women's Emancipation. The nuns were invited to return to the convent in 1994, with services recommencing the following year.

CEMETERY MAP

If you want to investigate Novodevichy Cemetery, buy the Russian map (on sale at the kiosk), which pinpoints nearly 200 graves of notable citizens. There is also a map posted near the entrance.

NOVODEVICHY CONVENT & CEMETERY

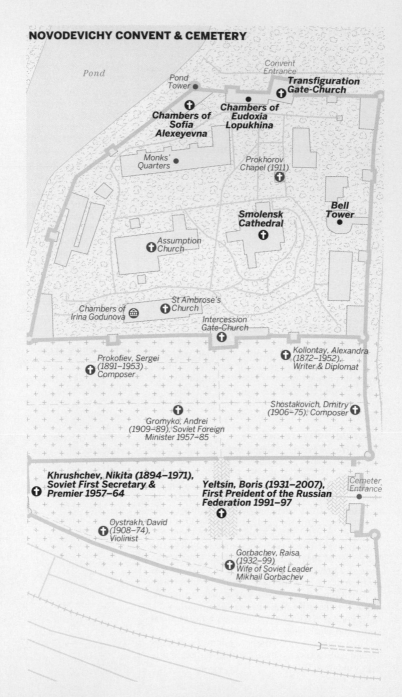

Pond

Pond Tower

Convent Entrance

Transfiguration Gate-Church

Chambers of Sofia Alexeyevna

Chambers of Eudoxia Lopukhina

Monks' Quarters

Prokhorov Chapel (1911)

Bell Tower

Smolensk Cathedral

Assumption Church

Chambers of Irina Godunova

St Ambrose's Church

Intercession Gate-Church

Prokofiev, Sergei (1891–1953) Composer

Kollontay, Alexandra (1872–1952), Writer & Diplomat

Shostakovich, Dmitry (1906–75), Composer

Gromyko, Andrei (1909–89), Soviet Foreign Minister 1957–85

Khrushchev, Nikita (1894–1971), Soviet First Secretary & Premier 1957–64

Yeltsin, Boris (1931–2007), First Preident of the Russian Federation 1991–97

Cemeter Entrance

Oystrakh, David (1908–74), Violinist

Gorbachev, Raisa (1932–99) Wife of Soviet Leader Mikhail Gorbachev

TOP SIGHT
PUSHKIN MUSEUM OF FINE ARTS

This is Moscow's premier foreign-art museum, split over three branches and showing off a broad selection of European works, including masterpieces from ancient civilisations, the Italian Renaissance and the Dutch Golden Age, not to mention an incredible collection of Impressionist and post-Impressionist paintings in the 19th and 20th Century Art Gallery.

Main Building

The main building opened in 1912 as the museum of Moscow University. It now exhibits the bulk of the holdings that date from antiquity through to the 18th century.

The excellent Ancient Civilisation exhibits in rooms 1 and 2 contain ancient Egyptian weaponry, jewellery, ritual items and tombstones. Most of the items were excavated from burial sites, including two haunting mummies. Room 3 houses the impressive Treasures of Troy exhibit, with excavated items dating back to 2500 BC.

The highlight of the museum is the selection of Dutch masterpieces from the 17th century, located in rooms 9 through 11. Rembrandt is the star of the show, with many paintings on display, including his moving Portrait of an Old Woman.

The Greek and Italian Courts (rooms 14 and 15) contain examples from the museum's original collection, which was made up of plaster-cast reproductions of masterpieces from ancient Greece and Rome, as well as from the Renaissance. You'll find more plaster casts upstairs, including a room devoted to Michelangelo (29).

The 17th and 18th centuries dominate the 2nd floor. Room 17 contains a diverse collection of Italian paintings, including some formidable large-scale canvases. Rooms

DON'T MISS

➡ Treasures of Troy

➡ Golden Age of Dutch Art

➡ Impressionist and post-Impressionist collections

PRACTICALITIES

➡ Музей изобразительных искусств им Пушкина

➡ Map p276, G3

➡ ☑ 495-697 9578

➡ www.arts-museum.ru

➡ ul Volkhonka 12

➡ single/combined galleries ₽300/550

➡ ⊙11am-7pm Tue-Sun, to 9pm Thu

➡ Ⓜ Kropotkinskaya

MUSEUM TOWN

In 2017 the Pushkin Museum of Fine Arts commenced a vast expansion and redesign known as 'Museum Town'. The project will revamp the existing museum buildings, connecting them with underground galleries. Exhibition space is expected to double and ul Volkhonka will be transformed into a tree-lined boulevard. The surrounding parkland will host concerts, festivals and public art.

The Museum Town project is supposed to be completed in 2019. In the meantime, the main building and the 19th and 20th Century Art Gallery are open, as usual. The Museum of Private Collections is closed during the construction of the new complex.

Audio guides in English are available for the main building (₽350) and the 19th and 20th Century Art Gallery (₽300).

A combination ticket (adult/student ₽550/300) includes admission to both the main building and the 19th and 20th Century Art Gallery.

21 through 23 are devoted to France, with a separate gallery for the rococo period, featuring some appropriately dreamy paintings by Boucher.

19th & 20th Century Art Gallery

The separate **19th and 20th Century Art Gallery** (Map p276; www.arts-museum.ru; ul Volkhonka 14; adult/student ₽300/150; ⊘11am-7pm Tue-Sun, to 9pm Thu; ⓂKropotkinskaya) contains a famed assemblage of Impressionist and post-Impressionist works, based on the collections of two well-known Moscow art patrons, Sergei Shchukin and Ivan Morozov.

The Impressionists occupy rooms 10 and 11, with paintings by Degas, Manet, Renoir and Pissarro. Rodin's sculptures include pieces from the *Gates of Hell* and the *Monument to the Townspeople of Calais*. Room 14 is entirely dedicated to Monet.

Rooms 15 to 17 are dedicated to post-Impressionism. Room 15 is almost exclusively Cézanne, featuring his sensuous *Bathers*. Room 16 contains some lesser-known gems by Van Gogh, including the scorching *Red Vineyards* and the tragic *Prison Courtyard,* painted in the last year of his life. Room 17 is devoted to works by Gauguin, representing his prime period.

Upstairs, rooms 19 and 20 display many of the most famous paintings by Matisse, such as *Goldfish*. There are a few exquisite, primitive paintings by Rousseau in room 21, and some lesser-known pieces by Picasso in room 22. The final rooms complete the rich collection of 20th-century art, featuring Miró, Kandinsky, Chagall, Arp and others.

Museum of Private Collections

The **Museum of Private Collections** (Музей личных коллекций; Map p276; www.artprivatecollections.ru; ul Volkhonka 10; entry prices vary; ⊘noon-8pm Wed-Sun, to 9pm Thu; ⓂKropotkinskaya) shows off art collections donated by private individuals. The centrepiece is the collection of Ilya Silberstein, the museum's founder and an accomplished historian of Russian literature and art. This collection is especially rich in pieces by early-20th-century 'Mir Iskusstva' artists such as Benois, Serebryakova, Serov and Kustodiev.

Other highlights include the Inna Koretskaya and Boris Mikhailovsky Collection featuring works by Rerikh, Golovin and Kuznetsov; the Lemkul room, with graphic art by Fyodor Lemkul, as well as the artist's collection of glassworks from Russia and Europe; the Sergei Solovyov Collection, with paintings by Perov and Repin; and the impressive collection of Old Believer icons from the 16th to 20th centuries.

TOP SIGHT
PARK POBEDY AT POKLONNAYA HILL

Magnificent Park Pobedy (Victory Park) at Poklonnaya Hill is a huge memorial complex commemorating the sacrifice and celebrating the triumph of the Great Patriotic War – as WWII is known in Russia. Unveiled on the 50th anniversary of the victory, the park includes endless fountains, monuments and museums, as well as a memorial church, synagogue and mosque.

Obelisk

The park's dominant monument is an enormous obelisk, topped with a sculpture of St George slaying the dragon (the work of contemporary Moscow artist Zurab Tsereteli). Its height is exactly 141.8m, with every 10cm representing one day of the war. At the 60th-anniversary Victory Day celebrations in 2005, President Vladimir Putin unveiled 15 mighty bronze cannons, symbolic of the war's 15 fronts. The ensemble is surrounded by fountains and benches, as well as the sweet Church of St George.

Museum of the Great Patriotic War

The **Museum of the Great Patriotic War** (Центральный музей Великой Отечественной Войны; www.poklonnayagora.ru; ul Bratiev Fonchenko 10; adult/child ₽300/200; ⊙10am-6pm Tue-Sun Nov-Mar, to 8pm Apr-Oct; Ⓜ Park Pobedy) is the centrepiece of Park Pobedy.

The massive museum has hundreds of exhibits, including dioramas of every major WWII battle the Russians fought in, as well as weapons, photographs, documents and other wartime memorabilia.

The museum building also contains two impressive memorial rooms: the Hall of Glory honours the many heroes of the Soviet Union, while the moving Hall of Remembrance and Sorrow is hung with strings of glass-bead 'teardrops' in memory of the fallen.

DON'T MISS

➡ Towering obelisk
➡ Hall of Remembrance and Sorrow
➡ Memorial to the Victims of the Holocaust

PRACTICALITIES

➡ Парк Победы
➡ www.poklonnaya-gora.ru
➡ Kutuzovsky pr
➡ admission free
➡ ⊙dawn-dusk
➡ ♿
➡ Ⓜ Park Pobedy

METRO STATION

Check out the artwork in Park Pobedy metro station. Created by the tireless Moscow artist Zurab Tsereteli, the two mosaics depict events from the War of 1812 and the Great Patriotic War, respectively. This station rivals the more central stations for artistry – and it is also the deepest metro station in the city.

Just east of Park Pobedy, the Triumphal Arch (Kutuzovsky pr) celebrates the defeat of Napoleon in 1812. The original arch was demolished at its site in front of the Belorusskaya metro station during the 1930s and reconstructed here in a fit of post-WWII public spirit.

GETTING AROUND

Park Pobedy covers a vast area, so a thorough tour of its monuments, museums and other features entails a lot of walking. Bicycles are available to rent (from ₽250 per hour).

Exposition of Military Equipment

Tucked into a corner of the vast Park Pobedy, the **Exposition of Military Equipment** (Площадка боевой техники; www.poklonnayagora.ru; adult/child ₽300/200; ☺11am-6pm Tue-Sun) displays weapons and military equipment from the WWII era. There are plenty of Red Army tanks, armoured cars and self-propelled artillery, not to mention the famous Katyusha rocket launcher. You'll also see train cars, used by the civil engineering unit, fighter planes and naval destroyers.

In addition to the Soviet weaponry, the exhibit includes equipment captured from Germany and Japan, and other equipment that was used by the Allies.

Memorial Synagogue

The **Memorial Synagogue at Poklonnaya Hill** (Мемориальная синагога на Поклонной горе; ☑499-148 1907; www.poklonnaya.ru; Kutuzovsky pr 53; ☺by appointment) FREE opened in 1998 as a memorial to Holocaust victims, as well as a museum of the Russian Jewry. Admission is with a guide only, so you must make arrangements in advance, especially if you want a tour in English. Not far from the synagogue, a moving sculpture commemorates the victims of the Holocaust.

Borodino Panorama

Park Pobedy is a monument to the Great Patriotic War, but historians find many parallels with the War of 1812, not the least of which is the route taken by attacking and retreating armies. Following the vicious, inconclusive battle at Borodino in August 1812, Moscow's defenders retreated along what is now Kutuzovsky pr, pursued by Napoleon's Grand Army. Less than 1km east of Park Pobedy is a museum commemorating this event.

The centrepiece of the museum is the **Borodino Panorama** (Музей-панорама 'Бородинская битва'; www.1812panorama.ru; Kutuzovsky pr 38; adult/child ₽250/100; ☺10am-6pm Sat-Wed, to 9pm Thu), a pavilion with a giant 360-degree painting of the Borodino battle. Painted by Franz Roubaud, the canvas is 115m around and 15m high. Standing inside this tableau of bloodshed – complete with sound effects – is a powerful way to visualise the event. The museum also contains other artefacts and artwork related to the battle.

In honour of the 200th anniversary of the battle, the museum opened a two-room exhibit dedicated to 'Man & War'. It displays hundreds of items – including paintings, weapons and uniforms, with additional audio-visual effects.

TOP SIGHT
CATHEDRAL OF CHRIST THE SAVIOUR

Dominating the skyline along Prechistenskaya nab, the gargantuan Cathedral of Christ the Saviour was completed in 1997 – just in time to celebrate Moscow's 850th birthday. It is amazingly opulent, garishly grandiose and truly historic, guaranteeing its role as a love-it-or-hate-it landmark.

The contemporary cathedral sits on the site of an earlier and similar church of the same name, built in the 19th century to commemorate Russia's victory over Napoleon. The original was destroyed in 1931, during Stalin's orgy of explosive secularism. His plan to replace the church with a 315m-high Palace of Soviets never got off the ground. Instead, for 50 years the site served as the world's largest swimming pool. An on-site museum details the history of the original church, its destruction and reconstruction.

The central altar of the main church is dedicated to the Nativity, with two side altars dedicated to Sts Nicholas and Alexander Nevsky. Frescoes around the main gallery depict scenes from the War of 1812, while marble plaques remember the participants.

The smaller (but no less stunning) Church of the Transfiguration on the cathedral's ground level contains the venerated icon *Christ Not Painted by Hand*, by Sorokin, which was miraculously saved from the original cathedral.

DON'T MISS

➡ Fresco-covered interior dome

➡ *Christ Not Painted by Hand* in the Church of the Transfiguration

➡ Views from the Patriarshy footbridge

PRACTICALITIES

➡ Храм Христа Спасителя

➡ Map p276, F4

➡ www.xxc.ru

➡ ul Volkhonka 15

➡ admission free

➡ ☻1-5pm Mon, from 10am Tue-Sun

➡ Ⓜ Kropotkinskaya

⦿ SIGHTS

The Pushkin Museum of Fine Arts anchors a neighbourhood that's packed with art museums and galleries. It's not far from the atmospheric old Arbat, making this an exceptional area for strolling and discovering the city's artistic side. Novodevichy Convent occupies the southern end of the neighbourhood, but it's a long haul to get out here (four metro stops). There are few other attractions in the vicinity. Park Pobedy is 10km west of Red Square (4km outside the Garden Ring).

⦿ Arbat

CATHEDRAL OF CHRIST
THE SAVIOUR   CHURCH
See p127.

PUSHKIN MUSEUM OF
FINE ARTS   MUSEUM
See p123.

HOUSE OF FRIENDSHIP
WITH PEOPLES OF
FOREIGN COUNTRIES   NOTABLE BUILDING
Map p276 (Дом дружбы с народами зарубежных стран; Vozdvizhenka ul 16; МArbatskaya) Studded with seashells, this 'Moorish Castle' was built in 1899 for an eccentric merchant, Arseny Morozov, who was inspired by a real Moorish castle in Spain. The inside (not open to the public) is sumptuous and equally over the top. Morozov's mother, who lived next door, apparently declared of her son's home, 'Until now, only I knew you were mad; now everyone will.'

BULAT OKUDZHAVA STATUE   STATUE
Map p276 (cnr ul Arbat & Plotnikov per) Bulat Okudzhava was a poet turned songwriter who lived and often performed on the Arbat in the 1960s. He inspired a whole movement of liberal-thinking poets to take their ideas to the streets, including Vladimir Vysotsky and others.

PUSHKIN HOUSE-MUSEUM   MUSEUM
Map p276 (Дом-музей Пушкина; www.pushkin museum.ru; ul Arbat 53; ₽300; ⊙10am-6pm Tue-Sun, noon-9pm Thu; МSmolenskaya) After Alexander Pushkin married Natalia Goncharova at the nearby Church of the Grand Ascension, they moved to this charming blue house on the old Arbat. The museum provides some insight into the couple's home life, a source of much Russian romanticism. (The lovebirds are also featured in a statue across the street.) The ground floor contains a broader exhibit about Pushkin in Moscow.

The price also includes admission to the Adrei Beliy apartment, which is in the same building.

ARBAT, MY ARBAT
....

Arbat, my Arbat, you are my calling. You are my happiness and my misfortune.
– Bulat Okudzhava

For Moscow's beloved bard Bulat Okudzhava, the Arbat was not only his home, it was his inspiration. Although he spent his university years in Georgia dabbling in harmless verse, it was only upon his return to Moscow – and to his cherished Arbat – that his poetry adopted the free-thinking character for which it is known.

He gradually made the transition from poet to songwriter. While Bulat and his friends enjoyed his songs, composers, singers and guitarists did not, resenting the fact that somebody with no musical training was writing songs. The ill feeling subsided when a well-known poet announced that it was just another way of presenting poetry.

And so a new form of art was born. The 1960s were heady times, in Moscow as elsewhere, and Okudzhava inspired a whole movement of liberal-thinking poets to take their ideas to the streets. Vladimir Vysotsky and others – some political, others not – followed in Okudzhava's footsteps, their iconoclastic lyrics and simple melodies drawing enthusiastic crowds all around Moscow.

The Arbat today, crowded with tacky souvenir shops and overpriced cafes, bears little resemblance to the hallowed haunt of Okudzhava's youth. But its memory lives on in the bards and buskers, painters and poets who still perform for strolling crowds on summer evenings.

RERIKH MUSEUM

Nikolai Rerikh (known internationally as Nicholas Roerich) was a Russian artist from the late 19th and early 20th centuries, whose fantastical artwork is characterised by rich colours, primitive style and mystical themes. He is beloved for his commitment to global harmony, represented by a peace sign of his own design, a pyramid of three solid-red circles. In 1989 Rerikh's son founded a museum to display his father's paintings, as well as personal items and family heirlooms. Housed in the grand 17th-century Lopukhin manor, the Rerikh Museum was operated by the nongovernmental International Centre of Roerichs (ICR).

In recent years, however, the independent Rerikh Museum has felt increasing pressure from state forces, which came in the form of unexpected building inspections, lease revocations and eviction notices. In 2017 the museum was raided by special forces in riot gear, who seized nearly 200 works of art, and the building was locked shut.

State officials claim that the seized property is evidence in a fraud case against Boris Bulochnik, a fallen oligarch who donated the art to the museum. No angel himself, Bulochnik is the former chairman of the now-defunct Master Bank, which earned the title of 'Russia's seediest bank' from one Bloomberg columnist.

At the same time, officials from the Ministry of Culture have indicated that they intend to open a state Rerikh museum on the premises of the Lopukhin estate. Some experts claim that the artwork will be safer in the hands of the state. But the ICR wonders how the state, as it is, can protect the spiritual legacy of mystical, peace-loving Nikolai Rerikh.

This place should not be confused with the Pushkin Literary Museum, which focuses on the poet's literary influences.

MELNIKOV HOUSE   NOTABLE BUILDING

Map p276 (Дом Мельникова; ☑495-697 8037; Krivoarbatsky per 10; ☺courtyard 10am-7pm Mar-Oct, to 5pm Nov-Feb, house by appointment; ⓂArbatskaya) The only private house built during the Soviet period, the home of Konstantin Melnikov stands as testament to the innovation of the Russian avant-garde. The architect created his unusual home from two interlocking cylinders – an ingenious design that employs no internal load bearing wall. It was also experimental in its designation of living space, as the whole family slept in one room, divided by narrow wall screens.

BURGANOV HOUSE   MUSEUM

Map p276 (Дом Бурганова; ☑495-695 0429; www.burganov.ru; Bolshoy Afanasyevsky per 15; adult/child ₽150/100; ☺11am-7pm Sat-Wed, noon-9pm Thu; ⓂKropotkinskaya) Part studio, part museum, the Burganov House is a unique venue in Moscow, where the craft goes on around you, as you peruse the sculptures and other artwork on display. Comprising several interconnected courtyards and houses, the works of surrealist sculptor Alexander Burganov are artfully displayed alongside pieces from the artist's private collection. The surrounding streets of the Arbat and Khamovniki districts also contain many examples of the artist's work.

TOCHKA-G MUSEUM
OF EROTIC ART   MUSEUM

Map p276 (Музей эротического искусства 'Точка-G'; www.tochkag.net; ul Novy Arbat 15; ₽500; ☺noon-midnight; ⓂArbatskaya) The name means G spot, in case you didn't already guess. Among this gigantic display of erotica, you're bound to find something that will titillate yours. Look for 'artistic' interpretations of sex through the ages, from ancient Kama Sutra–style carvings to contemporary (and perhaps controversial) sexual-political commentary. Also on site: a sex shop and cafe! Enter from Maly Nikolopeskovsky per.

FOREIGN AFFAIRS
MINISTRY   NOTABLE BUILDING

Map p276 (Smolenskaya-Sennaya pl 32/34; ⓂSmolenskaya) One of the Stalinist skyscrapers known as the 'Seven Sisters', the Ministry of Foreign Affairs building is a 27-storey landmark that was completed in 1953.

⊙ Khamovniki

NOVODEVICHY CONVENT
CONVENT

See p120.

PARK POBEDY
MEMORIAL

See p125.

SHILOV GALLERY
MUSEUM

Map p276 (Галерея Шилова; www.shilov.su; ul Znamenka 5; adult/student ₽200/80; ⊘11am-7pm Tue-Sun, noon-9pm Thu; ⓜBiblioteka imeni Lenina) 'What is a portrait? You have to attain not only an absolute physical likeness… but you need to express the inner world of the particular person you are painting.' So Alexander Shilov described his life work as contemporary Russia's most celebrated portrait painter in an interview posted on the gallery's website. Known for his startling realism, the artist provides great insight into his subjects, with some high-level political figures among them.

GLAZUNOV GALLERY
MUSEUM

Map p276 (Галерея Глазунова; www.glazunov.ru; ul Volkhonka 13; ⊘11am-7pm Tue-Sun, to 9pm Thu; ⓜKropotkinskaya) This elaborate Russian Empire–style mansion, opposite the Pushkin Museum of Fine Arts, houses a gallery dedicated to the work of Soviet and post-Soviet artist Ilya Glazunov. Glazunov is famous for his controversial, colourful paintings that depict hundreds of people, places and events from Russian history in one monumental scene. His most famous work is *Eternal Russia (Bechnaya Rossiya)*.

PUSHKIN LITERARY MUSEUM
MUSEUM

Map p276 (Литературный музей Пушкина; www.pushkinmuseum.ru; ul Prechistenka 12/2; ₽200; ⊘10am-5pm Tue-Sun, noon-9pm Thu; ⓜKropotkinskaya) Housed in a beautiful Empire-style mansion dating from 1816, this museum is devoted to the life and work of Russia's favourite poet. Personal effects, family portraits, reproductions of notes and handwritten poetry provide insight into the work of the beloved bard. Perhaps the most interesting exhibit is 'Pushkin and His Time', which puts the poet in a historical context, demonstrating the influence of the Napoleonic Wars, the Decembrists' revolt and other historic events. Exhibits are in Russian.

This literary museum provides more in-depth insights than the Pushkin House-Museum (p128) on ul Arbat.

TOLSTOY LITERARY MUSEUM
MUSEUM

Map p276 (Литературный музей Толстого; www.tolstoymuseum.ru; ul Prechistenka 11; adult/student ₽250/100; ⊘noon-6pm Tue-Sun; ⓜKropotkinskaya) The Tolstoy Literary Museum is supposedly the oldest literary memorial museum in the world (founded in 1911). In addition to its impressive reference library, the museum contains exhibits of manuscripts, letters and artwork focusing on Leo Tolstoy's literary influences and output. Family photographs, personal correspondence and artwork from the author's era all provide insight into his work.

This museum undoubtedly contains the largest collection of portraits of the great Russian novelist. Entire exhibits (in Russian) are dedicated to his major novels such as *Anna Karenina* and *War and Peace*. The museum does not contain much memorabilia from Tolstoy's personal life, which is on display at the Tolstoy Estate-Museum (p132).

MULTIMEDIA ART MUSEUM
MUSEUM

Map p276 (Мультимедиа Арт Музей; www.mamm-mdf.ru; ul Ostozhenka 16; ₽500; ⊘noon-9pm Tue-Sun; ⓢ; ⓜKropotkinskaya) This slick, modern gallery is home to an impressive photographic library and archives of contemporary and historic photography. The facility usually hosts several simultaneous exhibits, often featuring works by prominent photographers from the Soviet period, as well as contemporary artists. The complex also hosts several month-long festivals: Photobiennale and Fashion and Style in Photography (held in alternating years).

TSERETELI GALLERY
MUSEUM

Map p276 (Галерея Церетели; www.tsereteli.ru; ul Prechistenka 19; ₽300; ⊘noon-8pm Tue-Sun, to 9pm Thu; ⓜKropotkinskaya) Housed in the 18th-century Dolgoruky mansion is this endeavour of the tireless Moscow architect and artist Zurab Tsereteli. The gallery shows how prolific this guy is. The rooms are filled with his often over-the-top sculptures and primitive paintings. If you don't want to spend the time or money exploring the gallery, just pop into the Galereya Khudozhnikov cafe (p135), which is an exhibit in itself.

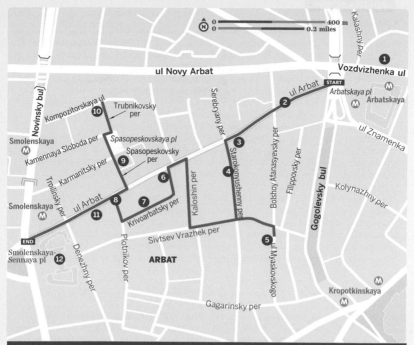

🏃 Neighbourhood Walk
Stary Arbat

START ARBATSKAYA PL
END SMOLENSKAYA-SENNAYA PL
LENGTH 3KM; TWO HOURS

Take note of the **1** **House of Friendship with Peoples of Foreign Countries**, flaunting its incongruous Moorish style.

Strolling up **2** **ul Arbat**, sidewalk art and street performers stand beside souvenir stalls and costumed characters. There are many treasures on display (and for sale) at the **3** **Association of Artists of the Decorative Arts** (p138).

Wander down some of the quiet lanes **4**, such as **5** **Starokonyushenny per**, which has exemplary art nouveau architectural details. Look out for strange and beautiful sculptures dotting the yards and courtyards. They are the work of Alexander Burganov, whose nearby **6** **studio** is filled with whimsical treasures.

Get a glimpse of the counterculture of the old Arbat at the corner of Krivoarbatsky per and ul Arbat, where the **7** **Viktor Tsoy memorial wall** is dedicated to the lead singer of the Soviet rock band Kino. Further along Krivoarbatsky per, the cylindrical **8** **Melnikov House** is an important constructivist architectural site.

Back on the Arbat, you can't miss the statue of **9** **Bulat Okudzhava**, the beloved bard who lived and performed on this storied street. Cross and continue north on Spasopeskovsky per. This little lane contains architectural gems such as the lovely 17th-century **10** **Church of the Saviour in Peski**. The handsome neoclassical mansion at No 10 is **11** **Spaso House**, famous as the scene of Satan's ball in Bulgakov's *The Master and Margarita*.

Return to the Arbat and the **12** **Pushkin House-Museum**. Continue to Smolenskaya-Sennaya pl – the towering skyscraper that houses the Ministry of Foreign Affairs (p129) is one of Stalin's 'Seven Sisters'. The Arbat is lined with restaurants and cafes where you can pause for a break along the way. Some of our favourites include Varenichnaya No 1 (p133) and Rukkola (p133).

WORTH A DETOUR

SPARROW HILLS

Head to the hills south of the city for one of the best views of Moscow. **Vorobyovy Gory** (Воробьевы горы; Sparrow Hills Nature Reserve; www.vorobyovy-gory.ru; Ⓜ Vorobyovy Gory) **FREE**, is the green hilly area south of the Moscow River, opposite the tip of the Khamovniki peninsula. This wooded hillside is a less developed, less crowded extension of Gorky Park and Neskuchny Garden. The paved path that originates near Gorky Park continues along the river for several kilometres, and bikes and skates are available to rent. Walking trails from the riverbank wind up to Universitetskaya pl for a lookout.

From the square in front of **Moscow State University** (Московский Государственный Университет; MGU; Universitetskaya pl; Ⓜ Universitet), most of the city spreads out before you. It is an excellent vantage point to see Luzhniki, the huge stadium complex (p136) built across the river for the 1980 Olympics, as well as Novodevichy Convent (p120) and the Cathedral of Christ the Saviour (p127).

Behind Universitetskaya pl is the Stalinist spire of Moscow State University, one of the 'Seven Sisters'. The building is the result of four years of hard labour by convicts between 1949 and 1953. It boasts an amazing 36 floors and 33km of corridors. The shining star that sits atop the spire is supposed to weigh 12 tonnes. Among other socialist-realist frills on the facade, look for the eager students looking forward to communism. The building is not open to the public, which is a shame, because the lobby is equally elaborate, featuring bronze statues of distinguished Soviet scientists.

ARBAT & KHAMOVNIKI SIGHTS

RUSSIAN ACADEMY OF ARTS
GALLERY

Map p276 (Российская академия художеств; www.rah.ru; ul Prechistenka 21; adult/student ₽100/50; ⊙noon-9pm Tue, to 8pm Wed-Sun; Ⓜ Kropotkinskaya) The Russian Academy of Arts hosts rotating exhibits in the historic 19th-century mansion of the Morozov estate. Despite the institutional-sounding name, this is part of the empire of contemporary Moscow artist and architect Zurab Tsereteli; it puts on inspired and varied shows featuring mostly contemporary Russian and foreign artists.

MOSCOW MUSEUM
MUSEUM

Map p281 (Музей Москвы; www.mosmuseum. ru; Zubovsky bul 2; adult/student ₽200/100; ⊙10am-8pm Tue-Wed & Fri-Sun, 11am-9pm Thu; Ⓜ Park Kultury) The permanent history exhibit here demonstrates how the city has spread from its starting point at the Kremlin. It is heavy on artefacts from the 13th and 14th centuries, especially household items and weapons, although there is little information in English. More exciting, the museum has space to launch thought-provoking temporary exhibits, including artists' and other locals' perspectives on the city.

The museum is housed in the former warehouses and garages of the Defence Ministry, with a central courtyard that displays outdoor art and interactive exhibits.

CHURCH OF ST NICHOLAS IN KHAMOVNIKI
CHURCH

Map p281 (Церковь Святого Николая в Хамовниках; ul Lva Tolstogo 2; Ⓜ Park Kultury) This church, commissioned by the weavers' guild in 1676, is among the most colourful in Moscow. The ornate green-and-orange-tapestry exterior houses an equally exquisite interior, rich in frescoes and icons. Leo Tolstoy, who lived up the street, was a parishioner at St Nicholas, which is featured in his novel *Resurrection*. Look also for the old white stone house, built in 1689, which housed the office of the **weavers' guild and textile shop** (Бывшая ткацкая гильдия; ul Lva Tolstogo 10).

TOLSTOY ESTATE-MUSEUM
MUSEUM

Map p281 (Музей-усадьба Толстого 'Хамовники'; www.tolstoymuseum.ru; ul Lva Tolstogo 21; adult/student ₽400/200; ⊙10am-6pm Tue, Wed & Fri-Sun, noon-8pm Thu; Ⓜ Park Kultury) Leo Tolstoy's winter home during the 1880s and 1890s now houses an interesting museum dedicated to the writer's home life. While it's not particularly opulent or large, the building is fitting for junior nobility – which Tolstoy was. Exhibits here demonstrate how Tolstoy lived, as opposed to his literary influences, which are explored at the Tolstoy Literary Museum (p130). See the salon where Sergei Rachmaninov and Nikolai Rimsky-Korsakov played piano, and the study where Tolstoy wove his epic tales.

 EATING

Arbat and Khamovniki do not offer the city's best dining, but visitors will not suffer for lack of choices. Nowadays, there are some excellent eateries in the streets around the museums. Even the old Arbat – long a culinary wasteland – now has a few noteworthy restaurants that merit a trip. Options are more limited outside the Garden Ring, but ul Lva Tolstogo has emerged as a dining hotspot, with many restaurant openings in recent years.

✖ Arbat

★ VARENICHNAYA NO 1   RUSSIAN €

Map p276 (www.varenichnaya.ru; ul Arbat 29; business lunch ₽290-340, mains ₽220-490; ⊙10am-midnight; ✈🔲🚻; MArbatskaya) Retro Soviet is all the rage in Moscow, and this old-style restaurant does it right, with books lining the walls, old movies on the B&W TV, and Cold War–era prices. The menu features tasty, filling *vareniki* and *pelmeni* (Russian-style dumplings), with sweet and savoury fillings. Bonus: an excellent house-made pickled veggie plate to make you pucker.

LAVKALAVKA   MARKET €

Map p276 (ЛавкаЛавка; www.lavkalavka.ru; Bldg 2, Plotnikov per 19/38; mains ₽200-500; ⊙10am-10pm Mon-Sat, to 8pm Sun; MSmolenskaya) After taking the Moscow culinary world by storm with its farm-to-table restauran, LavkaLavka has opened a network of small 'farmer's shops' like this one. Here, patrons can purchase handmade cheese and sausages, pickled vegetables and mushrooms, wild honey and more. A select and ever-changing menu of prepared foods is served at a tiny cafe.

RUKKOLA   ITALIAN €

Map p276 (Руккола; http://rucola.com.ru; ul Arbat 19; mains ₽320-640; ⊙10am-midnight; ✈✈🚻; MArbatskaya) Rukkola offers perfectly crispy, artfully topped thin-crust pizza that you'd be happy to eat in Napoli, let alone Moscow. A stylish interior, friendly service and affordable prices make this a great find. Lounge on comfy couches and watch the pizza chef toss his pies high in the sky; or grab an outdoor seat to watch the action on the Arbat.

BLACK STAR BURGERS   BURGERS €

Map p276 (www.blackstarburger.ru; ul Novy Arbat 15; burgers ₽240-777; ✈✈; MArbatskaya) Music and burger lovers line up out the door and down the sidewalk for a taste of the burgers being touted by Russian rapper Timati. There's a bit of gimmickry going on here (burgers are served with black gloves so patrons don't get their hands dirty) but most people agree that Timati knows how to make a good patty.

Bonus: three kinds of veggie burgers.

PRIME STAR   FAST FOOD €

Map p276 (www.prime-star.ru; ul Arbat 9; mains ₽100-200; ⊙8am-11pm; ✈🔲🔲; MArbatskaya) Stop in for a quick bite along the old Arbat. Enjoy fresh (and healthy!) salads and sandwiches, premade and ready to take out to the outdoor seating.

MOO-MOO   CAFETERIA €

Map p276 (My-My; www.cafemumu.ru; ul Arbat 45/24; mains ₽200-300; ⊙10am-11pm; ✈; MSmolenskaya) You will recognise this popular cafeteria by its black-and-white Holstein-print decor. The cafeteria-style service offers an easy approach to all the Russian favourites. There are other outlets all over town.

★ ELARDZHI   GEORGIAN €€

Map p276 (Эларджи; ☎495-627 7897; www.ginza.ru; Gagarinsky per 15a; mains ₽600-800; ⊙noon-midnight; 🔲🚻; MKropotkinskaya) Moscow's Georgian restaurants are all very tasty, but this one is also tasteful. You'll be charmed from the moment you enter the courtyard, where live rabbits and lambs greet all comers. Sink into a sofa in the romantic dining room or on the light-filled porch; then feast on delicacies, such as the namesake dish, *elarji* (cornmeal with *suluguni* cheese).

BALKON   ASIAN, ITALIAN €€

Map p276 (Балкон; www.balkon-restaurant.ru; 7th fl, Novinsky bul 8; mains ₽500-1000; ⊙noon-midnight; ✈🔲; MSmolenskaya) On the 7th floor of the Lotte Plaza, this trendy spot has the requisite outdoor terrace (the largest in the city) and superb city views. But it also gives you something to look at right in the dining area: various islands of activity give a glimpse of the preparation of different kinds of food – a 'gastronomic show'.

GENATSVALE ON ARBAT   GEORGIAN €€

Map p276 (Генацвале на Арбате; ☑495-697 9453; www.genatsvale-restoran.ru; Bldg 2, ul Novy Arbat 11; meals ₽600-1000; ◷noon-midnight; ◫; MArbatskaya) Subtle, it is not. Bedecked with fake trees and flowing fountains, this restaurant conjures up the Caucasian countryside, leaving little to the imagination. But what better setting to feast on favourites such as *khachapuri* (cheesy bread) and lamb dishes.

VOSTOCHNY KVARTAL   UZBEK €€

Map p276 (Восточный квартал; www.vkvartal-arbat.ru; ul Arbat 45/24; mains ₽400-800; ◷noon-11pm; ☑◫; MSmolenskaya) Vostochny Kvartal lives up to its name, acting as the 'Eastern Quarter' of the Arbat. Uzbek cooks and plenty of Uzbek patrons are a sign that this is a real-deal place to get your *plov*, an Uzbek pilaflike dish of meat and rice. Despite the Arbat address, the restaurant is actually on Plotnikov per, behind the Bulat Okudzhava statue (p128).

★CHEMODAN   RUSSIAN €€€

Map p276 (Чемодан; ☑495-695 3819; www.chemodan-msk.ru; Gogolevsky bul 25; mains ₽900-1950; ✽☑◫; MKropotkinskaya) A unique opportunity to sample Siberian cuisine (rare, that is, for those of us who don't frequent Siberia). The menu highlights game meat, regional seafood and wild fruits and berries (and pine cones). The dining room is decorated with old photos and antiques, creating a romantic atmosphere that any adventurer would be happy to return home to. Highly recommended.

✖ Khamovniki

USACHEVSKY MARKET   MARKET €

Map p281 (☑8-999-003 0030; www.usachevsky.ru; ul Usachyova 26; mains ₽200-600; ◷9am-9pm; MSportivnaya) An old market has been taken over by hipster foodies, who instantly filled the premises with little eateries serving Georgian, Uzbek, Italian, Israeli and you-name-it cuisine, as well as shops representing small-scale Russian food producers, such as Kostroma Cheese. It's a great place for lunch and shopping, if you happen to be nearby.

PROFESSOR PUF   RUSSIAN €

Map p276 (www.professorpuf.ru; Bldg 1, ul Volkhonka 9; breakfast ₽150-200, lunch ₽350-500;

◷8am-10pm Mon-Fri, from 10am Sat & Sun; ☑◫; MKropotkinskaya) A select menu of Russian classics shows off fresh ingredients, old-fashioned cooking methods and contemporary flare. Pleasant, efficient service and a super-central location make this a great option before or after a morning at the museum. Unfortunately named, but otherwise delightful, especially the house-made bread and pastries.

GOLUBKA   RUSSIAN €

Map p281 (Голубка; www.golubka-msk.ru; Bolshaya Pirogovskaya ul 53/55; mains ₽300-500; ◷9am-11pm; ☑◫; MSportivnaya) Opposite the entrance to Novodevichy Convent is this sweet place where you can snuggle into big armchairs, enjoy the view out the picture windows, and feast on fresh bread, hot soup and other old-fashioned goodness. The menu is mostly Russian cuisine, but includes pasta, sandwiches and other international favourites.

BB&BURGERS   BURGERS €

Map p281 (www.bbburgers.ru; ul Lva Tolstogo 20; mains ₽380-480; ◷11am-10pm; ☑; MPark Kultury) If you're wondering what all the Bs stand for, it's 'beer' and 'buns', as well as burgers. The latter is the star of the show, of course, with seven original burger creations (including a tasty mushroom veggie burger) and five additional sandwiches on the menu. Good, quick tasty lunch stop.

VORONEZH   STEAK €€

Map p276 (Воронеж; ☑495-695 0641; www.voronej.com; ul Prechistenka 4; sandwiches ₽250-750, restaurant mains from ₽580; ◷8am-midnight; ☑; MKropotkinskaya) When Voronezh first opened, foodies couldn't stop talking about how a classy new restaurant in the capital was named after a provincial town. Bold move by esteemed chef Alexander Rapoport. The fact is that Voronezh (the restaurant) is a celebration of meat, and all of this meat comes from the owner's ranch in Voronezh (the city).

The place is set on multiple floors: the ground floor has a butcher shop and a sandwich counter, while the 2nd floor contains the proper, stylish restaurant, serving every cut of meat your carnivorous heart desires.

ZHURFAK CAFE   RUSSIAN €€

Map p276 (Кафе Журфак; ☑8-985-212 5050; www.jurfak-cafe.ru; Bolshoy Afanasyevsky per 3; mains ₽500-800; ◷9.30am-11pm; ☑; MKropot-

WORTH A DETOUR

INDIAN FOOD WITH A VIEW

Darbars (www.darbar.ru; 16th fl, Leninsky pr 38; business lunch ₽400, meals ₽600-1000; ⊙noon-midnight; ⚡📶; ⓂLeninsky Prospekt) is a long-standing favourite of spice-loving Muscovites, who are willing to make the trek south of the centre to feast on samosas, dhal and curries. The fancy digs on the 16th floor of the Hotel Sputnik offer wonderful panoramic views. Still a favourite destination for Indian families.

kinskaya) One of our favourite secret spots, this smart cafe is named for the Moscow State University Journalism Faculty, which is located nearby. In summer, there's a shady outside eating area. Otherwise, descend into the comfy basement quarters for lively conversation, traditional food, jazz music (Monday and Wednesday) and a hint of Soviet nostalgia.

TIFLIS DVORIK
GEORGIAN €€

Map p276 (Тифлисский дворик; www.tiflis.ru; ul Ostozhenka 32; mains ₽500-900; 📶; ⓂKropotkinskaya) The name of this restaurant comes from the Russian word for the Georgian capital, Tbilisi, and when you enter this restaurant you might think you are there. Its airy balconies and interior courtyards recall a 19th-century Georgian mansion – an atmospheric setting for tasty Georgian fare.

AKADEMIYA
ITALIAN €€

Map p276 (Академия; www.semifreddo-group.com; Volkhonka ul 15/17; breakfast ₽290-530, pizzas ₽340-650, mains ₽510-860; ⊙8am-midnight Mon-Fri, from 10am Sat & Sun; ✳️📶📶; ⓂKropotkinskaya) Sip fancy coffee drinks or munch on crispy-crust pizza and watch the world go by. Steps from the Pushkin Museum of Fine Arts (p123) and the Cathedral of Christ the Saviour (p127), this is the perfect place to recover from a day of art and architecture.

BABA MARTA
BULGARIAN €€

Map p276 (www.babamarta.ru; Bldg 2, Gogolevsky bul 8; business lunch ₽430, mains ₽490-860; ⊙noon-11pm; 📶⚡📶📶; ⓂKropotkinskaya) With its colourful, folksy decor, this basement dining room is an atmospheric spot for filling Balkan food and sweet wine. The excellent-value lunch special makes it a popular option for a midday meal, when service can be harried.

BLACK MARKET
AMERICAN €€

Map p281 (www.blackmarketcafe.ru; ul Usachyova 2/1; burgers ₽620-720, mains ₽560-920, steaks ₽800-1800; ⊙10am-11pm; ✳️📶📶; ⓂFrunzenskaya) Whether you come for the 'burger bar' or the 'meat market', you'll get your protein at this upscale American bar and grill. The preparation of the meat is perfect, down to the fresh, homemade burger rolls. You'll also appreciate the well-stocked bar, superslick interior and good-looking patrons.

PANE & OLIO
ITALIAN €€€

Map p281 (📞499-246 2622; www.paneolio.ru; ul Timura Frunze 22; pastas ₽520-920, mains ₽660-1440; ⊙noon-11pm; ⚡📶; ⓂPark Kultury) Forgoing the trends that characterise many Moscow restaurants, Pane & Olio is a classic Italian trattoria, offering homemade pasta and fine grilled meats and fish. A chef named Giuseppe makes the rounds to ensure his guests are sated and happy.

GALEREYA KHUDOZHNIKOV
FUSION €€€

Map p276 (Галерея художников; 📞495-637 2866; www.gal-h.ru; ul Prechistenka 19; mains ₽800-1500; ⊙noon-midnight; ⚡📶; ⓂKropotkinskaya) This fantastical restaurant next to the Tsereteli Gallery (p130) lives up to its name, which means 'Artist Gallery'. The huge, light-filled atrium is wallpapered with stained glass and primitive paintings. The menu is a fusion of European and Asian influences. Though it is secondary to the art, the food is well prepared and, appropriately enough, artistically presented.

🍷🍸 DRINKING & NIGHTLIFE

There are bars clustered along ul Arbat and ul Novy Arbat, as well as ul Lva Tolstogo in Khamovniki. In other areas, this cultural district might feel a little staid when it comes to nightlife.

🍷 Arbat

BALALAECHNAYA CRAFT BEER

Map p276 (Балалаечная; www.balaykabar.ru; ul Arbat 23; ⊘noon-midnight; MArbatskaya) There is nothing too complicated going on here, and that's the beauty of it. Lovely handcrafted *balalaikas* (traditional Russian stringed instruments) for sale on the wall, and tasty handcrafted beer on tap. Live acoustic music on 'Spiritual Thursdays'.

ZHIGULI BEER HALL BREWERY

Map p276 (Пивной зал Жигули; www.zhiguli. su; ul Novy Arbat 11; beer ₽210-350; ⊘10am-2am Sun-Thu, to 4am Fri & Sat; ♠; MArbatskaya) It's hard to classify this old-style *stolovaya* (cafeteria) that happens to brew great beer. The place harks back to the Soviet years, when a popular *pivnaya* beer joint with the same name was a Novy Arbat institution. The minimalist decor and cafeteria-style service recalls the heyday, although it's been updated with big-screen TVs and a separate table-service dining room.

🍷 Khamovniki

DOM 12 WINE BAR

Map p276 (www.dom12cafe.ru; Mansurovsky per 12; ⊘noon-6am; MPark Kultury) Eclectic and atmospheric, Dom 12 may be the perfect place to attend an event or chat with friends over a glass of wine. The cosy interior is enhanced by natural materials, comfy chairs and low lighting. Besides the excellent wine list, the place offers poetry nights, lectures, concerts and dancing. Delightful!

SOHO ROOMS CLUB

Map p281 (☑495-988 7474; www.sohorooms. com; Savvinskaya nab 12; ⊘restaurant from noon Tue-Sat, pool terrace from 9pm Thu-Sat, club from midnight Fri & Sat; MSportivnaya) Still a hotspot in Moscow, this uber-exclusive nightclub offers dressed-up women, cool music and expensive cocktails. Of course, many clubs in Moscow can boast such things, but only Soho Rooms has a swimming pool and a poolside terrace, too. Face control is tight, so you'd best look sharp.

I LIKE WINE WINE BAR

Map p281 (www.perelmanpeople.com; ul Timura Frunze 11; ⊘10am-midnight Sun-Thu, to 2am Fri & Sat; ♠; MPark Kultury) The name choice is truly regrettable (especially with the thumbs-up 'like' symbol). But if you can get past that, this is an inviting and enjoyable place. It is stylish but not pretentious, with exposed brick walls and an expansive outdoor terrace. You'll find dozens of vintages from around the world, with a menu of Mediterranean-style small plates to complement them.

ANDERSON CAFE

Map p276 (АндерСон; www.cafe-anderson.ru; Gagarinsky per 6; desserts ₽200-400; ⊘9am-11pm Mon-Fri, from 10am Sat & Sun; ♠; MKropotkinskaya) There are a few lunch items on the menu, but this is really a place to come to indulge in rich pastries and sweet drinks. Stuffed animals available to keep you (or your kids) company.

☆ ENTERTAINMENT

LUZHNIKI STADIUM SPECTATOR SPORT

Map p281 (Олимпийский Комплекс Лужники; ☑495-780 0808; www.luzhniki.ru; Luzhnetskaya nab 24; MSportivnaya) This giant stadium (home to football club FC Torpedo) is the capital's largest, seating nearly 81,000 people. The stadium is part of the Luzhniki Olympic Complex, which was the chief venue for the 1980 Summer Olympics. In recent years, it underwent a major upgrade, in preparation for hosting the 2018 World Cup Final.

BOLSHOI CIRCUS ON VERNADSKOGO CIRCUS

(☑495-930 0300; www.greatcircus.ru; pr Vernadskogo 7; tickets ₽600-3000; ⊘shows 7pm Wed, 1pm & 5pm Sat, 3pm Sun; ♠; MUniversitet) This huge circus holds 3400 spectators, but the steep pitch means that everyone has a view of the action. The company includes hundreds of performers – mostly acrobats, but some animals too (bears, sea lions, monkeys). It is a great spectacle that is certain to entertain and amaze.

KUKLACHEV CAT THEATRE THEATRE

(Театр кошек Куклачёва; ☑495-243 4005; www.kuklachev.ru; Kutuzovsky pr 25; tickets ₽500-2500; ⊘box office 11am-7pm; ♠; MKutuzovskaya) At this unusual theatre, acrobatic cats do all kinds of stunts for the audience's delight. Director Yury Kuklachev bristles at the use of the word 'train', claiming that the

THE BRAINS

High up on the top floor of the Russian Academy of Sciences building (fondly known as 'the Brains'), chic restaurant **Sky Lounge** (www.skylounge.ru; Fl 22, Leninsky prospekt 29; ⊘1pm-midnight Sun-Wed, to 1am Thu-Sat; ⊠Leninsky Pr) is a sweet spot to go for a sundown drink. Service is variable and food is overpriced, but the city views are unbeatable.

animals cannot be forced to do anything. Instead, he says, handlers simply 'play' with the cats.

PIONER CINEMA   CINEMA
(Кинотеатр Пионер; ☑499-240 5240; http://pioner-cinema.ru; Kutuzovsky pr 21; ⊠Kievskaya) Almost all of the films shown in Russia are dubbed into the Russian language, but this cinema theatre is a pleasant exception. Apart from sticking with the original language, it screens festival and art-house films that you won't be able to see elsewhere.

RHYTHM BLUES CAFE   LIVE MUSIC
Map p276 (Блюз Кафе Ритм; ☑499-697 6008; www.rhythm-blues-cafe.ru; Starovagankovsky per; cover ₽500-1000; ⊘shows from 7.30pm; ⊠Aleksandrovsky Sad) If your dog got run over by a pickup truck, you might find some comfort at the Rhythm Blues Cafe, with down-and-out live music every night, plus cold beer and a whole menu of salty cured meats. Great fun and a friendly vibe, with people actually listening to the music. Book a table if you want to sit down.

ARBAT 13   JAZZ, KARAOKE
Map p276 (Арбат 13; ☑499-6494225; http://arbal-13.obiz.ru; ul Arbat 13; ⊘noon-midnight Sun-Thu, to 4am Fri & Sat; ⊠Arbatskaya) The retro decor and friendly service create a great vibe at this cool underground music club. There are live jazz performances on Thursday and Sunday, and karaoke on the other nights. Food, wine and cocktails are fairly straightforward but satisfactory. Reservations recommended.

**MOSCOW CHILDREN'S
MUSICAL THEATRE**   THEATRE
(Детский Музыкальный театр им. Н.И.Сац; ☑495-120 2515; www.teatr-sats.ru; pr Vernadskogo 5; tickets ₽500-1500; ⊘box office noon-7pm; ⛹; ⊠Universitet) Founded by theatre legend Natalya Sats in 1965, this was the country's first children's theatre. Sats, apparently, was the inspiration for Prokofiev's famous rendition of *Peter and the Wolf,* which is still among the most popular performances here. But all shows are entertaining and educational, with actors appearing in costume beforehand to talk with the children.

🛍 SHOPPING

We have to admit that tourist streets and centres are good for souvenir shopping. That is certainly the case on ul Arbat, which is lined with souvenir shops – mostly tacky and overpriced, but there are a few gems along the way.

DOM KNIGI   BOOKS
Map p276 (Дом Книги; www.mdk-arbat.ru; ul Novy Arbat 8; ⊘9am-11pm Mon-Fri, from 10am Sat & Sun; ⊠Arbatskaya) Among the largest bookstores in Moscow, Dom Knigi has a selection of foreign-language books to rival any other shop in the city, not to mention travel guidebooks, maps, and reference and souvenir books. This huge, crowded place hosts regularly scheduled readings, children's programs and other bibliophilic activities.

**RUSSIAN EMBROIDERY
& LACE**   GIFTS & SOUVENIRS
Map p276 (Русская вышивка и кружево; ul Arbat 31; ⊘11am-8pm Mon-Sat, to 5pm Sun; ⊠Smolenskaya) Considering the lack of flashy signs and kitsch, it would be easy to miss this plain storefront on the Arbat. But inside there are treasures galore, from elegant tablecloths and napkins to delicate handmade sweaters and embroidered shirts.

**RUSSKIE CHASOVYE
TRADITSII**   JEWELLERY
Map p276 (Русские часовые традиции; www.smirs.com; ul Arbat 11; ⊘10am-9pm;

ℹ FUN FOR KIDS

Russia's rich tradition of theatre and entertainment extends to all segments of the population, even the little people. If you are travelling with children, you are likely to find yourself in the southwest corner of the city, which is home to some of the best options for kids' entertainment, including a huge circus, an acrobatic-cat show and a children's musical theatre.

Ⓜ Arbatskaya) If you're in the market for a fancy timepiece, pop into the Arbat outlet of 'Russian Watch Traditions'. On this touristy drag, these small shops carry exclusively Russian brands, including Aviator, Buran, Vostok, Poljot, Romanoff and Denissov.

ASSOCIATION OF ARTISTS OF THE DECORATIVE ARTS   GIFTS & SOUVENIRS

Map p276 (Ассоциация художников декоративно-прикладного искусства; AHDI; www.ahdi.ru; ul Arbat 21; ⊙11am-8pm; Ⓜ Arbatskaya) Look for the ceramic number plate and the small sign indicating the entrance to this 'exposition hall', which is actually a cluster of small shops, each showcasing arts and crafts by local artists. In addition to paintings and pottery, the most intriguing items are the gorgeous knit sweaters, woolly coats and embroidered dresses – all handmade and unique.

BURO NAHODOK   ART

Map p276 (Бюро находок; www.buro-nahodok.ru; Smolensky bul 7/9; ⊙10am-9pm; Ⓜ Park Kultury) 🖉 In 2003 three Moscow artists opened this shop to sell their fun and funky gifts and souvenirs. You'll find quirky knick-knacks, clothing and home decor, most exhibiting more than a hint of irony.

VASSA & CO   FASHION & ACCESSORIES

Map p276 (www.vassatrend.com; Nikitsky bul 5/1; ⊙10am-9pm Mon-Sat, noon-8pm Sun; Ⓜ Arbatskaya) Elena Vassa is a Russian designer but was trained in New York City. Her designs reflect a classical and classy sense of style. Catering to modern Moscow men and women, Vassa offers suits, shirts, skirts, dresses and other professional clothing that stylish folks might wear at the office or out on the town.

ARTEFACT GALLERY CENTRE   ART

Map p276 (ul Prechistenka 30; ⊙10am-6pm, individual gallery hours vary; Ⓜ Kropotkinskaya)

Near the Russian Academy of Arts (p132), the Artefact Gallery Centre is a sort of art mall, housing a few dozen galleries under one roof. Look for paintings, sculptures, dolls, pottery and other kinds of art that people actually buy, as opposed to the more avant-garde exhibits at other art centres.

CHAPURIN BOUTIQUE   FASHION & ACCESSORIES

Map p281 (www.chapurin.com; Savvinskaya nab 21; ⊙10am-10pm; Ⓜ Sportivnaya) Fashion maven Igor Chapurin got his start designing theatre costumes, but his creativity knows no bounds: in addition to men's and women's clothing, he has lines of children's clothing and sportswear. Rich fabrics, playful textures and solid colours.

🏃 SPORTS & ACTIVITIES

LUZHNIKI AQUA COMPLEX   SWIMMING

Map p281 (Аквакомплекс Лужники; www.aqua-luzhniki.ru; Luzhnetskaya nab 24; per hr ₽1200-1500; ⊙7am-11pm; Ⓜ Vorobyovy Gory) On the grounds of the Luzhniki Olympic Complex, the main venue for the 1980 Olympics, this aquatic facility includes a collection of swimming pools that are open year-round. There is a 50m lap pool and a kid-friendly recreational area, as well as table tennis, volleyball and a training room and sauna.

BIG FUNNY   AMUSEMENT PARK

Map p276 (www.big-funny.com; ul Arbat 16; per attraction ₽300-350) You can't miss this colourful, kid-friendly fun house on the old Arbat. Each floor has a different attraction, including an upside-down house, a ribbon maze, a house of giants and a very tricky mirror maze. Enquire about a few other attractions in the surrounding streets.

Zamoskvorechie

Neighbourhood Top Five

1 **Gorky Park** (p143) Strolling, cycling, roller-blading, dancing, drinking, playing pétanque – being as active or as lazy as you wish in this wonderfully gentrified and iconic park.

2 **State Tretyakov Gallery** (p141) Admiring the Tretyakov's superb collection of Russian icons, the cutting social commentary of the Peredvizhniki (Wanderers) and the pre-revolutionary decadence of the Symbolists.

3 **Bar Strelka** (p152) Watching the day and short summer night go by at the city's best open-terrace bar.

4 **Art Muzeon** (p145) Walking through the park's forest of sculptures, including fallen Soviet idols.

5 **Danilovsky Market** (p151) Gorging on delicious food at an old Soviet market converted into a gourmet paradise.

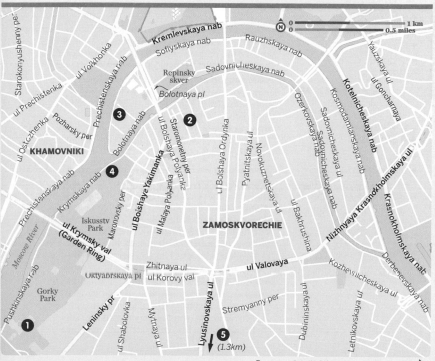

For more detail of this area see Map p282 ➡

Lonely Planet's Top Tip

The northern part of Zamoskvorechie – including the Red October complex on Bolotny Island – is easiest to access by walking over the Bolshoy Moskvoretsky most (bridge) from the Kremlin or walking over the Patriarshy most from the Cathedral of Christ the Saviour.

✕ Best Places to Eat

➜ Mizandari (p148)

➜ Björn (p152)

➜ Chugunny most (p151)

➜ Danilovsky Market (p151)

➜ Bardeli (p151)

For reviews, see p148.➜

🍷 Best Places to Drink

➜ Bar Strelka (p152)

➜ Le Boule (p152)

➜ Parka (p153)

➜ Underdog (p152)

➜ MOJO (p153)

For reviews, see p152.➜

🍬 Best Sweet Shops

➜ Alyonka (p154)

➜ RotFront (p154)

For reviews, see p154.➜

Explore Zamoskvorechie

Novokuznetskaya and Tretyakovskaya metro stations provide the best access to the core parts of Zamoskvorechie. A scenic way to access the area is by walking across one of two bridges on both sides of the Kremlin or the pedestrian bridge near the Cathedral of Christ the Saviour.

The core of Zamoskvorechie is squeezed between ul Pyatnitskaya and ul Bolshaya Polyanka, with the district's crown gem – the Tretyakov Gallery – positioned in the very middle. North of the Tretyakov Gallery, a pedestrian bridge across the canal connects historical Zamoskvorechie with Bolotny Island, home to the fledgling hipster cluster of Red October. The latter serves as a starting point for exploring a chain of beautifully renovated parks filled with modern art spaces, cool eateries and sport facilities. Travelling south you can explore several important fortified monasteries and palaces, stopping for a meal at Danilovsky Market.

You'll need at least a full day to explore the core of Zamoskvorechie and the riverside parks.

Local Life

➜**Eating at the market** A vestige of the Soviet era, the Danilovsky Market has jumped on the wave of gentrification and is now filled to the brim with little eateries representing all imaginable (and barely imaginable) cuisines. Worth the trek from the centre.

➜**Outdoor activities** Closed to vehicles, but welcoming cyclists, rollerbladers and pedestrians, Moscow's answer to London's South Bank stretches 8km from Red October to Vorobyovy Gory via Gorky Park.

➜**Gorging on art** Muscovites' hunger for artistic education manifests itself in weekend crowds pouring into Zamoskvorechie's large and famous galleries, especially when exhibitions are under way.

➜**Pub crawling** The area between Tretyakovskaya and Novokuznetskaya metro stations is dotted with bars and craft-beer pubs.

Getting There & Away

➜**Inner Zamoskvorechie** Three different metro lines cut through Zamoskvorechie in a north–south direction. The green Zamoskvoretskaya line and the orange Kaluzhsko-Rizhskaya line intersect at Novokuznetskaya. The grey Serpukhovsko-Timiryazevskaya line has a station at Polyanka.

➜**Outer Zamoskvorechie** Along the Ring line, the green Zamoskvoretskaya line stops at Paveletskaya; the orange Kaluzhsko-Rizhskaya line stops at Oktyabrskaya; and the grey Serpukhovsko-Timiryazevskaya line stops at Serpukhovskaya.

TOP SIGHT
STATE TRETYAKOV GALLERY

The exotic boyar castle on a little lane in Zamoskvorechie contains the world's best collection of Russian icons and an outstanding collection of other prerevolutionary Russian art. The building was designed by Viktor Vasnetsov between 1900 and 1905. The gallery started as the private collection of the 19th-century industrialist brothers Pavel and Sergei Tretyakov.

The tour of the gallery begins on the 2nd floor, where 18th- to 20th-century artists are exhibited. On the 1st floor, visitors are treated to more *fin-de-siècle* art before finding themselves surrounded by medieval icons.

Second Floor

Rooms 1 through 7 display paintings and sculpture from the 18th century, including many portraits and commissioned paintings. Things get more interesting in rooms 8 through 15, which display landscapes, character paintings and portraits from the 19th century.

The real gems of the collection start in room 16. In the 1870s, daring artists started to use their medium to address social issues, thus founding the Peredvizhniki movement.

Room 17 is dedicated to Vasily Perov, one of the founders of the movement. Look for his portrait of Dostoevsky and the moving painting *Troika,* with its stark depiction of child labour. Ivan Kramskoi (room 20) was another of the original Wanderers, and Ivan Shishkin (room 25) was a landscape painter closely associated with the movement.

Viktor Vasnetsov (room 26) paints fantastical depictions of fairy tales and historical figures. His painting *Bogatyry* (*Heroes*) is perhaps the best example from the revivalist movement, although *A Knight at the Crossroads* is more dramatic. By contrast, Vasily Vereshchagin (room 27) is known for

DON'T MISS

➡ Mikhail Vrubel's mural *The Princess of the Dream*
➡ *A Knight at the Crossroads* by Viktor Vasnetsov
➡ *Ivan the Terrible and his Son Ivan* by Ilya Repin

PRACTICALITIES

➡ Государственная Третьяковская Галерея
➡ Map p282, E3
➡ www.tretyakov gallery.ru
➡ Lavrushinsky per 10
➡ adult/child ₽500/200
➡ ⊙10am-6pm Tue, Wed & Sun, to 9pm Thu-Sat, last tickets 1hr before closing
➡ Ⓜ Tretyakovskaya

TRETYAKOV GALLERY

First Floor

Second Floor

his harsh realism, especially in battle scenes. *The Apotheosis of War,* for example, is far from subtle.

Vasily Surikov (room 28) excels at large-scale historical scenes. *Boyarina Morozova* captures the history of the schism in the Orthodox Church and how it tragically played out for one family. Ilya Repin (rooms 29 and 30) is perhaps the most beloved Russian realist painter. *Ivan the Terrible and his Son Ivan* is downright chilling.

Room 31 has a few masterpieces by Nicholas Ge. Mikhail Vrubel (rooms 32 to 34) was a Symbolist-era artist who defies classification. One entire wall is covered with his fantastic art nouveau mural *The Princess of the Dream.* More famous though is the melancholy *Demon Seated.*

First Floor

A selection of Isaac Levitan's landscapes is in room 37. Mikhail Nesterov (room 39) combines Symbolism with religious themes. *The Vision of the Youth Bartholomew* depicts an episode from the childhood of St Sergius of Radonezh (patron saint of Russia). In rooms 41 and 42, Valentin Serov was the most celebrated portraitist of his time. Moving into the 20th century, artists began to reject the rules of realism. Room 43 displays Konstantin Korovin's foray into Impressionism. Alexander Golovin and Boris Kustodiev represent the 'World of Art' art nouveau movement in room 44. In room 46, Pavel Kuznetsov was the founder of the Blue Rose, the Moscow group of Symbolist artists. Nikolai Rerikh (Nicholas Roerich) shows off his fantastical storytelling style in room 47.

Rooms 49 to 54 contain drawings, watercolours, pastels and prints, with rotating exhibits of works from the museum's permanent collection. Room 55 houses the Treasury, with its collection of metals, jewellery and embroidery.

Icons are found in rooms 56 to 62. Andrei Rublyov's *Holy Trinity* (1420s) from Sergiev Posad, regarded as Russia's greatest icon, is in room 60. Within the museum grounds is the **Church of St Nicholas in Tolmachi** (Map p282; ☺noon-4pm Tue-Sun), which was transferred to this site and restored in 1997. The centrepiece is the 12th-century *Vladimir Icon of the Mother of God,* protector of all Russia.

TOP SIGHT
GORKY PARK

Moscow's main city getaway is not your conventional expanse of nature preserved deep inside an urban jungle. Its mission is to mix leisure and culture in equal proportions. Designed in the 1920s by avant-garde architect Konstantin Melnikov as a piece of communist utopia, these days it showcases the enlightened transformation Moscow has undergone in recent years.

Activities

The list of activities on offer could easily cover the Rosetta Stone, although on sunny days thousands opt for complete inactivity atop one of the giant cushions scattered around the park.

Cyclists and rollerbladers create a bit of a traffic jam in the park during weekends, but they can enjoy a vehicle-free, 16km riverside ride to Vorobyovy Gory and back. There are several bicycle- and skate-rental places around the park, with one conveniently located under the pedestrian bridge.

Sport fans will find dedicated areas for beach volleyball, urban and extreme sports, table tennis and even pétanque – played by local Francophones and hipsters at Le Boule (p152) bar.

Pionersky pond near the park entrance now comes with a small sandy beach (Olive Beach, pictured), where you can sunbathe and not so much bathe as walk in shallow water.

In summer, the park is totally engulfed in the dance craze – young people gather in their hundreds to learn every conceivable type of dance, including acrobatic rock 'n' roll, salsa and polka. The epicentre of this madness is located on the boardwalk under Andreyevsky Bridge, but there are a few more dancing venues inside the park.

DON'T MISS

➡ Garage Museum of Contemporary Art

➡ Dancing under Andreyevsky Bridge

➡ View from the top of the arch that contains Gorky Park Museum

➡ Boules at Le Boule

PRACTICALITIES

➡ Парк Горького

➡ Map p282, B5

➡ admission free

➡ ⊙24hr

➡ 🛜♿

➡ Ⓜ Oktyabrskaya

GORKY PARK MUSEUM

You can observe the park as well as much of Moscow from the top of the giant Stalin-era arch at the entrance. Access is via the Gorky Park Museum. See p146 for more.

Neskuchny literally means 'not dull', which sounds as weird in Russian as it does in English. 'Sad' simply means 'gardens' – it's not sad at all!

TAKE A BREAK

The whole place is designed for taking a break from work and urban madness! The park is dotted with eateries, such as AC/DC in Tbilisi (p148), and there are also numerous small kiosks, the main cluster being the Gorky Park Food Row (p150). For drinks (and a game of pétanque) head to Le Boule (p152).

When temperatures drop, Gorky Park becomes a winter wonderland. The ponds are flooded, turning the park into the city's biggest ice-skating rink (p155). Ice skates are available to rent; bring your passport.

Culture

After decades as a tacky and neglected fun fair, Gorky Park is once again a real Park Kultury (or park of culture) as Muscovites normally call it. It is the venue for almost weekly musical, theatre, art and culinary festivals.

Art objects pop up throughout the park as part of various exhibitions and festivals, but Darya Zhukova's Garage Museum of Contemporary Art (p146) plays the flagship role. Unfortunately, little is preserved of the prewar Soviet sculptures that adorned the park's walkways, but if you walk southwest to the adjoining gardens of Neskuchny Sad, you will find a bronze female swimmer about to jump into the Moscow River.

Also at Neskuchny Sad, the open-air Stas Namin Theatre (p154) hosts concerts as well as its own performances, mostly from the rock opera genre. Back in Gorky Park, the open-air Pioner cinema shows films after dark, although almost all are entirely in Russian. Its new competitor, Garage Screen, is located in front of Garage Museum of Contemporary Art.

Neskuchny Sad

As you head southwest along the river, past Andreyevsky Bridge, you'll find yourself in what looks more like a conventional park. Neskuchny Sad is much less crowded than Gorky Park, full of shade, and criss-crossed by walking and cycling paths that go up and down through deep ravines. It contains several sports facilities, including tennis courts, as well as open-air table tennis and chess clubs. There is also an open-air gym.

⊙ SIGHTS

On top of its multitude of trademark churches, Zamoskvorechie contains two major collections of Russian art (the old and new Tretyakov galleries), a gentrified park belt along the Moscow River and the reconstructed Danilovsky Market, a magnet for foodies from all over the city.

STATE TRETYAKOV GALLERY

MAIN BRANCH   GALLERY
See p141.

GORKY PARK   PARK
See p143.

BOLOTNAYA PLOSHCHAD   SQUARE
Map p282 (Болотная площадь) Named after the swamp it used to be, Bolotnaya has a lot to tell about those who rebelled against the Kremlin, which views it warily from the other side of the river. Comprised of gardens and a bulging section of the city's main avenue, flanked by the grim constructivist **Dom na Naberezhnoy** (Map p282; ☑495-959 0317; www.museumdom.narod.ru; ul Serafimovicha 2; adult/child ₽100/50; ◷10am-6.30pm Tue, Wed & Fri, 11am-9pm Thu, 11am-6pm Sat & Sun; ⓂKropotkinskaya), it was the scene of the public executions of the leaders of two of Russia's main peasant uprisings – Stepan Razin and Yemelyan Pugachev.

Centuries later, prominent Bolsheviks who proudly moved into the newly built Dom na Naberezhnoy in the 1920s were disappearing from their flats almost every night during Stalin's purges. A small museum tells the story of the house's most prominent inhabitants. The walls of the house are adorned with numerous plaques commemorating its famous residents. If the year of the death is 1937 or 1938, it most likely means that the person was executed during the most brutal wave of terror.

The Repinsky skver gardens across the square draw punks, hippies and *Lord of the Rings* re-enactment fans on summer nights. The gardens contain an intriguing sculpture by Mikhail Shemyakin, *Children are Victims of Adults' Vices* (with the vices depicted in delightful detail). In 2012 Bolotnaya Sq became the site of anti-Putin protests commonly known as the Bolotnaya movement.

RED OCTOBER   ARTS CENTRE
Map p282 (Завод Красный Октябрь; Bersenevskaya nab; ⓂKropotkinskaya) **FREE** This defiant island of Russian modernity and Europeanness is a vibrant arts centre filled with cool bars, restaurants and galleries. With an aptly revolutionary name, the former Red October chocolate factory looks straight into the Kremlin's eyes – a vivid reminder that Russia is not all about totalitarian control and persecution.

Made of red brick, like its imperial vis-à-vis across the river, the factory was built by German national Theodor Ferdinand von Einem and proudly bore his name until the Bolshevik takeover. Production ended in the noughties, when its conversion into Moscow's hottest restaurant and entertainment area began. These days it is a key part of the hipster belt stretching along the river into Gorky Park and beyond. Come here to rub shoulders with Moscow's smart, cool and beautiful in one of the rooftop bars or check out an exhibition at Lumiere Brothers Photography Centre.

A huge power-station building here was under reconstruction at the time of writing, slated to open as another major modern art venue in 2019 under the name of GES-2.

LUMIERE BROTHERS PHOTOGRAPHY CENTRE   GALLERY
Map p282 (www.lumiere.ru; Bolotnaya nab 3, bldg 1, ₽200-430, ◷noon-9pm Tue-Fri, to 10pm Sat & Sun) One of the main pilgrimage destinations for photography fanatics, this modern and competently curated space frequently hosts changing exhibitions of Russian and Western photo artists. There is a nice shop selling photo albums and postcards on the premises.

ART MUZEON & KRYMSKAYA NABEREZHNAYA   PUBLIC ART
Map p282 (ⓂPark Kultury) **FREE** Moscow's answer to London's South Bank, Krymskaya Nab (Crimea Embankment) features wave-shaped street architecture with Scandinavian-style wooden elements, beautiful flowerbeds and a moody fountain, which ejects water randomly from many holes in the ground to the excitement of children and adults alike. It has merged with the Art Muzeon park and its motley collection of Soviet stone idols (Stalin, Sverdlov, a selection of Lenins and Brezhnevs) that were ripped from their pedestals in the post-1991 wave of anti-Soviet feeling.

The embankment is now fully revamped from the pedestrian Patriarshy bridge – which links it to the Red October (p145) gentrified industrial area on Bolotny Island – to the wide passage under Krymsky bridge that provides access to Gorky Park (p143). A mammoth-sized eyesore, the statue of Peter the Great authored by the controversial sculptor Zurab Tsereteli, surveys the area from a giant column standing at the tip of Bolotny Island. A similarly huge shoebox-shaped Brezhnev-era concrete edifice in the middle of the park contains the New Tretyakov Gallery and the Central House of Artists, a major exhibition space. Next to it, the Vernisage market is the place where artists exhibit their work – mostly commercial kitsch, but you can find a gem or two here, if you are lucky.

We'd call this area fully pedestrianised, if not for the cyclists and inline skaters who often create what resembles a typical Moscow traffic jam. There is a shop renting bicycles and inline-skating equipment. This is the starting point of the vehicle-free 8km route that runs through Gorky Park, Neskuchny Sad and Vorobyovy Gory.

NEW TRETYAKOV GALLERY GALLERY

Map p282 (Новая Третьяковская галерея; www.tretyakovgallery.ru; ul Krymsky val 10; adult/child ₽500/200; ☺10am-6pm Tue, Wed & Sun, to 9pm Thu-Sat, last tickets 1hr before closing; MPark Kultury) Moscow's premier venue for 20th-century Russian art, this branch of the Tretyakov Gallery (p141) has much more than the typical socialist-realist images of muscle-bound men wielding scythes and busty women milking cows (although there's that, too). The exhibits showcase avant-garde artists such as Malevich, Kandinsky, Chagall, Goncharova and Popova, as well as nonconformist artists of the 1960s and 1970s who refused to accept the official style.

In the same building, **Central House of Artists** (Центральный дом художника; ЦДХ; Map p282; www.cha.ru; admission ₽350; ☺11am-7pm Tue-Sun; MOktyabrskaya), also known as **TsDKh**, is a huge exhibit space used for contemporary-art shows. A number of galleries are also housed here on a permanent basis.

GORKY PARK MUSEUM MUSEUM

Map p282 (Музей Парка Горького; ☏495-995 0020; ul Krymsky val 9, str 11; adult/student ₽300/150; MOktyabrskaya, Park Kultury) The grandiose colonnaded arch that serves as Gorky Park's front entrance now contains a museum, its exhibition largely comprised of old photographs and screens showing Soviet-era newsreels about the park. The main reason for paying the hefty entrance fee is to access the roof of the arch, from where one can observe the entire park and much of central Moscow.

★GARAGE MUSEUM OF CONTEMPORARY ART MUSEUM

Map p282 (☏495-645 0520; www.garagemca.org; ul Krymsky val 9/32; adult/student ₽400/200; ☺11am-10pm; MOktyabrskaya) The brainchild of Moscow art fairy Darya Zhukova, Garage is one of the capital's hottest modern-art venues. In mid-2015 the museum moved to spectacular new digs in Gorky Park – a derelict Soviet-era building, renovated by the visionary Dutch architect Rem Koolhaas. It hosts exhibitions, lectures, films and interactive educational programs, featuring Russian and international artists. A good cafe and a bookstore are also on the premises.

As you enter, pay attention to the part-ruined Soviet-era wall mosaics, conserved in the manner of ancient mosaics. Lectures and film screenings regularly occur here and at Garage Screen open-air cinema, located across the square favoured by inline skaters. The museum's large bookstore is mostly dedicated to art.

CHURCH OF ST JOHN THE WARRIOR CHURCH

Map p282 (Церковь Иоанна Воина; ul Bolshaya Yakimanka 48; MOktyabrskaya) The finest of all Zamoskvorechie's churches mixes Moscow and European baroque styles, resulting in a melange of shapes and colours. It was commissioned by Peter the Great in thanks for his 1709 victory over Sweden at Poltava. The gilt, wood-carved iconostasis was originally installed in the nearby Church of the Resurrection at Kadashi.

BAKHRUSHIN THEATRE MUSEUM MUSEUM

Map p282 (Театральный музей Бахрушина; www.gctm.ru; ul Bakhrushina 31/12; adult/student ₽300/150; ☺noon-7pm Tue & Fri-Sun, 1-9pm Wed & Thu; MPaveletskaya) Russia's foremost stage museum, founded in 1894, is in the neo-Gothic mansion on the north side of Paveletskaya pl. The museum exhibits all things theatrical – stage sets, costumes,

TSARITSYNO PALACE

On a wooded hill in far southeast Moscow, **Tsaritsyno Palace** (Музей-заповедник Царицыно; ☑495-355 4844; www.tsaritsyno-museum.ru; Great Palace & Khlebny Dom adult/student ₽350/100, all exhibition spaces ₽800; ⊙grounds 6am-midnight, exhibits 11am-6pm Tue-Fri, to 8pm Sat & Sun; ⓂOrekhovo) is a modern-day manifestation of the exotic summer home that Catherine the Great began in 1775 but never finished. Architect Vasily Bazhenov worked on the project for 10 years before he was sacked. She hired another architect, Matvey Kazakov, but the project eventually ran out of money. For hundreds of years, the palace was little more than a shell, until the Russian government finally decided to finish it in 2007.

Nowadays, the Great Palace is a fantastical building that combines old Russian, Gothic, classical and Arabic styles. Inside, exhibits are dedicated to the history of Tsaritsyno, as well as the life of Catherine the Great. The nearby kitchen building, or khlebny dom (Хлебный дом), also hosts rotating exhibits, sometimes culinary and sometimes covering topics such as icons and art. The khlebny dom is a pleasant place to hear classical concerts in summer.

The extensive grounds include some other lovely buildings, such as the Small Palace, the working Church of Our Lady Lifegiving Spring, the cavalier buildings, greenhouses with tropical plants and some interesting bridges. A pond is bedecked with a fantastic fountain set to music. The English-style wooded park stretches all the way south to the Upper Tsaritsynsky Pond, which has rowing boats available for hire in summer, and west to the Tsaritsyno Palace complex.

Tsaritsyno park is best accessed from Orekhovo metro station – the entrance is right by the station. From there, walk towards the ponds past an open-air stage, where old folks gather to dance to 1960s tunes in summer, then turn right towards the palace.

scripts and personal items belonging to some of Russia's stage greats. The exhibits are not limited to drama, also tracing the development of opera, ballet and puppetry.

Highlights include the costumes and stage set from *Boris Godunov* (starring the famous bass, Fyodor Chaliapin) and the ballet shoes worn by Vaslav Nijinsky.

DANILOV MONASTERY   MONASTERY
(Даниловский монастырь; www.msdm.ru; ul Danilovsky val; ⊙7am-7pm; ⓂTulskaya) FREE
The headquarters of the Russian Orthodox Church stands behind white fortress walls. On holy days this place seethes with worshippers murmuring prayers, lighting candles and ladling holy water into jugs at the tiny chapel inside the gates. The Danilov Monastery was built in the late 13th century by Daniil, the first Prince of Moscow, as an outer city defence.

The monastery was repeatedly altered over the next several hundred years, and served as a factory and a detention centre during the Soviet period. It was restored in time to replace Sergiev Posad as the Church's spiritual and administrative cen-

tre, and became the official residence of the Patriarch during the Russian Orthodoxy's millennium celebrations in 1988.

Enter beneath the pink St Simeon Stylite Gate-Church on the north wall. The oldest and busiest church is the Church of the Holy Fathers of the Seven Ecumenical Councils, where worship is held continuously from 10am to 5pm daily. Founded in the 17th century and rebuilt repeatedly, the church contains several chapels on two floors: the main one upstairs is flanked by side chapels to St Daniil (on the northern side) and Sts Boris and Gleb (south). On the ground level, the small main chapel is dedicated to the Protecting Veil, and the northern one to the prophet Daniil.

The yellow neoclassical Trinity Cathedral, built in the 1830s, is an austere counterpart to the other buildings. West of the cathedral are the patriarchate's External Affairs Department and, at the far end of the grounds, the Patriarch's official residence. Against the north wall, to the east of the residence, there's a 13th-century Armenian carved-stone cross, or *khachkar,* a gift from the Armenian Church. The church guesthouse, in the southern part of the monastery grounds, has been turned into the elegant Danilovskaya Hotel (p197).

DONSKOY MONASTERY
MONASTERY

(Донской монастырь; ☑495-952 1646; www. donskoi.org; Donskaya ul; Ⓜ Shabolovskaya) Moscow's youngest monastery, Donskoy was founded in 1591 as the home of the *Virgin of the Don* icon, now in the Tretyakov Gallery (p141). This icon is credited with the victory in the 1380 battle of Kulikovo; it's also said that, in 1591, the Tatar Khan Giri retreated without a fight after the icon showered him with burning arrows in a dream.

Most of the monastery, surrounded by a brick wall with 12 towers, was built between 1684 and 1733 under Regent Sofia and Peter the Great. The Virgin of Tikhvin Church over the north gate, built in 1713 and 1714, is one of the last examples of Moscow baroque. In the centre of the grounds is the large brick New Cathedral, built between 1684 and 1693. Just to its south is the smaller Old Cathedral, dating from 1591 to 1593.

When burials in central Moscow were banned after the 1771 plague, the Donskoy Monastery became a graveyard for the nobility, and it is littered with elaborate tombs and chapels.

Donskoy Monastery is a five-minute walk from Shabolovskaya metro. Go south along ul Shabolovka, then take the first street west, 1-y Donskoy proezd.

✖️ EATING

You'll find the main cluster of restaurants in the area between Tretyakovskaya and Novokuznetskaya metros. The hipster belt between Red October and Gorky Park is also filled with cafes.

⭐ MIZANDARI
GEORGIAN €

Map p282 (☑8-903-263 9990; www.mizandari. ru; Bolotnaya nab 5, str 1; mains ₽300-500; ◎11am-11pm Sun-Thu, to midnight Fri & Sat; Ⓜ Kropotkinskaya) Georgian restaurants in Moscow tend to be either expensive or tacky. This small family-run place is neither. Come with friends and order a selection of appetisers, such as *pkhali* and *lobio* (both made of walnut paste), *khachapuri* (cheese bread) and *kharcho* (spicy lamb soup). Bless

you if you can still accommodate a main course after all that!

A bottle of Kindzmarauli red wine might help to increase your consumption capacity.

AC/DC IN TBILISI
GEORGIAN €

Map p282 (☑8-909-955 4043; www.facebook. com/acdcintbilisi; Gorky Park; mains ₽250-350; ◎10am-10pm; Ⓜ Oktyabrskaya) Burgers and Georgia (the one in the Caucasus) seem to inhabit parallel universes, but they get together in this summer-only Gorky Park kiosk. An otherwise very ordinary burger turns Georgian with the help of hot *adjika* sauce and *suluguni* cheese. The meatballs in *satsivi* (walnut, garlic and pomegranate paste) are another thing to try here.

VAY ME
GEORGIAN €

Map p282 (Вай Мэ; ☑495-951 7016; http:// vaimecafe.com; Pyatnitsky per 8, str 1; mains ₽180-250; ◎10am-11pm; Ⓜ Novokuznetskaya) Georgian food has never been known to be fast, but this fledgling chain is bringing about a revolution. The stylishly designed little eatery has all the famous staples, like *khachapuri* (cheese pastry), *kharcho* (beef or lamb soup) and *khinkali* (dumplings), but you order at the counter and eat in the discomfort of tall bar tables and stools.

That's not quite how they do it in Georgia, but it fits into Moscow's crazy lifestyle just fine.

DOM KAFE
RUSSIAN €

Map p282 (Очень домашнее кафе; ☑495-951 1734; http://homecafe.rest; Pyatnitskaya ul 9/28, str 1; mains ₽420-580; ◎9am-midnight; Ⓜ Novokuznetskaya) The name, which translates as 'a very homey cafe', is also its motto. This is as close as it gets to the kind of food Russians eat at home, which inevitably means borsch (beetroot soup) or mushroom soup for starters, and all kinds of *kotlety* (meat, chicken or fish cutlets) as the main course.

Portions are fairly small, and appetisers go for about the same price as main courses, which may bring the cost of the entire meal close to ₽1000 per person.

MARUKAME
JAPANESE €

Map p282 (Марукамэ; www.marukame.ru; Pyatnitskaya ul 29; mains ₽170-310; ◎11am-11pm; Ⓜ Novokuznetskaya) This superpopular and conveniently located self-service noodle shop draws crowds of office workers during lunch break – hence a long, but fast-moving queue. Apart from udon noodles, the menu

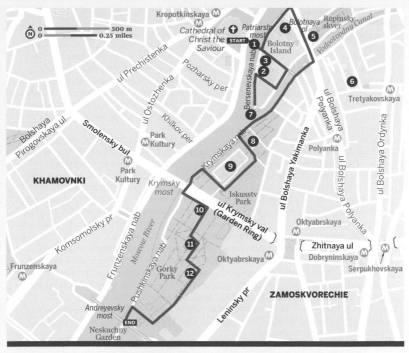

Neighbourhood Walk
Zamoskvorechie

START CATHEDRAL OF CHRIST THE
SAVIOUR
END ANDREYEVSKY BRIDGE
LENGTH 3KM; TWO TO FOUR HOURS

From Cathedral of Christ the Saviour a pedestrian bridge crosses the Moscow River
to Bolotny Island. The ❶**Patriarshy most**
offers a fantastic panorama of the Kremlin
towers and of the cathedral itself. South of
the bridge on the islands is the old ❷**Red
October chocolate factory** (p145), now
housing a heaving art and entertainment
cluster, and its centrepiece ❸**Strelka Institute** (p154).

Detour north along Sofiyskaya nab to ❹
Dom na Naberezhnoy (p145), which was a
prestigious residential building during Soviet
times, but became one of Moscow's most
infamous addresses during Stalin's purges. It
faces ❺**Bolotnaya ploshchad** (p145), the
scene of anti-Putin protests in 2012.

Walk across the Maly Kamenny most. The
❻**State Tretyakov Gallery** (p141) is a few
blocks to the east, but if you don't want to
be sidetracked for the rest of the day, head

south along the pedestrianised embankment passing Zurab Tsereteli's sculpture of
❼**Peter the Great**. From the embankment
enter the ❽**Art Muzeon sculpture park**
(p145), an art museum and history lesson all
in one. From here, you can enter the ❾**New
Tretyakov Gallery** (p146), dedicated to
20th-century art.

Proceed to Gorky Park via the passage
under Krymsky most, then turn left and walk
towards the park's official entrance, where
a large colonnaded arch contains ❿**Gorky
Park Museum** (p146). Take an elevator to
the roof of the arch to admire the views of
the park and examine your route from this
perfect vantage point. Back on earth, walk
past the large ⓫**musical fountain** towards
the ⓬**Garage Museum of Contemporary
Art** (p146). Check out an exhibition or two
and proceed to the corner of the park where
AC/DC in Tbilisi (p148) and Le Boule will
save you from hunger and thirst. Continue
towards Andreyevsky pedestrian bridge
(p143). If you time your arrival to coincide
with sunset you'll probably find hundreds of
people dancing on the embankment.

KOLOMENSKOE MUSEUM-RESERVE

Set amidst 4 sq km of picturesque parkland, on a bluff above a bend in the Moscow River, **Kolomenskoe** (Музей-заповедник "Коломенское"; www.mgomz.com; ⊘grounds 8am-9pm; ⓂKolomenskaya, Kashirskaya) FREE is an ancient royal country seat and a Unesco World Heritage Site. Shortly after its founding in the 14th century, the village became a favourite destination for the princes of Moscow. The royal estate is now an eclectic mix of churches and gates, as well as other buildings that were added to the complex over the years.

From Bolshaya ul, enter at the rear of the grounds through the 17th-century Saviour Gate to the whitewashed Our Lady of Kazan Church, both built in the time of Tsar Alexey. The church faces the site of his great wooden palace, which was demolished in 1768 by Catherine the Great. Ahead, the white, tent-roofed 17th-century front gate and clock tower mark the edge of the old inner-palace precinct. The golden double-headed eagle that tops the gate is the symbol of the Romanov dynasty. The adjacent buildings house an interesting museum with a bit of everything: a model of Alexey's wooden palace, material on rebellions associated with Kolomenskoe, and Russian handicrafts from clocks and tiles to woodcarving and metalwork.

Built in the mid-17th century, the **wooden palace of Tsar Alexey** (Дворец царя Алексея Михайловича; pr Andropova 39; ₽400; ⊘10am-6pm Tue-Sun; ⓂKashirskaya) was dubbed 'the eighth wonder of the world'. This whimsical building was famous for its mishmash of tent-roofed towers and onion-shaped eaves, all crafted from wood and structured without a single nail. Unfortunately, the legendary building fell into disrepair and was demolished in 1768 by Catherine the Great, until some 230 years later, a kitschy gingerbread replica, complete with its opulent interior based on historic records, was built in the grounds.

Outside the front gate, overlooking the river, rises Kolomenskoe's loveliest structure, the quintessentially Russian **Ascension Church** (pr Andropova 39; ⊘10am-6pm Tue-Sun; ⓂKolomenskaya). Built between 1530 and 1532 for Grand Prince Vasily III, it probably celebrated the birth of his heir, Ivan the Terrible. It is actually an important development in Russian architecture, reproducing the shapes of wooden churches in brick for the first time, and paving the way for Moscow's great St Basil's Cathedral (p76) 25 years later. Immediately west of it are the round 16th-century St George's Bell Tower and a 17th-century tower. About 300m further southwest, across a gully, the white St John the Baptist Church was built for Ivan the Terrible in the 1540s or 1550s. It has four corner chapels that make it a stylistic 'quarterway house' between the Ascension Church and St Basil's.

Among the old wooden buildings on the grounds is Peter the Great's cabin, where he lived while supervising ship- and fort-building at Arkhangelsk. The cabin is surrounded by a recreation of the tsar's orchards and gardens.

also features *donburi* rice dishes, tempura skewers and rolls.

SOK   VEGETARIAN €

Map p282 (Сок; ☑495-953 7963; http://cafe-cok.ru; Lavrushinsky per 15; mains ₽340-400; ⊘11am-11pm; 🛜🍴🆓; ⓂTretyakovskaya) Citrus-coloured walls and delicious fresh-squeezed juices are guaranteed to brighten your day. All the soups, salads, pasta and fabulous desserts are vegetarian, with many vegan options too. The menu even features a few Russian classics such as beef stroganoff, made with seitan (a wheat-based meat substitute).

GORKY PARK FOOD ROW   INTERNATIONAL €

Map p282 (Gorky Park; mains ₽200-400; ⊘all day; ⓂOktyabrskaya) The kind of food row you'd find at a Christmas market, but with a strong hipster flavour – hence the inevitable gourmet burgers and falafels, as well as delicious *khachapuri* (cheese pastry) and *churchkhela* (Georgian sweet made of grape syrup and walnuts).

GRABLY   CAFETERIA €

Map p282 (Грабли; www.grably.ru; Pyatnitskaya ul 27; mains ₽200-300; ⊗10am-11pm; 🛜📶♿; ⓂNovokuznetskaya) This big buffet features an amazing array of fish, poultry and meat, salads, soups and desserts. After you run the gauntlet and pay the bill, take a seat in the elaborate winter-garden seating area. This Zamoskvorechie outlet is particularly impressive, with two levels of tiled floors, vines draped over wrought-iron rails, and chandeliers suspended from the high ceilings.

⭐**DANILOVSKY MARKET**   MARKET €€

(www.danrinok.ru; Mytnaya ul 74; mains ₽400-600; ⊗8am-8pm; ⓂTulskaya) A showcase of the area's ongoing gentrification, this giant Soviet-era farmers' market is now largely about deli food cooked and served in myriad little eateries, including such gems as a Dagestani dumpling shop and a Vietnamese pho-soup kitchen. The market itself looks very orderly, if a tiny bit artificial, with uniformed vendors and thoughtfully designed premises.

Even if you're not shopping, it's entertaining to peruse the tables piled high with multicoloured produce: homemade cheese and jam, golden honey straight from the hive, vibrantly coloured spices pouring out of plastic bags, slippery silver fish posing on beds of ice, and huge slabs of meat hanging from the ceiling.

BARDELI   INDIAN €€

Map p282 (📞8-968-665 5114; Pyatnitskaya ul 56, str 4; set lunch ₽400-600, set dinner ₽1200-1500; ⊗noon-midnight) Bardeli's well-travelled owner (also responsible for the Jean-Jacques and John Donn restaurant chains) has a playful and ironic attitude to the notion of authenticity, resulting in this pretty cafe with funny painted-wood decor, funny paired plastic chairs and thali sets served in dabba metal pots. Portions are tiny and service is pretty authentic in both attentiveness and slow delivery.

SYROVARNYA   EASTERN EUROPEAN €€

Map p282 (📞495-727 3880; www.novikovgroup.ru/restaurants/syrovarnya; Bersenevsky per 2, str 1; mains ₽400-700; ⊗noon-midnight Mon-Thu, 24hr Fri-Sun; ⓂPolyanka, Kropotkinskaya) Domestic cheese production is all the rage in Russia, which has banned cheese imports from the EU in retaliation for Western sanctions. This restaurant serves hearty, homey meals, most of which contain cheese produced right here – in a micro-creamery that you see first thing after coming inside. A shop selling top-quality cheese is also on the premises.

MITZVA BAR   ISRAELI €€

Map p282 (📞495-532 4224; www.facebook.com/mitzva.msk; Pyatnitskaya ul 3/4, str 1; mains ₽750-820; ⊗3pm-3am; ⓂNovokuznetskaya) A baby of the recent Israeli food craze, this restaurant-cum-bar hides in an atmospheric vaulted cellar decorated with Judaic and Masonic symbols. The talented chef's wild imagination turns Jewish standards, such as gefilte fish (stuffed carp), into art objects fit for the fusion cuisine of the future. There are great cocktails, too.

FEDYA, DICH!   FUSION €€

(Федя, дичь!; 📞8-916-747 0110; Mytnaya ul 74; mains ₽650-820; ⊗11am-11pm; ⓂTulskaya) Let's take a walk on the wild side of the Moscow food scene. This place gets fresh supplies of fish and game from faraway corners of Siberia. Sea of Japan oysters and Arctic fish tartare are fresh and delicious despite crossing eight time zones to land on your table; so are wild-boar cutlets and deer steaks with forest berries.

CORREA'S   EUROPEAN €€

Map p282 (📞495-725 6035; ul Bolshaya Ordynka 40/2, mains ₽450-650; ⊗8am-11pm; 🍽🛜📶📱; ⓂPolyanka) Correa's has outlets all over the city, and though none are quite as cosy and quaint as the original in Presnya (p113), a restaurant with a bit more space has its advantages. This one is oddly located in a cement courtyard, but it offers outdoor seating and a spacious, light-filled interior. Fresh ingredients and simple preparations guarantee the food is impeccable.

CHUGUNNY MOST   BISTRO €€

Map p282 (Чугунный мост; 📞495-959 4418; www.facebook.com/chugunniimost; Pyatnitskaya ul 6; mains ₽700-1000; ⊗9am-midnight; ⓂTretyakovskaya) This place illustrates the direction in which the entire Moscow restaurant scene seems to be heading – a bistro-cum-bar that would not be out of place in somewhere like Prenzlauer Berg, Berlin. The subdued, wood-dominated decor is almost therapeutic and the inventive, postethnic food makes you want to live or work in the vicinity, just so it can be your local.

ZAMOSKVORECHIE EATING

The ₽550 set-lunch deal is about the best value for money in town. The place is a good breakfast choice, too.

★BJÖRN
SCANDINAVIAN €€€

Map p282 (☑495-953 9059; http://bjorn.rest; Pyatnitskaya ul 3; mains ₽600-1200; ⓜNovokuznetskaya) A neat cluster of fir trees on a busy street hides a Nordic gem that deserves a saga to glorify its many virtues. This is not an 'ethnic' restaurant, but a presentation of futuristic Scandinavian cuisine straight out of a science fiction movie. From salads to desserts, every dish looks deceptively simple, visually perfect and 23rd century.

PANCHO VILLA
MEXICAN €€€

Map p282 (☑499-238 7913; www.panchovilla.ru; ul Bolshaya Yakimanka 52; meals ₽850-1500; ⓢ24hr; 🛜☑⏾; ⓜOktyabrskaya) Near Oktyabrskaya pl, this is Moscow's top choice for 'Meksikansky' food. If the fajitas and margaritas aren't enough of a draw, come for breakfast burritos, happy-hour specials or live Latin music nightly (from 8pm).

🍷🍸 DRINKING & NIGHTLIFE

The area between Tretyakovskaya and Novokuznetskaya metros is best for a pub crawl.

★BAR STRELKA
CAFE, CLUB

Map p282 (www.barstrelka.com; Bersenevskaya nab 14/5, bldg 5a; ⓢ9am-midnight Mon-Thu, to 3am Fri, noon-3am Sat, noon-midnight Sun; 🛜; ⓜKropotkinskaya) Located just below the Patriarshy most, the bar-restaurant at the Strelka Institute (p154) is the ideal starting point for an evening in the Red October (p145) complex. The rooftop terrace has unbeatable Moscow River views, but the interior is equally cool in a shabby-chic sort of way. The bar menu is excellent and there is usually somebody tinkling the ivories.

★GIPSY
CLUB, CAFE

Map p282 (www.bargipsy.ru; Bolotnaya nab 3/4; ⓢ6pm-1am Sun-Thu, 2pm-6am Fri & Sat) Euphoria reigns in this postmodern nomad camp of a bar with its strategic rooftop position on Red October (p145). The decor is bright-coloured kitsch, which among other oddi-

ties means fake palm trees and toilet doors covered with artificial fur. The DJ and live-music repertoires are aptly eclectic. You don't have to be rich to pass the face control, but some natural coolness does help.

ROLLING STONE
CLUB

Map p282 (www.facebook.com/pg/BarRolling Stone; Bolotnaya nab 3; ⓢ6pm-1am Mon-Thu, 6am-10am Fri, 2pm-10am Sat, 2pm-7am Sun; ⓜKropotkinskaya) Plastered with covers of the namesake magazine and lit by naked bulbs, this place has the feel of an upscale dive bar. The music spans all genres and there is a small dance floor if you are so inclined. What makes it upscale is its location in the ultratrendy Red October (p145) complex, and of course the clientele.

They might be dressed in casual gear but they still have to look impeccable to get past the face control.

UNDERDOG
CRAFT BEER

Map p282 (Klimentovsky per 12, str 14; ⓢ2pm-2am; ⓜTretyakovskaya) This cosy little pub hidden away from the perpetually crowded Klimentovsky per has the melancholy of an Edward Hopper painting or a good road movie. The beer menu is an all-encompassing list of IPAs, APAs, lagers, krieks and whatnot – mostly produced at local microbreweries. Some Russian beers come with crazy names like Shaman Has Three Hands.

LE BOULE
BAR

Map p282 (☑495-518 8412; Gorky Park; ⓢnoon-midnight; 🛜; ⓜOktyabrskaya) The goatee and moustache factor is high in this hipster-ridden verandah bar that comes with a dozen pétanque lanes. Grab a pitcher of sangria or a pint of cider and have a go at what is arguably the most alcohol-compatible sport. Live bands often play on the verandah in the early evening.

DICTATURA ESTETICA
BAR

Map p282 (☑495-991 9946; www.facebook.com/dictaturabar; Bersenevskaya nab 6, str 1; ⓢ24hr; ⓜPolyanka, Kropotkinskaya) Aesthetics indeed rule this stylish little bar, but its main appeal lies in the gin cocktails based on secret potions, which its mixologists produce out of anything that grows. We tried the nettle mix and it tasted great. They serve quality food with South Asian motifs.

COFFEE BEAN
CAFE

Map p282 (www.coffeebean.ru; Pyatnitskaya ul 5; ☺8am-11pm; ⓂTretyakovskaya) One could claim that Coffee Bean started the coffee craze in Moscow. While the original location on Tverskaya ul is no longer open, there are a few of these excellent, affordable cafes around town. Try their trademark Raf coffee, invented years ago by a customer and now spreading around the world, without anyone realising it comes from Russia.

MOJO
BAR

Map p282 (☑495-999 0507; www.facebook.com/mojobarmoscow; ul Valovaya 26; ☺9am-midnight; ⓂDobryninskaya) The name may not sound original, but these guys do get your mojo working! Their magic formula includes outstanding cocktails, classily understated design with subdued lights, great deli food, modern art on the walls and DJ music. The expat owners mingle and drink with patrons – sometimes so hard, they can't open shop on Sunday.

BAGA BAR
BAR

Map p282 (☑495-532 5320; http://bagabar.com; Pyatnitskaya ul 25, str 1; ☺24hr; ⓂNovokuznetskaya) Ready to satisfy your thirst and hunger (both literal and social) at any time of day and night, this venue comes with human-sized maharaja dolls, waiters dressed in Indian army uniforms and a summer terrace that fills up with a crowd of office workers on the loose. Get a beer or a cocktail and watch Moscow corporates in their element.

Expertly cooked Indian and Uzbek food is also available.

PARKA
CRAFT BEER

Map p282 (☑8-926-160 6313; www.facebook.com/parkacraft; Pyatnitskaya ul 22, str 1; ☺1pm-2am; ⓂNovokuznetskaya) 'Parka' is a *banya* (bathhouse) term, hence the sauna-like decor, and just like a proper *banya*, this a very relaxing place. The friendly bartenders let you try any beer before you commit to buying a pint; the brews, many with crazy Runglish names, are mostly local.

KUSOCHKI
BAR

(Pieces; ☑495-114 5525; www.kusochki-cafe.ru; ul Shabolovka 63; ☺noon-midnight Sun-Thu, to 6am Fri & Sat; ⓂShabolovskaya) This Shabolovka district local is an alcohol-infused version of the Mad Hatter's tea party with a hint of BDSM. It features waitresses dressed as paramedics and policewomen, cocktails served in drip bags and a table inside a prison cell, where you can handcuff your drinking buddies if that sounds like a fun thing to do. Extensive drinks list and good food.

GARAGE CLUB
CLUB

Map p282 (Клуб Гараж; www.garageclub.ru; Brodnikov per 8; ☺24hr; ⓂPolyanka) This is the only place in Moscow you can drink and drive. Not to be confused with the Garage Museum of Contemporary Art, this is the reincarnation of a Yeltsin-era nightclub with the same car seats to lounge in as in the original. Nowadays, it's the place to strut your R&B stuff on the dance floor.

It gets packed in the early-morning hours of the weekend (technically Saturday and Sunday), when the clubbing crowd comes for the famous 'after party'.

KVARTIRA 44
BAR

Map p282 (☑499-238 8234; www.kv44.ru; ul Malaya Yakimanka 24/8; ☺noon-midnight Sun-Thu, to 4am Fri & Sat; 🛜; ⓂPolyanka) Back in the olden days, the best place to go for a drink was your neighbour's flat, which would be crowded with mismatched furniture and personal memorabilia. This is the atmosphere evoked at 'Apartment 44', where the drinks flow, the music plays and life is merry.

KARLSON
BAR

Map p282 (Карлсон; ☑8-985-751 1919; http://ginza.ru/msk/restaurant/karlson; Ovchinnikovskaya nab 20/1; ☺noon-midnight Sun-Thu, to 3am Fri & Sat; ⓂNovokuznetskaya) Karlson is posh (though not at all tasteless) and boasts a spectacular view of Moscow from its rooftop position, which is the main reason to throw a few thousand roubles on wine and cocktails, or even super-expensive food, here. Rest assured that quality will match the price. The bar is located inside a business centre.

Just say you are going to Karlson at the entrance.

PUEROPORT
TEAHOUSE

Map p282 (Chaynaya Vysota; ☑495-225 5996; http://cha108.ru; Pushkinskaya nab, Gorky Park; ☺11am-9pm Mon-Fri, 10am-11pm Sat & Sun; ⓂPark Kultury, Oktyabrskaya) Don't leave Gorky Park (p143) without trying one of the invigorating tea-based drinks at this kiosk-like outlet on the embankment. Here, they

ZAMOSKVORECHE DRINKING & NIGHTLIFE

mix tea with sweet syrups made in-house from such ingredients as fir-tree needles, pine cones and cloudberries. For a snack, get a pie with feijoa, a kiwi-like Brazilian fruit that's now massively cultivated in the Caucasus.

PITCHER PUB
CRAFT BEER

Map p282 (☑495-120 2417; www.pitcher.pub; Pyatnitskaya ul 82/34, str 1; ◉2pm-2am Sun & Mon, to 3am Tue-Thu, to 4am Fri & Sat; Ⓜ Dobryninskaya) This strategically located little bar is all about craft beer with a couple of dozen ales, stouts and lagers on tap, coming from Russian and European microbreweries. The attitude is near-academic, and if you feel like debating the merits of blackberry braggot or hazelnut brown ale, this is definitely your place.

 ENTERTAINMENT

MOSCOW INTERNATIONAL HOUSE OF MUSIC
CLASSICAL MUSIC

Map p282 (☑495-730 1011; www.mmdm.ru; Kosmodemyanskaya nab 52/8; tickets ₽200-2000; Ⓜ Paveletskaya) This graceful, modern glass building has three halls, including Svetlanov Hall, which holds the largest organ in Russia. Needless to say, organ concerts held here are impressive. This is the usual venue for performances by the National Philharmonic of Russia, a privately financed, highly lauded, classical-music organisation. Founded in 1991, the symphony is directed and conducted by the esteemed Vladimir Spivakov.

STRELKA INSTITUTE
ARTS CENTRE

Map p282 (www.strelkainstitute.ru; Bersenevskaya nab 14/5; Ⓜ Kropotkinskaya, Polyanka) This institute is the focal point of the development at the Red October (p145) chocolate factory. Aside from the course offerings and the popular bar (p152), Strelka brings a healthy dose of contemporary culture to Moscow, hosting lectures, workshops, film screenings and concerts.

NATIONAL PHILHARMONIC OF RUSSIA
CLASSICAL MUSIC

Map p282 (Национальный филармонический оркестр России; ☑495-730 3778; www.nfor.ru) The National Philharmonic is a new orchestra for the 21st century, founded in 2003. The NPR performs at the Moscow International House of Music.

STAS NAMIN THEATRE
THEATRE

Map p282 (Театр Стаса Намина; Green Theatre; www.stasnamintheatre.ru; ul Krymsky val 9, str 33; Ⓜ Oktyabrskaya) In Neskuchny Sad gardens, the open-air Stas Namin Theatre hosts concerts as well as its own performances, mostly from the rock opera genre.

🛍 SHOPPING

Although not a major commercial area, Zamoskvorechie has a couple of shops worth checking out.

GZHEL PORCELAIN
CERAMICS

Map p282 (http://farfor-gzhel.ru; Pyatnitskaya ul 10, str 1; ◉10am-9pm) Gzhel porcelain, with its signature white-and-blue folkloric decor, is sold here.

ALYONKA
CHOCOLATE

Map p282 (www.shop.alenka.ru; Bersenevskaya nab 6, str 1; ◉10am-8pm; Ⓜ Polyanka, Kropotkinskaya) Although the old Red October (p145) chocolate factory has long been converted into a hipster den, you can still sample the products of Russian chocolatiers at the shop located at the far end of the old factory. Alyonka is an iconic Soviet brand of chocolate candies with a picture of a rosy-cheeked peasant girl wearing a kerchief on the wrapper.

ROTFRONT
CHOCOLATE

Map p282 (2-y Novokuznetsky per 13/15; ◉9am-8pm Mon-Sat, to 5pm Sun; Ⓜ Novokuznetskaya) You know you're in an ex-Soviet country when a candy factory is named after a phrase German socialist workers greeted

EASY STEAMING: ESSENTIAL BANYA

The dos and don'ts of the *banya*:

➡ **Do** take advantage of the plunge pool (or at least the cold shower, if there is no pool on-site). It's important to bring your body temperature back down after being in the *banya*.

➡ **Don't** bother with a bathing suit. Most public *bani* are segregated by gender, in which case bathers steam naked. In mixed company, wrap yourself in a sheet (provided at the *banya*).

➡ **Do** rehydrate in between steams. Tea or even beer are common, but it is also important to drink water or juice.

➡ **Don't** stop at one! Most bathers will return to the *parilka* (steam room) several times over the course of an hour or two.

each other with in the 1920s. The factory is actually much older than its Soviet name, having catered to Moscow's sweet tooth since 1826. The shop sells largely the same toffees, caramel and chocolate candies as it did in the 1970s.

🏃 SPORTS & ACTIVITIES

GORKY PARK
SKATING RINK   ICE SKATING

Map p282 (Парк Горького; ☑495-237 1266; ul Krymsky val; ⊙10am-3pm & 5-11pm Tue-Sun; ⓂPark Kultury) When the temperatures drop, Gorky Park becomes a winter wonderland. The ponds are flooded, turning the park into the city's biggest ice-skating rink, which includes a smaller and safer rink for children. Tracks are created for cross-country skiers to circumnavigate the park. Ice skates and cross-country skis are available to rent. Bring your passport.

OLIVER BIKES   CYCLING

Map p282 (Оливер Байкс; ☑499-340 2609; www.bikerentalmoscow.com; Pyatnitskaya ul 3/4, str 2; per hr/day from ₽500/1200, tours per group ₽6000; ⊙10am-11pm; ⓂNovokuznetskaya) Oliver rents all kinds of two-wheeled vehicles, including cruisers, mountain bikes, folding bikes and tandem bikes, all of which are in excellent condition. Its location is convenient for rides along the Moscow River. Oliver also offers weekend bike tours, but only occasionally in English.

Meshchansky & Basmanny

Neighbourhood Top Five

1 **Winzavod** (p158) Contemplating Moscow's hot contemporary art scene at one of the gentrified old factories.

2 **Bunker-42** (p161) Descending 60m underground to explore the Cold War communications centre.

3 **Izmaylovsky Market** (p161) Stocking up on junk souvenirs and Soviet paraphernalia.

4 **Aptekarsky Ogorod** (p159) Escaping from the urban jungle into the dense vegetation of Moscow's quaintest gardens.

5 **Ukuleleshnaya** (p166) Sampling craft beer with a fair chance of witnessing a ukulele jam.

For more detail of this area see Map p286 ➡

Explore Meshchansky & Basmanny

Begin acquainting yourself with the area from Luby-anskaya pl, where the former KGB building looks over a modest stone that marks the millions of people who perished in the infamous Gulag camps. Before you start exploring, head up to the roof of Detsky Mir department store for a view over the neighbourhood.

Elegant ul Myasnitskaya leads to the Boulevard Ring, which creates a leafy pedestrian belt that runs all the way down to the Moscow River. With a beautiful pond that becomes a skating rink in winter, Chistoprudny bul is one of the loveliest parts of Moscow.

A short walk will take you to ul Pokrovka, which – together with ul Maroseyka – has in recent years transformed into one of the city's best restaurant rows. This a great place to sit back with a cup of coffee and indulge in some people-watching.

From here, make your way towards Kursky railway station through the quieter lanes between Chistoprudny bul and the Garden Ring, where you'll see some nice churches and early-20th-century houses.

Cross the Garden Ring and go around the station area before walking down ul Nizhnyaya Syromyatnich-eskaya. Two passages under the railway track lead to a belt of centenarian factories that are becoming one of Moscow's hottest art, shopping and start-up scenes. The flagship Winzavod (accessed via the first passage), a former winery, is packed with galleries, while the nearby ArtPlay area specialises in modern design.

Local Life

→**New Moscow** Watch the city's game changers plot new projects and start-ups at Winzavod and ArtPlay.

→**Anticafe** A cafe but not as you know it – you pay for time, and the coffee (and cookies) are free.

→**Outdoors** Whatever the weather, locals stroll and socialise around Chistye Prudy.

Getting There & Away

→**Meshchansky** Several metro lines pass through Meshchansky. Both the purple Tagansko-Krasnopresnenskaya line and the orange Kaluzhsko-Rizhskaya line have stops at Kitay-Gorod. Along the Boulevard Ring, Chistye Prudy is on the red Sokolnicheskaya line; Turgenevskaya is on the orange Kaluzhsko-Rizhskaya line; and Sretensky Bulvar is on the light green Lyublinskaya line.

→**Basmanny** The converted factories are best accessed from Kurskaya where the Ring line links with the dark blue Arbatsko-Pokrovskaya line and the light green Lyublinskaya line.

Lonely Planet's Top Tip

Trams departing from Chistye Prudy metro station are a nice way of touring this section of the Boulevard Ring. All of them go down to the river and across the bridge to Novokuznetskaya metro in Zamoskvorechie.

⚑ Best Places to Eat

→ Darbazi (p166)
→ Kitayskaya Gramota (p163)
→ Odessa-Mama (p165)
→ Levon's Highland Cuisine (p164)
→ Yuzhane (p163)

For reviews, see p163.➡

⚑ Best Places to Drink

→ Ukuleleshnaya (p166)
→ Solyanka (p167)
→ Chaynaya Vysota (p167)
→ Tsurtsum Cafe (p166)
→ Sisters Cafe (p166)

For reviews, see p166.➡

⚑ Best Places to Shop

→ Naivno? Ochen! (p168)
→ Khokhlovka Original (p168)
→ Russkaya Usadba (p169)

For reviews, see p168.➡

TOP SIGHT
WINZAVOD

A hundred years ago, industrialisation was a buzz word in Moscow, which is why the city is filled with rather imposing centenarian red-brick factories, all of them defunct. Today's buzz word is gentrification, which brings them back into the spotlight. The huge industrial area behind Kursky train station is being redeveloped as a hotspot for modern culture and start-ups.

It all began with Winzavod, a former wine-bottling factory. Its buildings still bear names such as 'Fermentation Workshop', but now they are packed with art galleries, funky shops and fashion showrooms. Sadly, politics has forced its flagship, M&J Guelman Gallery, to leave the area, but there are still a few good galleries to inspect, particularly the temporary exhibitions housed at Red & White Wine Workshops. The main courtyard is a great place to relax over a drink.

The nearby Manometer factory has also been touched by the magic wand of gentrification and is known as ArtPlay (opposite). It focuses on design, housing many furniture showrooms and antique stores. It's a bit of a maze, which is now expanding into adjacent industrial spaces. Halfway between it and the entrance, Edward's (p167) is a convenient pit stop for beer lovers.

DON'T MISS
➡ Red & White Wine Workshops
➡ Winzavod courtyard cafes
➡ Naivno? Ochen!

PRACTICALITIES
➡ Винзавод
➡ Map p286, E4
➡ www.winzavod.ru
➡ 4-y Syromyatnichesky per 1
➡ admission free
➡ Ⓜ Chkalovskaya

◉ SIGHTS

Swarming with galleries, places to eat and quirky shops, the revitalised old factories at the back of Kursky railway station are the district's main draw. The relatively quiet central part of the neighbourhood is perfect for strolling, with a few notable sights to check out on the way. Further out, vast Sokolniki park makes a great escape from the city, while Izmaylovsky Market is a diverse – if kitschy – place to shop.

◉ Meshchansky

SOKOLNIKI   PARK

(Сокольники; 🛜 🚻; Ⓜ Sokolniki) **FREE** Changed beyond recognition in recent years, Sokolniki park is criss-crossed by cycling paths, and blends into a proper forest bordering on Losiny Ostrov national park (Национальный парк Лосиный остров). The area by the entrance (a short walk from Sokolniki metro station), centred on a fountain, is full of cool places to eat and welcoming benches. Further away, to the left of the entrance, is a funfair with rides and carousels. Another attraction is the Rosarium (Розариум), a manicured rose garden.

At least three outlets in the central part of the park hire out bicycles and other sporting equipment. In summer, beach bums head to the Basseyn (Бассейн) open-air swimming pool, which turns into a party zone in the evening. Come winter, the park opens a skating rink and Moscow's longest (200m) sledding hill. Dozens of intriguing exhibitions are scattered around the park, including the Modern Museum of Calligraphy and a showroom of ZIL limos, which transported Soviet leaders. All kinds of urban culture and sport festivals, including the popular Equestrian Fest (Конный Фестиваль; 29 August to 1 September), take place year round, with the main events occurring during weekends.

APTEKARSKY OGOROD   GARDENS

(Аптекарский огород; www.hortus.ru; pr Mira 26; adult/student ₽300/200; ◉ 10am-10pm May-Sep, to 5pm Oct-Apr; Ⓜ Prospekt Mira) Moscow's lovely botanic garden was established in 1706. Originally owned by the Moscow general hospital to grow herbs and other medicinal plants, its name translates, unsurprisingly, as Pharmacy Garden. Visitors can wander along the trails, enjoy an exhibition of ornamental plants and explore three greenhouses containing plants from more southerly climes.

A glassy compound that separates the gardens from the street houses some of the city's best-loved cafe outlets, including Lavka Bratyev Karavayevykh, Lepim i Varim, Upside Down Cake & Co and Khachapuri. The latter comes with a garden-facing verandah, where you can linger over a meal or a bottle of wine. During weekends, Aptekarsky Ogorod becomes a venue for concerts, fashion shows and craft fairs.

HILTON MOSCOW
LENINGRADSKAYA   NOTABLE BUILDING

Map p286 (Гостиница Ленинградская; Kalanchevskaya ul 21/40; Ⓜ Komsomolskaya) The Leningradskaya – now owned and operated by Hilton – is the smallest of the Stalinist skyscrapers that dot the city. At 136m, it towers over Komsomolskaya pl, echoing the ornamentation on nearby Kazan Station (p245). The architect Leonid Polyakov was apparently stripped of his Stalin Prize when Khrushchev decided the hotel was an inefficient use of space.

KRASNYE VOROTA
APARTMENT BLOCK   NOTABLE BUILDING

Map p286 (Высотка на площади Красных Ворот; ul Sadovaya-Spasskaya; Ⓜ Krasnye Vorota) This 131m Stalinist skyscraper houses the Ministry of Transportation. The block is allegedly slightly lopsided, due to settling of the soil on one side of the building.

◉ Basmanny

WINZAVOD CENTER FOR
CONTEMPORARY ART   GALLERY

See p158.

★ ARTPLAY   GALLERY

Map p286 (✆ 495-620 0882; www.artplay.ru; ul Nizhny Syromyatnichesky per 10; ◉ noon-8pm Tue-Sun; Ⓜ Chkalovskaya) **FREE** A 'design centre', ArtPlay occupies the buildings of the former Manometer factory and is home to firms specialising in urban planning and architectural design, as well as furniture showrooms and antique stores. Considering the architectural emphasis, there is perhaps less for the casual caller to see, although there are always diverse and dynamic rotating exhibits in the display spaces. Come here to feel the pulse of new Moscow.

LUBYANKA
HISTORIC BUILDING

Map p286 (Лубянка; Lubyanskaya pl; Ⓜ Lubyanka) Easily the most feared edifice in Russia, looming on the northeastern side of Lubyanskaya pl is the brain centre behind Stalin's genocidal purges and the network of concentration camps known as Gulag. The building came into life circa 1900 as the headquarters of an insurance company, but was taken over by the CheKa (Bolshevik secret police) in 1919 and remained in the hands of its successors – OGPU, NKVD, MGB and finally KGB. The building is not open to the public.

The building's cellar contained an internal jail reserved for elite prisoners, such as Stalin's rival Nikolai Bukharin, Swedish Holocaust hero Raul Wallenberg, poet Osip Mandelshtam and Polish army commander Wladislaw Anders. Its last inmate, American pilot Gary Powers, captured during an ill-fated reconnaissance mission, was released in 1962.

In August 1991 a million-strong pro-democracy crowd was close to storming the building, but only succeeded in toppling the monument to CheKa founder Felix Dzerzhinsky, which stood in the middle square. You can now see it at the Art Muzeon Park (p145), along with other fallen communist idols. Later, a large granite boulder, known as the Solovetsky Stone, was brought from the original Gulag site in the Solovetsky Islands and laid on the southeast side of the square to commemorate the victims of terror. Every year on 30 October, thousands of people form a long queue here to read out the names of the victims.

The freshly restored compound now houses the Federal Security Service, or Federalnaya Sluzhba Bezopasnosti. The FSB is proud of its CheKa roots and keeps a pretty good eye on domestic goings on.

CHORAL SYNAGOGUE
NOTABLE BUILDING

Map p286 (Московская Хоральная Синагога; Bolshoy Spasoglinishchevsky per 10; ⊙9am-6pm; Ⓜ Kitay-Gorod) Construction of a synagogue was banned inside Kitay Gorod, so Moscow's oldest and most prominent synagogue was built just outside the city walls, not far from the Jewish settlement of Zaryadye. Construction started in 1881 but dragged on, due to roadblocks by the anti-Semitic tsarist government. It was finally completed in 1906 and was the only synagogue that continued to operate throughout the Soviet period, despite attempts to convert it into a workers' club.

Apparently, Golda Meir shocked the authorities when she paid an unexpected visit here in 1948.

CHISTYE PRUDY
PARK

Map p286 (Чистые пруды; Chistoprudny bul; Ⓜ Chistye Prudy) Clean Ponds is the lovely little pond that graces the Boulevard Ring at the ul Pokrovka intersection. The Boulevard Ring is always a prime location for strolling, but the quaint pond makes this a particularly desirable address. Paddle boats in summer and ice skating in winter are essential parts of the ambience. Buy a coffee, find a bench or sit on the grass, and watch the world go by.

Nearby on the boulevard, a little square with fountains and a monument to Kazakh poet Abay Kunanbayev became the unlikely venue of antigovernment protests in 2013. The little-known cultural figure became a protest icon, his face reproduced in graffiti art and on T-shirts.

SAKHAROV CENTRE
MUSEUM

Map p286 (☑495-623 4401; www.sakharov-center.ru; ul Zemlyanoy val 57; ⊙11am-7pm Tue-Sun; Ⓜ Chkalovskaya) **FREE** South of Kursky vokzal, by the Yauza River, is a small park with a two-storey house containing a human-rights centre named after Russia's most famous dissident. Inside is a museum recounting the life of Sakharov, the nuclear-physicist-turned-human-rights-advocate, detailing the years of repression in Russia and providing a history of the courage shown by the dissident movement. Free English-language tours are available on Wednesday, Friday and Saturday; book in advance.

The centre holds numerous presentations and debates on contemporary political and human-rights issues.

The park is dotted with unusual sculptures, most built from weapons and other military-industrial waste. Look out for a piece of the Berlin Wall that has been repurposed into a poignant display. Temporary exhibitions cover current human-rights issues and contemporary art.

WORTH A DETOUR

IZMAYLOVO

Never mind the kitschy faux 'tsar's palace' it surrounds, **Izmaylovsky Market** (www.kremlin-izmailovo.com; Izmaylovskoye sh 73; ☉10am-8pm; Ⓜ Partizanskaya) is the ultimate place to shop for *matryoshka* dolls, military uniforms, icons, Soviet badges and some real antiques. Huge and diverse, it is almost a theme park, including shops, cafes and a couple of not terribly exciting museums.

Serious antiquarians occupy the 2nd floor of the wooden trade row surrounding the palace, but for really good stuff you need to come here at an ungodly hour on Saturday morning and compete with pros from Moscow galleries. Keep in mind that Russia bans the export of any item older than 100 years. Feel free to negotiate, but don't expect vendors to come down more than 10%. This place is technically open every day, but many vendors come out only on weekends, when the selection is greater.

But the famous flea market is only part of the area that includes shops, restaurants, museums and monuments, all contained within a mock '**kremlin**' (Кремль в Измайлово; www.kremlin-izmailovo.com; Izmaylovskoe sh 73; ☉10am-8pm; Ⓜ Partizanskaya), complete with walls and towers that make a great photo op. Within the kremlin walls, the place recreates the workshops and trade rows of an old settlement. As well as the **Vodka History Museum** (www.vodkamuseum.ru; Izmaylovskoe sh 73; admission ₽200; ☉10am-8pm; Ⓜ Partizanskaya), other museums in the complex also include the Russian Costume & Culture Museum and a small Toy Museum. Kremlin in Izmaylovo is a 10-minute walk from Partizanskaya metro station along a plaza lined by high-rise hotels.

Nearby at a branch of the Central Museum of Armed Forces, **Stalin's Bunker** (Бункер Сталина; www.cmaf.ru; Sovietskaya ul 80; tours for 1/2/3 people ₽5000/2500/2000 per person; ☉by appointment only; Ⓜ Partizanskaya) was built under a sports stadium in the late 1930s in anticipation of the conflict with Germany. It was later designated the 'command centre of the Supreme commander-in-chief of Red Army'. You must make advance arrangements for a group tour of the facility, which includes the command room, dining room, an elegant marble meeting hall, and Stalin's office and living area.

YELOKHOVSKY CATHEDRAL   CHURCH
Map p286 (http://elohov.ru; Spartakovskaya ul 15; Ⓜ Baumanskaya) FREE Built between 1837 and 1845, the Church of the Epiphany in Yelokhovo has been Moscow's senior Orthodox cathedral since 1943. With five domes in a Russian eclectic style, the cathedral is full of gilt and icons, not to mention worshippers kneeling, polishing and lighting candles. In the northern part is the tomb of St Nicholas the Miracle Worker.

A shrine in front of the right side of the iconostasis contains the remains of St Alexey.

◉ Taganka

KOTELNICHESKAYA
APARTMENT BLOCK   NOTABLE BUILDING
Map p286 (Высотка на Котельнической набережной; Kotelnicheskaya nab 17/1; Ⓜ Taganskaya) Completed in 1940, this 176m Stalinist skyscraper towers over the south of the city, at the confluence of the Moscow and Yauza Rivers.

MUSEUM OF THE
RUSSIAN ICON   MUSEUM
Map p286 (Частный музей русской иконы; www.russikona.ru; ul Goncharnaya 3; ☉11am-7pm Thu-Tue; Ⓜ Taganskaya) FREE This museum houses the private collection of Russian art patron Mikhail Abramov. He has personally amassed a collection of more than 4000 pieces of Russian and Eastern Christian art, including some 600 icons. The collection is unique in that it represents nearly all schools of Russian iconography. Highlights include Simon Ushakov's 17th-century depiction of the Virgin Odigitria and an icon of St Nikolai Mirlikiisky.

BUNKER-42 COLD
WAR MUSEUM   MUSEUM
Map p286 (☏495-500 0554; www.bunker42.com; 5-y Kotelnichesky per 11; tours adult/student from ₽2200/1300; ☉by appointment; Ⓜ Taganskaya)

LOCAL KNOWLEDGE

IZMAILOVSKY PARK & ROYAL ESTATE

Across a lake from the Izmaylovsky Market (p161), Izmailovsky Park is a former royal estate developed by Peter the Great's father, Tsar Alexey Mikhaylovich. Its 15 sq km contain a recreation park and a much larger expanse of woodland (Izmailovsky Lesopark) east of Glavnaya alleya (the road that cuts north–south across the park). Trails wind throughout, making it a good place to escape the city by hiking or biking.

Tsar Alexey had an experimental farm here in the 17th century, where Western farming methods and cottage industries were sampled. It was on the farm ponds that his son Peter learned to sail in a little British boat, sparking his dream of creating the Russian navy and conquering the seas.

Past an extensive 18th-century barracks is the beautiful five-domed 1679 Intercession Cathedral, an early example of Moscow baroque. The nearby triple-arched, tent-roofed Ceremonial Gates (1682) and the squat brick bridge tower (1671) are the only other original buildings remaining.

On a quiet side street near Taganskaya pl, a nondescript neoclassical building is the gateway to the secret Cold War–era communications centre. The facility was meant to serve as the communications headquarters in the event of a nuclear attack. As such, the building was just a shell, serving as an entryway to the 7000-sq-metre space 60m underground. Now in private hands, the facility has been converted into a sort of a museum dedicated to the Cold War.

Unfortunately, not much remains from the Cold War days. The vast place is nearly empty, except for a few exhibits set up for the benefit of visitors, such as a scale model of the facility. Visitors watch a 20-minute film about the history of the Cold War, followed by a guided tour of the four underground 'blocks'. Call beforehand to sign up for a tour.

VYSOTSKY CULTURAL CENTRE   MUSEUM

Map p286 (Культурный центр Высоцкого; www.vysotsky.ru; Nizhny Tagansky tupik 3; ₽150; ⏰11am-6pm Tue & Wed, Fri-Sun, 1-9pm Thu; Ⓜ️Taganskaya) Part museum, part performance space, part art exhibit, this cultural centre pays tribute to local legend Vladimir Vysotsky (1938–80). Singer and songwriter, poet and actor, Vysotsky was one of the Soviet Union's most influential pop-culture figures, thanks mostly to the witty lyrics and social commentary in his songs. The permanent exhibit features a slew of photos and documents, as well as personal items, such as the bard's guitar.

RUBLYOV MUSEUM OF EARLY RUSSIAN CULTURE & ART   MUSEUM

Map p286 (Музей древнерусской культуры и искусства им Андрея Рублёва; www.rublev-museum.ru; Andronevskaya pl 10; ₽250-400; ⏰11am-6pm Mon, Tue, Fri & Sat, 2-9pm Thu; Ⓜ️Ploshchad Ilycha) On the grounds of Andronikov Monastery, the Rublyov Museum exhibits icons from days of yore and present. Unfortunately, it does not include any work by its acclaimed namesake artist, though it is still worth visiting, not least for its romantic location. Andrei Rublyov, the master of icon painting, was a monk here in the 15th century. He is buried in the grounds, but no one knows quite where.

In the centre of the monastery grounds is the compact Saviour's Cathedral, built in 1427, the oldest stone building in Moscow. The cluster of *kokoshniki* (gables of colourful tiles and brick patterns) is typical of Russian architecture from the era. To the left is the combined rectory and 17th-century Moscow-baroque Church of the Archangel Michael; to the right, the old monks' quarters house the museum.

NOVOSPASSKY MONASTERY   MONASTERY

Map p286 (Новоспасский монастырь; ☏495-676 9570; www.spasnanovom.ru; Verkhny Novospassky proezd; ⏰7am-7pm; Ⓜ️Proletarskaya) FREE Novospassky Monastery, a 15th-century fort-monastery, is about 1km south of Taganskaya pl. The centrepiece of the monastery, the Transfiguration Cathedral, was built by the imperial Romanov family in the 1640s in imitation of the Kremlin's

Assumption Cathedral. Frescoes depict the history of Christianity in Russia, while the Romanov family tree, which goes as far back as the Viking Prince Rurik, climbs one wall. The other church is the 1675 Intercession Church.

Under the riverbank, beneath one of the towers of the monastery, is the site of a mass grave for thousands of Stalin's victims. At the northern end of the monastery's grounds are the brick Assumption Cathedral and an extraordinary Moscow-baroque gate tower.

ECCLESIASTIC RESIDENCE
HISTORIC BUILDING

(Крутицкое подворье; www.krutitsy.ru; 1-y Krutitsky per; ⊘10am-6pm Wed-Mon; Ⓜ Proletarskaya) FREE Across the road running south of Novospassky Monastery is the sumptuous Ecclesiastic Residence. It was the home of the Moscow metropolitans after the founding of the Russian patriarchate in the 16th century, when they lost their place in the Kremlin.

OLD BELIEVERS' COMMUNITY
MONASTERY

(Старообрядческая Община; http://starove.ru/rogozhskoe/sloboda/; ul Rogozhsky posyolok 29; ⊘9am-6pm Tue-Sun; Ⓜ Rimskaya/Ploshchad Ilyicha) One of Russia's most atmospheric religious centres is the Old Believers' Community, located at Rogozhskoe, 3km east of Taganskaya pl. The Old Believers split from the main Russian Orthodox Church in 1653, when they refused to accept certain reforms. They have maintained the old forms of worship and customs ever since. In the late 18th century, during a brief period free of persecution, rich Old Believer merchants founded this community, which is among the most important in the country.

The yellow, classical-style Intercession Church contains one of Moscow's finest collections of icons, all dating from before 1653, with the oldest being the 14th-century *Saviour with the Angry Eye* (Spas yaroe oko), protected under glass near the south door. The icons in the deesis row (the biggest row) of the iconostasis are supposedly by the Rublyov school, while the seventh, *The Saviour,* is attributed to Rublyov himself.

Visitors are welcome at the church, but women should take care to wear long skirts (no trousers) and headscarves. There is a popular cafeteria in the premises. To reach the community, take *marshrutka* 340 to Staroobryadcheskaya ulitsa stop from metro Rimskaya.

✖ EATING

Maroseyka and Pokrovka are perhaps the city's most important restaurant rows, with cool (and not so cool) cafes lining both streets.

✖ Meshchansky

★ KITAYSKAYA GRAMOTA
CHINESE €€

Map p286 (Китайская грамота; ☑495-625 4757; http://chinagramota.ru/; ul Sretenka 1; mains ₽400-1200; ⊘noon-midnight; Ⓜ Sretenskaya) Ignore the fact that the waiting staff are dressed as Mao's soldiers; this is the place to try outstanding Cantonese fare in an atmosphere echoing that of the Opium War's decadence. A true culinary magician, the Chinese chef turns any ingredient – from hog paw to octopus to simple milk – into a mouth-watering delicacy.

The sumptuous 'fried milk' dessert is to die for.

MADAM GALIFE
GEORGIAN €€

(☑495-775 2601; www.madamgalife.ru; Pr Mira 26/1; mains ₽430-850; ⊘noon-5am; 🛜; Ⓜ Prospekt Mira) A brainchild of famous Georgian film director Rezo Gabriadze, this is much more than just another Caucasian restaurant. It faces the charming Aptekarsky Ogorod gardens for starters, and the interior design – combining naive art with antiques brought from Georgia – is superb. Food is a mixture of Georgian and European. To avoid disappointment, stick to the former.

Also adding to the awesome atmosphere is the live music – mostly piano and some other jazzy ensembles – performed every night.

YUZHANE
MODERN EUROPEAN €€

Map p286 (☑495-926 1640; www.facebook.com/yuzhanemsk/; pr Akademika Sakharova 10; mains ₽450-1300; ⊘noon-midnight; Ⓜ Krasnye Vorota) A carnivore stronghold, Yuzhane (which means 'the Southerners') gets its meat from the Kuban area in southern Russia, hence the name. The chef's philosophy is to utilise every bit of an animal's body, so in addition to juicy steaks, the menu features all kinds of by-products. The southern theme is backed by seafood and a wealth of vegetables, including meaty tomatoes.

🍴 Basmanny

★ DUKHAN CHITO-RA GEORGIAN €

Map p286 (☎8-916-393 0030; www.chito-ra.ru; ul Kazakhova 10 str 2; mains ₽300-500; ☺noon-11pm; ⓜKurskaya) It's a blessing when one of the most revered Georgian eateries in town is also one of the cheapest. The object of worship here is *khinkali* – large, meat-filled dumplings – but the traditional veggie starters are also great. The rather inevitable downside is that the place is constantly busy and there is often a queue to get in.

Beware – there is a lot of delicious broth inside the dumplings, so bite a little and suck it out before proceeding with the rest.

LEVON'S HIGHLAND CUISINE ARMENIAN €

Map p286 (☎8-985-108 8947; http://levons cafe.com/; ul Pokrovka 3/7 str 1a; wraps ₽250; ☺10am-11pm; ⓜKitay-Gorod) You might be distracted by the crazy wall paintings, which depict Darth Vader and Chewbacca mingling with characters from the Soviet comedy *Prisoner of the Caucasus*, but the main part in this film-themed mayhem is reserved for *brtuch* – a wrap made of Armenian flat bread and chicken with a choice of gravy – pomegranate, walnut or garlicky yogurt. Drinks available include pomegranate or tarragon fizzy drinks or craft beer.

DOMOZHILOV INTERNATIONAL €

Map p286 (Доможилов; ☎499-678 0225; http://domogilov.ru; Nizhny Syromyatnichesky 10, bldg 10; mains ₽350-480; ☺11am-11pm; 🛜🍴🅟; ⓜChkalovskaya) On the grounds of ArtPlay gallery, this is an appropriately artistic venue, where creative types come to socialise or poke away on their laptops. The excellent fusion menu features local favourites, such as *shchi* (cabbage soup) and shashlyk (meat kebab), as well as tom yum and a variety of burgers.

LAFLAFEL ISRAELI €

Map p286 (☎499-346 7385; Maly Kazenny per 16; mains ₽350; 🍴; ⓜKurskaya) Halfway between Chistye Prudy and the gentrified factory area behind Kursky vokzal, this lovely joint combines Middle Eastern and Indian food, in a nod to young Israelis' gap year adventures after the army service. The rather minimalist menu consists of falafel/hummus combinations on the Israeli side, and paneer or fish curry on the Indian. Good for vegetarians.

EFESENKO / SHUTTERSTOCK ©

Izmaylovsky Market (p161)

LIUDI KAK LIUDI
FAST FOOD €

Map p286 (Люди как люди; www.ludikakludi.
ru; Solyansky tupik 1/4; mains ₽150-300; ⊙9am-
11pm Sun-Wed, 9am to dawn Thu-Sat; Ⓜ Kitay-
Gorod) 🍴 An old institution, for decades
this quaint cafe has served as a pit stop for
Kitay Gorod club-goers. During the day, it's
a pleasant place to get a quick bite and a
coffee or smoothie.

AVOCADO
VEGETARIAN €

Map p286 (☑495-621 7719; www.avocadocafe.
ru; Chistoprudny bul 12/2; mains ₽350-550;
⊙10am-11pm; 🛜 🍴 🚻; Ⓜ Chistye Prudy) With
a slightly austere interior, Avocado has a
diverse menu drawing on cuisines from
around the world. Meatless versions of
soups and salads, pasta and *pelmeni* (Russian-style ravioli) are all featured. Vegans
and rawists will find specially dedicated
sections on the menu.

KARAVAYEV BROTHERS
CULINARY SHOP
DELI €

Map p286 (Кулинарная лавка братьев
Караваевых; www.karavaevi.ru; ul Pokrovka 14
str 2; mains ₽200-300; ⊙8am-11pm; Ⓜ Chistye
Prudy, Kitay-Gorod) It's a deli and it's user-
friendly. Take a ticket at the entrance, then
– while waiting for your turn – browse the
ready-made meals on display and take your
pick. Russian classics, such as *vinegret*
beetroot salad, mingle on the menu with
Western European and Asian favourites.
It's a popular chain, so you may see other
outlets elsewhere in Moscow.

FILIAL
INTERNATIONAL €

Map p286 (Филиал; ☑495-621 2143; www.
filialmoscow.ru; per Krivokolenny 3 str 1; mains
₽370-620; ⊙noon-6am; Ⓜ Chistye Prudy) The
woodwork interior makes it look like a pub
or even a Gothic chapel, but the menu is a
bit of a culinary ping-pong with Japan and
China on one side and Italy on the other.
Italian pasta sits next to Asian noodles,
while risotto meets Thai curry in the same
section. DJs play all night on Fridays and
Saturdays.

ODESSA-MAMA
UKRAINIAN €€

Map p286 (☑8-964-647 1110; www.cafeodessa.
ru; per Krivokolenny 10 str 5; ₽400-800; ⊙10am-
11pm Sun-Thu, to 2am Fri & Sat; Ⓜ Chistye Prudy)
Come here to celebrate Odessa, affection-
ately called 'mama' by the residents of this
port city. What mama cooks is a wild fusion

of Jewish, Ukrainian and Balkan foods,
with a strong emphasis on Black Sea fish.
It's like island hopping – from *forshmak*
(Jewish herring pate) to Ukrainian borsch
and eventually to fried Odessa gobies.

If seafood is not your thing, try Ukrainian
Vareniki dumplings or Greek meatballs.
Also worth checking out – for cultural
as much as gastronomical reasons – are
makarony po-flotski (navy-style pasta),
a classic Soviet staple, filling locals with
nostalgia for the good old times.

SHCHERBET
UZBEK €€

Map p286 (☑495-621 4687; www.scherbet.
ru; ul Sretenka 32; main ₽350-650; ⊙24hr;
Ⓜ Sukharevskaya) Sitting amid plush pillows
and woven tapestries, you'll feel like a sheik
in this extravagantly decorated restaurant.
Feast on *plov* (rice mixed with lamb and
vegetables), shashlyk (meat kebabs) and
other Uzbek specialities. And of course, it
wouldn't be Moscow if it didn't also offer
hookahs and an evening belly-dance show.

EXPEDITION
RUSSIAN €€€

Map p286 (Экспедиция; ☑495-775 6075;
http://expedicia-restaurant.ru; Pevchesky per
6; mains ₽1200-3000; 🍴 🚻; Ⓜ Kitay-Gorod)
This outrageously themed restaurant takes
diners beyond the Polar circle, capturing
the adventure and excitement of Siberia.
With a helicopter in the centre of the dining room, you could almost imagine you'd
arrived by air. Feast on typical 'northern
cuisine' – *ukha* (famous Baikal fish soup);
pelmeni (Russian-style ravioli) stuffed with
wild boar or Kamchatka crab; and venison
stroganoff.

There is also an expensive but authentic
Siberian *banya* (hot bath) on the premises.

🍴 Taganka

DIZENGOF99
ISRAELI €

Map p286 (☑8-926-177 0206; www.facebook.
com/dizengof99; 1-y Goncharny per 4/2; mains
₽450-570; Ⓜ Taganskaya) Threadbare walls
half-covered by corrugated sheets and cacti
on the tables make this kiosk-like structure
look like an army outpost in the Negev de-
sert. In fact, this is a place to sample modern Middle Eastern food. Dishes include
shakshuka (eggs fried in vegetable sauce),
arayes (pita with chopped meat) and many
kinds of hummus.

★DARBAZI   GEORGIAN €€
Map p286 (☎495-915 3632; www.darbazirest.
ru; ul Nikoloyamskaya 16; mains ₽590-1500;
☺noon-midnight; 🛜🗐; ⓂTaganskaya) The
vast majority of Georgian restaurants focus on the most popular, tried-and-true
fare, such as shashlyk (meat kebabs) and
khinkali (dumplings). This classy place
goes far beyond these, listing less well-
known delicacies with almost encyclo-
paedic meticulousness. Our favourite is
chakapuli (lamb cooked in white wine
with tarragon) and megreli kharcho (duck
in walnut sauce).

Definitely go for one of the desserts,
such as pelamushi (red grape mousse).

🍷 DRINKING &
🍸 NIGHTLIFE

**You'll easily find a drinking den if you
head onto ul Maroseyka from Kitay-
Gorod metro station.**

★UKULELESHNAYA   BAR
Map p286 (Укулелешная; ☎495-642 5726;
www.uku-uku.ru; ul Pokrovka 17 str 1; ☺noon-
midnight Sun-Thu, noon-4am Fri & Sat; ⓂChistye
Prudy) In its new location, this is now more
of a bar than a musical instrument shop,
although ukuleles still adorn the walls,
prompting an occasional jam session.
Craft beer prevails on the drinks list, but
Ukuleleshnaya also serves experimental
cocktails of its own invention. Live concerts happen regularly and resident Po-
meranian spitz Berseny (cute dog) presides
over the resulting madness.

Enter from the boulevard side.

★SISTERS CAFE   CAFE
Map p286 (☎495-623 0932; www.cafesisters.
com; ul Pokrovka 6; ☺noon-11pm; 🛜; ⓂKitay-
Gorod) This cosy and quiet cafe-cum-bar
has a distinct feminine touch about it – as
if Chekhov's sisters have finally made their
way to Moscow and started a new life here.
Cheapish smoothies, lemonades and teas
are on offer, but the wine and cocktail lists
are equally impressive.

Retro furniture creates a homely feeling, but a striking mural with a girl facing a blue abyss suggests that this place is
about dreams and new horizons.

COFFEE BEAN   CAFE
Map p286 (www.coffeebean.ru; ul Pokrovka
21; ☺8am-11pm; ⓂChistye Prudy) Winds of
change brought US national Jerry Ru-
ditser to Moscow in the early 1990s on a
mission to create the nation's first coffee
chain, which he succeeded in doing long
before Starbucks found Russia on the map.
Some argue it's still the best coffee served
in the capital. That might be disputed, but
on the friendliness front Coffee Bean is
unbeatable.

TSURTSUM CAFE   CAFE
Map p286 (Цурцум кафе; 4-y Syromyatnichesky
per 1 str 6; ☺10am-11pm) Synonymous with
Winzavod (p158) art centre, where it is located, Tsurtsum is a watering hole where
all the beasts of the postindustrial savan-
nah at the back of Kursky vokzal gather to
sit on the verandah and plot new start-ups,
performances and revolutions. Great for
people-watching and nonmalicious, self-
educating eavesdropping – if you speak
Russian.

KHITRYE LYUDI   CAFE
Map p286 (Хитрые люди; 4-y Syromyatnichesky per str 10; ☺noon-midnight Sun-Thu, to 5am
Fri & Sat; ⓂKurskaya) Occupying what looks
like an abandoned classroom in its Winzavod premises, this easygoing cafe has
hip, likeable waiters, an intriguing list of
lemonades as well as alcoholic drinks, and
a Hemingway portrait hanging above the
bar that contributes to the slightly devil-
may-care atmosphere.

TSIFERBLAT   ANTICAFE
Map p286 (Циферблат; ☎8-962-964 6786;
www.domnadereve.ziferblat.net; ul Pokrovka
12 str 1; 1st hour ₽180, subsequent hours ₽120;
☺8.30am-midnight Mon-Thu, till 6am Fri, Sat,
10am-midnight Sun; 🛜; ⓂKitay-Gorod) How often do you head to a cafe just because you
need somewhere nice to spend some time
in, not because you are desperate to get a
coffee? Tsiferblat was the first establishment in Moscow that turned the idea of a
coffee shop upside down. Here you pay for
time, while coffee, as well as lemonade and
cookies, are free.

They call it an 'anticafe'. Looking like an
old flat, this place is good for chatting with
friends or for fiddling with your gadgets,
but it might be slightly too noisy if you need
to do some real work. Enter at the back of
the building, then walk to the 2nd floor.

CHAYNAYA VYSOTA   TEAHOUSE

Map p286 (Чайная высота; http://cha108.ru/; ul Pokrovka 27 str 1; ☎; ⓂChistye Prudy) Tea-room? Gelateria? This place looks more like an academic library of tea and ice cream, an impression enhanced by it sharing premises with a bookstore. The tea menu is an endless list of pu'ers and oolongs, while ice-cream flavours represent every-thing that grows in the former USSR – from gooseberry or fir-needle juice to chestnuts and Crimean rose petals.

The emphasis is on the most unusual and hard-to-find ingredients, which unfor-tunately makes the place quite pricey.

CAFE DIDU   BAR

Map p286 (☑495-624 1320; www.cafe-didu.ru; Myasnitskaya ul 24; ☉noon-6am; ☎; ⓂChistye Prudy) This playful club-cafe invites re-laxation and fun with lounge furniture, tantalising cocktails and colourful model-ling clay. Containers of pliable play dough are found on each table (right next to the condiments) and the sculpted results are on display all around the restaurant.

If that is not enough to keep you en-tertained, there are also late-night mov-ies (midnight Sunday to Thursday) and weekend dance parties (11pm Friday and Saturday).

SOLYANKA   CAFE, CLUB

Map p286 (☑8-903-745 1313; http://ε-11.ru; ul Solyanka 11; ☉11am-6am; ☎; ⓂKitay-Gorod) Solyanka is a historic 18th-century mer-chant's mansion that has been revamped into an edgy, arty club. Wide-plank floors, exposed brick walls, leather furniture and funky light fixtures transform the space. By day it's an excellent restaurant, serving contemporary, creative Russian and Euro-pean food.

In the evening, the big bar room gets cleared of tables and the DJ spins hip-hop, techno and rave. The music usually starts at 11pm (and so does the face control).

OMG! COFFEE   COFFEE

Map p286 (☑499-397 7758; www.omgcoffee. net; Arma, Nizhny Susalny per 5/10; ☉9am-10pm Mon-Fri, from 11am Sat & Sun; ⓂKurskaya) This smallish local is very scientific (or in its own words – psychotic) about coffee, which is purchased from trusted roasting specialists and brewed using seven different methods. It also serves delightful gourmet burgers and sandwiches.

SECRET   CLUB

Map p286 (www.secret-club.ru; Nizhny Susalny per 7, Bldg 8; ☉11pm-6am; ⓂKurskaya) The 'sliding scale' cover charge and cheap drinks attract a young, student crowd to this gay nightclub. The earlier you arrive, the cheaper the admission, but if you're a male aged 18 to 22, it's free any time. Two dance floors, plus live music or drag shows on weekends.

EDWARD'S   PUB

Map p286 (ArtPlay, ul Nizhnyaya Syromyatnich-eskaya 10, str 9; ☉8am-midnight; ⓂKurskaya) Ambushing unsuspecting visitors from its hidden location inside a strategic passage at the ArtPlay converted factory area, Ed-ward's is a tiny but noisy place with a few ales and lagers on tap and typical British pub grub. Great for watching artsy types rushing through the passage.

BEAVERS & DUCKS   BAR

Map p286 (Бобры и утки; www.bobryiutki.ru; Chistoprudny bul 1a; ☉24hr; ⓂChistye Prudy) This convivial bar is run by two joyful women who mingle with the punters and invent risqué names for cocktails, which we will not cite here for decency reasons. The place is open round the clock and starts serving breakfasts at 4am, which lures in herds of hungry party animals at the most ungodly hours.

TEMA BAR   BAR

Map p286 (☑495-624 2720; www.temabar.ru; Po-tapovsky per 5; ☉24hr; ⓂChistye Prudy) There are too many cocktails to count...but we do know that Tema serves more than 20 dif-ferent martinis, so that should give you an idea of the extent of the drinks menu. The talented bar staff are sure to serve up some-thing that you like. Popular among both expats and locals, Tema has a fun, friendly and sometimes raucous vibe.

LIGA PAP   SPORTS BAR

Map p286 (☑495-624 3636; www.ligapap.ru; ul Bolshaya Lubyanka 24; ☉24hr; ⓂTurgenevs-kaya) It's a sports bar, but it sure is a snazzy one. The gorgeous interior features big windows, tiled floors and Gothic arched ceilings, in addition to the 20-plus flat-screen TVs. The centrepiece of the main hall is the huge screen, complete with pro-jector, as well as dramatic auditorium-style seating.

PROPAGANDA
CAFE, CLUB

Map p286 (www.propagandamoscow.com; Bolshoy Zlatoustinsky per 7; ⊙noon-6am; 🛜; MKitay-Gorod) This long-time favourite looks to be straight from the warehouse district, with exposed brick walls and pipe ceilings. It's a cafe by day, but at night they clear the dance floor and let the DJ do his stuff. This is a gay-friendly place, especially on Sunday nights.

⭐ ENTERTAINMENT

GOGOL CENTRE
THEATRE

Map p286 (Гоголь-центр; ☎499-262 9214; www.gogolcenter.com; ul Kazakhova 8; MKurskaya) One of the most talked-about theatres in Moscow is under constant political pressure due to the nonconformist position of its director Kirill Serebrennikov. Gogol Centre is a modern venue that hosts many musical and dance performances as well as cutting-edge drama. The latter is difficult to appreciate without knowing Russian.

PIROGI ON MAROSEYKA
LIVE MUSIC, CINEMA

Map p286 (https://pirogicafe.ru; ul Maroseyka 9/2; ⊙24hr; 🛜; MKitay-Gorod) If you have ever visited Pirogi's earlier incarnations, you might be surprised by the club's slick storefront. Inside, it's not dark and it's not grungy. Do not fear, however, as the crucial elements have not changed: decent food, affordable beer, and movies and music every night, all of which draw the young, broke and beautiful.

NEW BALLET
DANCE

Map p286 (☎495-265 7510; www.newballet. ru; Novaya Basmannaya ul 25/2; ⊙box office 11am-7pm; MKrasnye Vorota) If you can't stand to see another *Swan Lake,* you will be pleased to know that the New Ballet performs innovative contemporary dance. This performance art, called 'plastic ballet', incorporates elements of classical and modern dance, as well as pantomime and drama. The theatre is tiny, providing an up-close look at original, cutting-edge choreography.

GAZGOLDER
LIVE MUSIC

Map p286 (☎495-741 8383; http://gazgolder. com; Nizhny Susalny per 5 str 26; MKurskaya) A popular concert venue, associated with a namesake label that's responsible for one of Russia's best-known rap acts, Basta.

🛍 SHOPPING

You'll find a number of quirky shops and commercial galleries at Winzavod and Artplay, and more scattered around Meshchansky district.

KHOKHLOVKA ORIGINAL
CLOTHING

Map p286 (http://hhlvk.ru; Khokhlovsky per 7; ⊙noon-10pm; MKitay-Gorod) This is about the most clandestine fashion store we've ever reviewed. To get in, enter a graffiti-covered courtyard, then look for a small gap between two single-storey buildings on your left – the door is inside the tiny passage. The small showroom displays clothes and accessories produced by dozens of young (but often stellar) Russian designers.

The designs may often seem controversial, but you can rest assured you'll never see anyone wearing the same item back home.

ODENSYA DLYA SCHASTYA
CLOTHING

Map p286 (Оденься для счастья; ul Pokrovka 31; ⊙11am-9pm; MKurskaya) This sweet boutique – encouraging shoppers to 'dress for happiness' – carries unique clothing by a few distinctive designers, including Moscow native Oleg Biryukov. The designer's eponymous label features refined styles with long, flowing lines and subdued, solid colours. The tastefulness and elegance exemplify the new direction of Russian fashion.

NAIVNO? OCHEN!
HOMEWARES

Map p286 (Наивно? Очень!; ☎499-678 0162; www.orz-design.ru; ArtPlay, ul Nizhnyaya Syromyatnicheskaya 10; ⊙11am-10pm; MKurksaya) These folks do a great service selling souvenirs – cups, plates and T-shirts – themed on inspired and whimsical drawings produced by children with special needs. Proceeds go to charities that help them. It's a big deal for a country that lags far behind the West on that front.

MIR KINO
MUSIC

Map p286 (Мир кино; ☎495-628 5145; ul Maroseyka 6/8 str 2; ⊙11am-9pm; MKitay-Gorod) This tiny shop that sells secondhand vinyl and CDs has a few shelves dedicated to Russian indie music from the 1980s to present. There is also a Korean dumpling shop in the same premises.

COSMOTHEKA
PERFUME

Map p286 (www.cosmotheca.com; 4-y Syromyatnichesky per 1/8, str 6; ⊙10am-10pm; ⓂKurskaya) Here you'll find perfume brands that you won't come by in a duty-free shop. All fringe international and Russian perfume producers are welcome, while Dior and the likes are not. The shop is located by the entrance to Winzavod art space.

BIBLIO-GLOBUS
BOOKS

Map p286 (☑495-781 1900; www.biblio-globus.ru; Myasnitskaya ul 6; ⊙9am-10pm Mon-Fri, 10am-9pm Sat & Sun; ⓂLubyanka) Moscow's favourite bookshop is huge, with lots of souvenir books devoted to language, art and history, and a good selection of maps and travel guides. A user-friendly computerised catalogue will help you find what you're looking for. Just to prove that Russia's consumer culture can keep up with the best of them, there's a coffee shop on the ground floor.

RUSSKAYA USADBA
ANTIQUES

Map p286 (http://sundook.ru; ArtPlay, ul Nizhnyaya Syromyatnicheskaya 10 str 9; ⊙11am-7pm Mon-Sat) One of Moscow's best antiques dealers, this gallery specialises in 19th century furniture salvaged from the mansion houses of the nobility, most of which were burned down or otherwise destroyed by the Bolsheviks. Quite a fascinating place to visit at ArtPlay (p159), even if you don't intend to buy.

FACTORY-EXPEDITION
SPORTS & OUTDOORS

Map p286 (Фактория-Экспедиция; www.expedicia.ru; Pevchesky per 6; ⊙10am-7pm; ⓂKitay-Gorod) For all your hunting expedition needs, head to this tiny shop below the restaurant of the same name. As well as guns, knives, camping equipment and outdoor expedition gear, you'll also find some strange and scary souvenir items from the great Russian countryside.

MAGAZIN CHAI-KOFE
FOOD & DRINKS

Map p286 (Магазин Чай-Кофе; ☑495-625 4656; https://chai-cofe.com/; Myasnitskaya ul 19; ⊙9am-9pm Mon-Fri, 10am-7pm Sat & Sun; ⓂTurgenevskaya) In 1894 the old Perlov Tea House was redecorated in the style of a Chinese pagoda. Today this fantastical facade contains the Tea-Coffee Store – a simple name for a place that is filled with coffee beans from Italy, Brazil, Costa Rica and Kenya, and tea leaves from China, India and South Africa.

🏃 SPORTS & ACTIVITIES

RUDIVE
DIVING

(☑495-925 7799; www.dive.ru; Suvorovskaya ul 19) In addition to operating a dive centre in Moscow, this club organises dive trips to the White Sea, Lake Baikal and other destinations around the world.

MOSGORBIKE
CYCLING

Map p286 (www.mosgorbike.ru; ArtPlay, ul Nizhnyaya Syromyatnicheskaya 10 str 8; ₽700; ⊙10am-7pm) Run by friendly Latvians, this bicycle shop at ArtPlay gallery has urban bikes to hire. It also serves coffee supplied by Riga's best roasters. From the last in the chain of ArtPlay's courtyards, walk through a passage inside a multistorey building on your left. The shop is in the newly incorporated area on the other side.

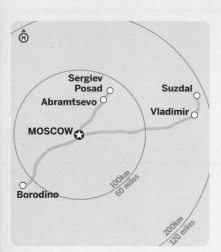

Day Trips from Moscow

Sergiev Posad p171

Home to the Trinity Monastery of St Sergius, Sergiev Posad's easy distance from Moscow and historic atmosphere ensure it's the most visited destination in the Golden Ring.

Abramtsevo p174

An artists colony and country estate, Abramtsevo was a font of artistic inspiration during the 19th-century renaissance of traditional Russian painting, sculpture, architecture and arts.

Vladimir p175

The 12th-century capital of medieval Rus was formative in establishing a distinctively Russian architectural style. Ancient Vladimir still shows off several remarkable structures that date back to its heyday.

Suzdal p180

Dating to the 11th century, Suzdal was a medieval capital and a spiritual centre. The village is still ringed with monasteries and peppered with merchant churches, making for an idyllic fairy-tale setting.

Borodino p184

The site of turning-point battles in the Napoleonic War of 1812 as well as the Great Patriotic War (WWII), Borodino battlefield is also an idyllic destination far from the crowds, traffic and smog.

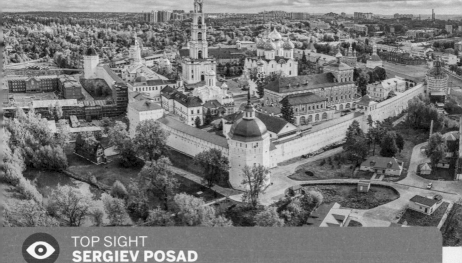

TOP SIGHT
SERGIEV POSAD

Blue-and-gold cupolas offset by snow-white walls – this colour scheme lies at the heart of the Russian perception of divinity and Sergiev Posad's monastery is a textbook example. It doesn't get any holier than this in Russia, for the place was founded in 1340 by the country's most revered saint, St Sergius of Radonezh. Since the 14th century, pilgrims have been journeying here to pay homage to him.

History

In 1340 St Sergei of Radonezh founded the Trinity Monastery of St Sergius, which soon became the spiritual centre of Russian Orthodoxy. St Sergei is credited with providing mystic support to Prince Dmitry Donskoy during his improbable victory over the Tatars in the battle of Kulikovo Pole in 1380. Soon after his death at the age of 78, Sergei was named Russia's patron saint.

Although the Bolsheviks closed the monastery, it was reopened following WWII as a museum, residence of the patriarch and a working monastery. The patriarch and the church's administrative centre moved to the Danilovsky Monastery in Moscow in 1988, but the Trinity Monastery of St Sergius remains one of the most important spiritual sites in Russia.

Spruced up on the occasion of St Sergius' 700-year anniversary in 2014, the monastery is an active religious centre with a visible population of monks in residence. This mystical place is a window into the age-old belief system that has provided Russia with centuries of spiritual sustenance.

DON'T MISS

➡ Trinity Cathedral
➡ Tomb of Boris Godunov
➡ Chapel-at-the-Well

PRACTICALITIES

➡ Свято-Троицкая Сергиева Лавра
➡ ☑info 496-544 5334, tours 496-540 5721
➡ www.stsl.ru
➡ admission free
➡ ⊙5am-9pm

EATING

There are two inexpensive cafes on the grounds of the monastery, just inside the front gate to the left. For a memorable sit-down meal, try **Gostevaya Izba** (Гостевая Изба; ☑496-541 4343; www. sergiev-kanon.ru; Aptekarsky per 2; meals ₽350-850; ⊙10am-11pm; ☑◨), just outside the monastery walls.

DRINKING

For something several steps up from a hotel-restaurant bar, try some of the local craft beer at **Bar Svoi** (Бар Свои; ☑8-963-787 3289; www. svoi.bar; 1-ya Rybnaya ul 9/26; ⊙noon-midnight Sun-Thu, to 4am Fri & Sat; ☎), around the corner from the bus station.

TOY MUSEUM

The multiple changing exhibits at the **Toy Museum** (Музей Игрушек; ☑496-540 4101; www. museumot.info; pr Krasnoy Armii 123; adult/child ₽200/100; ⊙10am-5pm Wed-Sun) feature toys from throughout Russian history and around the world; recent exhibits have included toys from the royal children of two centuries of the Romanov dynasty and toys with a naval theme. The museum has a good collection of nesting dolls, as Sergiev Posad was the centre of *matryoshka* production before the revolution.

Trinity Cathedral

Built in 1423, the squat, gold-domed Trinity Cathedral (Троицкий собор) is the heart of the monastery, as well as its oldest surviving building. The tomb of St Sergius stands in the church's southeastern corner, where a memorial service for him goes on all day, every day. The icon-festooned interior, lit by oil lamps, is largely the work of the great medieval painter Andrei Rublyov and his students.

Cathedral of the Assumption

The star-spangled Cathedral of the Assumption (Успенский собор) was modelled on the cathedral of the same name in the Moscow Kremlin. It was finished in 1585 with money left by Ivan the Terrible in a fit of remorse for killing his son. To the left of the main entrance is the rectangular tomb of Boris Godunov, the only tsar not buried in the Moscow Kremlin or St Petersburg's SS Peter & Paul Cathedral. Another notable grave is that of St Innokenty, known as the 'apostle of America' for founding the Russian Orthodox community in Alaska.

Nearby, the resplendent Chapel-at-the-Well (Накладезная часовня) was built over a spring that is said to have appeared during the Polish siege of 1608–10, in the Time of Troubles. The five-tier baroque bell tower (колокольня) – at 88.5m, the highest in Russia – took nearly 30 years to build (from 1741 to 1770), and once had 42 bells, the largest of which weighed 65 tonnes.

Sacristy

The sacristy (ризница), behind Trinity Cathedral, displays the monastery's extraordinarily rich treasury, bulging with 600 years of donations by the rich and powerful – tapestries, jewel-encrusted vestments, solid-gold chalices and more. At the time of research it was unavailable for tours due to restoration works, with no set date of return.

Refectory Church of St Sergei

The huge block with the 'wallpaper' paint job is the Refectory Church of St Sergei (Трапезная церковь преподобного Сергия), so called because it was once a dining hall for pilgrims. Now it's the Assumption Cathedral's winter counterpart, holding morning services in cold weather. It's closed outside services, except for guided tours. The green building next door is the metropolitan's residence.

TRINITY MONASTERY OF ST SERGIUS

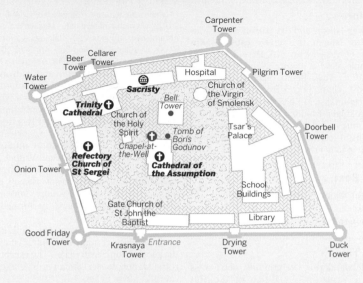

Getting There & Away

➡**Train** The fastest transport option is the express commuter train that departs from Moscow's Yaroslavsky vokzal (₽210 to ₽260, one hour); there are four daily during the week, three on weekends. Cheaper but slower *elektrichki* (₽164; 1½ hours) depart a few times per hour throughout the day. The **train station** (Сергиев Посад; Vokzalnaya pl) is 400m east of pr Krasnoy Armii, opposite the **bus station** (Автовокзал; Vokzalnaya pl 49a).

➡**Bus** A suburban route, Bus 388 to Sergiev Posad (₽200, 1½ hours) departs from Moscow's VDNKh metro station approximately every 15 minutes from 6.45am to 10.50pm.

Abramtsevo

Explore

Railway tycoon and art patron Savva Mamontov bought this lovely estate 45km north of Moscow in 1870. Here, he hosted a whole slew of painters and musicians, including Ilya Repin, landscape artist Isaak Levitan, portraitist Valentin Serov and ceramicist Mikhail Vrubel, as well as opera singer Fyodor Chaliapin. Today the Abramtsevo Estate Museum-Preserve is a delightful retreat from Moscow or addition to a trip to nearby Sergiev Posad.

The Best...

➡ **Sight** Saviour Church 'Not Made by Hand'

➡ **Place to Eat** Cafe Abramtsevo

Top Tip

While wandering the grounds, don't miss Viktor Vasnetsov's rendition of the Hut on Chicken Legs, the house of Baba Yaga, witch of fairy-tale fame.

Getting There & Away

➡ **Train** Suburban trains (headed to Sergiev Posad or Alexandrov) run every half-hour from Moscow's Yaroslavsky station (₽250, 1¼ hours). From the train platform, follow the foot trail through the woods, straight across the fire road, through a residential community and down a rough set of stairs. Before reaching the highway, turn left to cross the bridge and continue up into the parking area. The 1km walk is not well signposted.

➡ **Car** Turn west off the M8 Moscow–Yaroslavl highway just north of the 61km post (signs to Khotkovo and Abramtsevo mark the turn-off) and continue over the railroad tracks.

Need to Know

➡ **Area Code** ☑495

➡ **Location** Abramtsevo is 45km north of Moscow.

◉ SIGHTS

ABRAMTSEVO ESTATE
MUSEUM-PRESERVE   MUSEUM
(Музей-заповедник Абрамцево; ☑496-543 2470; www.abramtsevo.net; Museynaya ul 1, Abramtsevo; grounds ₽60, buildings & grounds ₽400; ◷10am-6pm Wed-Sun Apr-Sep, 10am-4pm Wed-Sun Oct-Mar) In 1870 Savva Mamontov – railway tycoon and patron of the arts – bought this lovely estate 45km north of Moscow. Here, he hosted a whole slew of artists, who sought inspiration in the gardens and forests: painter Ilya Repin; landscape artist Isaak Levitan; portraitist Valentin Serov; and the quite un-Slavic painter and ceramicist Mikhail Vrubel.

Other artists came to dabble in the woodworking and ceramics workshop, and musicians (including Fyodor Chaliapin, who made his debut here) performed in Mamontov's private opera.

You can enter most of the buildings, some of which contain exhibits, if you buy the general admission ticket. The exception is the Manor House, which requires a separate admission ticket.

MANOR HOUSE   MUSEUM
(Усадебный дом; adult/child ₽300/150) Several rooms of the manor house have been preserved intact, complete with artwork by various former resident artists. The main attraction is Mamontov's dining room, featuring Ilya Repin's portraits of the patron and his wife, as well as Valentin Serov's luminous *Girl with Peaches*. A striking maiolica bench by Mikhail Vrubel is in the garden.

SAVIOUR CHURCH
'NOT MADE BY HAND'   CHURCH
(Храм Спаса Нерукотворного) The prettiest building in the grounds is Saviour Church 'Not Made by Hand' (Khram Spasa Nerukotvorny). The structure epitomises Mamontov's intentions: it's a carefully researched homage by half a dozen artists to 14th-century Novgorod architecture. The iconostasis is by Ilya Repin and Vasily Polenov. The tiled stove in the corner, still working, is exquisite.

STUDIO   MUSEUM
(Мастерская и Кухня) Built in 1873 by Victor Gartman, the ornate Russian-style

wooden studio is notable for the carved art nouveau detailing on the exterior. It contains an exhibit of Mikhail Vrubel's ceramic works, including an exquisite tile stove.

BATHHOUSE   MUSEUM

(Баня-Теремок) Completed in 1878, this is a good example of old Russian architecture, with a wood-carved exterior and chequer-painted roof. When the Mamontovs lived on the estate, the building was used primarily as a guesthouse, and now houses an exhibit of carpentry and woodwork, including work by Yelena Polenova, who organised a wood-carving studio here back in the day.

KITCHEN   MUSEUM

(Кухня) Formerly the estate kitchen, this outpost now contains a small exhibit of folk art. Built in 1870, the building originally served as living quarters for the Mamontovs while the manor house was being renovated.

✖ EATING

CAFE ABRAMTSEVO   RUSSIAN €€

(Кафе Абрамцево; ☑8-915-177 3649; www.cafe-abramtsevo.ru; mains ₽340-640; ⊙10am-6pm) Across the street and down the lane from the main entrance to Abramtsevo Estate Museum-Preserve, you'll find this friendly cafe with outdoor seating and a full menu of Russian and international favourites. Portions are generous and preparations are tasty, making this a good stop before returning to the city.

Vladimir

••

Explore

Founded at the dawn of the 12th century on a bluff over the Klyazma River, Vladimir

---

RIDING THAT TRAIN

••

When taking trains from Moscow, note the difference between the long-distance and 'suburban' trains. Long-distance trains run to places at least three to four hours from Moscow, with limited stops and a range of classes. Suburban trains run to places within 100 to 200km of Moscow.

Long-distance Trains

The regular long-distance service is a *skory poezd* (fast train). It rarely gets up enough speed to really merit the 'fast' label. The best *skory* trains often have names, eg the Rossiya (the Moscow to Vladivostok service). These 'name trains', or *firmeny poezda*, generally have cleaner, more modern cars and more convenient arrival and departure hours; they sometimes also have fewer stops, more 1st-class accommodation and restaurant cars.

The new modern trains that are being gradually introduced on the busiest routes are generally classified as *skorostnoy poezd* (high-speed train), but generally they go under their brand names. Servicing the Moscow–St Petersburg route, Sapsan trains are the Russian equivalent of German ICE or Italian Pendolino. The slower Lastochka and Strizh trains feel more like an average Western European suburban train.

A *passazhirskiy poezd* (passenger train) is an intercity train, found mostly on routes of 1000km or less. Journeys on these can take longer, as the trains clank from one small town to the next. However, they are inexpensive and often well timed to allow an overnight sleep between neighbouring cities. Avoid trains numbered over 900. These are primarily baggage or postal services and are appallingly slow.

Suburban Trains

A *prigorodny poezd* (suburban train), commonly nicknamed an *elektrichka,* is a local service linking a city with its suburbs or nearby towns, or groups of adjacent towns – they are often useful for day trips, but can be fearfully crowded. There's no need to book ahead for these – just buy your ticket and go. In bigger stations there may be separate timetables, in addition to *prigorodny zal* (the usual name for ticket halls) and platforms, for these trains.

became the cradle of Russian history when Prince Andrei Bogolyubsky moved his capital there from Kyiv in 1169. Thus began Vladimir's Golden Age, when many of the beautifully carved white-stone buildings for which the area is renowned were built by Bogolyubsky and his brother, Prince Vsevolod the Big Nest. After a Mongol invasion devastated the town in 1238, power shifted some 200km west to a minor settlement called Moscow. Though Vladimir eventually rebounded from the ruins, it would never regain its former glory.

Today this bustling city is the administrative centre of Vladimir Oblast. It's not as charmingly bucolic as nearby Suzdal, but its cluster of Unesco-listed sights and its stunning river-valley panoramas make it an ideal stop on the way there.

The Best

→**Sight** Assumption Cathedral

→**Place to Eat** Restaurant Panorama (p178)

→**Place to Drink** Four Brewers Pub (p179)

Top Tip

If you intend to visit Vladimir and Suzdal in one trip, spend the night in Suzdal, which offers more (and better) accommodation.

Getting There & Away

→**Train** There are nine services a day from Moscow's Kursk Station (Kursky vokzal), with modern Strizh and slightly less comfortable Lastochka trains (₽600 to ₽1600, 1¾ hours).

→**Car** Vladimir is a 178km drive along the M7 from Moscow. Consider leaving in the morning (except Saturday) to lose less time at the exit from Moscow.

Need to Know

→**Area Code** ☑4922

→**Location** Vladimir is 178km east of Moscow.

→**Vladimir Tourist Information** (☑4922-377 000; www.invladimir.ru/en; Sobornaya pl; ◎10am-6pm Tue-Sun) Located in a small house on the western side of Sobornaya pl.

→**Vladimir Region Tourist Information** (www.tourism33.ru)

◉ SIGHTS

★**ASSUMPTION CATHEDRAL**   CHURCH
(Успенский собор; ☑4922-325 201; www.vlad museum.ru; Sobornaya pl; adult/child ₽100/free; ◎visitors 1-4.45pm Tue-Sun) Set dramatically high above the Klyazma River, this simple but majestic piece of pre-Mongol architecture is the legacy of Prince Andrei Bogolyubsky, the man who began shifting power from Kyiv to northeastern Rus (which eventually evolved into Muscovy). A white-stone version of Kyiv's brick Byzantine churches, the cathedral was constructed from 1158 to 1160, though it was rebuilt and expanded after a fire in 1185. It was added to Unesco's World Heritage List in 1992.

The seat of the Vladimir and Suzdal diocese, the cathedral has held services for its entire history except from 1927 to 1944. The cool, hushed interior is a riot of gold leaf – the baroque iconostasis was constructed with a donation from Catherine the Great. A few restored 12th-century murals of peacocks and prophets can be seen about halfway up the inner wall of the outer north aisle (originally an outside wall); the real treasures, though, are the *Last Judgement* frescoes by Andrei Rublyov and Daniil Chyorny, painted in 1408 in the central nave and inner south aisle (under the choir gallery towards the western end).

Comply with the standard church dress code (no shorts for men; covered head and long skirts for women) at all times, and be especially mindful of people's sensitivities outside the designated 'tourist time'. Tickets can be purchased at the small kiosk in the courtyard to the right of the cathedral.

CATHEDRAL OF ST DMITRY   CHURCH
(Дмитриевский собор; www.vladmuseum.ru; Bolshaya Moskovskaya ul 60; adult/child ₽100/free; ◎10am-6pm Mon-Thu, to 8pm Fri-Sun May-Sep, 11am-5pm Wed-Mon Oct-Apr) Built between 1193 and 1197, this exquisite, Unesco-listed white-stone cathedral represents the epitome of Russian stone carving. The attraction here is the cathedral's exterior walls, which are covered in an amazing profusion of images. At their top centre, the north, south and west walls all show King David bewitching the birds and beasts with music.

Vladimir prince Vsevolod III (nicknamed 'the Big Nest' thanks to the 14 children he had with his wife Maria) had this church built as part of his palace. He appears at the top left of the north wall,

Vladimir

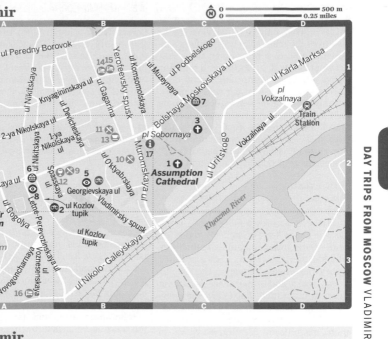

Vladimir

with a baby son on his knee and other sons kneeling on each side. Above the right-hand window of the south wall, Alexander the Great ascends to heaven, a symbol of princely might; on the west wall is a depiction of the Labours of Hercules.

HISTORY MUSEUM   MUSEUM
(Исторический музей; ☑4922-322 284; Bolshaya Moskovskaya ul 64; adult/child ₽100/ free; ⊙11am-6pm Mon-Thu, 10am-7pm Fri-Sun) This museum displays many remains and reproductions of the ornamentation from Vladimir's two cathedrals as part of an extensive exhibition covering the history of the town from Kyivan princes to the 1917 revolution. Particularly interesting are the artefacts upstairs, including a remarkable keyboard-less typewriter from 1905. The red-brick edifice was purpose-built in 1902.

GEORGIEVSKAYA ULITSA
STREET, VIEWPOINT

This pedestrian-only street curving south-west from the main strip was lovingly recreated in 2015 as a brick-paved thorough-fare from the old days, dotted with souvenir stores, whimsical bronze statues of 19th-century locals and working water pumps; at its far end is the former water tower, now Old Vladimir Museum. It's a lovely place for a stroll. Don't miss the broad viewing terraces at the eastern end, which offer stunning views of Assumption Cathedral (p176) – especially gorgeous floodlit at night.

★OLD VLADIMIR MUSEUM
VIEWPOINT, MUSEUM

(Музей 'Старый Владимир'; www.vladmuseum. ru; ul Kozlov; adult/child ₽100/free; ☺10am-6pm Mon-Thu, to 8pm Fri-Sun) This red-brick former water tower contains a multistorey exhibit of everyday objects from Vladimir's history (no English signage); the display of old clocks and stopwatches is among the most interesting. But follow the curving staircase all the way up to find the real draw here: the observation deck, which offers magnificent 360-degree views of Vladimir, with the Klyazma River curling lazily off into the distance and gold church domes set against the surrounding blue sky and green fields.

GOLDEN GATE
HISTORIC BUILDING, MUSEUM

(Золотые ворота; ☑4922-322 559; www.vlad museum.ru; Bolshaya Moskovskaya ul 1; adult/child ₽100/free; ☺9am-6pm) In the 1160s Andrei Bogolyubsky built five defensive gates to guard his city; only this former western entrance survives. It was later restored and expanded under Catherine the Great. Up the narrow stone staircase, a military museum displays weapons and armour from the 1200s through WWII (plus a 1970s cosmonaut suit); the centrepiece is a slightly fusty diorama of Vladimir being ravaged by Mongols in 1238, set to flashing lights and dramatic narration (English version available upon request).

Across the street is the grassy remnant of the old city wall that encircled the town in medieval times.

CRYSTAL, LACQUER MINIATURES & EMBROIDERY MUSEUM
MUSEUM

(Выставка хрусталя, лаковой миниатюры и вышивки; www.vladmuseum.ru; Dvoryanskaya ul 2; adult/child ₽100/free; ☺11am-7pm Sun-Fri, to 9pm Sat) Housed in the former Old Believers' Trinity Church (1916), this museum features the crafts of Gus-Khrustalny and other nearby towns. The 1st floor displays a huge variety of crystal pieces (old and new), while upstairs is a collection of embroidered cloth and 19th-century lacquer boxes painted with scenes from Russian history. Keep an eye out for the particularly detailed 10-piece *matryoshka* (nesting doll) that's over a century old. A basement shop has a decent selection of crystal for sale.

✕ EATING

SALMON & COFFEE
INTERNATIONAL €€

(Лосось и кофе; www.losos-coffee.ru; Bolshaya Moskovskaya ul 19a; mains ₽340-790; ☺11am-1am Sun-Thu, to 8am Fri & Sat; ☎) Salmon is yet to be found in the Klyazma, and coffee is not exactly what medieval princes had for breakfast. But instead of hinting at the city's past, this DJ cafe serving Asian and European dishes aims for a cosmopolitan touch in an ancient town. Lots of dark wood, dim lights and magenta-coloured metal railings create a cool, intriguing atmosphere.

PITEYNY DOM KUPTSA ANDREYEVA
RUSSIAN €€

(Питейный дом Купца Андреева; ☑4922-326 545; www.andreevbeer.com/dom; Bolshaya Moskovskaya ul 16; mains ₽350-685; ☺11am-midnight Sun-Wed, to 2am Thu-Sat; ☎▣) Merchant Andreyev's Liquor House, as the name translates, makes a half-hearted attempt to pass off as an old-world Russian *kabak* (pub), but its main virtues are the home-brewed beers on tap and hearty Russian meals, including all the classics – from *shchi* (cabbage soup) to bliny. Service can be slow, but the beer helps to make the time fly faster.

★RESTAURANT PANORAMA
RUSSIAN €€€

(Ресторан Панорама; ☑4922-464 746; Bolshaya Moskovskaya ul 44b; mains ₽380-1260; ☺noon-midnight Sun-Thu, to 2am Fri & Sat; ▣) This upscale restaurant, hidden down a lane off the main street, offers perhaps the fanciest meal in town, with attentive service, an elegant atmosphere and – true to its name – great views over the river val-

WORTH A DETOUR

BOGOLYUBOVO

Tourists and pilgrims all flock to Bogolyubovo, just 12km northeast of Vladimir, for **Church of the Intercession on the Nerl** (Церковь Покрова на Нерли; ☺10am-6pm Tue-Sun), a perfect little jewel of a 12th-century church standing amid a flower-covered floodplain. The Church of the Intercession on the Nerl is the golden standard of Russian architecture. Apart from ideal proportions, its beauty lies in a brilliantly chosen waterside location (floods aside) and the sparing use of delicate carving.

Legend has it that Prince Andrei Bogolyubsky had the church built in memory of his favourite son, Izyaslav, who was killed in battle against the Bulgars. As with the Cathedral of St Dmitry (p176) in Vladimir, King David sits at the top of three facades, the birds and beasts entranced by his music. The interior has more carvings, including 20 pairs of lions. If the church is closed (from October to April the opening hours are more sporadic), try asking at the house behind.

To reach this famous church, get bus 152 (₽20) from the Golden Gate or Sobornaya pl in Vladimir and get off by the massive, blue-domed Bogolyubsky Monastery, which contains remnants of Prince Andrei's palace. Walk past the monastery to Vokzalnaya ul, the first street on the right, and follow it down to the train station. Cross the pedestrian bridge over the railroad tracks and follow the stone path for 1km across the meadow. If driving, take the M7 east out of Vladimir until you get to the monastery, then turn right onto Vokzalnaya and park at the train station.

---

ley from your table. The menu features the usual salads, pasta and meat dishes, including a rabbit confit the restaurant insists is worth the wait.

🍷 DRINKING & 🍸 NIGHTLIFE

★**FOUR BREWERS PUB** CRAFT BEER

(Паб Четыре Пивовара; www.4brewers.ru; Bolshaya Moskovskaya ul 12; ☺2pm-midnight Sun-Thu, to 2am Fri & Sat) This pocket-sized pub offers 20 brews on tap and dozens more in bottles – porter, IPA, stout, ale, you name it – all from the brewers' own vats or other Russian microbreweries, with such unforgettable names as 'Banana Kraken', 'Santa Muerte', 'Roksana and the Endless Universe' and (our personal favourite) 'Black Jesus, White Pepper'. Bartenders happily offer recommendations and free tastes.

KOFEIN CAFE, COFFEE

(Кофеин; Gagarina ul 1; ☺8.30am-11pm Sun-Thu, to midnight Fri & Sat; 🛜) This smart cafe in the town centre offers a variety of delicious desserts and espresso-based coffees (as well as a full food menu). Vegans, rejoice – there's soy milk, too. Free wi-fi.

🛏 SLEEPING

NICE HOSTEL HOSTEL €

(Найс Хостел; ☏4922-421 231, 8-902-888 5004; www.nicehostel33.ru; Manezhney t 1; dm/d from ₽510/1500; 🛜🍴) This brand-new hostel won't win any design awards, but it's spotless and offers a free breakfast in the common kitchen. Dorm rooms (male-only, female-only and mixed) have four, six or eight beds; five doubles are available (three with private bathrooms), as well as a four-bed family room (₽2600). There's a washing machine and iron for guest use.

RUS HOTEL €€

(Русь; ☏4922-322 736; www.rushotel33. ru; ul Gagarina 14; s/d incl breakfast from ₽3000/3600; 🌀🛜) Occupying a large old house on a quiet corner just two blocks from Bolshaya Moskovskaya ul, this hotel offers nicely appointed and comfortable (if rather beige) rooms with extra towels and bathrobes. Reception staff are helpful and speak some English. Breakfast is included.

VOZNESENSKAYA SLOBODA HOTEL €€€

(Вознесенская слобода; ☏4922-325 494; www.vsloboda.ru; ul Voznesenskaya 14b; d ₽4800; 🅿🌀🛜) Perched on a bluff with tremendous views of the valley, this hotel has one of the most scenic locations in the area. Outside is a quiet neighbourhood of old wooden cottages and villas dominated by the elegant Ascension Church, whose bells chime idyllically throughout the day. The new building's interior is tastefully designed to resemble art nouveau style c 1900.

Suzdal

Explore

The sparkling diamond in the Golden Ring is undoubtedly Suzdal – if you have time for only one of these towns, this is the one to see. With rolling green fields carpeted with dandelions, a gentle river curling lazily through a historic town centre, sunlight bouncing off golden church domes and the sound of horse clops and church bells carrying softly through the air, you may feel like you've stumbled into a storybook Russia.

Suzdal served as a royal capital when Moscow was still a cluster of cowsheds, and was a major monastic centre and an important commercial hub for many years as well. But in 1864, local merchants failed to get the Trans-Siberian Railway built through here (it went to Vladimir instead). Suzdal was thus bypassed both by trains and 20th-century progress, preserving its idyllic character for future visitors.

The Best

➡**Sight** Kremlin
➡**Place to Eat** Gostiny Dvor (p183)
➡**Place to Sleep** Petrov Dom (p184)

Top Tip

Most long-distance buses from Vladimir or Moscow pass the central square on their way to the Suzdal bus station. Ask the driver to let you out at the square to avoid the 2km trek back into town.

Getting There & Away

➡**Bus** The **bus station** (Автовокзал; ☑49231-020 147; Vasilievskaya ul 44; ⊘4.30am-8pm) is 2km east of the centre on Vasilievskaya ul. There is no bus service to Suzdal from Moscow; you'll need to take

a train to Vladimir and then switch to a Suzdal-bound bus there. Buses run very regularly throughout the day to and from Vladimir (₽95, 45 minutes).

Need to Know

➡**Area Code** ☑49231
➡**Location** Suzdal is 35km north of Vladimir.

◉ SIGHTS

★KREMLIN   FORTRESS
(Кремль; ☑49231-21 624; www.vladmuseum.ru; ul Kremlyovskaya; joint ticket adult/child ₽350/free; ⊘exhibitions 9am-6pm Sun-Thu, to 9pm Fri & Sat, grounds to 9pm) The grandfather of the Moscow Kremlin, this citadel was the 12th-century base of Prince Yury Dolgoruky, who ruled the vast northeastern part of Kyivan Rus (and, among other things, founded a small outpost that would eventually become the Russian capital). The 1.4km-long earthen ramparts of Suzdal's kremlin enclose a few streets of houses and a handful of churches, as well as the main cathedral group on ul Kremlyovskaya.

The Unesco-listed **Nativity of the Virgin Cathedral** (Церковь Казанской иконы Божьей Матери; Suzdal kremlin, ul Kremlyovskaya; adult/child ₽100/free; ⊘9am-7pm Sun-Thu, to 9pm Fri & Sat), its deep blue domes spangled with gold stars, was built in 1225 (only its richly carved lower section is original white stone, though, the rest being 16th-century brick). The inside is sumptuous, with 13th- and 17th-century frescoes and 13th-century damascene (gold on copper) west and south doors.

Within the kremlin, the Archbishop's Chambers (Архиерейские палаты) house the Suzdal History Exhibition, which includes the original 13th-century door from the cathedral, photos of its interior and a visit to the 18th-century Cross Hall (Крестовая палата), which was used for receptions. The tent-roofed 1635 kremlin bell tower (Звонница), directly across the yard from the cathedral, contains additional exhibits, including the 17th-century Jordan Canopy (Иорданская сень), the only one of its kind left in Russia; every January on Epiphany Day, this 28m-tall painted wooden structure would be placed over a cross-shaped hole in the ice on the Kamenka for the annual rite of blessing the river water.

To the southwest, between the cathedral and the river, is the 1766 Nikolskaya Wooden Church (Никольская деревянная церковь), which was moved to Suzdal from a nearby village in 1960. (Other rural wooden buildings were subsequently moved for preservation to the excellent Museum of Wooden Architecture & Peasant Life (p183), across the river.)

If you don't want to see all of the exhibitions, you can pay for admission to the cathedral separately; to walk around the grounds only costs ₽50 (children get in free).

TORGOVAYA
PLOSHCHAD   SQUARE
(Торговая Площадь) Suzdal's Torgovaya pl (Market Sq) is dominated by the pillared Trading Arcades (Торговые ряды; 1806–11) along its western side. There are several churches in the immediate vicinity, including the 1739 Kazan Church (Казанская церковь) and the 1720 Resurrection Church (Воскресенская церковь) right on the square; the latter's hours are irregular but if it's open you can take the precarious climb to the top of the bell tower to be rewarded with wonderful views of Suzdal's gold-domed skyline.

Across ul Lenina, the five-domed 1707 Tsar Constantine Church (Цареконстантиновская церковь) in the square's northeastern corner is a working church with an ornate interior; next door is the 1750 Church of Our Lady of Sorrows (Скорбященская церковь).

HOLY INTERCESSION
CONVENT   CONVENT
(Свято-Покровский монастырь; www.spokrov mon.ru; Pokrovskaya ul; ⏰7am-7pm) FREE It's a classic Suzdal picture: the whitewashed beauty of monastic walls surrounded by green meadows on the banks of the lazily meandering river. Inside are beds of brightly coloured flowers tended by the nuns, who live in wooden cottages left over from a rustic hotel built here when the convent was closed after the revolution (it was revived in 1992). Founded in 1364, this convent was originally a place of exile for the unwanted wives of tsars.

★SAVIOUR MONASTERY
OF ST EUTHYMIUS   MONASTERY
(Спасо-Евфимиев монастырь; ☏49231-20 746; ul Lenina; adult/child ₽400/free; ⏰10am-7pm Sun-Thu, to 9pm Fri & Sat) Founded in the 14th century to protect the town's northern entrance, Suzdal's biggest monastery grew mighty in the 16th and 17th centuries after Vasily III, Ivan the Terrible and the noble Pozharsky family funded impressive new stone buildings and made large land and property acquisitions. It was girded with its great brick walls and towers in the 17th century.

Right at the entrance, the Annunciation Gate Church (Благовещенская надвратная церковь) houses an interesting exhibit on Dmitry Pozharsky (1578–1642), leader of the Russian army that drove the Polish invaders from Moscow in 1612.

A tall 16th- to 17th-century cathedral bell tower (Звонница) stands before the seven-domed Cathedral of the Transfiguration of the Saviour (Спасо-Преображенский собор); every hour on the hour from 11am to 5pm a short concert of chimes is played on its bells. The cathedral was built in the 1590s in 12th- to 13th-century Vladimir–Suzdal style. Inside, restoration has uncovered some bright 1689 frescoes by the school of Gury Nikitin from Kostroma. The tomb of Prince Dmitry Pozharsky is by the cathedral's east wall.

The 1525 Assumption Refectory Church (Успенская церковь), facing the bell tower, adjoins the old Father Superior's chambers (Палаты отца-игумена), which house a display of Russian icons and an excellent naive-art exhibition showcasing works by local amateur painters from the Soviet era.

The old Monastery Dungeon (Монастырская тюрьма), set up in 1764 for religious dissidents, is at the north end of the complex. It now houses a fascinating exhibit on the monastery's prison history, including displays of some of the better-known prisoners who stayed here. The Bolsheviks used the monastery as a concentration camp after the 1917 revolution. During WWII, German and Italian officers captured in the Battle of Stalingrad were kept here.

To the northeast of the main cathedral group, the combined Hospital Chambers & St Nicholas Church (Больничные кельи и Никольская церковь) feature a rich collection of gold church treasures.

Suzdal

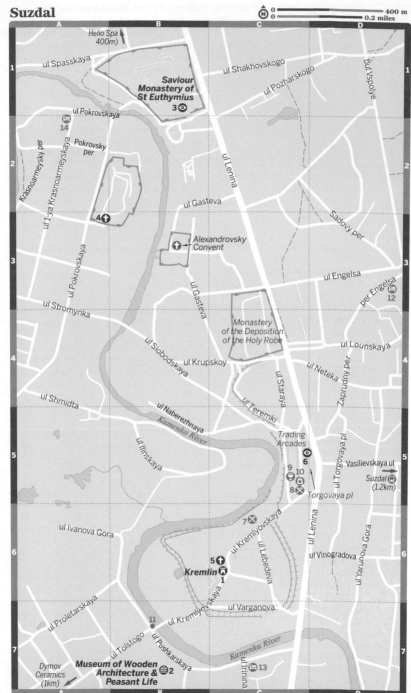

Helio Spa
400m)

ul Spasskaya

**Saviour
Monastery of
St Euthymius**
3 ◎

ul Shakhovskogo

ul Pozharskogo

bul Vspolye

ul Pokrovskaya

14

Krasnoarmeysky per

Pokrovsky
per

ul 1-ya Krasnoarmeyskaya

ul Lenina

ul Gasteva

4 ⊕

**Alexandrovsky
Convent**

ul Pokrovskaya

Sadovy per

ul Engelsa

per Engelsa
12

ul Stromynka

ul Gasteva

**Monastery
of the Deposition
of the Holy Robe**

ul Lounskaya

ul Slobodskaya

ul Krupskoy

ul Neteka

Zap_rudny per

ul Shmidta

ul Naberezhnaya

Kamenka River

ul Teremki

ul Staraya

ul Ilinskaya

Trading
Arcades

6 ◎

9 ⊕
10
8 ✕

Torgovaya pl

ul Torgovaya pl

Vasilievskaya ul →

Suzdal 🚌
(1.2km)

ul Ivanova Gora

7 ✕

ul Kremlyovskaya

ul Lenina

ul Vinogradova

ul Yarunova Gora

5 ⊕
Kremlin 🏛
1

ul Lebedeva

ul Kremlyovskaya

ul Varganova

ul Proletarskaya

11

ul Kremlyovskaya

ul Tolstogo

ul Pushkarskaya

Kamenka River

**Museum of Wooden
Architecture &
Peasant Life**

🏛 2

ul Irinina

13

Dymov
Ceramics
(1km) ↙

Suzdal

✗ EATING & DRINKING

★ **CHAYNAYA** — RUSSIAN €
(Чайная; www.tea-suzdal.ru; ul Kremlyovskaya 10g; mains ₽130-450; ⏰10am-9pm; 🖶) It's hidden behind a kitsch crafts market, but this place is a gem. Russian standards – bliny, *shchi* (cabbage soup), mushroom dishes and pickles – are prominently represented, but it's all the unusual (and rather experimental) items on the menu that make Chaynaya so special. Red-buckwheat pancakes, anyone?

★ **GOSTINY DVOR** — RUSSIAN €€
(Гостиный дворъ; ☎49231-021 190; www. suzdal-dvor.ru; Trading Arcades, Torgovaya pl; mains ₽450-550; ⏰10am-10pm Mon-Thu, 9am-11pm Fri-Sun; 🛜🖶🖶) There are so many things to like about this place: eclectic decor of rustic antiques and warm wood; outside terrace tables offering river views;

hearty Russian dishes (chicken, pike, *pelmeni* dumplings) prepared with modern flair; and friendly, attentive service, to start. Finish up with a tasting set of housemade *medovukha* (honey ale) while the kids amuse themselves in the playroom.

GRAF SUVOROV &
MEAD-TASTING HALL — BEER HALL
(Граф Суворов и зал дегустаций; ☎8-905-734 5404, 49231-20 803; Trading Arcades, Torgovaya pl; tasting menu ₽300-500; ⏰10am-6pm Mon-Fri, to 8pm Sat & Sun) Sit beneath vaulted ceilings and contemplate kitsch murals of Russian military hero Count Suvorov's exploits in the Alps as you make your way through a tasting set (10 samples) of the few dozen varieties of locally produced *medovukha,* a mildly alcoholic honey ale. Flavours also include berry and herb infusions. Located on the back (river) side of the Trading Arcades.

🔒 SHOPPING

DYMOV CERAMICS — CERAMICS, SOUVENIRS
(Дымов керамика; ☎49231-21 190; www. dymovceramic.ru/en; Trading Arcades, Torgovaya pl; ⏰10am-7pm) If you're after souvenirs a level up from the Russo-kitsch found everywhere else, check out these lovely handmade ceramic creations: mugs, tiles, vases, brightly patterned plates and even ceramic ice-cream cones. The shop also sells handmade clothing, toys and foodstuffs, and Dymov offers classes in pottery and tile-making at its suburban **workshop** (Дымов керамика; ☎8-980 752 3555, 495-500 0173; www.dymovceramic.ru/en; Solnechnaya ul 7, Ivanovskoye; 🖶).

MARIA FROLOVA — ARTS & CRAFTS
(Мария Фролова; ☎8-920-936 3063; www. frolmaster-nn.ru) The affable Maria learned the rare and delicate traditional art of filigree embroidery from her grandmother; she often sells her beautiful wares – jewellery and miniature framed needleworks of flowers, birds and rustic patterns – at the **Museum of Wooden Architecture & Peasant Life** (Музей деревянного зодчества и крестьянского быта; www.vladmuseum.ru; ul Pushkarskaya; adult/child ₽300/free; ⏰9am-7pm Sun-Thu, to 9pm Fri & Sat; 🖶). Contact her directly about workshops for adults and

kids in embroidery, woodcarving, lacework and other traditional crafts.

🏃 SPORTS &ACTIVITIES

HELIO SPA   BATHHOUSE

(☎49231-23 939; www.suzdal.heliopark.ru; ul Korovniki 14) Cleanse body and soul with a visit to a Russian *banya*. Beautiful lakeside *bani* can be rented at Helio Park Hotel for ₽1600/1800 per hour on weekdays/weekends (minimum two hours) for up to six to eight people; attendant services, such as a gentle thrashing with *veniki* (birch branches), are available at extra cost. Advance booking is necessary.

BOAT TRIPS   CRUISE

(☎8-916-423 2541; ul Pushkarskaya, at ul Tostogo; adult/child ₽350/free; ⊙hourly noon-7pm) Once an hour a boat takes tourists on a 40-minute cruise up and down the Kamenka River, leaving from the bridge by the Museum of Wooden Architecture (p183). It's a good chance to look at and take pictures of Suzdal's many monasteries and churches from a different perspective. Call to enquire about evening charters. Children under 10 ride for free.

🛏 SLEEPING

★PETROV DOM   GUESTHOUSE €€

(Петров дом; ☎8-919-025 6884; www.petrovdom.ru; per Engelsa 18; r from ₽2000; P🛜🚳) Vlad and Lena offer three nicely furnished rooms in their wooden dacha-style house with a lovely garden on a quiet side street. It's a great option for travellers with children. A sumptuous breakfast costs just ₽200; self-caterers can use the kitchen and garden grill. There's also a private *banya* (hot bath) built by Vlad himself, available for guest rental.

★SURIKOV GUEST HOUSE   GUESTHOUSE €€

(Гостевой дом Суриковых; ☎8-915-752 4950, 49231-21 568; ul Krasnoarmeyskaya 53; d incl breakfast ₽2500; P🛜) This 11-room boutique guesthouse is positioned at a particularly picturesque bend of the Kamenka River across from the walls of the St Euthymius Monastery (p181). It has modestly sized but comfortable rooms equipped with rustic-style furniture (some made by the owner himself) and a Russian restaurant (for guests only) on the 1st floor. Visitors rave about this place.

PUSHKARSKAYA SLOBODA   RESORT €€€

(Пушкарская слобода; ☎49231-23 303; www.pushkarka.ru; ul Lenina 45; d from ₽4950; P❄🛜🖥🚳) This attractive riverside holiday village has everything you might want for a Russian idyll, including accommodation options in traditionally styled log cabins (from ₽7900). It has three restaurants (including a rustic country tavern and a formal dining room) and a spa centre with pool. The staff can also arrange all sorts of tours and classes around Suzdal.

Borodino

Explore

Borodino battlefield was the site of the turning-point Battle of Borodino in 1812, during the Napoleonic Wars. Two hundred years later, the rural site presents a vivid history lesson. Start at the Borodino Museum, which provides a useful overview, then spend the rest of the day exploring the 100-sq-km preserve. If you have your own car, you can see monuments marking the sites of the most ferocious fighting, as well as the headquarters of both the French and Russian armies. If you come by train, you'll probably be limited to the monuments along the road between the train station and the museum (which are many).

The rolling hills around Borodino and Semyonovskoe are largely undeveloped, due to their historic status. Facilities are extremely limited; be sure to bring a picnic lunch.

The Best

➤**Sight** Borodino Field

Top Tip

Over the first weekend in September, the Borodino Field Museum-Preserve hosts a **re-enactment of the historic Battle of Borodino** (День Бородина; www.borodino.ru), complete with Russian and French participants, uniforms and weapons.

Getting There & Away

→**Train** A suburban train leaves from Moscow's Belorussky station to Borodino (₽255, 2½ hours) at 7.51am (with additional trains departing at 9.52am and 11.22am on weekends). There are return trains at 3.29pm and 8.22pm. It's a 4km walk from Borodino station through the battlefield to Borodino Museum.

→**Car** Since the area is rural, visiting by car is more convenient and probably more rewarding. If driving from Moscow, stay on the M1 highway (Minskoe sh) until the Mozhaysk turn-off, 95km beyond the Moscow outer ring road. It's 5km north to Mozhaysk, then 13km west to Borodino village.

Need to Know

→**Area Code** ☑49638

→**Location** Borodino is 130km west of Moscow.

SIGHTS

BORODINO MUSEUM   MUSEUM
(Музей-панорама 'Бородинская битва'; www.borodino.ru; adult/student ₽200/100; ◎10am-6pm Tue-Sun May-Oct, 9am-5pm Tue-Sun Nov-Apr) This museum is an excellent place to start when you arrive in Borodino. You can study an interactive diorama of the Battle of Borodino before setting out to see the site in person. Otherwise, the main exhibits feature original objects from the battle, including uniforms, weapons, documents and personal items. The displays, created by soldiers and their contemporaries, demonstrate the perception of the battle and the Napoleonic Wars at the time. There is also an exhibit dedicated to the WWII battle at this site.

BORODINO FIELD   HISTORIC SITE
(Бородинское поле; www.borodino.ru; museum & all exhibits ₽400) The entire battlefield – more than 100 sq km – is now part of the Borodino Field Museum-Preserve, its vast fields dotted with dozens of memorials to specific divisions and generals. The hilltop monument in front of Borodino Museum is Bagration's tomb (Могила Багратиона),

the grave of Prince Bagration, a heroic Georgian infantry general who was mortally wounded in battle. The front line was roughly along the 4km road from Borodino train station to the museum: you'll see many monuments close to the road.

Further south, a concentration of monuments around Semyonovskoe marks the battle's most frenzied fighting. Here, Bagration's heroic Second Army, opposing far more numerous French forces, was virtually obliterated. Apparently, Russian commander Mikhail Kutuzov deliberately sacrificed Bagration's army to save his larger First Army, opposing lighter French forces in the northern part of the battlefield. Kutuzov's headquarters are marked by an obelisk in the village of Gorky. Another obelisk near Shevardino to the southwest, paid for in 1912 with French donations, marks Napoleon's camp.

The battle scene was recreated during WWII, when the Red Army confronted the Nazis on this very site. Memorials to this battle also dot the fields, and WWII trenches surround the monument to Bagration. Near the train station are two WWII mass graves.

SAVIOUR BORODINO MONASTERY   MUSEUM
(Спасо-Бородинский монастырь; www.borodino.ru; per exhibit ₽50; ◎10am-6pm Wed-Sun May-Oct, 9am-5pm Wed-Sun Nov-Apr) This monastery was built by widows of the Battle of Borodino, and there are several exhibits on the grounds related to the 1812 battle. Leo Tolstoy stayed here when he was writing about the events that transpired nearby for his novel *War and Peace*. Nowadays, the building where he stayed contains an exhibit dedicated to the historical and fictional characters that populate his pages.

EATING

ART CAFE BORODINO   CAFE €€
(Арт-Кафе Бородино; mains ₽400-600) Do not be alarmed if you forgot to pack your picnic. On the grounds of Borodino Museum, there is now a small cafe serving bliny (crepes), *pelmeni* (Russian-style ravioli) and other Russian standards. Fuel up before or after exploring the preserve.

ANTON MARTYNOV / SHUTTERSTOCK ©

1. Abramtsevo Estate Museum-Preserve (p174) Wooden workshop in the grounds of a 19th-century artists' colony.

2. Re-enactment of the Battle of Borodino (p184) The 1812 Battle of Borodino was a turning point in the Napoleonic Wars.

3. Assumption Cathedral (p176), Vladimir Its pre-Mongol architectural legacy dates this church's beginnings to the mid-12th century.

4. Museum of Wooden Architecture & Peasant Life (p183), Sudzal An open-air museum offering a glimpse into the traditional lives of rural people.

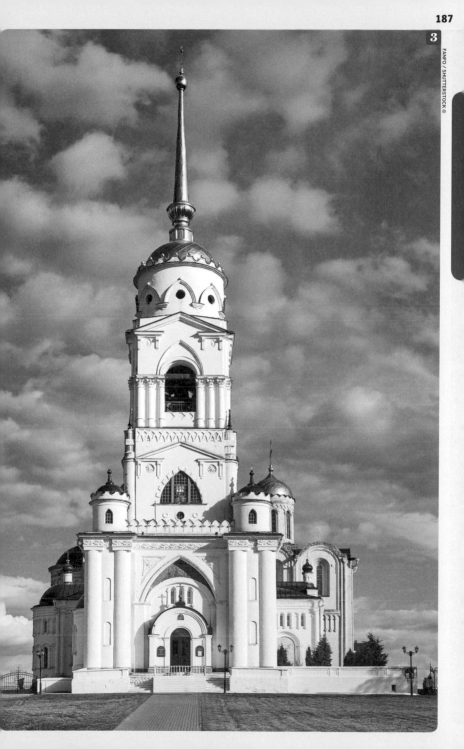

Sleeping

Hotels have become more affordable for foreigners, due to the weak rouble, but Moscow is still not a cheap place to sleep. The city is flush with international luxury hotels, but more affordable hotels are harder to find. Fortunately, a slew of hostels have opened, and more midrange accommodation is now also appearing, usually in the form of 'mini-hotels'.

Hotels

The most visible type of accommodation in Moscow is the palatial four- or five-star hotel, which proliferated in the 2000s. Priced for the business market, they may be prohibitively expensive for some travellers.

At the other end of the spectrum is the Soviet *gostinitsa* (hotel). These old-style institutions have gradually adapted to the needs of the modern traveller, and most have undertaken some degree of renovation. As a result, the quality of rooms can vary widely, and prices usually do too (even within the same hotel).

In recent years, some smaller private hotels have opened in Moscow. Many are housed in historic buildings, and their smaller size means they offer more intimacy than the larger chain hotels. However, the level of comfort and service at these smaller hotels can vary widely.

Mini-Hotels

Privately owned 'mini-hotels' usually occupy a few floors in an apartment building. The rooms have been renovated to comfortably accommodate guests, but the hotel itself (which might have a dozen rooms or less) does not usually offer other facilities. Considering the shortage of midrange options, mini-hotels are among the best-value accommodation in the city.

Hostels

In recent years, dozens of hostels have opened in Moscow, much to the delight of budget travellers. Many have been converted from flats or *kommunalky* (communal apartments), so they are often located in innocuous, unmarked buildings on residential streets. All hostels offer English-speaking staff, internet access, linen, kitchens and laundry facilities. Hostel prices do not usually include breakfast.

Room Rates

Moscow doesn't provide much value for money when it comes to the hospitality industry. Luxury hotels are indeed top notch, but they have prices to match. Expect to pay upwards of ₽10,000 for a night at one of Moscow's top-end hotels. If you can forgo a degree of luxury, you can stay in a classy, comfortable and centrally located hotel for ₽8000 to ₽10,000 for a double.

Midrange travellers can choose from a range of hotels, which offer decent rooms and amenities for ₽3000 to ₽8000 for a double. This wide-ranging category includes some Soviet-era properties that have been upgraded to varying degrees, as well as mini-hotels and three-star Western chains. Budget accommodation is usually dorm-style, although there are a few private rooms available for less than ₽3000.

Accommodation is harder to find during the week than on weekends, and prices are usually lower on Friday and Saturday nights. Seasonal fluctuations are not significant.

Lonely Planet's Top Choices

Hotel National (p194) The ultimate in turn-of-the-century luxury, sitting pretty a few steps from Red Square.

Hotel de Paris (p193) Chic rooms, super service and a vibrant neighbourhood – all at an affordable price.

Godzillas Hostel (p191) A wide range of rooms and services for anyone watching their roubles.

Best By Budget

€

Godzillas Hostel (p191) The long-standing favourite that's more of a travellers' social club than hostel.

Loft Hostel 77 (p193) Friendly service in an urban chic setting.

Jedi Hostel (p194) The force is with you at this fun-loving hostel.

€€

Bulgakov Mini-Hotel (p195) Literary-themed accommodation in an excellent location.

Danilovskaya Hotel (p197) Comfortable accommodation on the grounds of a monastery.

Hotel de Paris (p193) Central, stylish, reasonably priced.

€€€

Hotel Baltschug Kempinski (p197) Ultimate luxury in the historic hotel facing the Kremlin across the river.

Hotel National (p194) Artistic and historic, the National offers a uniquely Moscow experience.

Russo Balt Hotel (p195) Intimate, elegant and indulgent accommodation.

Hotel Grafskiy (p195) A top-notch boutique hotel at the lower end of the price range.

Best Historic Hotels

Hotel Metropol (p191) An architectural marvel operating since 1907 that is steps from Moscow's most historic sites.

Hotel Baltschug Kempinski (p197) The recent renovation adds a modern touch to this 1898 beaut.

Radisson Royal Hotel Ukraina (p195) Housed in a Stalinist skyscraper, this luxury hotel evokes the grandeur of an earlier era.

Four Seasons Moscow (p191) A recreation of a Stalin original, brought up to scratch with top-notch rooms and amenities.

Best Hideaways

Bulgakov Mini-Hotel (p195) Enter through the back door to find this homey place on the Arbat.

Hotel de Paris (p193) Hidden in a side-street courtyard, but still close to the action.

People Business Novinsky (p195) Tucked into the courtyard of a palace dating to 1913.

Seven Hills at Lubyanka (p191) Hidden amid the narrow streets of Kitay Gorod.

Best Unique Lodgings

High Level Hostel (p193) A hostel in a skyscraper in Moskva-City.

Danilovskaya Hotel (p197) You don't have to be a monk to sleep in a monastery.

Hilton Moscow Leningradskaya (p198) Sleep in high Soviet style.

NEED TO KNOW

Price Ranges
The following prices refer to a double room with a private bathroom. Breakfast is not included unless otherwise indicated.

€   less than ₽3000

€€   ₽3000–15,000

€€€   more than ₽15,000

Price Units
Most hotels accept credit cards, but some hostels do not. Many hotels set their prices in dollars or euros. So-called *uslovie yedenitsiy* (often abbreviated as 'y.e.'), or standard units, are usually equivalent to euros. You will always be required to pay in roubles.

Taxes
Prices include the 18% value-added tax (VAT), but not the 5% sales tax, which is charged mainly at luxury hotels.

Reservations
Reservations are highly recommended. Unfortunately, some old-style hotels still charge a reservation fee, usually 20% but sometimes as much as 50% of the first night's tariff.

SLEEPING

Where to Stay

Neighbourhood	For	Against
Kremlin & Kitay Gorod	Close to the city's most prominent historic sites, including the Kremlin and Red Square. Beautiful and atmospheric location. Good transport connections.	Touristy and few inexpensive options. Heavy traffic in city centre.
Tverskoy	Excellent dining and entertainment options. Easy access to Sheremetyevo from Belorussky vokzal.	Can be noisy; heavy traffic.
Presnya	Excellent dining and entertainment options, and lots of green space. Easy access to Sheremetyevo from Belorussky vokzal.	Plenty of traffic and noise on larger roads.
Arbat & Khamovniki	Close to Pushkin Museum of Fine Arts and other art venues. Excellent dining and entertainment options, and lots of green space. Easy access to Vnukovo from Kievsky vokzal.	Metro lines three and four are confusing (due to multiple stations with the same name) and not as convenient as some others.
Zamoskvorechie	Close to Tretyakov Gallery. Excellent dining and entertainment options. Easy access to Domodedovo from Paveletskaya vokzal. Lots of green space.	The area around Paveletskaya is often congested with traffic.
Meshchansky & Basmanny	Plenty of dining and entertainment options in Basmanny. Easy access to Yaroslavsky vokzal (train station); good transport connections.	The area surrounding Taganska-ya pl can be noisy due to heavy traffic and multiple metro lines.

🛏 Kremlin & Kitay Gorod

There is much to be said for staying in the middle of Moscow's most historic neighbourhood, especially if you are here for a short period of time. There are some fancy digs right on Red Square and nearby Teatralnaya pl, as well as some more affordable places to stay in Kitay Gorod.

⭐HOTEL METROPOL   HISTORIC HOTEL €€

Map p271 (📞499-501 7800; www.metropol-moscow.ru; Teatralny proezd 1/4; r from ₽10,000; ⊖❄🛜❄; Ⓜ Teatralnaya) Nothing short of an art nouveau masterpiece, the 1907 Metropol brings an artistic, historic touch to every nook and cranny, from the spectacular exterior to the grand lobby and the individually decorated (but small) rooms. The breakfast buffet (₽2250) is quite an affair, with an extravagant feast served under the restaurant's gorgeous stained-glass ceiling.

KITAY-GOROD HOTEL   HOTEL €€

Map p271 (Отель Китай-Город; 📞495-991 9971; www.otel-kg.ru; Lubyansky proezd 25; s ₽2900-6500, d ₽3700-8000; ❄🛜; Ⓜ Kitay-Gorod) A rare chance for budget-conscious travellers to stay this close to Red Square, with easy access to the metro and many nearby restaurants. Forty-six small but comfortable rooms are situated on two floors of this residential building. The location can be noisy: it's worth requesting air-con as you'll want to keep your windows closed. Prices are lower on weekends.

SEVEN HILLS AT LUBYANKA   HOTEL €€

Map p271 (Seven Hills на Лубянке; 📞495-606 7091; www.sevenhillshotels.ru; Bol Cherkassky per 4, bldg 1; s/d from ₽3700/5900; ❄🛜; Ⓜ Lubyanka) It feels a little sketchy when you enter through the courtyard, off a side street in the heart of Kitay Gorod. The surrounding buildings are rather decrepit, but the interior of this mini-hotel is fresh, with 17 simple rooms on the first two floors. It's nothing fancy, but you'll find acceptable, Ikea-style furnishings, high ceilings and plenty of natural light.

Breakfast (₽300) is served in the rooms.

FOUR SEASONS MOSCOW   HISTORIC HOTEL €€€

Map p271 (📞499-277 7100; www.fourseasons.com; Okhotny ryad 2; r from ₽27,000; ❄🛜❄🛜; Ⓜ Okhotny Ryad) Long a fixture on the Moscow skyline, the infamous Hotel Moskva was demolished in 2003, but Four Seasons reconstructed the old exterior, complete with architectural quirks. The updated interior, of course, is contemporary and classy, with over 200 luxurious rooms and suites, as well as a fancy spa and a glass-roofed swimming pool.

The story goes that Stalin was shown two possible designs for the Hotel Moskva on Manezhnaya pl. Not realising they were alternatives, he approved both. The builders did not dare point out his error, and so built half the hotel in constructivist style and half in Stalinist style. The incongruous result became a familiar and beloved feature of the Moscow landscape, even gracing the label of Stolichnaya vodka bottles.

🛏 Tverskoy

Tverskoy has the highest concentration of luxury hotels in the whole of Moscow, but curiously there are also many good hostels around even prestigious areas. Finding a midrange hotel can be much more problematic, though not impossible. Note that many hotels offer large discounts over weekends.

GODZILLAS HOSTEL   HOSTEL €

Map p274 (📞495-699 4223; www.godzillashostel.com; Bolshoy Karetny per 6; dm ₽700-950, s/d ₽2200/2800; ❄@🛜; Ⓜ Tsvetnoy Bulvar) Tried and true, Godzillas is Moscow's best-known hostel, with dozens of beds spread out over four floors. The rooms come in various sizes, but they are all spacious and light-filled and painted in different colours. To cater to the many guests, there are bathroom facilities on each floor, three kitchens and a big living room with satellite TV.

BOLSHOI HOSTEL   HOSTEL €

Map p274 (📞8-926-135 4687; www.hostelbolshoi.ru; ul Petrovskiye Linii 1; dm from ₽700; Ⓜ Trubnaya) It might be just a hostel – bunk beds, shared showers and all that – but the location is indeed five-star, amid boutiques, fancy restaurants and luxury hotels in the city's ritziest district. This new establishment, with circa 50 beds and a large kitchen area, occupies a former communal flat in a stately 19th-century residential building.

CHOCOLATE HOSTEL   HOSTEL €

Map p274 (📞8-910-446 1778; www.chocohostel.com; Degtyarny per 15, apt 4; dm ₽600-700, tw/tr

₽2600/3300; @🛜; MPushkinskaya) Chocolate lovers rejoice – this charming hostel will soothe your craving. Bring your favourite brand from home for their collection. In return you'll get simple, friendly accommodation – colourfully painted rooms with metal furniture and old-style parquet floors. Bonus: bikes available for rent!

GUEST HOUSE AMELIE GUESTHOUSE €€

Map p274 (📞495-650 1789; www.hotel-amelie. ru; Strastnoy bul 4, str 3, apt 17; r from ₽5000; 🛜; MChekhovskaya) Amelie benefits from its superb location right by Pushkinskaya pl – it's unlikely you will find a room much cheaper than this in the vicinity, and it's a very nicely furnished room, too! On the downside, the hotel is a converted apartment, which means shared bathrooms and an unmarked entrance located on per Kozitsky.

Once you find this lane, look out for the entrance in the building marked as per Kozitsky 3. Dial 17 and they will let you in.

GOLDEN APPLE BOUTIQUE HOTEL €€

Map p274 (📞495-980 7000; www.golden apple.ru; ul Malaya Dmitrovka 11; d from ₽5100; ⊜❄🛜; MPushkinskaya) A classical edifice fronts the street, but the interior is sleek and sophisticated. The rooms are decorated in a minimalist, modern style – subdued whites and greys punctuated by contrasting coloured drapes and funky light fixtures. Comfort is paramount, with no skimping on luxuries such as heated bathroom floors and down-filled duvets.

PUSHKIN HOTEL HOTEL €€

Map p274 (Отель Пушкин; 📞495-201 0222; http://otel-pushkin.ru; Nastasyinsky per 5 1; r from ₽4500; ❄🛜; MPushkinskaya) Just off the eponymous square, this hotel strives to fuse 19th-century style with the modern perception of comfort. We'd call it plush, if not for the tiny, B&B-style reception area. There is a restaurant on the premises, but no need to use it since the area is packed with great places to eat and drink.

ARARAT PARK HYATT HOTEL €€€

Map p274 (📞495-783 1234; www.moscow.park. hyatt.com; ul Neglinnaya 4; r from ₽20,000; ⊜❄🛜❄; MTeatralnaya) This deluxe hotel is an archetype of contemporary design: its glass-and-marble facade is sleek and stunning, yet blends effortlessly with the classical and baroque buildings in the surrounding area. The graceful, modern appearance extends inside to the atrium-style lobby and the luxurious rooms. Guests enjoy every

---

SERVICED APARTMENTS

Some entrepreneurial Muscovites rent out apartments on a short-term basis. Flats are equipped with kitchens and laundry facilities, and they almost always offer wi-fi access. The rental agency usually makes arrangements for the flat to be cleaned every day or every few days. Often, a good-sized flat is available for the price of a hotel room, or less. It is an ideal solution for families or travellers in a small group.

Prices for apartments start at around ₽5000 per night. Expect to pay more for fully renovated, Western-style apartments. Although there are usually discounts for longer stays, they are not significant, so these services are not ideal for long-term renters.

➜ **Moscow Suites** (📞495-233 6429; www.moscowsuites.ru; studios from US$100; 🛜) Slick apartments in central locations on Tverskaya or Novy Arbat. Airport pick-up and visa support are included in the price.

➜ **Intermark Hospitality** (📞495-221 8922; www.intermarksa.ru; 1-/2-room apt from ₽5800/6800; 🛜) Catering mostly to business travellers, Intermark offers four-star accommodation in the city centre.

➜ **Enjoy Moscow** (📞8-916-976 4807; www.enjoymoscow.com; apt from US$120; 🛜) Has a range of apartments in the Tverskoy district. Apartments vary in size and decor, but the company provides responsive, reliable service.

➜ **HOFA** (📞8-911-766 5464; www.hofa.ru; s/d from €33/52, apt €44-67; 🛜) Authentic (and affordable) stays in a Russian family's apartment (with or without the family).

➜ **Moscow4rent.com** (📞495-225 5405; www.moscow4rent.com; studios from US$83) Centrally located flats, with internet, satellite TV and unlimited international phone calls.

imaginable amenity, and the service is top-notch (twice-daily housekeeping!).

HOTEL SAVOY
BOUTIQUE HOTEL €€€

Map p274 (Отель Савой; ☑495-620 8500; www.savoy.ru; ul Rozhdestvenka 3; r from ₽13,000; ⊛✻🔊🖳; ⓂLubyanka) Built in 1912, the Savoy maintains an atmosphere of tsarist-era privilege for its guests, and is more intimate and affordable than other luxury hotels. All rooms are equipped with marble bathrooms and Italian fittings and furnishings. The state-of-the-art health club includes a glass-domed 20m swimming pool, complete with geysers and cascades to refresh tired bodies.

🛏 Presnya

The Presnya neighbourhood offers loads of accommodation options in all price ranges. Inner Presnya is an excellent home base, with easy access to sights, restaurants, nightlife and transportation. The area around Patriarch's Ponds (p106) is particularly atmospheric, while Belorussky station (p245) provides easy access to Sheremetyevo airport. The outer regions of Presnya are not quite as attractive, although there is some appeal to staying in the skyscrapers of the Moscow International Business Centre (p246).

★LOFT HOSTEL 77
HOSTEL €

Map p278 (☑499-110 4228; www.hostel-77.com; Bldg 3a, Maly Gnezdnikovsky per 9; dm ₽1000-1400; 🔊; ⓂPushkinskaya) This sweet spot offers stylish dorm rooms, fully equipped with lockers, individual lights, orthopaedic mattresses and privacy curtains. Exposed brick walls and leather furniture create an attractive shabby-chic atmosphere. Multilingual staff and a super-central locale are added pluses. The only drawback is the lack of a kitchen, but the surrounding streets are packed with eateries.

HIGH LEVEL HOSTEL
HOSTEL €

(☑+87-963-757 9533; www.hostelhl.ru; 43rd fl, bldg 2, Presnenskaya nab 6, Imperia Tower; dm ₽1500-1700, d ₽3800; ✻🔊; ⓂDelovoy Tsentr) Located 170m above the city, this place claims to be the world's first and only sky-scraper hostel. What does this mean for you? An incredible panoramic city view from the common area. Rooms are furnished with sturdy wooden bunks, desks and lockers. Service is excellent, with breakfast and laundry included in the price.

The location in the Moscow International Business Centre (p246) is not the most convenient, but it's certainly a novelty. The metro will whisk you to the centre in three or four stops.

FRESH HOSTEL ARBAT
HOSTEL €

Map p278 (☑8-967-037 1314; www.hostelfresh.ru; Merzlyakovsky per 16; dm ₽640-690, d from ₽2800; ✻@🔊; ⓂArbatskaya) This quiet, well-hidden gem near the Arbat is clean and cosy with a great air-conditioned kitchen/hang-out area. It offers eight- and 10-bed dorms, with 50 beds in total. Look for the distinctive 'F' in the courtyard and get the door code before showing up.

★HOTEL DE PARIS
BOUTIQUE HOTEL €€

Map p278 (☑495-777 0052; www.cityhotelgroup.ru; Bldg 3, Bolshaya Bronnaya ul 23; d from ₽6800; 🅿✻🔊; ⓂPushkinskaya) Steps from the hustle and bustle of Tverskaya, this is a delightfully stylish hotel tucked into a quiet courtyard off the Boulevard Ring. Situated on the lower floors, the rooms do not get much natural light, but they feature king-sized beds, whirlpool tubs and elegant design. Service is consistently friendly. Prices drop on weekends, offering terrific value.

MARCO POLO PRESNJA
HOTEL €€

Map p278 (Марко Поло Пресня; ☑495-660 0606; www.presnja.ru; Spiridonevsky per 9; d from ₽6800; ✻🔊; ⓂMayakovskaya) If you could choose your best location – any location in the whole city – it might just be a quiet, leafy side street in the midst of Moscow's best restaurants. If that's what you chose, look no further. This place has a bit of that old-style institutional feel, but it's comfortable enough. And it's great value for your hard-earned cash.

HOTEL GENTALION
BOUTIQUE HOTEL €€

Map p278 (☑495-926 7900; www.hotelgentalion.ru; Bldg 1, 1ya-Brestskaya ul 38; s/d from ₽8500/9500) This elegant, old-fashioned hotel has a few things going for it – its ornate marble lobby, complete with crystal chandelier, and its central location, convenient to Belorusskaya station (and train to Sheremetyevo airport). The rooms are rather pedestrian, but comfortable enough. Service is accommodating. Breakfast is included but meagre.

KEY ELEMENT HOTEL
HOTEL €€

Map p278 (Отель Элемент; ☑495-988 0064; www.key-element.ru; Bldg 5, Bolshaya Nikitskaya ul 24/1; d ₽3800-4500; ❋ 🛜; Ⓜ Arbatskaya) The location on trendy Bolshaya Nikitskaya is prime, and prices are unbeatable, so you'll forgive the side-street entrance and the fact that rooms can be rented by the hour. It's actually a perfectly respectable place, with spotless rooms, pleasant decor and helpful staff. The cheapest rooms are tiny, so unless you're travelling solo, you'll probably want to upgrade.

ARBAT HOUSE HOTEL
HOTEL €€

Map p278 (Отель Арбат Хаус; ☑495-695 5136, 495-697 0864; www.arbat-house.com; Skatertny per 13; d from ₽3000; ❋ 🛜; Ⓜ Arbatskaya) The Arbat House is popular with tour groups and business travellers, who appreciate the decent price and quaint location. It is not all that close to the Arbat, but tucked into a quiet residential street surrounded by embassies. The rooms are small but comfortable places to crash.

PEKING HOTEL
HOTEL €€

Map p278 (Гостиница Пекин; ☑495-650 0900; www.hotelpeking.ru; Bolshaya Sadovaya ul 5/1; r from ₽7600; ❋ 🛜; Ⓜ Mayakovskaya) Towering over Triumfalnaya pl, this Stalinist building is blessed with high ceilings, parquet floors and a marble staircase. The rooms vary, but they have all been renovated in attractive jewel tones with relatively modern furniture. But the place can't shake its Soviet mood: sour reception staff really put a damper on things.

SEVEN HILLS NA BRESTSKOY
HOTEL €€

Map p278 (Seven Hills на Брестской; ☑495-790 7905; www.sevenhillshotels.ru; 1-ya Brestskaya ul 44; d from ₽6000; ❋ 🛜; Ⓜ Belorusskaya) This solid affordable option is perfectly situated for travellers who want easy access to Belorussky station (p245) and Sheremetyevo airport. Nineteen renovated rooms are furnished in a simple, contemporary fashion. Street noise can be an issue and the included breakfast is skimpy, but it's a suitable, comfortable base for exploring the city.

★ HOTEL NATIONAL
HISTORIC HOTEL €€€

Map p278 (☑495-258 7000; www.national.ru; Mokhovaya ul 15/1; d with/without Kremlin views from ₽14,600/9700; ❋ 🛜; Ⓜ Okhotny Ryad) Now operated by Starwood Resorts, this 1903 beauty occupies a prime location at the base of Tverskaya ul, just across from Alexander Garden. As such, some rooms have magnificent views of the Kremlin (worth the extra roubles). Original artwork lines the walls and antique-style furnishings grace the premises. The rooms themselves are classically luxurious.

NIKITSKAYA HOTEL
BOUTIQUE HOTEL €€€

Map p278 (Гостиница Никитская; ☑495-933 5001; www.assambleya-hotels.ru; Bolshaya Nikitskaya ul 12; s/d ₽10,900/12,900; ❋ 🛜; Ⓜ Okhotny Ryad) If you like small hotels in quaint neighbourhoods you'll love the Nikitskaya. While the building and rooms are spacious and perfectly maintained, the hotel preserves an old-fashioned atmosphere of cosiness and comfort. And you can't beat the location, amidst the excellent restaurants and grand architecture of Bolshaya Nikitskaya. Breakfast (₽500) is served in the popular attached restaurant, Ugolyok (p111).

Despite its superb location and Russian charm, we can't help feeling that this place is overpriced, unless you can take advantage of the special offers that are available at weekends and other low-occupancy times.

🛏 Arbat & Khamovniki

Arbat and Khamovniki are both lively neighbourhoods with plenty of great options for dining and drinking. Arbat is sort of a hub for budget accommodation, with several hostels around or near the pedestrian street.

JEDI HOSTEL
HOSTEL €

Map p276 (☑929-681 0041; http://jedihostel. com; 4th fl, 2-y Smolensky per 1/4; dm/d from US$11/40; ❋ @ 🛜; Ⓜ Smolenskaya) This place exudes (and requires) good vibes, with its wacky and wonderful mural-painted walls and pillow-strewn 'lounge zone'. Dorm beds are actually little 'pods' with shades that ensure complete privacy. Lockers, kitchen and laundry facilities are available. Get the door code before you show up.

HOSTEL RUS
HOSTEL €

Map p276 (Хостел Рус; ☑8-905-588 0058, 495-691 5577; www.arbathostelrus.ru; ul Arbat 11; dm ₽550-950, q ₽3200; ⊖ @ 🛜 🚹; Ⓜ Arbatskaya) The best part of this friendly place is the wide-open, spacious common area and kitchen, painted in bold colours. Clean dorm rooms (four to 10 beds) are located on two floors. If you want to experience old-fashioned communal living, ask for one of the upstairs rooms, which are part of an unofficial 'Museum of Soviet Life'.

Enter the courtyard from Starokonnyushenny per and look for the sign.

BEAR HOSTEL ON ARBAT HOSTEL €

Map p276 (☑495-649 6736; Bolshaya Molchanovka ul 23; dm ₽750-1500, tw ₽4000; ❄@🛜; MArbatskaya) Remove your shoes before entering this spotless, efficiently run hostel. Don't worry if you forgot your *tapochki* (slippers); you can buy some from the vending machine here. You can also buy a toothbrush, underwear and breakfast-in-a-box. Prices vary according to room size (two to 10 beds). The place is rather soulless but there are no surprises.

★BULGAKOV MINI-HOTEL HOTEL €€

Map p276 (☑495-229 8018; www.bulgakovhotel. com; ul Arbat 49; s/d from ₽3600/4000; ❄@🛜; MSmolenskaya) The classy rooms, graced with high ceilings and *Master and Margarita* inspired art, are as good as it gets in Moscow for this price, especially considering the primo location. The bathrooms are tiny but they are private. Enter the courtyard from Plotnikov per and use entrance No 2.

★HOTEL GRAFSKIY BOUTIQUE HOTEL €€

Map p281 (Отель Графский; ☑499-677 5727; www.grafskiyhotel.ru; Bldg 5, ul I va Tolstogo 23; s ₽6000-8000, d ₽7700-9000; ❄❄🛜; MPark Kultury) Live next door to Leo Tolstoy (p132) at this new boutique hotel, in a building dating from 1866. Both service and style are simple but quite delightful. Some of the 38 rooms have exposed brick walls or loft-style ceilings. Outside the Garden Ring, this neighbourhood is still pretty lively, with a number of restaurants and bars in the immediate vicinity.

MERCURE ARBAT HOTEL BOUTIQUE HOTEL €€

Map p276 (Гостиница Меркурий Арбат; ☑495-225 0025; www.mercure.com; Smolenskaya pl 6; r from ₽6200, ❄❄🛜, MSmolenskaya) We're charmed by this sweet and stylish hotel. Rooms are attractive and rather plush to boot. The most affordable ones have two twins or one queen-size bed, plus work space, flat-screen TVs and chic bathrooms with basin sinks. It's surprisingly quiet for its location right on the Garden Ring. Excellent value, especially on weekends. You'll pay extra for the big buffet breakfast.

BLUES HOTEL BOUTIQUE HOTEL €€

Map p281 (☑495-961 1161; www.blues-hotel.ru; ul Dovatora 8; s/d from ₽7000/8000; ❄❄🛜; MSportivnaya) This boutique hotel is perhaps overpriced for the location (five metro stops to Red Square), but it's only a few blocks from Novodevichy, with several worthwhile restaurants in the vicinity. Otherwise, this friendly place is a gem, offering stylish, spotless rooms with king-sized beds and flat-screen TVs. Prices include breakfast. Discounts available on weekends.

ARBAT HOTEL HOTEL €€

Map p276 (Гостиница Арбат; ☑499-271 2801; http://arbat.president-hotel.ru; Plotnikov per 12; d from ₽8500; P❄❄🛜; MSmolenskaya) The location is the selling point here. On a quiet residential street, just steps from the Arbat, the neighbourhood offers both convenience and character. The hotel itself is pretty standard fare, but the 104 rooms are fine and service is friendly. Prices include breakfast.

PEOPLE BUSINESS NOVINSKY HOTEL €€

Map p276 (☑495-363 4580; www.hotel-people. ru; Novinsky bul 11; d ₽3500-3900, without bathroom from ₽2500; ❄@🛜; MSmolenskaya) This affordable option occupies three wings in a stately neoclassical palace on the Garden Ring. Rooms are small and sparse and the place is noisy, but the sunlit, modern rooms represent rare good value in Moscow. Service is exceptionally friendly.

★RUSSO BALT HOTEL BOUTIQUE HOTEL €€€

Map p276 (☑495-645 3873; www.russo-balthotel. com; Gogolevsky bul 31; s ₽13,500-15,000, d ₽15,400-16,900; ❄@🛜; MArbatskaya) With 15 rooms in an exquisite art deco building, the Russo Balt is as intimate and elegant as it gets in Moscow. Standard rooms are on the small side, but the whole place is beautifully decorated with period furnishings and original artwork, with the utmost attention to detail. Highly recommended.

RADISSON ROYAL HOTEL UKRAINA HISTORIC HOTEL €€€

(Гостиница Украина; ☑495-221 5555; www. radissonblu.com; Kutuzovsky pr 2/1; r from ₽11,700; ❄❄🛜❄; MKievskaya) Housed in one of Stalin's 'Seven Sisters', this bombastic beauty sits majestically on the banks of the Moscow River facing the White House. It has retained its old-fashioned ostentation, with crystal chandeliers, polished marble and a ceiling fresco in the lobby. Heavy drapes, textured wallpaper and reproduction antiques give the guest rooms a similar atmosphere – with all the modern amenities.

🛏 Zamoskvorechie

Many travellers choose Zamoskvorechie as a base because of its laid-back character and easy access to the centre. Although it really boasts only one luxury hotel, the district has a selection of midrange and budget options.

THREE PENGUINS
HOSTEL €

Map p282 (Три Пингвина; ☑8-910-446 1778; www.3penguins.ru; Pyatnitskaya ul 20, str 2; dm/d ₽750/₽2600; 🛜; ⓂNovokuznetskaya) This very small hostel is located in a converted flat with a comfy (we'd even say intimate) common area in the building best identified by Illarion cafe, just off Pyatnitskaya ul. Apart from the dorms, it features four doubles – two regular and two with bunk beds.

The Penguins scores high on friendliness and has a prime location in Zamoskvorechie's busiest area (also convenient for the Kremlin). Numerous cafes and the Tretyakov Gallery are in close proximity.

TROIKA
HOTEL €€

Map p282 (☑495-204 2226; www.hoteltroyka.ru; Sadovnicheskaya ul 5; r from ₽4000; ✴; ⓂNovokuznetskaya) This tourist hotel has a top-notch location across the bridge from Red Square, which makes it great value for money. All rooms are on the 1st floor of an 18th-century building with bare-brick walls and vaulted ceilings typical of that age.

OZERKOVSKAYA HOTEL
BOUTIQUE HOTEL €€

Map p282 (Озерковская гостиница; ☑495-783 5553; www.ozerkhotel.ru; Ozerkovskaya nab 50; s/d incl breakfast from ₽2900/3500; 🌐🛜; ⓂPaveletskaya) This comfy, cosy hotel has only 27 rooms, including three that are tucked up under the mansard roof. The rooms are simply decorated, but parquet floors and comfortable queen-sized beds rank it above the standard post-Soviet fare. Add in attentive service and a central location (convenient for the express train to Domodedovo airport), and you've got an excellent-value accommodation option.

NA KAZACHYEM
HOTEL €€

Map p282 (На Казачьем; ☑495-745 2190; 1-y Kazachy per 4; s/d from ₽7600/8600; 🌐✴🛜🅿; ⓂPolyanka) Set in the historic heart of Zamoskvorechie, Na Kazachyem recreates the atmosphere of an 18th-century estate. The light-filled atrium, bedecked with a crystal chandelier, and 15 classically decorated rooms provide a perfect setting for old-fashioned Russian hospitality. Reduced rates on weekends.

PARK INN SADU
HOTEL €€

Map p282 (☑495-644 4844; www.parkinn.ru; ul Bolshaya Polyanka 17; s/d incl breakfast from ₽6500/7500; ✴🛜; ⓂPolyanka) This very regular branch of the Park Inn chain – think slightly impersonal, predictable comforts – boasts a prime location within walking distance of the Kremlin and the Red October cluster of bars and galleries. Prices fall to a jaw-dropping low in the middle of summer.

MERCURE MOSCOW PAVELETSKAYA
HOTEL €€

Map p282 (☑495-720 5301; www.mercure.com; ul Bakhrushina 11; r from ₽3600; 🛜; ⓂPaveletskaya) This Mercure chain hotel seems to consist entirely of virtues. Convenient for Domodedovo airport trains and close to Paveletskaya metro station, it is a quality hotel with plush rooms (purple colour prevailing), located on a quiet street of portly 19th-century houses, offering four-star comforts for a price that's hard to come by in Moscow.

IBIS BAKHRUSHINA
HOTEL €€

Map p282 (☑495-720 5301; www.ibis.com; ul Bakhrushina 11; d from ₽3200; 🌐🛜; ⓂPaveletskaya) Yes, it's just another IBIS; but in Moscow, knowing exactly what you're getting is a big deal: affordable, comfortable rooms and professional, reliable service. Also convenient for the metro and trains to Domodedovo airport. Spa facilities in the adjacent Mercure hotel are available at extra charge.

WEEKEND INN APARTMENTS
GUESTHOUSE €€

Map p282 (☑495-648 4047; Pyatnitskaya ul 10, str 1; d/tr without bathroom from ₽3900/4500; 🛜; ⓂNovokuznetskaya) A short walk from the Kremlin across the river, this modest establishment occupies two upper floors of a 19th-century building. Rooms are spacious, with whitewashed walls and minimalist design. Shared bathrooms are immaculately clean and there is a common kitchen area, but there's no reason to bother cooking – the neighbourhood is packed with cafes.

DANILOVSKAYA HOTEL HOTEL €€

(Даниловская гостиница; ☑495-954 0503; www.danilovsky.ru; Bul Starodanilovsky per; s/d ₽4400/4900; ✉❄@☎; ⓂTulskaya) Moscow's holiest hotel is on the grounds of the 12th-century monastery of the same name – the exquisite setting comes complete with 18th-century churches and well-maintained gardens. The modern five-storey hotel was built so that nearly all the rooms have a view of the grounds. The recently renovated rooms are simple but clean, and breakfast is modest: no greed, gluttony or sloth here.

WARSAW HOTEL HOTEL €€

Map p282 (Гостиница Варшава; ☑495-238 7701; www.hotelwarsaw.ru; Leninsky pr 2/1; r from ₽7000; ✉❄☎; ⓂOktyabrskaya) In a traffic-ridden square dominated by a giant Lenin statue, but convenient for Gorky Park, this Soviet-era oldie has been fully renovated, as evidenced by the sparkling, space-age lobby adorned with lots of chrome, blue leather furniture and spiderlike light fixtures. The new rooms are decent value for the location. Rooms are about 40% cheaper during weekends.

★HOTEL
BALTSCHUG KEMPINSKI HISTORIC HOTEL €€€

Map p282 (Балчуг Кемпински; ☑495-287 2000; www.kempinski-moscow.com; ul Balchug 1; r with/without view from ₽13,600/12,000; ✉❄☎⌧; ⓂKitay-Gorod, Ploshchad Revolyutsii) If you want to wake up to views of the sun glinting off the Kremlin's golden domes, this luxurious property on the Moscow River is the place for you. It is a historic hotel, built in 1898, with 230 high-ceilinged rooms that are sophisticated and sumptuous in design.

SWISSÔTEL
KRASNYE HOLMY HOTEL €€€

Map p282 (☑495-787 9800; www.moscow. swissotel.com; Kosmodemyanskaya nab 52; s/d ₽17,000/19,800; ✉❄☎⌧; ⓂPaveletskaya) The metallic skyscraper towering over the Moscow River is the swish Swissôtel Krasnye Holmy, named for this little-known neighbourhood of Moscow. Rooms are sumptuous, subtle and spacious. The decor is minimalist: rich, dark hardwood floors and a few modernist paintings, but nothing to detract from the striking city skyline. There is a 20% discount for advance booking.

🛏 Meshchansky & Basmanny

The neighbourhood around Chistye Prudy is one of the nicest areas to stay in the city, with a good choice of both upmarket and midrange hotels, as well as a few nice hostels.

FASOL HOSTEL HOSTEL €

Map p286 (☑495-240 9409; http://fasol.co; Arkhangelsky per 11/16 str 3; dm from ₽900, d with shared bathroom ₽3100; ⓂChistye Prudy) The entrance to this hostel, hidden in the courtyards amid 19th-century apartment blocks, looks unassuming. However, with over 80 beds, this popular and professionally run place is a major-league player. Dorms, sleeping six to eight, are decorated with psychedelic wall paintings; bunk beds come with body-friendly mattresses, curtains and individual lights, allowing guests to enjoy full autonomy.

COMRADE HOSTEL HOSTEL €

Map p286 (☑499-709 8760; www.comrade hostel.com; ul Maroseyka 11; dm/s/d ₽750/2400/2900; ✉@☎; ⓂKitay-Gorod) It's hard to find this tiny place – go into the courtyard and look for entrance No 3, where you might spot a computer-printed sign in the 3rd-floor window. Inside is a great welcoming atmosphere, although the place is usually packed. Ten to 12 beds are squeezed into the dorm rooms, plus there are mattresses on the floor if need be.

There is not really any common space, except the small foyer and kitchen, but everybody seems to get along like comrades.

★BRICK DESIGN HOTEL BOUTIQUE HOTEL €€

Map p286 (☑499-110 2470; www.brickhotel. ru; Myasnitskaya ul 24/7 str 3/4; s/d from ₽6200/7100; ❄☎; ⓂChistye Prudy) Not only is this boutique hotel cosy, thoughtfully designed and very centrally located, it also doubles as an art gallery, with original works by Russian 20th-century conceptualist artists adorning the walls. That's in addition to a very tasteful combination of modern and antique furniture. Visitors also rave about the breakfast, which comes fresh from farms near Moscow.

SRETENSKAYA HOTEL
HOTEL €€

Map p286 (Сретенская гостиница; ☑495-933 5544; www.hotel-sretenskaya.ru; ul Sretenka 15; s/d from ₽4200/5200; ⊜ ❋ @ ☎; Ⓜ Sukharevskaya) Special for its small size and friendly staff, the Sretenskaya boasts a romantic Russian atmosphere. Rooms have high ceilings and tasteful, traditional decor. This place is particularly welcoming in winter, when you can warm your bones in the sauna, or soak up some sun in the tropical 'winter garden'.

GARDEN EMBASSY
HOTEL €€

(☑495-124 4095; http://ge-hotel.com; Botanichesky per 5; s/d from ₽6200/6700; ❋ ☎; Ⓜ Prospekt Mira) In a street lined with foreign embassies, this apartment hotel is indeed an embassy of style, with large and fully equipped apartments facing beautiful Aptekarsky Ogorod. A calming respite from the city.

HILTON MOSCOW LENINGRADSKAYA
HISTORIC HOTEL €€

Map p286 (☑495-627 5550; www.hilton.ru/hotels/hilton-moscow-leningradskaya; Kalanchevskaya ul 21/40; d from ₽6500; ⊜ ❋ ☎; Ⓜ Komsomolskaya) Occupying one of the iconic Stalinist skyscrapers, the old Leningradskaya Hotel is now part of the Hilton empire. The American chain has maintained the Soviet grandiosity in the lobby, but has updated the rooms with contemporary design and state-of-the-art amenities.

This is the most convenient option if you are arriving or departing by train, due to its proximity to three stations. This beauty overlooks Komsomolskaya pl, in all its chaotic, commotion-filled glory.

ELOKHOVSKY HOTEL
HOTEL €€

Map p286 (Отель Елоховский; ☑495-632 2300; www.elohotel.ru; ul Spartakovskaya 24; s/d ₽4500/5300; ❋ ☎; Ⓜ Baumanskaya) Admittedly not very central and occupying the top floor of a shopping arcade, this hotel is nevertheless about the best value for money in Moscow. Rooms are painted in soothing colours, complemented by cityscapes of the world's major cities. The coffee machine in the lobby is available 24 hours. Baumanskaya metro and Yelokhovsky Cathedral are a stone's throw away.

HOTEL SVERCHKOV 8
HOTEL €€

Map p286 (Сверчков 8; ☑495-625 4978; www.sverchkov-8.ru; Sverchkov per 8; s/d from ₽4200/4800; ⊜ ❋ ☎; Ⓜ Chistye Prudy) This tiny 11-room hotel in a graceful 19th-century building is situated on a quiet residential lane. The hallways are lined with plants, and paintings by local artists adorn the walls. Though rooms have old-style bathrooms and faded furniture, this place is a rarity for its intimacy and homely feel.

BENTLEY HOTEL
HOTEL €€

Map p286 (☑495-917 4436; www.bentleyhotel.ru; ul Pokrovka 28; s/d from ₽4900/7000; ⊜ ❋ ☎ ⛲; Ⓜ Kurskaya) Upstairs from a popular American-style diner, Bentley goes all out to make its guests feel right at home. This small hotel is a warm and inviting place, with a dozen spacious and richly decorated rooms. Bonus: guests receive a discount on massages and other services at a nearby spa – the perfect way to recover after a day of sightseeing.

MOSS BOUTIQUE HOTEL
BOUTIQUE HOTEL €€€

Map p286 (☑495 114 5572; www.mosshotel.ru; Krivokolenny per 10 str 4; r from ₽13,800; ❋ ☎; Ⓜ Chistye Prudy) You get to see real moss growing in the elevator shaft of this elegant boutique hotel, with aged wood and black concrete surfaces dominating the interior. There's also a cool, relaxed ambience. Rooms – some really small, others bigger – are all equipped with superbly comfortable beds and formidable music centres that you can connect to your phone.

Understand Moscow

Moscow Today

Nearly three decades into its reign as the capital of the Russian Federation, Moscow has proven itself. In this time the city has weathered economic crises and political transitions, building sprees and demolition derbies, terrorist attacks and festive celebrations. Now – with a stable middle class and a new look to boot – the city has settled into an upbeat but sustainable rhythm. Stalin's words ring true: 'Life has become better, comrades. Life has become more joyous.'

Best on Film

Elena (2011) Winner of a Jury Prize at Cannes, this drama examines the meaning of love, family and class in modern Moscow.

Hipsters (2008) A cult-classic musical about an underground Soviet youth movement.

Moscow Doesn't Believe in Tears (1980) Great chick flick that bagged an Oscar for best foreign-language film.

My Perestroika (2010) An insightful documentary about coming of age during the perestroika era and navigating life in contemporary Moscow.

Night Watch (2004) A fantasy thriller set in modern-day Moscow.

Best in Print

Anna Karenina (Leo Tolstoy; 1877) A legitimate alternative for readers who don't have time for War and Peace.

The Master and Margarita (Mikhail Bulgakov; 1967) The most telling fiction to come out of the Soviet Union.

The Big Green Tent (Ludmila Ulitskaya; 2015) An epic tale of three friends in post-Stalinist Moscow.

A Gentleman in Moscow (Amor Towles; 2016) A former count is placed under house arrest by the fledgling Soviet government, living out his years in the Hotel Metropol.

The Patriots (Sana Krasikov; 2017) A multigenerational family is caught between two countries.

Liveability

When Sergei Sobyanin became mayor of Moscow, he promised a shift in focus – away from big business and huge construction projects towards improving the city for regular-guy residents. Almost a decade down the line, the results are visible. Moscow is gradually but noticeably becoming an easier, cleaner, more pleasant place to live.

Recently, urban development in the centre has focused on parks and pedestrian ways, making it easier to navigate on foot – or even on bike. Indeed, hundreds of kilometres of bike lanes have been painted. The 'My Street' initiative has revitalised the city's pedestrian zones with wider pavements and more trees. Kitay Gorod is being transformed by the creation of Park Zaryadye and improvements to the surrounding streets. The same sort of metamorphosis is expected on ul Volkhonka with the creation of a 'Museum Quarter'.

In 2017 Sobyanin announced his grandest plan yet – the demolition of dilapidated khrushchevki (low-rise Soviet-era housing) and relocation of residents to modern blocks. The housing relocation program would affect some 5000 apartment buildings and 1.6 million people. Residents took to the streets in protest, fearing they would be forced to move to high-rise buildings in far-flung locations (although Sobyanin promised otherwise). The city administration responded by allowing tenants to vote on the fate of their own buildings, and residents of some 4000 blocks voted in favour of relocation. Hopefully this initial victory for the city administration will prove to be a long-term benefit for the many affected residents.

Social Mood

There's something to be said for political stability and financial security. That seems to be the conclusion that many Muscovites have drawn, as they grin and bear the low-grade economic crisis and authoritarian regime that have persisted in recent years.

This is not to say that they are complacent. But after three decades of economic instability and political upheaval, most folks have had enough. They want to concentrate on raising their families and advancing their careers. They are enjoying their new more liveable city, with its many cultural offerings and consumer choices. Of course, their roubles don't go as far as they used to, since the introduction of international sanctions and the devaluation of the rouble in 2014. And they may have their gripes with their president-for-life. But things could be worse. In fact, they *were* worse...

Not all Muscovites are satisfied to sit back and accept politics as usual. In 2017, for the first time in years, a wave of anticorruption protests took place in Moscow (and around the country). With the presidential election in 2018 – and Putin's certain participation – there are bound to be more. But most Muscovites are not in the mood for revolution.

On the contrary. The capital is feeling patriotic. Flag-waving viewers flock to military parades and historical exhibits celebrating Russia's glorious past. In a single day, some 25,000 believers lined up to venerate the relics of St Nicholas at the Cathedral of Christ the Saviour (at least double the number of protesters that took to the streets a few weeks later). And Putin's approval ratings are soaring.

Creative Capital

Despite the conservative mood, Moscow has still managed to become one of Europe's coolest and most creative capitals. Gone are the days when the city was defined by New Russians' excessive displays of wealth. Nowadays, the capital's movers and shakers are the innovators – the artists, architects, designers and chefs – who are shaping the aesthetic and atmosphere of the city.

All around Moscow, industrial spaces are being transformed into buzzing creative centres, with space for art exhibitions, design studios, lectures and live performances. Would-be ruins are turned into hothouses for experimentation and innovation. There is unprecedented opportunity for artists to express themselves and for viewers to witness their work. Meanwhile, boutiques are busting with clothing, jewellery and housewares designed by local fashionistas. Restaurants are experimenting with new ingredients and inventing new ways to serve the staples. The capital continues to surprise and delight anybody who's up for it.

The balance between conservatism and creativity is a tricky one, of course. To paraphrase one young journalist, where is there room for freshness and innovation when all the signs are in the same font and the same colour?

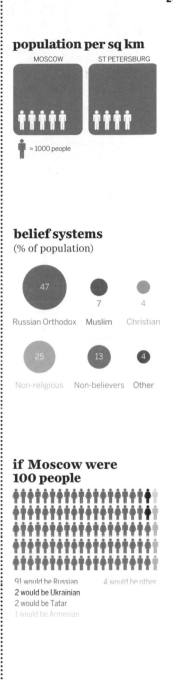

population per sq km

MOSCOW   ST PETERSBURG

≈ 1000 people

belief systems
(% of population)

47 — Russian Orthodox
7 — Muslim
4 — Christian

25 — Non-religious
13 — Non-believers
4 — Other

if Moscow were 100 people

91 would be Russian
2 would be Ukrainian
2 would be Tatar
1 would be Armenian
4 would be other

History

'Come to me, brother, please come to Moscow.' With these words, Yury Dolgoruky invited his allies to a celebratory banquet at the fortification he had erected on Borovitsky Hill, at the confluence of two rivers. The year was 1147. The settlement would prosper, eventually gaining power in the region and establishing itself as the capital of Ancient Rus. Nine centuries later – even as Russia has gone through multiple transformations – it is still ruled from the fortress that crowns Borovitsky Hill.

Medieval Moscow

> Prince Daniil became the first Grand Prince of Moscow at the end of the 13th century. Revered for his humbleness and diplomacy, he was canonised by the Russian Orthodox Church in 1652.

Early Settlement

Moscow began as a trading post, set up by eastern Slav tribes who had migrated eastward from Kyivan Rus. Back in Kyiv, Grand Prince Vladimir I was anxious to secure his claim of sovereignty over all the eastern Slavs. He made his son Yaroslav the regional vicelord, overseeing the collection of tribute and conversion of pagans.

After Vladimir's death, the descendants of Yaroslav inherited the northeastern territories of the realm, where they established a series of towns, fortresses and monasteries that is today known as the Golden Ring.

Political power gradually shifted eastward to these new settlements. During his reign, Grand Prince Vladimir Monomakh appointed his youngest son, Yury Dolgoruky, to look after the region. Legend has it that on his way back to Vladimir from Kyiv, Prince Yury stopped at Moscow. Believing that Moscow's Prince Kuchka had not paid him sufficient homage, Yury put the impudent boyar (high-ranking noble) to death and placed the trading post under his direct rule. Moscow's strategic importance prompted Yury to construct a moat-ringed wooden palisade on the hilltop and install his personal vassal on-site.

With its convenient access to rivers and roads, Moscow soon blossomed into a regional economic centre, attracting traders and artisans to the merchant rows just outside the Kremlin's walls. In the early 13th century, Moscow became the capital of a small, independent principality, though it remained a prize contested by successive generations of boyar princes.

TIMELINE	10th century	1015	1113–25
	Eastern Slav tribes migrate from the Kyivan Rus principality further west, eventually assimilating or displacing the Ugro-Finnic tribes that had previously populated the region.	Vladimir I's realm is divided among his sons, leading to a violent period of family feuds. His son Yaroslav's descendants gain control over the eastern territories.	The Vladimir-Suzdal principality becomes a formidable rival in the medieval Russian realm. Grand Prince Vladimir appoints his son, Yury Dolgoruky, to look after the region.

The Rise of Muscovy

In the 13th century, Eastern Europe was overwhelmed by the marauding Golden Horde, a Mongol-led army of nomadic tribespeople who appeared out of the eastern Eurasian steppes and were led by Chinggis (Genghis) Khaan's grandson, Batu. The ferocity of the Golden Horde raids was unprecedented, and quickly Russia's ruling princes acknowledged the region's new overlord. The Golden Horde's khan would constrain Russian sovereignty for the next two centuries, demanding tribute and allegiance from the Slavs.

The years of Mongol domination coincided with the rise of medieval Muscovy in a marriage of power and money. The Golden Horde was mainly interested in tribute, and Moscow was conveniently situated to monitor the river trade and road traffic. With Mongol backing, Muscovite officials soon emerged as the chief tax collectors in the region.

As Moscow prospered economically, its political fortunes rose as well. Grand Prince Ivan Danilovich earned the moniker of 'Moneybags' *(Kalita)* because of his remarkable revenue-raising abilities. Ivan Kalita used his good relations with the khan to manoeuvre Moscow into a position of dominance in relation to his rival princes. By the middle of the 14th century, Moscow had absorbed its erstwhile patrons, Vladimir and Suzdal.

Soon Moscow became a nemesis rather than a supplicant to the Mongols. In the 1380 Battle of Kulikovo, Moscow's Grand Prince Dmitry, Kalita's grandson, led a coalition of Slav princes to a rare victory over the Golden Horde on the banks of the Don River. He was thereafter immortalised as Dmitry Donskoy. This feat did not break the Mongols, who retaliated by setting Moscow ablaze only two years later. From this time, however, Moscow acted as champion of the Russian cause.

Towards the end of the 15th century, Moscow's ambitions were realised as the once-diminutive duchy evolved into an expanding autocratic state. Under the long reign of Grand Prince Ivan III, the eastern Slav independent principalities were forcibly consolidated into a single territorial entity.

After a seven-year assault, Ivan's army finally subdued the prosperous merchant principality of Novgorod and evicted the Hansa trading league. After Novgorod's fall, the 'gathering of the lands' picked up pace as the young Muscovite state annexed Tver, Vyatka, Ryazan, Smolensk and Pskov.

In 1480 Ivan's army faced down the Mongols at the Ugra River without a fight. Ivan now refused outright to pay tribute or deference to the

The Arbat is one of Moscow's oldest streets, dating to the 15th century. Linguists believe the name comes from the Arabic word *arbad*, which means 'outskirts'. The Arabic word might have entered the Russian language by way of the Crimean Khanate, which was frequently attacking Moscow at this time.

1147	1156	1237–38	1282
Moscow is first mentioned in the historic chronicles when Yury Dolgoruky invites his allies to a banquet there: 'Come to me, brother, please come to Moscow.'	Moscow is fortified with a wooden fence and surrounded by a moat as protection against rival principalities and other attackers from the east.	The Mongols raze the city and kill its governor. Their menacing new presence levels the political playing field in the region, creating an opportunity for a small Muscovite principality.	On the southern outskirts of Moscow, Daniil founds the town's first monastery as a defensive outpost – now the Danilovsky Monastery.

Medieval Sights

....

Kremlin (Kremlin & Kitay Gorod)

....

Kitay Gorod (Kremlin & Kitay Gorod)

....

St Basil's Cathedral (Kremlin & Kitay Gorod)

Golden Horde, and the 200-year Mongol yoke was lifted. A triumphant Ivan had himself crowned 'Ruler of all Russia' in a solemn Byzantine-style ceremony, earning him the moniker Ivan the Great.

Ivan the Terrible

At the time of Ivan the Great's death, the borders of Muscovy stretched from the Baltic region in the west to the Ural Mountains in the east and the Barents Sea in the north. The south was still the domain of hostile steppe tribes of the Golden Horde.

In the 16th century, the Golden Horde fragmented into four Khanates, which continued to raid Russian settlements. At this time, the grandson of Ivan the Great, Ivan IV (the Terrible), led the further expansion and consolidation of the upstart Muscovy state, defeating three out of four Khanates, securing control over the Volga River and opening up a vast wilderness east of the Urals. Ivan was less successful against the Crimean Tatars, who dominated the southern access routes to the Black Sea.

On the home front, the reign of Ivan IV spelt trouble for Moscow. Ivan came to the throne at age three with his mother as regent. Upon reaching adulthood, 13 years later, he was crowned 'Tsar of all the Russias'. (The Russian word 'tsar' is derived from the Latin term 'caesar'.) Ivan's marriage to Anastasia, a member of the Romanov boyar family, was a happy one, unlike the five that followed her early death.

When his beloved Anastasia died, it marked a turning point for Ivan. Believing her to have been poisoned, he started a reign of terror against the ever-intriguing and jealous boyars, earning himself the sobriquet 'the terrible'. Later, in a fit of rage, he even killed his eldest son and heir to the throne.

Ivan suffered from a fused spine and took mercury treatments to ease the intense pain. The cure, however, was worse than the ailment; it gradually made him insane.

The last years of Ivan's reign proved ruinous for Moscow. In 1571 Crimean Tatars torched the city, burning most of it to the ground. Ivan's volatile temperament made matters worse by creating political instability. At one point he vacated the throne and concealed himself in a monastery.

Upon his death, power passed to his feeble-minded son, Fyodor. For a short time, Fyodor's brother-in-law and able prime minister, Boris Godunov, succeeded in restoring order to the realm. By the beginning of the 17th century, however, Boris was dead, Polish invaders occupied the Kremlin, and Russia slipped into a 'Time of Troubles'. Finally, Cossack

In Russian, Ivan IV is called Ivan Grozny, which usually gets translated as 'terrible'. It actually means something like 'dreadfully serious', in reference to the tsar's severity and strictness.

1303	1326	1328	1327–33
Having become a monk before his death, Prince Daniil is buried in the cemetery at Danilovsky Monastery.	Moscow emerges as a political stronghold and religious centre. The head of the Russian episcopate departs Vladimir and moves into the Kremlin.	Grand Prince Ivan I (Kalita) gains the right to collect taxes from other Russian principalities, effectively winning control of the Vladimir-Suzdal principality.	The first stone structures are built within the Kremlin walls, including three elaborate limestone churches and a bell tower, each topped with a single dome.

soldiers relieved Moscow of its uninvited Polish guests and political stability was achieved with the coronation of Mikhail as tsar, inaugurating the Romanov dynasty.

Imperial Moscow

The Spurned Capital

Peter I, known as 'Peter the Great' for his commanding frame (reaching over 2m) and equally commanding victory over the Swedes, dragged Russia kicking and screaming into modern Europe. Peter spent much of his youth in royal residences in the Moscow countryside, organising his playmates in war games. Energetic and inquisitive, he was eager to learn about the outside world. As a boy, he spent hours in Moscow's European district; as a young man, he spent months travelling in the West. In fact, he was Russia's first ruler to venture abroad. Peter briefly shared the throne with his half-brother, before taking sole possession of it in 1696.

Peter wilfully imposed modernisation on Moscow. He ordered the boyars to shave their beards, imported European advisers and craftspeople, and rationalised state administration. He built Moscow's tallest structure, the 90m-high Sukharev Tower, and next to it founded the College of Mathematics and Navigation.

Yet Peter always despised Moscow for its scheming boyars and archaic traditions. Alexander Pushkin later wrote that 'Peter I had no love for Moscow, where, with every step he took, he ran into remembrances of mutinies and executions, inveterate antiquity and the obstinate resistance of superstition and prejudice'. In 1712 he startled the country by announcing the relocation of the capital to a swampland, recently acquired from Sweden in the Great Northern War. St Petersburg would be Russia's 'Window on the West' and everything that Moscow was not – modern, scientific and cultured.

The spurned former capital quickly fell into decline. With the aristocratic elite and administrative staff departing for marshier digs, the population fell by more than a quarter in the first 25 years. The city suffered further from severe fires, a situation exacerbated by Peter's mandate to direct all construction materials to St Petersburg.

In the 1770s Moscow was devastated by an outbreak of bubonic plague, which claimed more than 50,000 lives. It was decreed that the dead had to be buried outside the city limits. Vast cemeteries, including Danilovskoye and Vagankovskoye, were the result. The situation was so desperate that residents went on a riotous looting spree that was violently put down by the army. Empress Catherine II (the Great)

Imperial Sights

Kremlin Armoury (Kremlin & Kitay Gorod)

Cathedral of Christ the Saviour (Arbat & Khamovniki)

Bolshoi Theatre (Tverskoy)

Triumphal Arch (Arbat & Khamovniki)

HISTORY IMPERIAL MOSCOW

In 1682 Peter I was installed as tsar. His half-sister, Sophia Alekseyevna, acted as regent, advising from her hiding place behind the throne. This two-seated throne – complete with a hidden compartment – is on display at the Kremlin Armoury.

1360	1380	1450s	1475–1495
The Kremlin is refortified and expanded. As the small village grows into an urban centre, Grand Prince Dmitry replaces the wooden walls with a limestone edifice.	Grand Prince Dmitry mounts the first successful Russian challenge to Tatar authority, earning his moniker Donskoy after defeating the Tatars in the Battle of Kulikovo on the Don River.	A Russian Orthodox Church is organised. When Constantinople falls to heathen Turks, Moscow is said to be the 'Third Rome', the rightful heir of Christendom.	Ivan III launches a rebuilding effort, importing Italian artisans and masons to construct the Kremlin's thick brick walls and imposing watchtowers.

THE BATTLE OF MOSCOW – 1812

In 1807 Tsar Alexander I negotiated the Treaty of Tilsit. It left Napoleon emperor of the west of Europe and Alexander emperor of the east, united (in theory) against England. The alliance lasted until 1810, when Russia resumed trade with England. A furious Napoleon decided to crush the tsar with his Grand Army of 700,000 – the largest force the world had ever seen for a single military operation.

The vastly outnumbered Russian forces retreated across their own countryside throughout the summer of 1812, scorching the earth in an attempt to deny the French sustenance, and fighting some successful rearguard actions.

Napoleon set his sights on Moscow. In September, with the lack of provisions beginning to bite the French, Russian general Mikhail Kutuzov finally decided to turn and fight at Borodino, 130km from Moscow. The battle was extremely bloody, but inconclusive, with the Russians withdrawing in good order. More than 100,000 soldiers lay dead at the end of a one-day battle.

Before the month was out, Napoleon entered a deserted Moscow. Defiant Muscovites burned down two-thirds of the city rather than see it occupied by the French invaders. Alexander, meanwhile, ignored Napoleon's overtures to negotiate.

With winter coming and supply lines overextended, Napoleon declared victory and retreated. His badly weakened troops stumbled westward out of the city, falling to starvation, disease, bitter cold and Russian snipers. Only one in 20 made it back to the relative safety of Poland. The tsar's army pursued Napoleon all the way to Paris, which Russian forces briefly occupied in 1814.

The Kremlin sat abandoned and empty from 1712 until 1773, when Catherine the Great commissioned a residence there. Construction did not move forward due to lack of funding, but several years later, architect Matvey Kazakov did build the handsome neoclassical Senate building that stands today.

responded to the crisis by ordering a new sanitary code to clean up the urban environment and silencing the Kremlin alarm bell that had set off the riots.

By the turn of the 19th century, Moscow had recovered from its gloom; Peter's exit had not caused a complete rupture. The city retained the title of 'First-Throned Capital' because coronations were held there. When Peter's grandson, Peter III, relieved the nobles of obligatory state service, many returned to Moscow. Moreover, many of the merchants had never left. After the initial shock of losing the capital, their patronage and wealth became visible again throughout the city.

The late 18th century also saw the construction of the first embankments along the Moscow River, which were followed by bridges. Russia's first university and first newspaper were started in Moscow. This new intellectual and literary scene would soon give rise to a nationalist-inspired cultural movement, which would embrace those features of Russia that were distinctly different from the West.

1478–80	1505–08	1508–16	1524
Moscow subdues its rival principalities, and the Russian army defeats the Mongols at the Ugra River. Ivan III is crowned Ruler of all Russia, earning him the moniker 'Ivan the Great'.	Construction within the Kremlin continues, with the erection of the Ivan the Great Bell Tower, which would remain the highest structure in Moscow until the 20th century.	Alevizov moat is built outside the eastern wall of the Kremlin. The area outside the moat – present-day Red Square – is the town's marketplace.	Novodevichy Convent is founded in honour of the conquest of Smolensk 10 years before. The fortress is an important link in the city's southern defence.

Moscow Boom Town

Moscow was feverishly rebuilt in just a few years following the Napoleonic War. Monuments were erected to commemorate Russia's hard-fought victory and Alexander's 'proudest moment'. A Triumphal Arch (p126), inspired by their former French hosts, was placed at the top of Tverskaya ul on the road to St Petersburg, and the immensely grandiose Cathedral of Christ the Saviour, which took almost 50 years to complete, went up along the river embankment outside the Kremlin.

The building frenzy did not stop with national memorials. In the city centre, engineers diverted the Neglinnaya River into an underground canal and created two new urban spaces: the Alexander Garden (p72), running alongside the Kremlin's western wall; and Teatralnaya pl, featuring the glittering Bolshoi Theatre (p88) and later the opulent Hotel Metropol (p191). The rebuilt Manezh, the 180m-long imperial stables, provided a touch of neoclassical grandeur to the scene.

A postwar economic boom changed the city forever. The robust recovery was at first led by the big merchants, long the mainstay of the city's economy. In the 1830s, they organised the Moscow Commodity Exchange. By midcentury, industry began to overtake commerce as the city's economic driving force. Moscow became the hub of a network of railroad construction, connecting the raw materials of the east to the manufacturers of the west. With a steady supply of cotton from Central Asia, Moscow became a leader in the textile industry. By 1890 more than 300 of the city's 660 factories were engaged in cloth production and the city was known as 'Calico Moscow'. While St Petersburg's industrial development was financed largely by foreign capital, Moscow drew upon its own resources. The Moscow Merchant Bank, founded in 1866, was the country's second-largest bank by century's end.

The affluent and self-assured business elite extended its influence over the city. The eclectic tastes of the nouveau riche were reflected in the multiform architectural styles of the mansions, salons and hotels. The business elite eventually secured direct control over the city government, removing the remnants of the old boyar aristocracy. In 1876 Sergei Tretyakov, artful entrepreneur and art patron, started a political trend when he became the first mayor who could not claim noble lineage.

The increase in economic opportunity in the city occurred simultaneously with a decline in agriculture and the emancipation of the serfs. As a result, the city's population surged, mostly driven by an influx of rural job seekers. In 1890 Moscow claimed over one million inhabitants. The population was growing so rapidly that the number increased by another 50% in less than 20 years. Moscow still ranked second to St

Historic Estates

Kolomenskoe

Tsaritsyno

Arkhangelskoe

HISTORY IMPERIAL MOSCOW

Tolstoy's most famous novel, *War and Peace* tells the story of five aristocratic families in the lead-up to the Napoleonic invasion. The author used letters, journals, interviews and other first-hand materials to create the realist masterpiece, which includes some 160 real-life historical characters.

1560	1571	1592	1591–1613
Provoked by the death of his wife, the ever-suspicious Ivan IV commences a reign of terror over the boyars (high-ranking nobles), thus earning him the moniker 'Ivan the Terrible'.	Moscow is burned to the ground by Crimean Tatars. As the city rebuilds, a stone wall is erected around the commercial quarters outside the Kremlin.	An earthen rampart is constructed around the city, punctuated by some 50 towers, marking the city limits at the location of the present-day Garden Ring.	Ivan IV dies with no capable heir, leaving the country in chaos. His death ushers in the so-called 'Time of Troubles', when Russia is ruled by a string of pretenders to the throne.

Shortly after the Napoleonic War, the city's two outer defensive rings were replaced with the tree-lined Boulevard Ring and Garden Ring roads. The Garden Ring became an informal social boundary line: on the inside were the merchants, intellectuals, civil servants and foreigners; on the outside were the factories and dosshouses.

Petersburg in population, but unlike the capital, Moscow was a thoroughly Russian city – its population was 95% ethnic Russian.

By 1900 more than 50% of the city's inhabitants were first-generation peasant migrants. They settled in the factory tenements outside the Garden Ring and south of the river in the Zamoskvorechie district. The influx of indigents overwhelmed the city's meagre social services and affordable accommodation. At the beginning of the 20th century, Moscow's teeming slums were a breeding ground for disease and discontent. The disparity of wealth among the population grew to extremes. Lacking a voice, the city's less fortunate turned an ear to the outlawed radicals.

Red Moscow
Revolution

The tsarist autocracy staggered into the new century. In 1904 the impressionable and irresolute Tsar Nicholas II was talked into declaring war on Japan over some forested land in the Far East. His imperial forces suffered a decisive and embarrassing defeat, touching off a nationwide wave of unrest.

Taking their cue from St Petersburg, Moscow's workers and students staged a series of demonstrations, culminating in the October 1905 general strike, forcing political concessions from a reluctant Nicholas. In December the attempt by city authorities to arrest leading radicals provoked a new round of confrontation, which ended in a night of bloodshed on hastily erected barricades in the city's Presnya district.

Vladimir Ilych Ulyanov (Lenin) later called the failed 1905 Revolution the 'dress rehearsal for 1917'. He had vowed that next time Russia's rulers would not escape the revolutionary scourge. Exhausted by three years of fighting in WWI, the tsarist autocracy meekly succumbed to a mob of St Petersburg workers in February 1917. Unwilling to end the war and unable to restore order, the provisional government was itself overthrown in a bloodless palace coup, orchestrated by Lenin's Bolshevik Party.

In Moscow, regime change was not so easy – a week of street fighting left more than 1000 dead. Radical socialism had come to power in Russia.

Fearing a German assault, Lenin ordered that the capital return to Moscow. In March 1918 he set up shop in the Kremlin and the new Soviet government expropriated the nicer city hotels and townhouses to conduct affairs. The move unleashed a steady stream of favour-seeking sycophants on the city. The new communist-run city government

1601–03	1610–12	1613	1600s
Russia suffers from widespread famine, which kills up to two-thirds of the population. Over 100,000 people are buried in mass graves around Moscow.	The army of the Polish-Lithuanian Commonwealth occupies Moscow, until the arrival of a Cossack army, led by Dmitry Pozharsky and Kuzma Minin, which expels the Poles.	The Zemsky Sobor, a sort of parliament, elects Mikhail Romanov tsar. He is rescued from his exile in Kostroma and crowned, inaugurating the Romanov dynasty.	In the first half of the 17th century, the capital's population doubles to approximately 200,000 as settlements grow up outside the ramparts.

CHECK YOUR CALENDAR

For hundreds of years Russia was out of sync with the West. Until 1700 Russia dated its years from 'creation', which was determined to be approximately 5508 years before the birth of Christ. So at that time, the year 1700 was considered the year 7208 in Russia. Peter the Great – westward-looking as he was – instituted a reform to date the years from the birth of Christ, as they did in the rest of Europe.

Things got complicated again in the 18th century, when most of Europe abandoned the Julian calendar in favour of the Gregorian calendar, and Russia did not follow suit. By 1917 Russian dates were 13 days out of sync with European dates, which explains how the October Revolution could have taken place on 7 November.

Finally, the all-powerful Soviet regime made the necessary leap. The last day of January 1918 was followed by 14 February 1918. All dates since 1918 have been identical to dates in the West.

We try to use dates corresponding to the current Gregorian calendar that is used worldwide. However, even history is not always straightforward, as other accounts may employ the calendars that were the convention at that time. Tell *that* to your history professor.

authorised the redistribution of housing space, as scores of thousands of workers upgraded to the dispossessed digs of the bourgeoisie.

The revolution and ensuing civil war, however, took its toll on Moscow. Political turmoil fostered an economic crisis. In 1921 the city's |factories were operating at only 10% of their prewar levels of production. Food and fuel were in short supply. Hunger and disease stalked the darkened city. The population dropped precipitously from two million in 1917 to just one million in 1920. Wearied workers returned to their villages in search of respite, while the old elite packed up its belongings and moved beyond the reach of a vengeful new regime.

Stalin's Moscow

In May 1922 Lenin suffered the first of a series of paralysing strokes that removed him from effective control of the Party and government. He died, aged 53, in January 1924. His embalmed remains were put on display in Moscow, St Petersburg was renamed Leningrad in his honour, and a personality cult was built around him – all orchestrated by Josef Stalin.

The most unlikely of successors, Stalin outwitted his rivals and manoeuvred himself into the top post of the Communist Party. Ever-paranoid, Stalin later launched a reign of terror against his former

Many of Moscow's 'historic' sights are new buildings modelled after structures that were destroyed in the past. Kazan Cathedral and the Cathedral of Christ the Saviour were built in the 1990s, while the Great Wooden Palace at Kolomenskoe and the Great Palace at Tsaritsyno are both 21st-century constructions.

1654–62	1682	1712	1700s
Wars with Poland and Sweden spur financial crisis. The production of copper coinage causes further economic hardship, sparking a massive uprising of 10,000 people on the streets.	A power struggle between two clans stirs up unrest among the Kremlin guard, which spreads to the Moscow mobs. Sophia Alekseyevna is installed as regent for her two brothers.	Peter I (the Great) surprises the country by moving the Russian capital from Moscow to St Petersburg.	Moscow falls into decline in the first half of the century, when bureaucrats and aristocrats relocate to the north. By mid-century the population has dropped to 130,000.

party rivals, which eventually consumed nearly the entire first generation of Soviet officialdom. Hundreds of thousands of Muscovites were systematically executed and secretly interred on the ancient grounds of the old monasteries.

In the early 1930s, Stalin launched Soviet Russia on a hell-bent industrialisation campaign. The campaign cost millions of lives, but by 1939 only the USA and Germany had higher levels of industrial output. Moscow set the pace for this rapid development. Political prisoners became slave labourers. The building of the Moscow-Volga Canal was overseen by the secret police, who forced several hundred thousand 'class enemies' to dig the 125km-long ditch.

The brutal tactics employed by the state to collectivise the countryside created a new wave of peasant immigrants who flooded into Moscow. Around the city, work camps and bare barracks were erected to shelter the huddling hordes who shouldered Stalin's industrial revolution. At the other end, Moscow also became a centre of a heavily subsidised military industry, whose engineers and technicians enjoyed a larger slice of the proletarian pie. The party elite, meanwhile, moved into new spacious accommodation such as the Dom na Naberezhnoy (p145), on the embankment opposite the Kremlin.

Under Stalin, a comprehensive urban plan was devised for Moscow. On paper, it appeared as a neatly organised garden city; unfortunately, it was implemented with a sledgehammer. Historic cathedrals and bell towers were demolished in the middle of the night.

New monuments marking the epochal transition to socialism went up in place of the old. The first line of the marble-bedecked metro was completed in 1935. The enormous Cathedral of Christ the Saviour was razed with the expectation of erecting the world's tallest building, upon which would stand an exalted 90m statute of Lenin. This scheme was later abandoned and the foundation hole instead became the world's biggest municipal swimming pool. Broad thoroughfares were created and neo-Gothic skyscrapers girded the city's outer ring.

In the 1940s the medieval Zaryadye district in Kitay Gorod was razed to make room for Stalin's 'Eighth Sister'. The skyscraper was never built, and the foundation eventually became the base of the gargantuan Hotel Rossiya (now demolished). The latest development on this plot is the much-anticipated Park Zaryadye.

Post-Stalinist Moscow

When Stalin died, his funeral procession brought out so many gawkers that a riot ensued and scores of mourners were trampled to death. The system he built, however, lived on, with a few changes.

Nikita Khrushchev, a former mayor of Moscow, curbed the powers of the secret police, released political prisoners, introduced wide-ranging reforms and promised to improve living conditions. Huge housing estates grew up around the outskirts of Moscow; many of the hastily constructed low-rise projects were nicknamed *khrushchoby,* after

1746	1755	1756	1770–80
The road to Tver becomes the road to St Petersburg, or Peterburskoye shosse, connecting the two capitals.	Compelled by Mikhail Lomonosov and Minister of Education Ivan Shuvalov, Empress Elizabeth establishes Moscow State University, the first university in Russia.	The country's first newspaper – the *Moscow News (Moskovskiye Vedemosti)* – is published at the new university, coming out on a weekly basis.	The bubonic plague breaks out in Moscow, killing as many as 50,000 people. By the end of the decade, the population of St Petersburg surpasses that of Moscow.

trushchoby (slums). Khrushchev's populism and unpredictability made the ruling elite a bit too nervous and he was ousted in 1964.

Next came the long, stagnant reign of ageing Leonid Brezhnev. Overlooking Lenin's mausoleum, he presided over the rise of a military superpower and provided long-sought-after political stability and material security.

During these years, the Cold War shaped Moscow's development as the Soviet Union enthusiastically competed with the USA in the arms and space races. The aerospace, radio-electronics and nuclear weapons ministries operated factories, research laboratories and design institutes in and around the capital. By 1980 as much as one-third of the city's industrial production and one-quarter of its labour force was connected to the defence industry. Moscow city officials were not

LENIN UNDER GLASS

Red Square is home to the world's most famous mummy, that of Vladimir Ilych Lenin. When he died of a massive stroke on 22 January 1924, aged 53, a long line of mourners gathered in the depths of winter for weeks to glimpse the body as it lay in state. Inspired by the spectacle, Stalin proposed that the father of Soviet communism should continue to serve the cause as a holy relic. So the decision was made to preserve Lenin's corpse for perpetuity, against the vehement protests of his widow, as well as Lenin's own expressed desire to be buried next to his mother in St Petersburg.

Boris Zbarsky, a biochemist, and Vladimir Voribov, an anatomist, were issued a political order to put a stop to the natural decomposition of the body. The pair worked frantically in a secret laboratory in search of a long-term chemical solution. In the meantime the body's dark spots were bleached, and the lips and eyes sewn tight. The brain was removed and taken to another secret laboratory, to be sliced and diced by scientists for the next 40 years in the hope of uncovering its genius.

In July 1924 the scientists hit upon a formula to successfully arrest the decaying process, a closely guarded state secret. This necrotic craft was passed on to Zbarsky's son, who ran the Kremlin's covert embalming lab for decades. After the fall of communism, Zbarsky came clean: the body is wiped down every few days and then, every 18 months, thoroughly examined and submerged in chemicals, including paraffin wax. The institute has now gone commercial, offering its services and secrets to wannabe immortals for a mere million dollars.

In the early 1990s Boris Yeltsin expressed his intention to heed Lenin's request and bury him in St Petersburg, setting off a furore from the political left as well as more muted objections from Moscow tour operators. It seems that the mausoleum, the most sacred shrine of Soviet communism, and the mummy, the literal embodiment of the Russian Revolution, will remain in place for at least several more years.

1810–12	1824	1839–60	1861
Russia defies its treaty with France, provoking Napoleon and his Grand Army to invade Russia. According to some, Muscovites burn down their own city in anticipation of the invasion.	The Bolshoi Theatre and the Maly Theatre are built on the aptly named Theatre Square, with the inauguration of the historic venues taking place the following year.	To celebrate the heroic victory over France in the Napoleonic Wars, the Cathedral of Christ the Saviour is built on the banks of the Moscow River.	The 'liberator tsar' Alexander II enacts the Emancipation Reform, which liberates the serfs. Moscow's population surges as thousands of peasants descend on the big city.

Red Moscow Sights

....

Lenin's Mausoleum (Kremlin & Kitay Gorod)

....

Moscow metro

VDNKh (Tverskoy)

....

Bunker-42 Cold War Museum (Meshchansky & Basmanny)

In the 1970s Moscow's most devastating social problem was alcoholism, cited as the major factor behind the high rate of absenteeism, abuse and truancy. Alcoholism was so rampant that Gorbachev tried to limit consumption to two bottles of vodka per week per family, which was not a popular policy initiative.

privy to what went on in these secretly managed facilities. As a matter of national security, the KGB discreetly constructed a second subway system, Metro-2, under the city.

Still, the centrally planned economy could not keep pace with rising consumer demands. While the elite lived in privilege, ordinary Muscovites stood in line for goods. For the Communist Party, things became a bit too comfortable. Under Brezhnev the political elite grew elderly and corrupt, while the economic system slid into a slow, irreversible decline. And the goal of turning Moscow into a showcase socialist city was quietly abandoned.

Nonetheless, Moscow enjoyed a postwar economic boom. Brezhnev showed a penchant for brawny displays of modern architecture. Cavernous concrete-and-glass slabs, such as the now-defunct Hotel Rossiya, were constructed to show the world the modern face of the Soviet Union. The city underwent further expansion, accommodating more and more buildings and residents. The cement pouring reached a frenzy in the build-up to the 1980 Summer Olympics. However, Russia's invasion of Afghanistan caused many nations to boycott the Games and the facilities mostly stood empty.

Appreciation for Moscow's past began to creep back into city planning. Most notably, Alexander's Triumphal Arch (p126) was reconstructed, though plans to re-erect Peter's tall Sukharev Tower were not realised. Residential life continued to move further away from the city centre, which was increasingly occupied by the governing elite. Shoddy high-rise apartments went up on the periphery and metro lines were extended outward.

The attraction for Russians to relocate to Moscow in these years was, and continues to be, very strong. City officials tried desperately to enforce the residency permit system, but to no avail. In 1960 the population topped six million, and by 1980 it surpassed eight million. The spillover led to the rapid growth of Moscow's suburbs. While industry, especially the military industry, provided the city's economic foundation, many new jobs were created in science, education and public administration. The city became a little more ethnically diverse, particularly with the arrival of petty-market traders from Central Asia and the Caucasus.

Transitional Moscow

The Communist Collapse

The Soviet leadership showed it was not immune to change when Mikhail Gorbachev came to power in March 1985 with a mandate to revitalise the ailing socialist system. Gorbachev soon launched a multi-

1862	1905	1905	1914–17
Ivan Turgenev's novel *Fathers and Sons* kicks off the nihilist movement, an early forerunner of populism, anarchism and eventually Bolshevism.	Upon institution of the new position of 'city governor', the tsar appoints Alexander Adrianov as the first mayor of Moscow.	The unpopular Russo-Japanese War provokes general strikes in Moscow and St Petersburg. In Moscow street barricades are set up, and fighting takes place in Presnya.	Russia suffers immeasurably from losses in WWI. By 1916 it has sustained as many as 1.6 million casualties. High prices and food shortages affect the population.

THE BATTLE OF MOSCOW – 1941

In the 1930s Stalin's overtures to enter into an anti-Nazi collective security agreement were rebuffed by England and France. Vowing that the Soviet Union would not be pulling its 'chestnuts out of the fire', Stalin signed a nonaggression pact with Hitler instead.

Thus, when Hitler launched Operation Barbarossa in June 1941, Stalin was caught by surprise and did not emerge from his room for three days.

The ill-prepared Red Army was no match for the Nazi war machine, which advanced on three fronts. History repeated itself with the two armies facing off at Borodino. By December, the Germans were just outside Moscow, within 30km of the Kremlin. Only an early, severe winter halted the advance. A monument now marks the spot, near the entrance road to Sheremetyevo airport, where the Nazis were stopped in their tracks. Staging a brilliant counteroffensive, Soviet war hero General Zhukov staved off the attack and pushed the invaders back.

faceted program of reform under the catchphrase 'perestroika' (restructuring), recognising that it would take more than bureaucratic reorganisations and stern warnings to reverse economic decline. He believed that the root of the economic crisis was society's alienation from the socialist system. Thus, he sought to break down the barrier between 'us' and 'them'.

His reforms were meant to engage the population and stimulate initiative. Glasnost (openness) gave new voice to both a moribund popular culture and a stifled media. Democratisation introduced multicandidate elections and new deliberative legislative bodies. Cooperatives brought the first experiments in market economics in over 50 years. Gorbachev's plan was to lead a gradual transition to reform socialism, but in practice, events ran ahead of him. Moscow set the pace.

In 1985 Gorbachev promoted Boris Yeltsin from his Urals bailiwick into the central leadership as the new head of Moscow. Yeltsin was given the assignment of cleaning up the corrupt Moscow party machine and responded by sacking hundreds of officials. His populist touch made him an instant success with Muscovites, who were often startled to encounter him riding public transport or berating a shopkeeper for not displaying their sausage. During Gorbachev's ill-advised anti-alcohol campaign, Yeltsin saved Moscow's largest brewery from having to close its doors.

More importantly, Yeltsin embraced the more open political atmosphere. He allowed 'informal' groups, unsanctioned by the Communist Party, to organise and express themselves in public. Soon Moscow streets, such as those in the Arbat district, were hosting

It is well known that Mikhail Gorbachev won the Nobel Peace Prize, in 1990, for his efforts to end the Cold War. It is less known that he also won a Grammy Award in 2004, for his spoken word album for children Peter and the Wolf, Wolf Tracks.

1917	1918	1922–24	1930s
Tsar Nicholas II succumbs to a mob of workers in St Petersburg and abdicates the throne. A provisional government is set up in an attempt to restore order.	The Bolshevik Party seizes power from the ineffective provisional government. In fear of a German attack, Vladimir Ilych Ulyanov (Lenin) moves the capital back to Moscow.	Lenin dies after a series of strokes and is succeeded by Josef Stalin. Nearly one million mourners arrive to pay their respects while Lenin lies in state.	Stalin launches a campaign of modernisation and a reign of terror. Moscow becomes an industrial city, complete with poor workers and smoke-billowing factories.

214

History Museums

Jewish Museum & Centre of Tolerance (Tverskoy)

....

State History Museum (Kremlin & Kitay Gorod)

....

Contemporary History Museum (Tverskoy)

....

Gulag History Museum (Tverskoy)

demonstrations by democrats, nationalists, reds and greens. Yeltsin's renegade style alienated the entire party leadership, one by one. He was summarily dismissed by Gorbachev in 1987, though he would be heard from again.

Gorbachev's political reforms included elections to reformed local assemblies in the spring of 1990. By this time, communism had already fallen in Eastern Europe and events in the Soviet Union were becoming increasingly radical. In their first free election in 88 years, Muscovites turned out in large numbers at the polls and voted a bloc of democratic reformers into office.

The new mayor was economist Gavril Popov, and the vice-mayor was Yury Luzhkov. Popov immediately embarked on the 'decommunisation' of the city, selling off housing and state businesses and restoring prerevolutionary street names. He clashed repeatedly with the Soviet leadership over the management of city affairs. Popov soon acquired a key ally when Yeltsin made a political comeback as the elected head of the new Russian Supreme Soviet.

On 18 August 1991, the city awoke to find a column of tanks in the street and a 'Committee for the State of Emergency' claiming to be in charge. This committee was composed of leaders from the Communist Party, the KGB and the military. They had already detained Gorbachev at his Crimean dacha and issued directives to arrest Yeltsin and the Moscow city leadership.

But the ill-conceived coup quickly went awry and confusion ensued. Yeltsin, Popov and Luzhkov made it to the Russian parliament building, the so-called White House, to rally opposition. Crowds gathered at the White House, persuaded some of the tank crews to switch sides and started to build barricades. Yeltsin climbed on a tank to declare the coup illegal and call for a general strike. He dared the snipers to shoot him, and when they didn't, the coup was over.

The following day, huge crowds opposed to the coup gathered in Moscow. Coup leaders lost their nerve, one committed suicide, some fell ill and the others simply got drunk. On 21 August the tanks withdrew; the coup was foiled. Gorbachev flew back to Moscow to resume command, but his time was up as well. On 23 August Yeltsin banned the Communist Party in Russia.

Gorbachev embarked on a last-ditch bid to save the Soviet Union with proposals for a looser union of independent states. Yeltsin, however, was steadily transferring control over everything that mattered from Soviet hands into Russian ones. On 8 December, Yeltsin and the leaders of Ukraine and Belarus, after several rounds of vodka toasts, announced that the USSR no longer existed. They proclaimed a new Commonwealth of Independent States (CIS), a vague alliance of fully

1931	1935	1941–44	1953
The massive Cathedral of Christ the Saviour is destroyed by dynamite to make way for the Palace of Soviets, a Lenin-topped monument to socialism.	Members of the Komsomol pitch in to construct their Komsomolskaya metro station. The first line of the metro, the Sokolniki line, starts operation.	Hitler defies a German-Soviet nonaggression pact and attacks Russia. The Nazi advance is halted by a severe winter, allowing the embattled Red Army to fight back.	Stalin dies and is entombed on Red Square. Nikita Khrushchev becomes first secretary. His main rival, Lavrenty Beria, is arrested, tried for treason and executed.

independent states with no central authority. Gorbachev, a president without a country or authority, formally resigned on 25 December, the day the white, blue and red Russian flag replaced the Soviet red flag over the Kremlin.

Rebirth of Russian Politics

Buoyed by his success over Gorbachev and the coup plotters, Yeltsin (now Russia's president) was granted extraordinary powers by the parliament to find a way out of the Soviet wreckage. Yeltsin used these powers to launch radical economic reforms and rapprochement with the West. In so doing, he polarised the political elite. As Yeltsin's team of economic reformers began to dismantle the protected and subsidised command economy, the parliament finally acted in early 1992 to seize power back from the president. A stalemate ensued that lasted for a year and a half.

The executive–legislative conflict at the national level was played out in Moscow politics as well. After the Soviet fall, the democratic bloc that had brought Popov to power came apart. In Moscow a property boom began, as buildings and land with no real owners changed hands at a dizzying rate with dubious legality. Increasingly, the mayor's office was at odds with the city council, as well as the new federal government. Popov began feuding with Yeltsin, just as he had previously with Gorbachev.

In June 1992 the impulsive Popov resigned his office in a huff. Without pausing to ask him to reconsider, Vice-Mayor Yury Luzhkov readily assumed the mayor's seat. The city council passed a vote of no confidence in Luzhkov and called for new elections, but the new mayor opted simply to ignore the resolution.

Throughout 1993, the conflict between President Yeltsin and the Russian parliament intensified. Eight different constitutional drafts were put forward and rejected. In September 1993 parliament convened with plans to remove many of the president's powers. Before it could act, Yeltsin issued a decree that shut down the parliament and called for new elections.

Events turned violent. Yeltsin sent troops to blockade the White House, ordering the members to leave it by 4 October. Many did, but on 2 and 3 October a National Salvation Front appeared, in an attempt to stir popular insurrection against the president. They clashed with the troops around the White House and tried to seize Moscow's Ostankino TV Tower.

The army, which until this time had sought to remain neutral, intervened on the president's side and blasted the parliament into

Post-Soviet Sights
....
Art Muzeon (Zamoskvorechie)
....
White House (Presnya)

1956	1958	1961	1964
Khrushchev makes a 'secret speech' at the Party Congress, denouncing Stalin's repressive regime and justifying his execution of Beria three years earlier.	Nearly three decades after the destruction of the Cathedral of Christ the Saviour, the massive hole in the ground becomes the world's largest swimming pool.	Stalin is removed from the mausoleum on Red Square and buried in the Kremlin wall.	A coup against Khrushchev brings Leonid Brezhnev to power, ushering in the so-called 'years of stagnation'.

In 2005 Yelena Baturina, property magnate and wife of Mayor Luzhkov, became Russia's first female billionaire. The wife of the current mayor, Irina Sobyana, is also in the construction industry, although she has yet to register on any lists of richest people.

submission. In all, 145 people were killed and another 700 wounded – the worst such incident of bloodshed in the city since the Bolshevik takeover in 1917. Yeltsin, in conjunction with the newly subjugated parliament, put together the 1993 constitution that created a new political system organised around strong central executive power.

Throughout the 1990s Yeltsin suffered increasingly from heart disease. But come 1996, he was not prepared to step down from his 'throne'. Russia's newly rich financiers, who backed Yeltsin's campaign, were rewarded with policy-making positions in the government and with state-owned assets in privatisation auctions. In a scene reminiscent of the medieval boyars, the power grabs of these 'oligarchs' became more brazen during Yeltsin's prolonged illness.

Economic Prosperity

In the new Russia, wealth was concentrated in Moscow. While the rest of Russia struggled to survive the collapse of the command economy, Moscow emerged quickly as an enclave of affluence and dynamism. By the mid-1990s Moscow was replete with all the things Russians had expected capitalism to bring, but had yet to trickle down to the provinces: banks, shops, restaurants, casinos, BMWs, bright lights and nightlife.

The city provided nearly 25% of all tax revenues collected by the federal government. Commercial banks, commodity exchanges, big businesses and high-end retailers all set up headquarters in the capital. By the late 1990s, Moscow had become one of the most expensive cities in the world.

When the government defaulted on its debts and devalued the currency in 1998, it appeared that the boom had gone bust. But as the panic subsided, it became clear that it was less a crisis and more a correction for a badly overvalued rouble. Russian firms became more competitive and productive with the new exchange rate. Wages started to be paid again and consumption increased.

History Books

....

Alexander Rodchenko: The New Moscow (Margarita Tupitsyn)

....

The Greatest Battle (Andrew Nagorski)

....

Lenin's Tomb (David Remnick)

....

Midnight Diaries (Boris Yeltsin)

Millennium Moscow

Cops in the Kremlin

In December 1999 Boris Yeltsin delivered his customary televised New Year's greeting to the nation. On this occasion the burly president shocked his fellow countryfolk yet again by announcing his resignation from office and retirement from politics. The once-combative Yeltsin had grown weary from a decade full of political adversity and physical infirmity.

Yeltsin turned over the office to his recently appointed prime minister, Vladimir Putin. As an aide to the president, Putin had im-

1979–80	1982–85	1985	1991
Russia invades Afghanistan to support its communist regime against US-backed Islamic militants. Relations between the superpowers deteriorate.	Brezhnev's death ushers in former KGB supremo Yury Andropov as president for 15 months until his death. His successor, Konstantin Chernenko, dies 13 months later.	Mikhail Gorbachev is elected general secretary of the Communist Party. Intent on reform, he institutes policies of *perestroika* (restructuring) and *glasnost* (openness).	A failed coup in August seals the end of the USSR. Gorbachev resigns and Boris Yeltsin becomes the first popularly elected president of the Russian Federation.

pressed Yeltsin with his selfless dedication, shrewd mind and principled resolve. It was Yeltsin's plan to spring this holiday surprise on the unprepared political opposition to bolster Putin's chances in the upcoming presidential election. The plan worked. In March 2000 Putin became the second president of the Russian Federation.

Mystery surrounded the cop in the Kremlin: he was a former KGB chief, but an ally of St Petersburg's democratic mayor; well versed in European culture, but nostalgic for Soviet patriotism; diminutive in stature, but a black belt in judo.

In his first term, Putin's popular-approval ratings shot through the onion domes. He brought calm and stability to Russian politics after more than a decade of crisis and upheaval. The economy finally began to show positive growth. The improved economic situation led to budget surpluses for the first time since the 1980s, and wages and pensions were paid in full and on time.

Putin vowed to restore the authority of the Moscow-based central state, engineering a constitutional reform to reduce the power of regional governors and launching a second war against radical Chechen separatists. His second term accelerated the trend towards a more authoritarian approach to politics. Former police officials were named prime minister and speaker of the parliament. Restraints on mass media, civil society and nongovernmental agencies were further tightened.

After years of deteriorating health, Boris Yeltsin died of congestive health failure in 2007. He is buried in Novodevichy Cemetery, where his grave is marked by an enormous Russian flag, which is sculpted out of stone but gives the appearance that it is rippling in the wind.

Terror in the Capital

Though the origins of the Russian–Chechen conflict date to the 18th century, it is only in recent times that Moscow has felt its consequences so close to home. In September 1999 mysterious explosions in the capital left more than 200 people dead. Chechen terrorists were blamed for the bombings, although the evidence was scant. Conspiracy theorists had a field day.

In 2002 Chechen rebels wired with explosives seized a popular Moscow theatre, demanding independence for Chechnya. Nearly 800 theatre employees and patrons were held hostage for three days. Russian troops responded by flooding the theatre with immobilising toxic gas, disabling hostage-takers and hostages alike and preventing the worst-case scenario. The victims' unexpectedly severe reaction to the gas and a lack of available medical facilities resulted in 130 deaths and hundreds of illnesses. The incident refuelled Russia's campaign to force the Chechens into capitulation.

Chechen terrorists responded in kind, with smaller-scale insurgencies taking place regularly over the next several years. Between 2002 and 2005, suicide bombers in Moscow made strikes near Red Square,

Since the beginning of the Second Chechen War in 1999, nearly 900 people have been killed by terrorist attacks in and around Moscow.

1992	1993	1997	1998
The former Chairman of the Moscow City Council, Yury Luzhkov is appointed Mayor of Moscow, replacing his patron Gavril Popov.	Yeltsin sends in troops to deal with dissenters at Moscow's White House and Ostankino TV Tower. It is Russia's most violent political conflict since 1917.	To celebrate the 850th anniversary of the founding of Moscow, the Cathedral of Christ the Saviour is rebuilt in its original location.	An artificially high exchange rate and fiscal deficit bring on a financial crisis, resulting in the devaluation of the rouble and the government's default on international loans.

Modern Moscow

....

Gorky Park (Zamoskvorechie)

....

Red October (Zamoskvorechie)

....

Winzavod & ArtPlay (Meshchansky & Basmanny)

....

Moscow International Business Centre (Presnya)

on the metro, on airplanes and at rock concerts, leaving hundreds of people dead and injured.

Things settled down for a few years, but the terror was not over. Towards the end of the decade, attacks resumed in full force, occurring on an annual basis in and around the capital. Again, the metro, the airport and other means of transportation were key targets.

The capital has been relatively quiet since 2011, but nothing has been resolved and nobody believes that this is over. Newspapers regularly report on FSB successes at foiling terrorist plots. Federal officials promise retribution, city officials increase security, and the violence continues.

The Party After the Party

Starting from 1999, Russia recorded positive economic growth. After the devaluation of the rouble, domestic producers became more competitive and more profitable. A worldwide shortage of energy resources heaped benefits on the economy. The Russian oil boom enabled the government to run budget surpluses, pay off its foreign debt and lower tax rates.

Moscow, in particular, prospered. The city continued to undergo a massive physical transformation, with industry emptying out of the historic centre and skyscrapers shooting up along the Moscow River. The city's congested roadways were replete with luxury vehicles. The new economy spawned a small group of 'New Russians', who were alternately derided and envied for their garish displays of wealth. Following decades of an austere and prudish Soviet regime, Muscovites revelled in their new-found freedom. Liberation, libation, defiance and indulgence were all on open display.

By the start of the 2010s, the economic rhythms of the city steadied. More than a decade of economic growth meant that wealth was trickling down beyond the 'New Russians'. In Moscow, the burgeoning middle class endured a high cost of living, but enjoyed unprecedented employment opportunities and a dizzying array of culinary, cultural and consumer choices.

Sobyanin's early initiatives included a crack-down on corruption and a halt to construction. One of his first acts in office was, controversially, to do away with some 2000 kiosks that were scattered over Moscow's streets and squares.

Moscow Under Medvedev

In 2008 Putin's second term as president came to an end and the constitution did not allow him to run for a third consecutive term. Putin's hand-picked presidential successor was law professor and Deep Purple fan Dmitry Medvedev, who made haste to install his predecessor as prime minister.

The change in power registered barely a blip on Russia's political lifeline. Four years later, Medvedev declined to run for re-election.

1999	2002–05	2008–09	2008–12
On New Year's Eve, Yeltsin announces his immediate resignation, entrusting the caretaker duties of president to Prime Minister Vladimir Putin.	Chechen rebels take 800 hostages in a Moscow theatre. Suicide bombers strike the metro, airplanes and rock concerts, leaving hundreds dead and injured.	A worldwide financial crisis hits Russia hard. The economic recession is exacerbated by the falling price of oil and military entanglements with Georgia.	Putin's chosen successor, Dmitry Medvedev, is elected president and serves one term. Putin acts as prime minister, until he is eligible to return to the presidency.

Putin stepped up, and suggested his main man Medvedev would make an excellent PM. They switched places in 2012.

For about six months between the election and the inauguration, Moscow's streets and squares saw regular protests 'for fair elections'. The demonstrations morphed into broader antigovernment unrest, sometimes called the 'Snow Revolution'. The larger of these events attracted 100,000 participants and more, according to organisers.

But this energy fizzled. Once in office, Putin enacted legislation that severely restricted such actions, making it more difficult to get permission to assemble, and levying harsh fines on anyone who participated in unsanctioned demonstrations. The opposition movement suffered from a lack of unity and organisation. Muscovites had jobs to do and families to support and sporting events and art exhibitions to attend. The capital returned to business as usual.

A New Era

Since the mayor of Moscow became a full-time bureaucratic job, rather than an honorary aristocratic title, no one held the position longer than Yury Luzhkov. And certainly no one was more influential in shaping postcommunist Moscow than the 'mayor in the cap'. During Luzhkov's 18-year run, Moscow realised its claim of being a global centre of power and wealth. The skyline was transformed, the economy boomed and international culture thrived. In the tradition of urban political bosses, Luzhkov provided plenty of bread and circuses, bluster and cronyism.

In 2010 long-simmering tension between the Kremlin and the mayor's office finally boiled over. After a semipublic spat, then-president Medvedev simply fired the unrepentant chieftain. Just to make sure that everyone knew it was personal, Medvedev's decree explained that the mayor had 'lost the trust of the president'.

Luzhkov's replacement, Sergei Sobyanin, was previously the head of the presidential administration under Putin. Like other prized possessions in Putin's Russia, Moscow now belongs to the Kremlin.

In 2013 American whistleblower Edward Snowden became Moscow's most mysterious resident, when he spent 39 days in the transit area at Sheremetyevo airport while seeking asylum from the US Department of Justice. He was finally granted temporary asylum in Russia, and he's been there ever since.

HISTORY MILLENNIUM MOSCOW

2009–11	2010	2011	2017
Chechen terrorists continue their deadly campaign. Attacks claim hundreds of victims, as bombs are detonated on trains, in metro stations and at the airport.	The long-serving, popular Moscow mayor Yury Luzhkov is removed from office. He is replaced by Sergei Sobyanin.	Moscow negotiates a land deal, whereby the city acquires a huge tract of sparsely populated land, more than doubling its geographic area.	Moscow's first major new park in 50 years, Park Zaryadye opens in Kitay Gorod on the site of the former Hotel Rossiya.

Performing Arts

Moscow has always been known for the richness of its culture, ranging from the traditional to the progressive. Whether a Tchaikovsky opera or an Ostrovsky drama, the classical performing arts in Moscow are among the best in the world. But New Russia comes with new forms of art and entertainment. This bohemian side of Moscow – be it a beatnik band or experimental theatre – provides a glimpse of Russia's future.

Music

Above: New Year's performance of the Nutcracker

The classics never go out of style. This is certainly true for music in Moscow, where Mussorgsky, Stravinsky and especially Tchaikovsky still feature in concert halls on an almost daily basis. The atmosphere in these places is a little stuffy, but the musicianship is first rate and the compositions are timeless. However, music in Moscow takes many forms, and these days rock, blues and jazz are ubiquitous in the capital;

you can also hear alternative contemporary styles like funk, ska, house, hip hop, trip-hop and more.

Classical Music & Opera

The defining period of Russian classical music was from the 1860s to 1900. As Russian composers (and painters and writers) struggled to find a national identity, several influential schools formed, from which some of Russia's most famous composers and finest music emerged. The so-called Group of Five, which included Modest Mussorgsky (1839–81) and Nikolai Rimsky-Korsakov (1844–1908), believed that a radical departure from Europe was necessary, and they looked to *byliny* (folk music) for themes. Mussorgsky penned *Pictures at an Exhibition* and the opera *Boris Godunov;* Rimsky-Korsakov is best known for *Scheherazade.*

Pyotr Tchaikovsky (1840–93) also embraced Russian folklore and music, as well as the disciplines of Western European composers. Tchaikovsky is widely regarded as the father of Russian national composers. His compositions – which include the magnificent *1812 Overture;* concertos and symphonies; ballets *Swan Lake, Sleeping Beauty* and *The Nutcracker*; and the opera *Yevgeny Onegin* – are among the world's most popular classical works. They are certainly the shows that are staged most often at theatres around Moscow.

Following in Tchaikovsky's romantic footsteps was Sergei Rachmaninov (1873–1943) and the innovative Igor Stravinsky (1882–1971). Both fled Russia after the revolution. Stravinsky's *The Rite of Spring,* which created a furore at its first performance in Paris, and *The Firebird* were influenced by Russian folk music. Sergei Prokofiev (1891–1953), who also left Soviet Russia but returned in 1934, wrote the scores for Sergei Eisenstein's films *Alexander Nevsky* and *Ivan the Terrible,* the ballet *Romeo and Juliet,* and *Peter and the Wolf,* so beloved by music teachers of young children. His work, however, was condemned for 'formalism' towards the end of his life.

Similarly, Dmitry Shostakovich (1906–75) was alternately praised and condemned by the Soviet government. He wrote brooding, bizarrely dissonant works, in addition to more accessible traditional classical music. After official condemnation by Stalin, Shostakovich's *7th Symphony* (also known as the *Leningrad Symphony*) brought him honour and international standing when it was performed by the Leningrad Philharmonic during the Siege of Leningrad. The authorities changed their minds again and banned his formalist music in 1948, then 'rehabilitated' him after Stalin's death.

Classical opera was performed regularly during the Soviet period, and continues to be popular. Nowadays, the top theatres – especially

Classical Music Venues

············

Tchaikovsky Concert Hall (Presnya)

············

Moscow Tchaikovsky Conservatory (Presnya)

············

Moscow International House of Music (Zamoskvorechie)

Rock & Pop Venues

············

Gazgolder (Meshchansky & Basmanny)

············

Sixteen Tons (Presnya)

············

Svobody (Tverskoy)

MOSCOW PLAY LIST

Eto bylo tak davno (Mashina Vremeni; 1993) *It Was So Long Ago* was the first studio recording of Mashina Vremeni (Time Machine).

Horowitz in Moscow (Vladimir Horowitz; 1986) World-renowned pianist Horowitz returns to his homeland after almost 60 years away.

Mergers & Acquisitions (Mumiy Troll; 2005) This album provides sharp commentary and social criticism.

Peter & the Wolf (Sergei Prokofiev; 1936) A children's classic written by Prokofiev after his return to Moscow.

the Bolshoi – are attempting to showcase new works by contemporary composers, as well as unknown works that were censored or banned in the past.

Contemporary Music

Russian music is not all about classical composers. Ever since the 'bourgeois' Beatles filtered through in the 1960s, Russians both young and old have been keen to sign up for the pop revolution. Starved of decent equipment and the chance to record or perform to big audiences, Russian rock groups initially developed underground. All music was circulated by illegal tapes known as *magizdat,* passed from listener to listener; concerts were held in remote halls in city suburbs. By the 1970s – the Soviet hippie era – such music had developed a huge following among the disaffected, distrustful youth.

Andrei Makarevich was the leader of Mashina Vremeni (Time Machine), now considered one of the patriarch groups of Soviet rock. Inspired by the Beatles, the band formed in 1968, playing simple guitar riffs and singable melodies. Even today, Mashina Vremeni remains popular across generations.

The god of *russky rok,* though, was Viktor Tsoy, front person of the group Kino; the band's classic album is 1988's *Gruppa Krovi (Blood Group)*. Tsoy's early death in a 1990 car crash sealed his legendary status. To this day, there is a graffiti-covered wall on ul Arbat that is dedicated to Tsoy, and fans gather on the anniversary of his death (15 August) to play his music.

Many contemporary favourites on the Russian rock scene have been playing together since the early days. One of the most notable Moscow bands (originally from Vladivostok) is Mumiy Troll, led by the androgynous Ilya Lagutenko. After 25 years, the band continues to produce innovative stuff. Its latest studio album, *Piratskie Kopii,* was released in 2015.

Gaining worldwide renown is Bi-2, whose members Shura and Leva have lived in Israel and Australia. Their popularity soared with the release of their namesake album in 2000. The duo is famed for their collaborations with other Russian rock stars. Several years and several records later, this 'post-punk' duo often appears at Moscow rock festivals.

Making a name for herself in the folk scene, art-rock-folk vocalist Pelageya is apparently Putin's favourite. She sings rock arrangements of folk songs including one that she performed at the Sochi Olympics. Arkona represent the incongruous pagan metal movement – heavy metal music that incorporates Russian folklore, Slavic mythology and other pre-Christian rites. Arkona employs traditional Russian instruments and its lead singer is renowned for her death-growl singing style.

The likes of techno-pop girl duo tATu and pretty-boy singer Dima Bilan (winner of 2008's Eurovision Song Contest) are the tame international faces of Russia's contemporary music scene. tATu has been mostly on the fritz since 2011, although the duo did reunite long enough to perform at the Sochi Olympics.

At the other end of the spectrum, today's most renowned Moscow rockers are Pussy Riot, a feminist punk rock band, who famously staged a performance in the Cathedral of Christ the Saviour in protest of Putin's election in 2012. The one-minute performance was used in their music video *Punk Prayer,* and led to the arrest of three members of the band. The women were sentenced to two years in prison, which was widely considered too harsh for the crime, but they were released on amnesty after about six months.

Dance Venues

Bolshoi Theatre (Tverskoy)

Stanislavsky & Nemirovich-Danchenko Musical Theatre (Tverskoy)

New Ballet (Meshchansky & Basmanny)

Kremlin Ballet (Kremlin & Kitay Gorod)

Performance at the Moscow International House of Music (p154)

Ballet & Dance

Ballet in Russia evolved as an offshoot of French dance combined with Russian folk and peasant dance techniques. As a part of his efforts towards Westernisation, Peter the Great invited artists from France to perform this new form of dance. In 1738 French dance master Jean Baptiste Lande established a school of dance in St Petersburg's Winter Palace, the precursor to the famed Vaganova School of Choreography. The Bolshoi Opera & Ballet Company was founded a few years later in 1776.

The father of Russian ballet is considered to be the French dancer and choreographer Marius Petipa (1819–1910), who acted as principal dancer and premier ballet master of the Imperial Theatre. All told he produced more than 60 full ballets, including the classics *Sleeping Beauty* and *Swan Lake*.

At the turn of the 20th century, Sergei Diaghilev's Ballets Russes took Europe by storm. The stage decor was unlike anything seen before. Painted by artists such as Alexander Benois, Mikhail Larianov, Natalia Goncharova and Leon Bakst, it suspended disbelief and shattered the audience's sense of illusion.

Bolshoi Ballet

During Soviet rule ballet enjoyed a privileged status, which allowed companies such as the Bolshoi (p88) to maintain a level of lavish production and high performance standards. In the 1960s Yury Grigorovich emerged as a bright, new choreographer, with *Spartacus, Ivan the Terrible* and other successes.

Grigorovich directed the company for over 30 years, but not without controversy. In the late 1980s he came to loggerheads with some of his

Novaya Opera (p100) performing the *Passenger*

leading dancers. Many stars resigned, accusing him of being 'brutal' and 'Stalinist'. With encouragement from President Yeltsin, Grigorovich finally resigned in 1995, prompting his loyal dancers to stage the Bolshoi's first-ever strike.

In the next decade, the Bolshoi would go through three different artistic directors, all of them promising, but none able to pry Grigorovich's conservative grasp from the company. Finally, in 2004, rising star Alexei Ratmansky was appointed artistic director. Born in 1968 in Ukraine, Ratmansky was young but accomplished. Most notably, *The Bright Stream* – which received a National Dance Award in 2003 – earned him the promotion.

Ratmansky's productions were well received, even when he stretched the traditionally narrow focus of the Bolshoi. In 2006, in honour of the 100th anniversary of Dmitry Shostakovich's birthday, the Bolshoi ballet premiered the composer's ballet *The Bolt*. Prior to that, the ballet was performed exactly once – in 1931 – before it was banned by the Soviet regime for its formalist errors. Ratmansky earned the Golden Mask in 2007 for his staging of *Jeu de Cartes*. In 2008 he recreated the revolutionary ballet *Flames of Paris,* which was originally performed in the 1930s.

After Ratmansky's resignation, the Bolshoi again experienced rapid turnover in direction, with a fair amount of scandal to keep everybody's attention. Most dramatically, in 2013, artistic director Sergei Filin was attacked with sulphuric acid, causing severe disfiguration and loss of eyesight. A disgruntled dancer was charged with orchestrating the crime.

Since 2016 the Bolshoi has been operating under the artistic direction of Makhar Vaziev, a former Mariinsky director and a self-proclaimed autocrat. Vaziev promises to implement a well-practised strategy of promoting young talent and experimenting with innovative programming.

Meanwhile, controversies continue to swirl around the Bolshoi. In 2017, the company cancelled a show just three days before its premiere. The new production was about the life of Rudolf Nureyev, a celebrated Soviet dancer who defected to the West – and who also happened to be bisexual. Journalists have speculated that the show was cancelled due to its subject matter (which might violate the infamous 'gay propaganda' law). The company's director claimed it was just not good enough during rehearsals.

Will Vaziev be able to navigate the politics of Russia's most prominent ballet company? And will he be able to exercise his artistic licence as hoped? Stay tuned for the next episode...

Other Dance Companies

The Bolshoi is Moscow's best known (and therefore most political) ballet company, but other companies in the city have equally talented dancers and directors. Both the Kremlin Ballet (p84) and the Stanislavsky & Nemirovich-Danchenko Musical Theatre (p101) stage excellent performances of the Russian classics.

The New Ballet (p168), directed by Pavel Nestratov, stages a completely different kind of dance. Dubbed 'plastic ballet', it combines dance with pantomime and drama. Productions vary widely, incorporating elements such as folk tales, poetry and improvised jazz. This bizarre, playful performance art is a refreshing addition to Moscow's dance scene.

Theatre

Moscow's oldest theatre, the Maly Theatre (p101), was established in 1756 upon the decree of Empress Elizabeth. But Russia's theatre scene flourished under the patronage of drama lover Catherine the Great, who set up the Imperial Theatre Administration and herself penned several plays. During her reign Moscow playwright Denis Fonvizin wrote *The Brigadier* (1769) and *The Minor* (1791), satirical comedies that are still performed today.

Alexander Ostrovsky (1823–86) was a prominent playwright who lived in Zamoskvorechie and based many of his plays on the merchants and nobles who were his neighbours. As the director of the Maly Theatre, he is credited with raising the reputation of that institution as a respected drama theatre and school. Other 19th-century dramatists included Alexander Pushkin, whose drama *Boris Godunov* (1830) was later used as the libretto for the Mussorgsky opera; Nikolai Gogol, whose tragic farce *The Government Inspector* (1836) was said to be a favourite play of Nicholas I; and Ivan Turgenev, whose languid *A Month in the Country* (1849) paved the way for the most famous Russian playwright of all: Anton Chekhov (1860–1904).

Chekhov lived on the Garden Ring in Presnya, though he spent much of his time at his country estate in Melikhovo. In 1898 Konstantin Stanislavsky implemented his innovative approach of method acting and made Chekhov a success. Chekhov's *The Seagull, The Three Sisters, The Cherry Orchard* and *Uncle Vanya,* all of which take the angst of the provincial middle class as their theme, owed much of their success to their 'realist' productions at the Moscow Art Theatre (p101).

Through the Soviet period theatre remained popular, not least because it was one of the few areas of artistic life where a modicum of freedom of expression was permitted. Stalin famously said of Mikhail

The attack on Bolshoi artistic director Sergei Filin and the toxic politics that provoked it are the subject of the 2016 documentary *Bolshoi Babylon.*

THE THEATRE OF POLITICS & THE POLITICS OF THEATRE

Of Moscow's many talented theatre directors, none has garnered more attention of late than Kirill Serebrennikov, director of the Gogol Centre. Unfortunately, it's not the kind of attention that one would hope to receive.

Since its founding in 2013, the Gogol Centre has been lauded for its innovative design and its experimental productions, often tackling controversial social and political subjects. Serebrennikov himself is an outspoken critic of the Kremlin who has advocated for LGBTQI rights, demonstrated against Russia's foreign policy and signed a collective statement in support of Pussy Riot, after members of the all-girl punk group were arrested

Although Serebrennikov was appointed by the Ministry of Culture, he often found himself at odds with the administration. In 2013 the Ministry cancelled a Gogol Centre screening of the documentary film *Pussy Riot: A Punk Prayer*. And in 2017, the Bolshoi cancelled the premier of Serebrennikov's ballet *Nureyev*, about the life the celebrated bisexual ballet dancer.

Also in the summer of 2017 the Gogol Centre was raided as part of a Kremlin investigation of alleged embezzlement of state funds. Eventually, Serebrennikov and several colleagues were arrested. Kremlin representatives claim the crimes under investigation are purely financial – not political. But arts critics and other journalists argue that such a distinction is meaningless: the rules for recipients of state finances are notoriously complicated – purposefully so, some claim, to make the beneficiaries vulnerable to legal prosecution should the political need arise.

For his part, Serebrennikov has denied all allegations, and the theatre community has rallied around his cause. More than 20 theatre companies from around Russia participated in actions in solidarity with the Gogol Centre administrators, while artists and actors have collected over 300 signatures on a petition calling for their immediate release. International celebs from Ian McKellen to Cate Blanchett have spoken out against the arrests.

Bulgakov's play *White Guard* that, although it had been written by an enemy, it still deserved to be staged because of the author's outstanding talent. Bulgakov is perhaps the only person dubbed an 'enemy' by Stalin who was never persecuted.

Others were not so fortunate. The rebellious director of the Taganka Theatre, Yury Lyubimov, was sent into exile as a result of his controversial plays. The avant-garde actor-director Vsevolod Meyerhold suffered an even worse fate. Not only was his Moscow theatre closed down but he was imprisoned and later tortured and executed as a traitor.

Throughout the 1980s and 1990s, Pyotr Fomenko was unable to find permanent work until he set up his own theatre company, which became wildly popular almost immediately. The Pyotr Fomenko Studio Theatre moved into a proper (beautiful) home theatre in 2008, just a few short years before the beloved director died in 2012.

Drama Venues
....
Moscow Art Theatre (Tverskoy)
....
Moscow English Theatre (Presnya)
....
Gogol Centre (Meshchansky & Basmanny)

Today, Moscow's theatre scene is as lively as those in London and New York. The capital hosts more than 40 theatres, which continue to entertain and provoke audiences. Notable directors include Kirill Serebrennikov, who does not shy away from touchy subjects in his productions at the Gogol Centre (p168); Kama Ginkas, who works with the Moscow Art Theatre and the New Generation Theatre; and Oleg and Vladimir Presnyakov, who cowrite and direct their plays under the joint name Presnyakov Brothers.

Circus

While Western circuses grow smaller and scarcer, the Russian versions are like those from childhood stories – prancing horses with acrobats on their backs, snarling lions and tigers, heart-stopping high-wire artists and hilarious clowns. No wonder the circus remains highly popular, with around half the population attending a performance once a year.

The Russian circus has its roots in the medieval travelling minstrels *(skomorokhi),* and circus performers today still have a similar lifestyle. The Russian State Circus company, RosGosTsirk, assigns its members to a particular circus for a performance season, then rotates them around to other locations. What the members give up in stability they gain in job security. RosGosTsirk ensures them employment throughout their circus career.

Many circus performers find their calling not by chance but by ancestry. It is not unusual for generations of one family to practise the same circus skill, be it tightrope walking or lion taming. Long-time performers claim that once the circus is in their bones and blood, it's nearly impossible to leave it behind.

Moscow is home to several circuses, including the acclaimed Nikulin Circus on Tsvetnoy Bulvar (p101). Its namesake is the clown Yury Nikulin, an empathetic figure who was beloved by all, from the smallest children to the powers that be, until his death in 1997. (Apparently he was a friend of Mayor Luzhkov and President Yeltsin.)

Speaking of empathy, most of the major troupes have cleaned up their act with regard to the treatment of animals. In Moscow circuses, it is unlikely you will see animals treated cruelly, though their very presence in the ring is controversial.

Circuses
························
*Nikulin Circus on
Tsvetnoy Bulvar
(Tverskoy)*
························
*Bolshoi Circus
on Vernadskogo
(Arbat &
Khamovniki)*

PERFORMING ARTS CIRCUS

Art & Architecture

The Russian capital is an endless source of amusement and amazement for the art and architecture aficionado. Moscow has great visual appeal, from the incredible Moscow baroque and Russian-revival architecture to the world-famous collections of Russian and Impressionist art. Now the capital is experiencing a burst of creative energy as artists and architects experiment with integrating old and new forms in this timeless city.

Visual Arts

Art is busting out all over Moscow, with the ongoing expansion of the Pushkin Museum of Fine Arts (p123) and the countless new contemporary art galleries that are taking over the city's former industrial spaces.

Icons

Up until the 17th century, religious icons were Russia's key art form. Originally painted by monks as a spiritual exercise, icons are images intended to aid the veneration of the holy subjects they depict, and are sometimes believed able to grant luck, wishes or even miracles. They're most commonly found on the iconostasis (screen) of a church.

Traditional rules decreed that only Christ, the Virgin, angels, saints and scriptural events could be depicted by icons – all of which were supposed to be copies of a limited number of approved prototype images. Christ images include the Pantokrator (All-Ruler) and the Mandilion, the latter called 'not made by hand' because it was supposedly developed from the imprint of Christ's face on St Veronica's handkerchief. Icons were traditionally painted in tempera (inorganic pigment mixed with a binder such as egg yolk) on wood.

The beginning of a distinct Russian icon tradition came when artists in Novgorod started to draw on local folk art in their representation of people, producing sharply outlined figures with softer faces and introducing lighter colours, including pale yellows and greens. The earliest outstanding painter was Theophanes the Greek (1340–1405), or Feofan Grek in Russian. Working in Byzantium, Novgorod and Moscow, Theophanes brought a new delicacy and grace to the form. His finest works are in the Annunciation Cathedral (p70) of the Moscow Kremlin.

Andrei Rublyov (1370–1430), a monk at the Trinity Monastery of St Sergius and Andronikov Monastery, was the greatest Russian icon painter. His most famous work is the dreamy *Old Testament Trinity,* in Moscow's Tretyakov Gallery (p141).

The layperson Dionysius, the leading late-15th-century icon painter, elongated his figures and refined the use of colour. Sixteenth-century icons were smaller and more crowded, their figures more realistic and Russian-looking. In 17th-century Moscow, Simon Ushakov (1626–86) moved towards Western religious painting with the use of perspective and architectural backgrounds.

Andrei Tarkovsky's 1966 film *Andrei Rublyov* interpreted the life of the icon painter amid the harsh realities of medieval Russia. Addressing themes such as religious faith and artistic freedom, the film was heavily censored in the Soviet Union, but was awarded a prize at the Cannes Film Festival in 1969.

Besides the outstanding collection at the Tretyakov Gallery and the Rublyov Museum of Early Russian Culture & Art (p162), there is an impressive private collection on display at the Museum of the Russian Icon (p161), not to mention the many churches around town.

Peredvizhniki & Russian Revival

The major artistic force of the 19th century was the Peredvizhniki (Society of Wanderers) movement, in which art was seen as a vehicle for promoting national awareness and social change. The movement gained its name from the touring exhibitions with which it widened its audience. These artists were patronised by the brothers Pavel and Sergei Tretyakov (after whom the Tretyakov Gallery (p141) is named). Peredvizhniki artists included Vasily Surikov (1848–1916), who painted vivid Russian historical scenes; Nikolai Ghe (1831–94), who depicted Biblical and historical scenes; and Ilya Repin (1884–1930), perhaps the best loved of all Russian artists, whose works ranged from social criticism *(Barge Haulers on the Volga)* to history *(Zaporozhie Cossacks Writing a Letter to the Turkish Sultan)* to portraits. Many Peredvizhniki masterpieces are on display at the Tretyakov Gallery.

Later in the century, industrialist Savva Mamontov was a significant patron of the arts, promoting a Russian revivalist movement. His Abramtsevo estate near Moscow became an artists' colony. One frequent resident was Victor Vasnetsov (1848–1926), a Russian-revivalist painter and architect famous for his historical paintings with fairy-tale subjects. In 1894 Vasnetsov designed his own house in Moscow, which is now a small museum. He also designed the original building for the Tretyakov Gallery, as well as the chapel at Abramtsevo (p174).

Nikolai Rerikh (1874–1947) – known internationally as Nicholas Roerich – was an artist whose artwork is characterised by rich, bold colours, primitive style and mystical themes. In 2013 Rerikh's painting *Madonna Laboris* sold at auction in London for some £7.9 million, temporarily topping the ever-changing list of most expensive Russian paintings. In Moscow, Rerikh's paintings are on display at the Museum of Oriental Art (p105). The dedicated Rerikh Museum (p129) has closed due to a state takeover.

The work of late-19th-century genius Mikhail Vrubel (1856–1910) is unique in form and style. He was inspired by sparkling Byzantine and Venetian mosaics. His panels on the sides of the Hotel Metropol (p191) are some of his best work.

Avant-Garde Art

In the 20th century, Russian art became a mishmash of groups, styles and 'isms', as it absorbed decades of

TIMELINE

1405

Andrei Rublyov paints the icons in the Annunciation Cathedral in the Kremlin and in the Assumption Cathedral in Vladimir, representing the peak of Moscow iconography.

1555

Churches with tent roofs and onion domes represent a uniquely Russian architectural style, the pinnacle of which is St Basil's Cathedral on Red Square.

1757

The Imperial Academy of Arts is established to support romantic and classical painting and sculpture.

1870

After boycotting the Imperial Academy of Arts, a group of rebellious art students form the Peredvizhniki (Society of Wanderers), whose work focuses on social and political issues.

1900–03

Fyodor Shekhtel fuses Russian revival and art nouveau to create architectural masterpieces such as Yaroslavsky station and Ryabushinksy Mansion.

1915–20

Kazimir Malevich publishes a treatise on suprematism, as exemplified by his iconic painting *The Black Square*. Constructivist artists and architects explore the idea of art with a social purpose.

ART & ARCHITECTURE VISUAL ARTS

BOGATYRS

Among the most beloved of Russian paintings is the evocative *Bogatyrs,* by Viktor Vasnetsov –on display at the Tretyakov (p141). The oil painting depicts three characters from Russian folklore, or *bylina*. Heroic Ilya Muromets is supposedly based on an actual historic medieval warrior and monk; Dobrynya Nikitich is a noble warrior best known for defeating a dragon; and the cunning and crafty Alyosha Popovich often outsmarts his foes. *Bylina* was originally an oral tradition – a narrative song – that passed down legends of Kyivan Rus. The stories were published in written form starting in the 18th century. Vasnetsov's Russian-revival paintings are yet another recasting of these ancient tales.

European change in a few years. It finally gave birth to its own avant-garde futurist movements.

Mikhail Larionov (1881–1964) and Natalya Goncharova (1881–1962) developed neoprimitivism, a movement based on popular arts and primitive icons. Just a few years later, Kazimir Malevich (1878–1935) announced the arrival of suprematism. His utterly abstract geometrical shapes (with the black square representing the ultimate 'zero form') freed art from having to depict the material world and made it a doorway to higher realities. Another famed futurist, who managed to escape subordinate 'isms', was Vladimir Mayakovsky, who was also a poet. Works by all of these artists are on display at the New Tretyakov Gallery (p146), as well as the Moscow Museum of Modern Art (p89).

An admirer of Malevich, Alexander Rodchenko (1891–1956) was one of the founders of the constructivist movement. He was a graphic designer, sculptor and painter, but he is best known for his innovative photography. Rodchenko's influence on graphic design is immeasurable, as many of his techniques were used widely later in the 20th century.

Soviet-Era Art

Futurists turned to the needs of the revolution – education, posters and banners – with enthusiasm. They had a chance to enact their theories of how art shapes society. But, at the end of the 1920s, abstract art fell out of favour and was branded 'formalist'. The Communist Party wanted 'socialist realism', or realist art that advanced the goals of the glorious socialist revolution. Images of striving workers, heroic soldiers and inspiring leaders took over from abstraction. Plenty of examples of this realism are on display at the New Tretyakov Gallery (p146). Two million sculptures of Lenin and Stalin dotted the country. Kazimir Malevich ended up painting penetrating portraits and doing designs for Red Square parades; Vladimir Mayakovsky committed suicide.

After Stalin, an avant-garde 'conceptualist' underground was allowed to form. Ilya Kabakov (1933–) painted, or sometimes just arranged the debris of everyday life, to show the gap between the promises and realities of Soviet existence. The 'Sotsart' style of Erik Bulatov (1933–) pointed to the devaluation of language by ironically reproducing Soviet slogans and depicting words disappearing over the horizon.

In 1962 the Moscow artist union celebrated the post-Stalin thaw with an exhibit of previously banned 'unofficial' art. Cautious reformer Khrushchev was aghast by what he saw, declaring the artwork to be 'dog shit'. The artists returned to the underground.

Art Museums

Tretyakov Gallery (Zamoskvorechie)

New Tretyakov Gallery (Zamoskvorechie)

Museum of Russian Impressionism (Presnya)

Vasnetsov House-Museum (Tverskoy)

Moscow Museum of Modern Art (Tverskoy)

Contemporary Art

The best-known artists in post–Soviet Russia are individuals who have been favoured by politicians in power, meaning that their work appears in public places. You might not know the name Alexander Burganov (1935–), but you will certainly recognise his sculptures, which grace the Arbat and other locales. More notorious than popular is the artist and architect Zurab Tsereteli (1934–), whose monumental buildings and statues are ubiquitous in Moscow.

Religious painter Ilya Glazunov (1930–2017) was a staunch defender of the Russian Orthodox cultural tradition, while Alexander Shilov (1943–) is famous for his portraits of contemporary movers and shakers.

That said, the real stars of the era are the artists who had no resources and no expectations. Among these young and disenfranchised, a sort of destructive performance art came to the fore in the 1990s, known as 'Moscow Actionism'. Oleg Kulik and Anatoly Osmolovsky were pioneers of the movement, while Alexander Brenner was famously expelled from Russia after he vandalised a Malevich painting. Nowadays a new generation of artists – such as Pyotr Pavlensky – are practising such performance art with a more minimalist style and more meaningful symbolic action.

The most intriguing aspect of Moscow's contemporary art scene is not the established artists, but rather the up-and-coming creatives who are stashed at the city's art centres. Recently featured at Winzavod (p158), Evgeny Granilshikov uses video and other cinematic media to express his generation's disappointment with politics. Taus Makhacheva is a Dagestani whose art addressing national identity appeared at the Venice Biennale and other local venues.

Artists now have tremendous freedom to depict all aspects of Russian life. Many art professionals state categorically that there is no censorship in Russia, although most acknowledge a degree of self-censorship. That said, anecdotal evidence shows that contemporary artists and curators risk prosecution, especially if they tackle such sensitive topics as the war in Chechnya or the Russian Orthodox Church.

Nonetheless, contemporary art receives unprecedented support from the powers-that-be, with the government pitching in to fund prestigious events such as the Moscow Biennale of Contemporary Art (p25). Many oligarchs have also stepped in to foster homegrown talent and develop a vibrant art scene. Leonid Mikhelson, founder of Novatek and Russia's richest man (according to *Forbes*), started the V-A-C Foundation to support contemporary art. The foundation has sponsored countless exhibitions in Moscow and around the world since its inception, and its massive new art centre, GES-2, is now under construction on the site of a former power plant. Redesigned by Renzo Piano, the project is slated for completion in 2019.

Architecture

Moscow's streets are a textbook of Russian history, with churches, mansions, theatres and hotels standing as testament to the most definitive periods. Despite the tendency to demolish and rebuild (exhibited both in the past and in the present), Moscow has managed to preserve an impressive array of architectural gems.

1934
Avant-garde ideas are officially out of favour with the institution of socialist realism. Architecture tends towards bombastic neoclassicism.

1985
The policy of *glasnost*, or openness, gradually allows for more freedom of expression by artists and architects, who begin to explore diverse styles and themes.

ART & ARCHITECTURE ARCHITECTURE

Contemporary Art
....
Garage Museum of Contemporary Art (Zamoskvorechie)
....
Winzavod (Meshchansky & Basmanny)
....
Multimedia Art Museum (Arbat & Khamovniki)

Medieval Moscow

Moscow's oldest architecture has its roots in Kyivan Rus. The quintessential structure is the Byzantine cross-shaped church, topped with vaulted roofs and a central dome. In the 11th and 12th centuries, Russian culture moved from Kyiv to principalities further northeast. These towns – now comprising the so-called 'Golden Ring' – copied the Kyivan architectural design, developing their own variations on the pattern. Roofs grew steeper to prevent the crush of heavy snow; windows grew narrower to keep out the cold.

In many cases, stone replaced brick as the traditional building material. For example the white stone Assumption Cathedral and Golden Gate, both in Vladimir, are close copies of similar brick structures in Kyiv. In some cases, the stone facade became a tableau for a glorious kaleidoscope of carved images, such as the Cathedral of St Dmitry in Vladimir and the Church of the Intercession on the Nerl in Bogolyubovo.

Early church-citadel complexes required protection, so all of these settlements had sturdy, fortress-style walls replete with fairy-tale towers – Russia's archetypal kremlins. They are still visible in Suzdal and, of course, Moscow.

At the end of the 15th century, Ivan III imported architects from Italy to build two of the three great cathedrals in the Moscow Kremlin: Assumption Cathedral (p65) and Archangel Cathedral (p68). Nonetheless, the outsider architects looked to Kyiv for their inspiration, again copying the Byzantine design.

It was not until the 16th century that architects found inspiration in the tent roofs and onion domes on the wooden churches in the north of Russia. Their innovation was to construct these features out of brick, which contributed to a new, uniquely Russian style of architecture. The whitewashed Ascension Church (p150) at Kolomenskoe is said to be the earliest example of this innovative style, featuring open galleries at its base, tiers of *kokoshniki* (colourful tiles and gables laid in patterns) in the centre, and the pronounced tent roof up top. St Basil's Cathedral (p76) is the ultimate example of the Russian style, but there are plenty of other examples around Moscow.

In the 17th century, merchants financed smaller churches bedecked with tiers of *kokoshniki*. The Church of St Nicholas in Khamovniki (p132) and the Church of the Trinity in Nikitniki (p81) are excellent examples, as are most of the churches in Suzdal. Patriarch Nikon outlawed such frippery shortly after the construction of the Church of the Nativity of the Virgin in Putinki (p90).

Imperial Moscow

Embellishments returned at the end of the 17th century with the Western-influenced Moscow baroque. This style is sometimes called Naryshkin baroque, named after the boyar family that inhabited the western suburbs of Fili in the 17th century. There, in honour of his brothers' deaths, Lev Naryshkin commissioned the **Church of the Intercession** (Церковь Покрова в Филях; Novozavodskaya ul 6; Ⓜ Fili), the ornate beauty that would define the city's style for years to come. It featured exquisite white detailing against red-brick walls. Another example is the Epiphany Cathedral in the monastery (p82) of the same name in Kitay Gorod. Zamoskvorechie is a treasure chest of Moscow baroque churches.

Tsar Alexander I favoured the grandiose Russian Empire style, commissioning it almost exclusively. Moscow abounds with Empire-style buildings, since much of the city had to be rebuilt after the fire of 1812. The flamboyant decorations of earlier times were used on the huge new buildings erected to proclaim Russia's importance, such as the Triumphal Arch (p126) and the Bolshoi Theatre (p88).

The Russian revival of the end of the 19th century extended to architecture. The Cathedral of Christ the Saviour (p127) was inspired by Byzantine Russian architecture. The State History Museum (p78) and the Leningradsky vokzal (p245) (Leningrad station) were inspired by medieval Russian styles. The extraordinary Kazansky vokzal (p245) (Kazan station) embraces no fewer than seven earlier styles.

Meanwhile, Russia's take on art nouveau – Style Moderne – added wonderful curvaceous flourishes to many buildings across Moscow. Splendid examples include Yaroslavsky vokzal (p245), the Hotel Metropol (p191) and Ryabushinsky Mansion (p106).

Soviet Moscow

The revolution gave rise to young constructivist architects, who rejected superficial decoration; they designed buildings whose appearance was a direct function of their uses and materials – a new architecture for a new society. They used lots of glass and concrete in uncompromising geometric forms.

Konstantin Melnikov was probably the most famous constructivist, and his own house (p129) off ul Arbat is one of the most interesting and unusual examples of the style. The former bus depot that now houses the Jewish Museum & Centre of Tolerance (p90) is a more utilitarian example. In the 1930s constructivism was denounced, as Stalin had much grander predilections.

Stalin favoured neoclassical architecture, which echoed ancient Athens. He also favoured building on a gigantic scale to underline the might of the Soviet state. Monumental classicism inspired a 400m-high design for Stalin's pet project, a Palace of Soviets, which (mercifully) never got off the ground.

Stalin's architectural excesses reached their apogee in the seven wedding-cake-style skyscrapers that adorn the Moscow skyline, also known as the 'Seven Sisters (p236)'.

In 1955 a schizophrenic decree ordered architects to avoid 'excesses'. A bland modern style was introduced, stressing function over form. The State Kremlin Palace (p61) is representative of this period. The White House (p109) was built later, but harks back to this style.

Contemporary Planning & Development

At the end of the Soviet Union, architectural energies and civic funds were initially funnelled into the restoration of decayed churches and monasteries, as well as the rebuilding of structures such as the Cathedral of Christ the Saviour (p127) and Kazan Cathedral (p74).

In the 2000s Moscow was a hotbed of development. Skyscrapers and steeples changed the city skyline; the metro expanded in all directions; and office buildings, luxury hotels and shopping centres went up all over the city.

The most visible urban development is in Moscow-City, the flashy new International Business Centre (p246) that is sprouting up along the Moscow River in Presnya. The complex is impressive, with shiny glass-and-metal buildings on either side of the Moscow River and a cool pedestrian bridge connecting them. It includes two of Europe's tallest skyscrapers: at 374m, the 93-storey Tower East (Vostok) of the Federation complex is the tallest building in both Russia and Europe; the 85-storey OKO south tower is not far behind, at 354m.

The centrepiece of the former Red October chocolate factory is the Strelka Institute for Media, Architecture and Design (www.strelkainstitute.com), an exciting and innovative organisation that hosts all kinds of cultural events and activities for public consumption.

ART & ARCHITECTURE ARCHITECTURE

Moscow's Art & Architecture

From icons and onion domes to skyscrapers and socialist realism, Russia has always invented its own forms of art and architecture – incorporating European influences but remaining true to its Slavic heart. There is no better place than Moscow to witness the dramatic and divergent visual expressions of Russian culture.

1

1. Kremlin (p60) View of Sobornaya pl (Cathedral Sq) within the Kremlin walls, from Ivan the Great Bell Tower.

2. Cathedral of Christ the Saviour (p127) The stunning central altar of the main church is dedicated to the Nativity.

3. Pushkin Museum of Fine Arts (p123) Considered Moscow's premier foreign-art museum, it also features a collection of ancient Egyptian artefacts.

4. State Tretyakov Gallery (p141) Former boyar's castle turned gallery, now containing the world's best collection of pre-Revolutionary Russian art.

STALIN'S SEVEN SISTERS

The foundations for seven large skyscrapers were laid in 1947 to mark Moscow's 800th anniversary. Stalin had decided that Moscow suffered from a 'skyscraper gap' when compared to the USA, and ordered the construction of these seven behemoths to jump-start the city's skyline.

One of the main architects, Vyacheslav Oltarzhevsky, had worked in New York during the skyscraper boom of the 1930s, and his experience proved essential. (Fortunately, he'd been released from the Gulag in time to help.)

In addition to the 'Seven Sisters' listed here, there were plans in place to build an eighth Stalinist skyscraper in Zaryadye (near Kitay Gorod). The historic district was razed in 1947 and a foundation was laid for a 32-storey tower. It did not get any further than that – for better and for worse – and the foundation was later used for the gargantuan Hotel Rossiya (demolished in 2006). This is now the site of the new Park Zaryadye (p80).

With their widely scattered locations, the towers provide a unique visual reference for Moscow. Their official name in Russia is *vysotky* (high-rise) as opposed to *neboskryob* (foreign skyscraper). They have been nicknamed variously the 'Seven Sisters', the 'wedding cakes', 'Stalin's sisters' and more.

➡ Foreign Affairs Ministry (p129)

➡ Hilton Moscow Leningradskaya (p159)

➡ Radisson Royal Hotel Ukraina (p195)

➡ Kotelnicheskaya Apartment Block (p161)

➡ Kudrinskaya Apartment Block (p107)

➡ Moscow State University (p132)

➡ Transport Ministry (p159)

In the Works

Park Zaryadye construction (Kitay Gorod)

Museum Town (Arbat & Khamovniki)

Narkomfin restoration (Presnya)

With the appointment of Sergei Sobyanin, the pace of construction has slowed dramatically. Several large-scale shopping malls and other projects were called off, in favour of more enlightened endeavours. Urban planning has shifted to focus on the redevelopment of parks such as Gorky Park (p143), as well as increasing and improving pedestrian routes, such as the fountain- and art-filled Krymskaya Naberezhnaya (p145). Sobyanin's focus on public places – emphasising usability and liveability – is a radical departure from the policies of his predecessor.

The highest profile example, perhaps, is the site of the former Hotel Rossiya in Zaryadye near Kitay Gorod. The Soviet behemoth was destroyed in 2006, in anticipation of a new luxury hotel and commercial complex. When the recession hit two years later, investors pulled out and construction came to a halt. After six years, the city administration finally reached some conclusion about what to do with the prime real estate: turn it into a park. New in 2017, the green space recreates Russia's four micro-climates – taiga, steppe, forest and marsh – while other facilities include an outdoor amphitheatre and several new museums.

Literature & Cinema

Of Russia's rich cultural offerings, none is more widely appreciated than its traditions of literature and cinema, much of which originates in Moscow. The classics – *War and Peace* by Leo Tolstoy, *Battleship Potemkin* by Sergei Eisenstein – are masterpieces that have earned the admiration of international audiences across the ages. Contemporary Russian culture may be lesser known, but the electric atmosphere in the creative capital continues to stimulate the creation of innovative and insightful literature and film.

Literature

A love of literature is an integral part of Russian culture, and Ivans and Olgas will wax rhapsodic on the Russian classics without hesitation. With the end of Soviet censorship, the literati have figured out what to do with their new-found freedom and new authors have emerged, exploring literary genres from historical fiction to science fiction.

Romanticism in the Golden Age

Among the many ways that Peter the Great and Catherine the Great Westernised and modernised Russia was through the introduction of a modern alphabet. As a result it became increasingly acceptable during the Petrine era to use popular language in literature. This development paved the way for two centuries of Russian literary prolificacy.

Romanticism was a reaction against the strict social rules and scientific rationalisation of previous periods, exalting emotion and aesthetics. Nobody embraced Russian romanticism more than the national bard, Alexander Pushkin (1799–1837). Pushkin was born in Moscow and it was here that he met his wife, Natalia Goncharova. The two were wed at the Church of Grand Ascension and lived for a time on ul Arbat.

Pushkin's most celebrated drama, *Boris Godunov*, takes place in medieval Muscovy. The plot centres on the historical events leading up to the Time of Troubles and its resolution with the election of Mikhail Romanov as tsar. The epic poem *Yevgeny Onegin* is set, in part, in imperial Moscow. Pushkin savagely ridicules its foppish, aristocratic society, despite being a fairly consistent fixture of it himself.

Tolstoy (1828-1910) is one of the most celebrated novelists, not only in Russia but in the world. The depth of his characters and the vividness of his descriptions evoke 19th-century Russia. His novels *War and Peace* and *Anna Karenina,* both of which are set in Moscow, express his scepticism with rationalism, espousing the idea that history is the sum of an infinite number of individual actions.

Tolstoy spent most of his time at his estate in Yasnaya Polyana, but he also had property in Moscow, and he was a regular parishioner at the Church of St Nicholas of Khamovniki.

Although Fyodor Dostoevsky (1821–81) is more closely associated with St Petersburg, he was actually born in Moscow. He was among the first writers to navigate the murky waters of the human subconscious, blending powerful prose with psychology, philosophy and spirituality.

Literary Sights

··················

Tolstoy Estate-Museum (Arbat & Khamovniki)

··················

Mikhail Bulgakov Museum (Presnya)

··················

Gogol House (Presnya)

··················

Dostoevsky House-Museum (Tverskoy)

Dostoevsky's best-known works, such as *Crime and Punishment,* were all written (and to a large degree set) in his adopted city of St Petersburg. But bibliophiles assert that his early years in Moscow profoundly influenced his philosophical development.

Amid the epic works of Pushkin, Tolstoy and Dostoevsky, an absurdist short-story writer such as Nikolai Gogol (1809–52) can get lost in the annals of Russian literature. But this troubled genius created some of Russian literature's most memorable characters, including Akaki Akakievich, tragicomic hero of *The Overcoat.*

Gogol spent most of his years living abroad, but it was his hilarious satire of life in Russia that earned him the respect of his contemporaries. *Dead Souls* is his masterpiece. This 'novel in verse' follows the scoundrel Chichikov as he attempts to buy and sell deceased serfs, or 'dead souls', in an absurd money-making scam.

After the novel's highly lauded publication in 1841, Gogol suffered from poor physical and mental health. While staying at the Gogol House, in a fit of depression, he threw some of his manuscripts into the fire, including the second part of *Dead Souls,* which was not recovered in its entirety (the novel ends midsentence). The celebrated satirist died shortly thereafter and he is buried at Novodevichy Cemetery (p121).

Symbolism in the Silver Age

The late 19th century saw the rise of the symbolist movement, which emphasised individualism and creativity, and maintained that artistic endeavours were exempt from the rules that bound other parts of society. The outstanding figures of this time were novelists Vladimir Solovyov (1853–1900), Andrei Bely (1880–1934) and Alexander Blok (1880–1921), as well as poets Sergei Yesenin (1895–1925) and Vladimir Mayakovsky (1893–1930).

Although Bely lived in Moscow for a time, he is remembered for his mysterious novel *Petersburg.* His essays and philosophical discourses were also respected, making him one of the most important writers of the symbolist movement.

Mayakovsky was a futurist playwright and poet, and he acted as the revolution's official bard. He lived near Lubyanskaya pl, where his flat has been converted into a museum. He devoted his creative energy to social activism and propaganda on behalf of the new regime, but the romantic soul was unlucky in love and life. As is wont to happen, he became disillusioned with the Soviet Union, as reflected in his satirical plays. He shot himself in 1930 and is buried at Novodevichy Cemetery (p121). He is memorialised at Triumfalnaya pl, site of Mayakovskaya metro.

Revolutionary Literature

The immediate aftermath of 1917 saw a creative upswing in Russia. Inspired by social change, writers carried over these principles into their work, pushing revolutionary ideas and ground-breaking styles.

The trend was temporary, of course. The Bolsheviks were no connoisseurs of culture, and the new leadership did not appreciate literature unless it directly supported the goals of communism. Some writers managed to write within the system, penning some excellent poetry and plays in the 1920s; however, most found little inspiration in the prevailing climate of art 'serving the people'. Stalin announced that writers were 'engineers of the human soul' and as such had a responsibility to write in a partisan direction.

The clampdown on diverse literary styles culminated in the late 1930s with the creation of socialist realism, a literary form created to

Anton Chekhov describes his style: 'All I wanted to do was to say honestly to people: have a look at yourselves and see how bad and dreary your lives are! The important thing is that people should realise that, for when they do, they will most certainly create another and better life for themselves.'

An estimated 150,000 people attended Vladimir Mayakovsky's 1930 funeral – the third-largest display of public mourning in Soviet history (after the funerals of Lenin and Stalin).

promote the needs of the state, praise industrialisation and demonise social misfits. Alexey Tolstoy (1883–1945), for example, wrote historical novels comparing Stalin to Peter the Great and recounting the glories of the Russian civil war.

Literature of Dissent

While Stalin's propaganda machine was churning out novels with titles such as *How the Steel Was Tempered,* the literary community was secretly writing about life under a tyranny. Many accounts of Soviet life were printed in *samizdat* (underground) publications and secretly circulated among the literary community. Now-famous novels such as Rybakov's *Children of the Arbat* were published in Russia only with the loosening of censorship under *glasnost* (openness). Meanwhile, some of the Soviet Union's most celebrated writers were silenced in their own country, while their works received international acclaim. Boris Pasternak's *Dr Zhivago,* for example, was published in 1956, but it took 30 years for it to be officially printed in the Soviet Union.

Pasternak (1890–1960) lived in a country estate on the outskirts of Moscow. The title character in *Dr Zhivago* is torn between two lovers, as his life is ravaged by the revolution and the civil war. The novel was unacceptable to the Soviet regime, not because the characters were anti-revolutionary but because they were apolitical, valuing their individual lives over social transformation. The novel was awarded the Nobel Prize for Literature in 1958, but Pasternak was forced to reject it.

Mikhail Bulgakov (1890–1940) was a prolific playwright and novelist who lived near Patriarch's Ponds. He wrote many plays that were performed at the Moscow Art Theatre, some of which were apparently enjoyed by Stalin. But later his plays were banned, and he had difficulty finding work. Most of his novels take place in Moscow, including *Fatal Eggs, Heart of a Dog* and, most famously, *The Master and Margarita.*

The post-*glasnost* era of the 1980s and 1990s uncovered a huge library of work that had been suppressed during the Soviet period. Authors such as Yevgeny Zamyatin, Daniil Kharms, Anatoly Rybakov, Venedict Erofeev and Andrei Bitov – banned in the Soviet Union – are now recognised for their cutting-edge commentary and significant contributions to world literature.

Written in 1970 by Venedict Erofeev, *Moscow to the End of the Line* recounts a drunken man's train trip to visit his lover and child on the outskirts of the capital. As the journey progresses, the tale becomes darker and more hallucinogenic. *Moscow Stations,* by the same author, is another bleakly funny novella recounting alcohol-induced adventures.

Contemporary Literature

Russia's contemporary literary scene is largely based in Moscow and, to some degree, abroad, as émigré writers continue to be inspired and disheartened by their motherland.

Check out what your neighbour is reading as they ride the metro: more than likely, it's a celebrity rag or a murder mystery. Action-packed thrillers and detective stories have become wildly popular in the 21st century, with Polina Dashkova, Darya Dontsova, Alexandra Marinina and Boris Akunin rank among the best-selling and most widely translated authors. *The Winter Queen,* by Akunin, is just one in the series of popular detective novels featuring the foppish Erast Fandorin as a member of the 19th-century Moscow police force. Several of these have been made into movies.

Horror is another popular genre, as exemplified by the young novelist Anna Starobinets. She has earned acclaim for her collection of short

Explore the Moscow of *The Master and Margarita* on an English-language walking tour offered by the Mikhail Bulgakov Museum.

LITERATURE & CINEMA LITERATURE

Every year in June/July, the Moscow International Film Festival offers a venue for directors of independent films from Russia and abroad to compete for international recognition.

stories, *Awkward Age*, and for her several novels, especially the 2011 *Living One*, which was shortlisted for the National Bestseller Award in Russia. Ludmilla Petrushevskaya is famous for her 'scary fairy tales'. In 2017 she departed from this genre with the publication of *The Girl from the Metropol Hotel*, a memoir about her impoverished childhood in the Soviet Union.

Indeed, some of the most noteworthy contemporary fiction is set in Soviet Russia. Most significantly, Alexander Chudakov won the Russian Booker Prize for his fictionalised memoir, *A Gloom Descends upon the Ancient Steps*. Ludmila Ulitskaya is also beloved for her works of historical fiction, as well as her outspokenness on contemporary issues. She has written more than a dozen novels, her most recent being *The Big Green Tent*, which is an epic tale of three friends in post-Stalinist Moscow.

Multiple award-winning author Mikhail Shishkin is not bound by traditional literary devices. His novel *Taking of Izmael* is a mishmash of language, storylines and styles, yet it won the Booker Prize in 2001. His 2014 novel, *The Light & the Dark*, is a letter-book, comprised of the intimate correspondence between two lovers who are separated by thousands of miles but also by centuries.

Meanwhile, social critics continue the Soviet literary tradition of using dark humour and fantastical storylines to provide scathing social commentary. Vladimir Sorokin's works include *Day of the Oprichnik*, which describes Russia in the year 2028 as a nationalist country ruled with an iron fist that has shut itself off from the West by building a wall. His 2015 novel *Blizzard* is also set in the future. Victor Pelevin is the unrivalled master of Russian political fiction. Pelevin won the 1993 Russian 'Little Booker' for short stories, but he has written dozens of dark, abstract, comical novels. Most notably, the 2009 *Sacred Book of the Werewolf* is a supernatural love story that is also a satire of contemporary Russian politics.

Cinema

In the Hollywood hills they have Leo the MGM lion, and in Sparrow Hills they have the iconic socialist sculpture, *Worker and Peasant Woman*, the instantly recognisable logo of Mosfilm. Russia's largest film studio has played a defining role in the development of Soviet and Russian cinema.

Revolutionary Cinema

During the Soviet period, politics and cinema were always closely connected. The nascent film industry received a big boost from the Bolshevik revolution, as the proletarian culture needed a different kind of canvas. Comrade Lenin recognised that motion pictures would become the new mass medium for the new mass politics. By government decree,

MOSCOW DOES NOT BELIEVE IN TEARS

Three young women arrive in the capital in 1958, starting new careers and looking for love. They become friends. This is the simple premise of one of the most iconic films to come out of the Soviet Union, *Moscow Does Not Believe in Tears*, which won the Academy Award for Best Foreign Film in 1980. The three friends follow different paths, of course, and the film then flashes forward 20 years to show us how things turn out. Along the way, we get insights into class consciousness (yes, even in the Soviet Union) and romantic relationships – with plenty of shots of 1970s Moscow as a backdrop.

the film studio Mosfilm was officially founded in 1923, under the leadership of Alexander Khanzhokov, the pioneer of Russian cinema.

In this golden age, Soviet film earned an international reputation for its artistic experimentation and propaganda techniques. Legendary director Sergei Eisenstein, a socialist true believer, popularised a series of innovations, such as fast-paced montage editing and mounted tracking cameras, to arouse emotional response from the audience that could be used to shape political views. His *Battleship Potemkin* (1925) remains one of film history's most admired and most studied silent classics.

Socialist Realism

Under Stalin, the cinematic avant-garde was kept on a tight leash. Stylistic experimentation was repressed, and socialist realism was promoted. There was no mistaking the preferred social values of the political regime. Characters and plot lines were simple; the future looked bright.

Some directors were assigned 'partners' to ensure that they did not get too creative and stray into formalism. During this period, Eisenstein produced award-winning historical dramas such as *Alexander Nevsky* (1938) and *Ivan the Terrible* (1946).

When Stalin departed the scene, directors responded with more honest depictions of Soviet daily life and more creative styles. Russian productions again received international acclaim, earning top honours at all the most prestigious cinematic venues. During this period, the Academy Award for Best Foreign Language Film went to Mosfilm works multiple times, for films such as *War and Peace* (1968), *The Brothers Karamazov* (1969), *Tchaikovsky* (1971), *Dersu Uzala* (1975) and *Moscow Does Not Believe in Tears* (1980).

However, getting past the censors at home still posed challenges. The fate of any movie was decided by the risk-averse Goskino, the vast Moscow-based bureaucracy that funded and distributed films.

Elem Klimov's comedies were thinly veiled critiques of contemporary society. They were not exactly banned, but they were not exactly promoted. The dark and rather disturbing *Adventures of a Dentist* (1965) was shown in less than 100 theatres. Klimov's war drama *Come and See* was on the shelf for eight years before it was finally released in 1985 to commemorate the 40th anniversary of the Soviet victory in WWII.

Andrei Tarkovsky earned worldwide recognition for his films, including his first feature film *Ivan's Childhood* (1962), which won in Venice, and *Andrei Rublyov* (1966), which won in Cannes. The latter film was cut several times before a truncated version was finally released in the Soviet Union in 1971.

Glasnost & Transition

During a 1986 congress of Soviet filmmakers held in Moscow, *glasnost* touched the USSR's movie industry. By a large vote the old conservative directors were booted out of the leadership and renegades demanding more freedom were put in their place.

Over 250 previously banned films were released. As such, some of the most politically daring and artistically innovative works finally made it off the shelf and onto the big screen for audiences to see for the first time. By the end of the Soviet regime, Mosfilm was one of Europe's largest and most prolific film studios, with over 2500 films to its credit.

With the collapse of the Soviet Union, the film industry fell on hard times. Funding had dried up during the economic chaos of the early 1990s and audiences couldn't afford to go to the cinema anyway. Mosfilm was finally reorganised into a quasi-private concern, although it continued to receive significant state patronage.

Irony of Fate (1975) is a classic that's still screened on TV every New Year's Eve. After a mind-bending party in Moscow, the protagonist wakes up in St Petersburg, where his key fits into the lock of an identical building at the same address in a different town. Comedy ensues.

Vasily Pichul's ground-breaking film *Little Vera* (1988), produced by the Gorky Film Studio, caused a sensation with its frank portrayal of a family in chaos (exhausted wife, drunken husband, rebellious daughter) and with its sexual frankness – mild by Western standards but startling to the Soviet audience.

LITERATURE & CINEMA CINEMA

INDIE FILMS

In this age of corporate-sponsored cinema, some Russian directors are still turning out stimulating art-house films.

In 2003 Moscow director Andrei Zvyagintsev came home from Venice with the Golden Lion, awarded for his moody thriller *The Return*. His follow-up film, *The Banishment*, refers to the end of paradise for a couple whose marriage is falling apart. Zvyagintsev continues to earn accolades at Venice and in Cannes. *Elena* (2011) is an evocative, if disheartening portrait of relationships in modern Moscow. *Leviathan* (2014) is another starkly realistic drama about an everyday guy who tries to seek justice and takes on the system – with a tragic outcome.

In 2006 stage director Ivan Vyrypaev won the small Golden Lion for his cinematic debut, the tragic love story *Euphoria*. Vyrypaev wrote and directed several experimental follow-up films. Meanwhile, Alexei Popogrebsky has won a slew of lesser awards for *How I Ended this Summer* (2010), a compelling drama set at a remote Arctic research station.

Valery Todorovsky directed *Hipsters* (2008), about a rebellious Soviet counter-cultural group from the 1950s. With cool costumes and a big-name soundtrack, the film has turned into a sort of cult classic.

At this low point, ironically, Mosfilm produced one of its crowning achievements – the Cannes Grand Prize and Academy Award–winning film *Burnt by the Sun* (1994), featuring the work of actor and director Nikita Mikhalkov. The story of a loyal apparatchik who becomes a victim of Stalin's purges, the film demonstrated that politics and cinema were still inextricably linked.

Many consider the film industry's turning point came with the release of *Brother* (1997), a crime film that portrayed the stark realities of the St Petersburg underground.

Contemporary Cinema

Moscow's film industry has made a remarkable comeback since the lull in the 1990s. Mosfilm is one of the largest production companies in the world, producing almost all of Russia's film, TV and video programming. Moscow is indeed the Russian Hollywood. Unfortunately, just like its American counterpart, the industry does not leave much room for artsy, independent films that are not likely to be blockbusters.

But there is no shortage of blockbusters. *The Turkish Gambit,* a drama set during the Russo-Turkish War, broke all post-Soviet box-office records in 2005. In 2007 the prolific Nikita Mikhalkov directed *12*, a film based on Sidney Lumet's *12 Angry Men*. The Oscar-nominated film follows a jury deliberating over the trial of a Chechen teenager accused of murdering his father, who was an officer in the Russian army. Vladimir Putin is quoted as saying that it 'brought a tear to the eye'.

The glossy vampire thriller *Night Watch* (2004) struck box-office gold both at home and abroad, leading to an equally successful sequel, *Day Watch* (2006) – and to Kazakhstan-born director Timur Bekmambetov being lured to Hollywood. Bekmambetov's most successful effort since the *Night Watch* series is undoubtedly his direction of *Irony of Fate: Continuation* (2007), a follow-up to the classic 1970s comedy. Simultaneously released on 1000 screens across the nation, the movie was poorly reviewed but widely watched. It is still one of the highest grossing films of the era.

In 2013 Fedor Bondarchuk directed Russia's first IMAX production, a historical war film called *Stalingrad*. It was acclaimed for stunning visuals but derided for melodramatic plot line. Nonetheless, the film shattered all box-office records.

In 2010 Nikita Mikhalkov used the largest production budget ever seen in Russian cinema to make the sequel to his 1994 masterpiece. *Burnt by the Sun II* received universally negative reviews and was a box-office flop.

Survival Guide

Transport

ARRIVING IN MOSCOW

Travellers to Moscow will likely arrive by air or train. Flights, cars and tours can be booked online at lonely planet.com/bookings.

Air

Most travellers arrive in Moscow by air, flying into one of the city's four international airports: Domodedovo, Sheremetyevo, Vnukovo or Zhukovsky. The vast majority of international flights go in and out of Domodedovo and Sheremetyevo, both of which are about an hour from the city centre by car or train.

There are Aeroflot outlets all around town:

➡ **Aeroflot** (Map p274; ul Petrovka 20/1; MChekhovskaya)

➡ **Aeroflot** (Map p286; ul Kuznetsky most 3; MKuznetsky Most)

➡ **Aeroflot** (Map p282; Pyatnitskaya ul 37/19; MTretyakovskaya)

The three main airports – not yet including Zhukovsky – are accessible by the convenient **Aeroexpress Train** (☑8-800-700 3377; www. aeroexpress.ru; airport one way ₽420; ☺6am-midnight) from the city centre; reduced rates are available for online purchases. Alternatively,

order an official airport taxi from the dispatcher's desk in the terminal (₽2000 to ₽2500 to the city centre). You can save some cash by booking in advance to take advantage of the fixed rates offered by most companies (usually from ₽1500 to ₽1800 to/from any airport). Driving times vary wildly depending on the traffic.

Sheremetyevo

The largest airport in Moscow, **Sheremetyevo** (Шереметьево; ☑495-578 6565; www.svo.aero) international airport is 30km northwest of the city centre. The Aeroexpress Train makes the 35-minute trip between Sheremetyevo (located next to Terminal E) and Belorussky vokzal every half-hour from 5.30am to 12.30am.

Domodedovo

Llocated about 48km south of the city, **Domodedovo** (Домодедово; ☑495-933 6666; www.domodedovo.ru) international airport is Moscow's largest and most efficient international airport. The Aeroexpress Train leaves Paveletsky vokzal every half-hour between 6am and midnight for the 45-minute trip to Domodedovo.

Vnukovo

About 30km southwest of the city centre, **Vnukovo**

(Внуково; ☑495-937 5555; www.vnukovo.ru) international airport serves most flights to/from the Caucasus, Moldova and Kaliningrad, as well as domestic flights and a smattering of flights to Europe. The Aeroexpress Train makes the 35-minute run from Kievsky vokzal to Vnukovo airport every hour from 6am to 11pm.

Zhukovsky

Opened in 2016, Moscow's fourth international airport, **Zhukovsky** (Жуковский; ☑495-228 9600; http://zia. aero) is about 40km southeast of Moscow. The new airport mostly serves Central Asian destinations, and it is a hub for Ural Airlines.

Train

Rail riders will arrive at one of Moscow's central train stations: Kievsky or Belorussky vokzal if you're coming from Europe; Leningradsky vokzal if you're coming from St Petersburg; Yaroslavsky or Kazansky vokzal if you're coming from the east; and Paveletsky vokzal if you're arriving from the Volga region or Central Asia.

All of the train stations are located in the city centre, with easy access to the metro. Most taxi companies offer a fixed rate of ₽400 to ₽600 for a train station transfer.

CLIMATE CHANGE & TRAVEL

Every form of transport that relies on carbon-based fuel generates CO_2, the main cause of human-induced climate change. Modern travel is dependent on aeroplanes, which might use less fuel per kilometre per person than most cars but travel much greater distances. The altitude at which aircraft emit gases (including CO_2) and particles also contributes to their climate change impact. Many websites offer 'carbon calculators' that allow people to estimate the carbon emissions generated by their journey and, for those who wish to do so, to offset the impact of the greenhouse gases emitted with contributions to portfolios of climate-friendly initiatives throughout the world. Lonely Planet offsets the carbon footprint of all staff and author travel.

Leningradsky Vokzal

Located at busy Komsomolskaya pl, **Leningrad Station** (Ленинградский вокзал; http://leningradsky.dzvr.ru; Komsomolskaya pl; ☎; MKomsomolskaya) serves Tver, Novgorod, Pskov, St Petersburg, Vyborg, Murmansk, Estonia and Helsinki. Note that sometimes this station is referred to on timetables and tickets by its former name, Oktyabrsky (Октябрьский).

Belorussy Vokzal

At the top of Tverskaya ul, **Belarus Station** (Белорусский вокзал; http://belorussy.dzvr.ru; Tverskaya Zastava pl; ☎; MBelorusskaya) serves trains to/from northern and central Europe, as well as suburban trains to/from the west, including Mozhaysk and Borodino. This is also where you'll catch the Aeroexpress Train to Sheremetyevo international airport.

Kievsky Vokzal

Located in Dorogomilovo, **Kiev Station** (Киевский вокзал; www.kievsky-vokzal.ru; Kievskaya pl; ☎; MKievskaya) serves Kyiv and western Ukraine, as well as points further west, such as Moldova, Slovakia, Hungary, Austria, Prague, Romania, Bulgaria, Croatia, Serbia and Greece. This is also where you'll catch the Aeroexpress Train to Vnukovo international airport.

Yaroslavsky Vokzal

The main station for Trans-Siberian trains, **Yaroslav Station** (Ярославский вокзал; http://yaroslavsky.dzvr.ru; Komsomolskaya pl; ☎; MKomsomolskaya) serves Yaroslavl, Arkhangelsk, Vorkuta, the Russian Far East, Mongolia, China and North Korea; some trains to/from Vladimir, Nizhny Novgorod, Kostroma, Vologda, Perm, the Ural Mountains and Siberia; and suburban trains to/from the northeast, including Abramtsevo and Sergiev Posad.

Kazansky Vokzal

Kazan Station (Казанский вокзал; http://kazansky.dzvr.ru; Komsomolskaya pl; ☎; MKomsomolskaya) serves trains to/from Kazan and points southeast, as well as some trains to/from Vladimir, Nizhny Novgorod, the Ural Mountains and Siberia.

Paveletsky Vokzal

South of the city **Pavelets Station** (Павелецкий вокзал; http://paveletsky.dzvr.ru; Paveletskaya pl; MPaveletskaya) serves points south, including the Volga region and Central Asia. This is also the departure/arrival point for the Aeroexpress Train to Domodedovo international airport.

GETTING AROUND MOSCOW

Metro

The **Moscow Metro** (www.mosmetro.ru; per ride ₽55) is by far the easiest, quickest and cheapest way of getting around Moscow. Plus, many of the elegant stations are marble-faced, frescoed, gilded works of art. The 150-plus stations are marked outside by large 'M' signs.

Reliability The trains are generally reliable: you will rarely wait on a platform for more than three minutes. Nonetheless, they do get packed, especially during the city's rush hours.

Tickets Ediny and Troika cards are sold at ticket booths. Queues can be long, so it's useful (and slightly cheaper) to buy a multiple-ride ticket.

Maps & Signage Stations have maps of the system at the entrance and signs on each platform showing the destinations. The maps are generally in Cyrillic and Latin script, although the signs are usually only in Cyrillic. The carriages also have maps inside that show the stops for that line in both Roman and Cyrillic letters.

Transfers Interchange stations are linked by underground passages, indicated by *perekhod* signs, usually blue with a stick figure running up the stairs. Be aware that when two or more lines meet, the intersecting stations often (but not always) have different names.

Moscow Central Ring Operated by Russian Railways, the new ring line complements the existing metro system and is good for moving between such far-flung attractions as **Izmaylovsky Market** (www.kremlin-izmailovo.com; Izmaylovskoye sh 73; ⏰10am-8pm; MPartizanskaya), the **Botanical Gardens** (www.gbsad.ru; MBotanichesky Sad) FREE and **Moscow International Business Centre** (Москва-сити; MDelovoi Tsentr).

Taxi

Taxi cabs are affordable. Unfortunately, you can't really flag down an official metered taxi in the street and most taxi drivers and dispatchers do not speak English. That said, mobile phone apps are common and easy to use.

The most popular mobile phone app for ordering taxis is **Yandex.Taxi** (Яндекс. Такси; https://taxi.yandex.com). The interface is available in English, and you provide all details (including departure point and destination address) via the app.

Citymobil (☑495-500 5050; www.citymobil.com)

Detskoe Taxi (Детское Такси; ☑495-765 1180; www.detskoetaxi.ru) 'Children's Taxi' has smoke-free cars and car seats for your children.

Lingo Taxi (www.lingotaxi.com) Promises English-speaking drivers (and usually delivers).

New Yellow Taxi (Новое жёлтое такси; ☑495-940 8888; www.nyt.ru)

Taxi Blues (☑495-925 5115; www.taxi-blues.ru)

Boat

For new perspectives on Moscow's neighbourhoods, fine views of the Kremlin, or just good, old-fashioned transport, a boat ride on the Moscow River is one of the city's highlights.

Capital Shipping Co (ССК, Столичная Судоходная Компания; ☑495-225 6070; www.cck-ship.ru; adult/child 60min cruise ₽900/700, 2-day pass ₽2400/2000) offers a two-day pass, so you can get on and off wherever you wish.

The main route runs between the boat landings at Kievsky vokzal and Novospassky most, with several stops along the way:

Vorobyovy Gory Landing (Vorobyovskaya nab)

Gorky Park Landing

Krymsky Most Landing (Map p281)

Bolshoy Kamenny Most Landing (Map p282)

Ustinsky Most Landing (Map p286)

Bicycle

There are more and more bicycles on the streets and pavements of Moscow. Cycling in the centre of Moscow is still a dangerous prospect, as the streets are overcrowded with fast-moving cars and the exhaust fumes are nasty.

That said, the city has launched a campaign to make the city safer for cyclists. As of 2016, there were some 250km of bike lanes, with plans for an additional 500km to be painted in coming years. There are a few parks and other off-road areas that are suitable for pleasure riding, including Gorky Park (p143), Vorobyovy Gory Nature Preserve (p132), Sokolniki (p159) and VDNKh (p93).

If you're nervous about navigating the streets on your own (or if you just want some company), **Moscow Bike Tours** (☑8-916-970 1419; www.moscowbiketours.com; 2½hr tour US$40-60) are a great way to see the city by bicycle.

Bike Share

Moscow's new bike-share program is **VeloBike** (www.velobike.ru), an innovative system designed to cut down on traffic and encourage healthier living in the capital. It started in 2013 and now offers some 2700 bicycles at 350 stations around the city.

➡ Go online to purchase a membership (₽150 for a day, ₽600

GETTING OUT OF TOWN ON YOUR BIKE

➡ Bicycles are not allowed on the metro (with the exception of folding bikes).

➡ They are permitted on long-distance trains, but you must buy a special ticket to bring your bike on the *elektrichka* (suburban commuter train).

➡ Bicycles are allowed on intercity passenger trains as long as your total luggage does not exceed the weight limit (36kg). You should disassemble and package the bike to ensure that you will be able to find space to store it.

➡ The **Russian Cycle Touring Club** (www.rctc.ru) organises weekend rides around Moscow and longer-distance bicycle tours around Russia, including a popular tour of the Golden Ring.

for a month, plus deposit). Now you are ready to roll!

➡ Use your credit card to unlock a bike at any station, go for a ride, and return your bike to any station. The first 30 minutes incurs no additional charge, but after that you'll pay for use.

➡ The system is designed for transportation rather than recreation, so it's a good deal for short rides from point A to point B. For longer rides, you may be better off renting from **Oliver Bikes** (Оливер Байкс; Map p282; ☑499-340 2609; www.bikerentalmoscow.com; Pyatnitskaya ul 3/4, str 2; per hr/day from ₽500/1200, tours per group ₽6000; ☺10am-11pm; ⓂNovokuznetskaya).

Bus

Buses, trolleybuses and trams might be necessary for reaching some sights away from the city centre. *Marshrutki* (private buses and minibuses) are particularly useful to reach some destinations on the outskirts of Moscow. Buses can also be useful for a few cross-town or radial routes that the metro misses. In particular, there are several buses that run around the Kremlin Ring (Mokhovaya ul, ul Okhotny Ryad, Teatralny pr, Staray pl), which is useful for the city centre.

Enter through the first door, with your ticket prepared for validation at the turnstiles (people behind you may get pushy and impatient if you start looking for the ticket in your bag at the last moment). You can travel with Ediny, Troika or TAT cards. If you don't have a ticket, you can buy one or several single-trip Ediny tickets from the driver for ₽55 per ticket.

Car & Motorcycle

There's little reason for travellers to rent a car to get around Moscow, as public transport is quite adequate. However, you might want to consider car rental for trips out of the city. Be aware that driving in Russia is an unfiltered Russian experience, mainly due to poor signage and ridiculous traffic.

Requirements

➡ To drive in Russia, you must be at least 18 years old and have a full driving licence.

➡ In addition, you may be asked to present an International Driving Permit with a Russian translation of your licence, or a certified Russian translation of your full licence (you can certify translations at a Russian embassy or consulate) – though this is unlikely.

➡ For your own vehicle, you will also need registration papers and proof of insurance. Be sure your insurance covers you in Russia.

➡ Finally, a customs declaration, promising that you will take your vehicle with you when you leave, is also required.

Safety

➡ **Drinking & Driving** As of 2013, the maximum legal blood-alcohol content is 0.0356%. Prior to this change it was practically illegal to drive after consuming any alcohol at all, and this rule was strictly enforced. In any case, it is not advisable to drink and drive in Russia, even a small amount.

➡ **Road Patrol** Officers of the Road Patrol Service (Dorozhno-Patrulnaya Sluzhba), better known as DPS, skulk about on the roadsides all around

Moscow waiting for miscreant drivers. They are authorised to stop you (by pointing their striped stick at you and waving you towards the side), and the DPS also hosts the occasional speed trap. Fines are *not* payable on the spot: you'll have a set amount of time to pay at a local bank; make sure you keep your receipt.

Fuel

Moscow has no shortage of petrol stations that sell all grades of petrol. Most are open 24 hours and can be found on the major roads in and out of town.

Hire

While driving around Moscow is an unnecessary hassle, renting a car may be a reasonable option for trips out of the city. Be aware that some firms won't let you take their cars out of the Moscow Oblast (Moscow Region).

The major international car-rental firms have outlets in Moscow (at either Sheremetyevo or Domodedovo airports, as well as in the city centre). They'll usually pick up or drop off the car at your hotel for an extra fee.

Avis (☑495-988 6216; www.avis.com/en/locations/qc/moscow; Komsomolskaya pl 3; ☺10am-8pm; ⓂKomsomolskaya)

Hertz (☑495-775 8333; www.hertz.ru; Darklaya ul 6/3; ☺9am-9pm; ⓂPark Pobedy)

Thrifty Outer North (www.thrifty.com; Bldg 3, Leningradskoye shosse 16; ⓂVoykovskaya); Outer South (www.thrifty.com; Profsoyuznaya ul 65; ⓂKaluzhskaya)

Directory A–Z

Customs Regulations

➡ Searches beyond the perfunctory are quite rare, but clearing customs when you leave Russia by a land border can be lengthy.

➡ Visitors are allowed to bring in and take out up to US$10,000 (or its equivalent) in currency, and goods up to the value of €10,000, weighing less than 50kg, without making a customs declaration.

➡ Fill in a customs declaration form if you're bringing into Russia major equipment, antiques, artworks or musical instruments (including a guitar) that you plan to take out with you – get it stamped in the red channel of customs to avoid any problems leaving with the same goods.

➡ If you plan to export anything vaguely 'arty' – instruments, coins, jewellery, antiques, antiquarian manuscripts and books (older than 50 years) or art (also older than 50 years) – it should first be assessed by the **Expert Collegium** (Коллегия экспертизы; ☏499-391 4212; ul Akademika Korolyova 21, bldg 1, office 505, 5th fl; ⊙11am-5pm Mon-Fri; Ⓜ VDNKh); it is very difficult to export anything over 100 years old. Bring two photographs of your item, your receipt and your passport. If export is allowed, you'll be issued a receipt for tax paid, which you show to customs officers on your way out of the country.

Discount Cards

➡ **Moscow Pass** (www.moscowpass.com) Purchase a one- or three-day pass (€27/51) and get admission to more than 40 Moscow museums, plus a riverboat cruise. Extra €8 charge if you want to include the Kremlin. Additional savings at two dozen different restaurants, as well as **Moscow Free** (Map p271; ☏495-222 3466; www.moscowfreetour.com; Nikolskaya ul 4/5; guided walk free, paid tours from €31) walking tours.

➡ **Russia City Pass** (www.russiacitypass.com) Admission to the same 40 museums (more or less) and riverboat cruise, with a miniguide to show you where to go. Also promises that you can skip the line at the most popular sights. Prices range from US$50 for a one-day pass to US$111 for a five-day pass.

➡ **Pass City** (www.passcity.ru) Includes museums and cultural attractions in both Moscow and St Petersburg, as well as **Yandex.Taxi** (Яндекс.Такси; https://taxi.yandex.com) rides and free audio tours in both cities. Prices start at ₽5990 for a three-day pass.

Electricity

Access electricity (220V, 50Hz AC) with a European plug with two round pins. A few places still have the old 127V system.

Type C
220V/50Hz

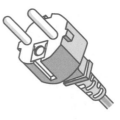

Type F
230V/50Hz

Embassies & Consulates

It's wise to register with your embassy, especially if you'll be in Russia for a long stay.

Australian Embassy
(Посольство Австралии; Map p286; ☑495-956 6070; www.russia.embassy.gov.au; Podkolokolny per 10a/2; Ⓜ Kitay-Gorod)

Belarusian Embassy
(Посольство Белорусии; Map p286; ☑495-777 6644; www.embassybel.ru; ul Maroseyka 17/6; Ⓜ Kitay-Gorod)

Canadian Embassy
(Посольство Канады; Map p276; ☑495-925 6000; http://russia.gc.ca; Starokonyushenny per 23, Moscow; ⊙8.30am-5pm; Ⓜ Kropotkinskaya)

Chinese Embassy
(Посольство Китая; ☑consular 499-951 8436; http://ru.chineseembassy.org/rus; ul Druzhby 6, Moscow; ⊙9am-noon Mon-Fri; Ⓜ Universitet)

French Embassy (Посольство Франции; Map p282; ☑495-937 1500; www.ambafrance-ru.org, ul Bolshaya Yakimanka 45, Moscow; Ⓜ Oktyabrskaya)

German Embassy
(Посольство Германии; ☑495-937 9500; www.germania.diplo.de; Mosfilmovskaya ul 56, Moscow; ⊙9am-3pm; ☐119, Ⓜ Universitet)

Irish Embassy (Посольство Ирландии; ☑495-937 5911; www.embassyofireland.ru; Grokholsky per 5; Ⓜ Prospekt Mira)

Kazakhstan Embassy
(Посольство Республики Казахстан (консульский отдел); Map p286; ☑495-627 1811; www.kazembassy.ru; Chistoprudny bul 3a; ⊙9.30am-12.30pm Mon, Tue, Thu & Fri)

Latvian Embassy
(Посольство Латвийской Республики; Map p286; ☑495-232 9760; www.mfa.gov.lv/en/moscow; ul Chaplygina 3; Ⓜ Chistye Prudy)

Mongolian Embassy
(Посольство Монголии; Map p278; ☑495-690 4636; http://embassymongolia.ru; Borisoglebsky per 11; Ⓜ Arbartskaya; Visa Section (Посольство Монголии (Визовый отдел); Map p276; ☑499-241 1557; http://embassymongolia.ru; Spasopeskovsky per 7/1; Ⓜ Smolenskaya)

Netherlands Embassy
(Посольство Королевства Нидерландов; Map p278; ☑495-797 2900; www.netherlands-embassy.ru; Kalashny per 6; Ⓜ Arbatskaya)

Tajik Embassy Russia (Consular Section) (Посольство Республики Таджикистан (Консульский отдел); Map p278; ☑495-690 5736; www.tajembassy.ru; 19 Skatertny pr; ⊙9am-5pm Mon, Thu & Fri; Ⓜ Barrikadnaya)

Turkmen Embassy (Consular Section) (Посольство Туркменистана (Консульский отдел); Map p276; ☑495-695 3716; https://russia.tm embassy.com.tm; Bldg 1, Maly Afanasyevsky per 14/34; ⊙9-11am & 2-5pm Mon, Tue, Thu & Fri; Ⓜ Arbatskaya)

UK Embassy (Посольство Великобритании; Map p276; ☑495-956 7200; www.gov.uk/government/world/russia; Smolenskaya nab 10, Moscow; ⊙9am-5pm; Ⓜ Smolenskaya)

Ukrainian Embassy
(Посольство Украины; Map p278; ☑495-629 3542, consular questions 495-629 9742; http://russia.mfa.gov.ua; Leontevsky per 18; Ⓜ Pushkinskaya)

US Embassy (Посольство США; Map p278; ☑495-728 5000; http://moscow.us embassy.gov; Bolshoy Devyatinsky per 8; Ⓜ Barrikadnaya)

Emergencies

Tourist Helpline	☑800-220 0001 /2
Universal Emergency Number	☑112

LGBTIQ Travel

➡ Russia is a conservative country and being gay is generally frowned upon. LGBTIQ people face stigma, harassment and violence in their everyday lives.

➡ Homosexuality isn't illegal, but promoting it (and other LGBTIQ lifestyles) is. What constitutes promotion is at the discretion of the authorities.

➡ Moscow Pride has not taken place since it was banned by city courts (despite fines from the European Court of Human Rights in 2010). Activists were

---

LGBTIQ TRAVELLERS

Although homosexuality is legal in Russia, this is a socially conservative country where open displays of affection may attract unwanted attention. Watchdog groups have reported an increase in violence since legislation banning 'gay propaganda' was enacted in 2011. There have also been reports of police harassment around gay clubs and cruising areas in Moscow. Exercise extra caution around LGBTIQ-specific venues (or avoid them) and you are unlikely to experience any problems.

violently attacked by extremists at the event in 2011.

➡ That said, Moscow is the most cosmopolitan of Russian cities, and the active gay and lesbian scene reflects this attitude. Newspapers such as the *Moscow Times* feature articles about gay and lesbian issues, as well as listings of gay and lesbian clubs.

➡ **Gay.ru** (http://english.gay.ru) is rather out-of-date but still has good links and resources for getting in touch with personal guides.

Health

While brushing your teeth with it is OK, assume that tap water isn't safe to drink. Stick to bottled water, boil water for 10 minutes or use water purification tablets or a filter.

Internet Access

➡ Almost all hotels and hostels offer wi-fi, as do many bars, restaurants and cafes. It isn't always free, but it is ubiquitous. There is also free wi-fi on the metro and at hotspots around the city.

➡ To use the free wi-fi, you will be obliged to register your phone number to obtain a pass code. Some services only accept Russian telephone numbers, in which case you may have to ask a local to use their number.

➡ Most hostels and hotels offer internet access for guests who are not travelling with their own device. Internet cafes are a thing of the past.

➡ Also popular is shared work space, which offers a comfortable work space, functional wi-fi, and sometimes drinks and snacks, for a per-minute or per-hour fee.

Ziferblat Tverskaya
(Циферблат; Map p274; www.ziferblat.net; Tverskaya ul 12c1;

⊙11am-midnight; MPushkinskaya)

Ziferblat Pokrovka
(Циферблат; Map p286; www.ziferblat.net; ul Pokrovka 12 c 1; per min ₽3; ⊙11am-midnight Sun-Thu, 11am-7pm Fri & Sat; MChistye Prudy)

Russian State Library (Map p276; ul Vozdvizhenka 3; ⊙9am-9pm; MBiblioteka imeni Lenina)

Legal Matters

You may spot 'tourist police' hanging around Red Square and other popular tourist haunts. No, they are not a special police force to harass tourists, but rather to *assist* tourists. Tourist police supposedly have a degree of foreign language proficiency and other training and communication skills.

That said, it's not unusual to see the regular police officers (*politsiya*) randomly stopping people on the street to check their documents. Often, the *politsiya* target individuals who look like they come from the Caucasus, and other people with darkish skin. But officers have the right to stop anyone, and they do exercise it.

Technically, everyone is required to carry a passport (*dokumenty*) at all times. Such reports have declined, but in the past travellers have complained about police pocketing their passports and demanding bribes. The best way to avoid such unpleasantness is to carry a photocopy of your passport, visa and registration, and present them when an officer demands to see your *dokumenty*.

If a police officer demands payment for some infraction, you have the right to insist that the 'fine' be paid the legal way, through Sberbank.

If you are arrested, the police are obliged to inform your embassy or consulate immediately and allow you to

communicate with it without delay. You can't count on the rules being followed, so be polite and respectful towards officials and hopefully things will go far more smoothly for you.

Medical Services

Moscow is well served by sparkling international-style clinics that charge handsomely for their generally excellent and professional service: expect to pay around US$100 for an initial consultation. Both the International Clinic MEDSI and the European Medical Centre accept health insurance from major international providers.

Botkin Hospital (✆495-945 0045; www.mosgorzdrav.ru; 2-y Botkinsky proezd 5; ⊙24hr; MBegovaya) The best Russian facility. From Begovaya metro station, walk 1km northeast on Khoroshevskoe sh and Begovoy pr. Turn left on Begovaya ul and continue to 2-y Botkinsky proezd.

European Medical Centre (Map p278; ✆495-933 6655; www.emcmos.ru; Spirodonevsky per 5; ⊙24hr; MMayakovskaya) Includes medical and dental facilities, which are open around the clock for emergencies. The staff speak 10 languages.

International Clinic MEDSI (✆495-933 7700; https://medsi.ru; Grokholsky per 1; ⊙24hr; MPr Mira) Offers 24-hour emergency service, consultations and a full range of medical specialists, including paediatricians and dentists. There is also an onsite pharmacy with English-speaking staff.

Pharmacies

36.6 Arbat (Map p276; ul Novy Arbat 15; ⊙9am-10pm; MArbatskaya)

PRACTICALITIES

Newspapers The *Moscow Times* (www.themoscow times.com) is a first-rate weekly and the last remaining publication for English-language news. It covers Russian and international issues, as well as sport and entertainment. Find it at hotels and restaurants around town.

Television TV channels include Channel 1 (Pervy Kanal; www.1tv.ru); NTV (www.ntv.ru); Rossiya (www.russia.tv); Kultura (www.tvkultura.ru); RenTV (www.ren-tv.com); and RT (http://rt.com), offering the 'Russian perspective' to overseas audiences in English, Arabic and Spanish.

Weights & Measures Moscow uses the metric system.

Smoking Banned in public places, including bars, hotels, restaurants, children's playgrounds, train station platforms and train carriages. If you're caught smoking in such places, you could be liable for fines of up to ₽1500.

36.6 Basmanny (Map p286; ul Pokrovka 1/13; ☺9am-9pm; ⓜKitay-Gorod)

36.6 Tverskaya (Map p274; Tverskaya ul 25/9; ☺24hr; ⓜMayakovskaya)

36.6 Zamoskvorechie (Map p282; Klimentovsky per 12; ☺8am-10pm; ⓜTretyakovskaya)

Opening Hours

Government offices 9am or 10am to 5pm or 6pm weekdays.

Banks and other services 9am–6pm weekdays; shorter hours Saturday.

Shops 10am–8pm daily. Department stores and food shops have longer hours.

Restaurants Noon–midnight daily.

Museums 10am or 11am to 6pm Tuesday to Sunday. Many museums have instituted evening hours one day a week, usually Thursday. Opening hours vary widely, as do the museums' weekly days off.

Post

Although the service has improved dramatically in recent years, the usual warnings about delays and disappearances of incoming and outgoing mail apply to Moscow. Airmail letters take at least two weeks from Moscow to Europe, and longer to the USA or Australasia. DHL, UPS and FedEx are all active in Moscow.

Should you decide to send mail to Moscow, or try to receive it, note that addresses should be written in reverse order: Russia, postal code, city, street address and then name.

Main Post Office (Map p286; Myasnitskaya ul 26; ☺24hr; ⓜChistye Prudy)

Public Holidays

New Year's Day 1 January
Russian Orthodox Christmas 7 January
International Women's Day 8 March
International Labour Day/ Spring Festival 1 and 2 May
Victory (1945) Day 9 May
Russian Independence 12 June
Day of Reconciliation and Accord (formerly Revolution Day) 7 November

Safe Travel

Moscow is mostly a safe city.

➡ As in any big city, be on guard against pickpockets, especially around train stations and in crowded metro cars.

➡ Always be cautious about taking taxis late at night, especially near bars and clubs. Never get into a car that already has two or more people in it.

➡ Always carry a photocopy of your passport and visa. If stopped by a member of the police force, it is perfectly acceptable to show a photocopy.

➡ Your biggest threat in Moscow is xenophobic or overly friendly drunks.

Telephone

Making telephone calls in Moscow is complicated, with four area codes and different dialling patterns for mobile phones and land lines.

Phone Codes

➡ Russia's country code is ☎7.

➡ There are now four area codes operating within Moscow. Both ☎495 and ☎499 are used in the city, while ☎496 and ☎498 are used on the outskirts.

➡ For all calls within Russia (including within Moscow), you must dial ☎8 plus the 10-digit number including the area code.

➡ To call internationally from Moscow, dial ☎810 plus the country code, city code and phone number.

➡ Russian mobile phones have a 10-digit number (no area code), usually starting with ☎9.

➡ For calls from a mobile

telephone, dial 🕿+7 plus the 10-digit number (mobile or land line).

Mobile Phones

There are several major phone networks, all offering pay-as-you-go deals.

➡ **Beeline** (http://moskva.beeline.ru)

➡ **Megafon** (http://moscow.megafon.ru)

➡ **MTS** (www.mts.ru)

➡ **Tele2** (https://msk.tele2.ru)

SIMs and phone-call-credit top-up cards, available at mobile phone shops and kiosks across the city (you'll usually find them in the airport arrival areas and train stations) and costing as little as ₽300, can be slotted into your regular (unlocked) mobile phone handset during your stay. Call prices are very low within local networks, but charges for roaming larger regions can mount up; cost-conscious locals switch SIM cards when crossing regional boundaries.

Topping up your credit can be done either via pre-paid credit cards bought from kiosks or mobile phone shops or, more commonly, via paypoint machines found in shopping centres, underground passes, and at metro and train stations. Choose your network, input your telephone number and the amount of credit you'd like, insert the cash and it's done, minus a 3% to 10% fee for the transaction. Confirmation of the top-up comes via a text message (in Russian) to your phone. You can also use the websites of mobile phone companies to top up your phone with a credit card.

Time

Moscow time is GMT/UTC plus three hours. Daylight Savings Time is no longer observed in Moscow.

Toilets

Pay toilets are identified by the words платный туалет (platny tualet). In any toilet Женский or Ж stands for women's (zhensky), while Мужской or М stands for men's (muzhskoy).

Plastic-cabin portable loos have become more common in public places. Toilets in hotels, restaurants and cafes are usually modern and clean, so public toilets need only be used for emergencies.

Tourist Information

Discover Moscow (https://um.mos.ru/en/discover-moscow) A comprehensive site organised by the City of Moscow.

Tourist Hotlines (🕿8-800-220 0001, 8-800-220 0002, 495-663 1393)

Travellers with Disabilities

Moscow is a challenging destination for wheelchair-bound visitors and travellers with other disabilities. Toilets are frequently accessed from stairs in restaurants and museums; distances are great; public transport is extremely crowded; and many footpaths are in poor condition.

This situation is changing (albeit very slowly) as buildings undergo renovations and become more accessible. Many hotels offer accessible rooms and all new metro stations are equipped with lifts and ramps.

Download Lonely Planet's free Accessible Travel guide from http://lptravel.to/AccessibleTravel.

All-Russian Society for the Blind (Всероссийское общество слепых; 🕿495-628

1374; www.vos.org.ru) Provides info and services for visually impaired people, including operating holiday and recreation centres.

All-Russian Society for the Deaf (Всероссийское общество глухих, www.voginfo.ru) Organises cultural activities and recreational facilities for its members.

All-Russian Society of Disabled People (Всероссийское общество инвалидов; 🕿495-935 0012; www.voi.ru) Does not offer any services to travellers, but may provide publications (in Russian) on legal issues or local resources.

Women Travellers

➡ Solo female travellers are unlikely to face any special challenges in Moscow, though they may attract friendly interest at the local bars.

➡ Although sexual harassment on the streets is rare, it is common in the workplace, in the home and in personal relations. Discrimination and domestic violence are hard facts of life for many Russian women. Alcoholism and unemployment are related problems.

➡ Activists ridicule as hypocritical the Women's Day celebrations (8 March) in Russia while such problems continue. Others say it is the one day in the year that men have to be nice to their mates.

➡ Russian women dress up on nights out. If you are wearing casual gear, you might feel uncomfortable in an upmarket restaurant, club or theatre (or you may not be allowed to enter).

➡ The **International Women's Club** (www.iwcmoscow.ru) is an active group of expat women. It is involved in organising social and charity events.

Language

Russian belongs to the Slavonic language family and is closely related to Belarusian and Ukrainian. It has more than 150 million speakers within the Russian Federation and is used as a second language in the former republics of the USSR, with a total number of speakers of more than 270 million people.

Russian is written in the Cyrillic alphabet (see the next page), and it's well worth the effort familiarising yourself with it so that you can read maps, timetables, menus and street signs. Otherwise, just read the coloured pronunciation guides given next to each Russian phrase in this chapter as if they were English, and you'll be understood. Most sounds are the same as in English, and the few differences in pronunciation are explained in the alphabet table. The stressed syllables are indicated with italics.

BASICS

Hello.	Здравствуйте.	zdrast·vuy·tye
Goodbye.	До свидания.	da svi·da·nya
Excuse me.	Простите.	pras·ti·tye
Sorry.	Извините.	iz·vi·ni·tye
Please.	Пожалуйста.	pa·zhal·sta
Thank you.	Спасибо.	spa·si·ba
You're welcome.	Пожалуйста.	pa·zhal·sta
Yes.	Да.	da
No.	Нет.	nyet

WANT MORE?

For in-depth language information and handy phrases, check out Lonely Planet's *Russian phrasebook*. You'll find it at **shop. lonelyplanet.com**, or you can buy Lonely Planet's iPhone phrasebooks at the Apple App Store.

How are you?

| Как дела? | kak di·la |

Fine, thank you. And you?

| Хорошо, спасибо. | kha·ra·sho spa·si·ba |
| А у вас? | a u vas |

What's your name?

| Как вас зовут? | kak vas za·vut |

My name is ...

| Меня зовут ... | mi·nya za·vut ... |

Do you speak English?

| Вы говорите по-английски? | vi ga·va·ri·tye pa·an·gli·ski |

I don't understand.

| Я не понимаю. | ya nye pa·ni·ma·yu |

ACCOMMODATION

Where's a ...?	Где ...?	gdye ...
boarding house	пансионат	pan·si·a·nat
campsite	кемпинг	kyem·ping
hotel	отель	o·tel
youth hostel	хостел	ho·stel
Do you have a ... room?	У вас есть ...?	u vas yest' ...
single	одно-местный номер	ad·na·myest·nih no·mir
double (one bed)	номер с двуспальной кроватью	no·mir z dvu·spal'·noy kra·va·tyu
How much is it for ...?	Сколько стоит за ...?	skol'·ka sto·it za ...
a night	ночь	noch'
two people	двоих	dva·ikh

The ... isn't working.	... не работает.	... ne ra·bo·ta·yit
heating	Отопление	a·ta·plye·ni·ye
hot water	Горячая вода	ga·rya·cha·ya va·da
light	Свет	svyet

CYRILLIC ALPHABET

Cyrillic	Sound	
А, а	a	as in 'father' (in a stressed syllable); as in 'ago' (in an unstressed syllable)
Б, б	b	as in 'but'
В, в	v	as in 'van'
Г, г	g	as in 'god'
Д, д	d	as in 'dog'
Е, е	ye	as in 'yet' (in a stressed syllable and at the end of a word);
	i	as in 'tin' (in an unstressed syllable)
Ё, ё	yo	as in 'yore' (often printed without dots)
Ж, ж	zh	as the 's' in 'measure'
З, з	z	as in 'zoo'
И, и	i	as the 'ee' in 'meet'
Й, й	y	as in 'boy' (not transliterated after ы or и)
К, к	k	as in 'kind'
Л, л	l	as in 'lamp'
М, м	m	as in 'mad'
Н, н	n	as in 'not'
О, о	o	as in 'more' (in a stressed syllable);
	a	as in 'hard' (in an unstressed syllable)
П, п	p	as in 'pig'
Р, р	r	as in 'rub' (rolled)
С, с	s	as in 'sing'
Т, т	t	as in 'ten'
У, у	u	as the 'oo' in 'fool'
Ф, ф	f	as in 'fan'
Х, х	kh	as the 'ch' in 'Bach'
Ц, ц	ts	as in 'bits'
Ч, ч	ch	as in 'chin'
Ш, ш	sh	as in 'shop'
Щ, щ	shch	as 'sh-ch' in 'fresh chips'
Ъ, ъ	–	'hard sign' meaning the preceding consonant is pronounced as it's written
Ы, ы	ih	as the 'y' in 'any'
Ь, ь	'	'soft sign' meaning the preceding consonant is pronounced like a faint y
Э, э	e	as in 'end'
Ю, ю	yu	as the 'u' in 'use'
Я, я	ya	as in 'yard' (in a stressed syllable);
	ye	as in 'yearn' (in an unstressed syllable)

DIRECTIONS

Where is ...?
Где ...?　gdye ...

What's the address?
Какой адрес?　ka·koy a·dris

Could you write it down, please?
Запишите, пожалуйста.　za·pi·shih·tye pa·zhal·sta

Can you show me (on the map)?
Покажите мне, пожалуйста (на карте).　pa·ka·zhih·tye mnye pa·zhal·sta (na kar·tye)

Turn ...	Поверните ...	pa·vir·ni·tye ...
at the corner	за угол	za u·gal
at the traffic lights	на светофоре	na svi·ta·fo·rye
left	налево	na·lye·va
right	направо	na·pra·va

behind ...	за ...	za ...
far	далеко	da·li·ko
in front of ...	перед ...	pye·rit ...
near	близко	blis·ka
next to ...	рядом с ...	rya·dam s ...
opposite ...	напротив ...	na·pro·tif ...
straight ahead	прямо	prya·ma

EATING & DRINKING

I'd like to reserve a table for ...	Я бы хотел/ хотела заказать столик на ... (m/f)	ya bih khat·yel/ khat·ye·la za·ka·zat' sto·lik na ...
two people	двоих	dva·ikh
eight o'clock	восемь часов	vo·sim' chi·sof

What would you recommend?
Что вы рекомендуете?　shto vih ri·ka·min·du·it·ye

What's in that dish?
Что входит в это блюдо?　shto fkho·dit v e·ta blyu·da

That was delicious!
Было очень вкусно!　bih·la o·chin' fkus·na

Please bring the bill.
Принесите, пожалуйста счёт.　pri·ni·sit·ye pa·zhal·sta shot

I don't eat ...	Я не ем ...	ya nye yem ...
eggs	яйца	yay·tsa
fish	рыбу	rih·bu
poultry	птицу	ptit·su
red meat	мясо	mya·so

Key Words

bottle	бутылка	bu·*tihl*·ka
bowl	миска	*mis*·ka
breakfast	завтрак	*zaf*·trak
cold	холодный	kha·*lod*·nih
dinner	ужин	u·zhihn
dish	блюдо	*blyu*·da
fork	вилка	*vil*·ka
glass	стакан	sta·*kan*
hot (warm)	горячий	go·*rya*·chiy
knife	нож	nosh
lunch	обед	ab·*yet*
menu	меню	min·*yu*
plate	тарелка	tar·*yel*·ka
restaurant	ресторан	ris·ta·*ran*
spoon	ложка	*losh*·ka
with/without	с/без	s/byez

Meat & Fish

beef	говядина	gav·*ya*·di·na
caviar	икра	i·*kra*
chicken	курица	*ku*·rit·sa
duck	утка	*ut*·ka
fish	рыба	*rih*·ba
herring	сельдь	syelt'
lamb	баранина	ba·*ra*·ni·na
meat	мясо	*mya*·sa
oyster	устрица	*ust*·rit·sa
pork	свинина	svi·*ni*·na
prawn	креветка	kriv·*yet*·ka
salmon	лосось	la·*sauce*
turkey	индейка	ind·*yey*·ka
veal	телятина	til·*ya*·ti·na

Fruit & Vegetables

apple	яблоко	*yab*·la·ka
bean	фасоль	fa·*sol'*
cabbage	капуста	ka·*pu*·sta
capsicum	перец	*pye*·rits
carrot	морковь	mar·*kof'*
cauliflower	цветная капуста	tsvit·*na*·ya ka·*pu*·sta
cucumber	огурец	a·gur·*yets*
fruit	фрукты	*fruk*·tih
mushroom	гриб	grip

Signs

Вход	Entrance
Выход	Exit
Открыто	Open
Закрыто	Closed
Информация	Information
Запрещено	Prohibited
Туалет	Toilets
Мужской (М)	Men
Женский (Ж)	Women

nut	орех	ar·*yekh*
onion	лук	luk
orange	апельсин	a·pil'·*sin*
peach	персик	*pyer*·sik
pear	груша	*gru*·sha
plum	слива	*sli*·va
potato	картошка	kar·*tosh*·ka
spinach	шпинат	shpi·*nat*
tomato	помидор	pa·mi·*dor*
vegetable	овощ	*o*·vash

Other

bread	хлеб	*khlyep*
cheese	сыр	sihr
egg	яйцо	yeyl·*so*
honey	мёд	myot
oil	масло	*mas*·la
pasta	паста	*pa*·sta
pepper	перец	*pye*·rits
rice	рис	ris
salt	соль	sol'
sugar	сахар	*sa*·khar
vinegar	уксус	*uk*·sus

Drinks

beer	пиво	*pi*·va
coffee	кофе	*kof*·ye
(orange) juice	(апельсиновый) сок	(a·pil'·*si*·na·vih) sok
milk	молоко	ma·la·*ko*
tea	чай	chey
(mineral) water	(минеральная) вода	(mi·ni·*ral'*·na·ya) va·*da*
wine	вино	vi·*no*

EMERGENCIES

Help!	Помогите!	pa·ma·*gi*·tye
Call ...!	Вызовите ...!	*vih*·za·vi·tye ...
a doctor	врача	vra·*cha*
the police	полицию	po·*li*·tsih·yu

Leave me alone!
проваливай! — pro·*va*·li·vai

There's been an accident.
Произошёл — pra·i·za·*shol*
несчастный случай. — ne·*shas*·nih *slu*·chai

I'm lost.
Я заблудился/ — ya za·blu·*dil*·sa/
заблудилась. (m/f) — za·blu·*di*·las'

Where are the toilets?
Где здесь туалет? — gdye zdyes' tu·al·*yet*

I'm ill.
Я болен/больна. (m/f) — ya *bo*·lin/bal'·*na*

It hurts here.
Здесь болит. — zdyes' ba·*lit*

I'm allergic to (antibiotics).
У меня алергия — u min·*ya* a·lir·*gi*·ya
на (антибиотики). — na (an·ti·bi·o·ti·ki)

SHOPPING & SERVICES

I need ...
Мне нужно ... — mnye *nuzh*·na ...

I'm just looking.
Я просто смотрю. — ya *pros*·ta smat·*ryu*

Can you show me?
Покажите, — pa·ka·*zhih*·tye
пожалуйста? — pa·*zhal*·sta

How much is it?
Сколько стоит? — *skol'*·ka *sto*·it

That's too expensive.
Это очень дорого. — e·ta o·*chen*' *do*·ra·ga

There's a mistake in the bill.
Меня обсчитали. — min·*ya* ap·shi·*ta*·li

bank	банк	bank
market	рынок	*rih*·nak
post office	почта	*poch*·ta
telephone office	телефонный пункт	ti·li·*fo*·nih punkt

Question Words		
What?	Что?	shto
When?	Когда?	kag·*da*
Where?	Где?	gdye
Which?	Какой?	ka·*koy*
Who?	Кто?	kto
Why?	Почему?	pa·chi·*mu*

TIME, DATES & NUMBERS

What time is it?
Который час? — ka·*to*·rih chas

It's (10) o'clock.
(Десять) часов. — (*dye*·sit') chi·*sof*

morning	утро	*ut*·ra
day	день	den
evening	вечер	*vye*·chir
yesterday	вчера	vchi·*ra*
today	сегодня	si·*vod*·nya
tomorrow	завтра	*zaft*·ra
Monday	понедельник	pa·ni·*dyel*'·nik
Tuesday	вторник	*ftor*·nik
Wednesday	среда	sri·*da*
Thursday	четверг	chit·*vyerk*
Friday	пятница	*pyat*·ni·tsa
Saturday	суббота	su·*bo*·ta
Sunday	воскресенье	vas·kri·*syen*·ye
January	январь	yan·*var*'
February	февраль	fiv·*ral*'
March	март	mart
April	апрель	ap·*ryel*'
May	май	mai
June	июнь	i·*yun*'
July	июль	i·*yul*'
August	август	*av*·gust
September	сентябрь	sin·*tyabr*'
October	октябрь	ak·*tyabr*'
November	ноябрь	na·*yabr*'
December	декабрь	di·*kabr*'

1	один	a·*din*
2	два	dva
3	три	tri
4	четыре	chi·*tih*·ri
5	пять	pyat'
6	шесть	shest'
7	семь	syem'
8	восемь	*vo*·sim'
9	девять	*dye*·vyat'
10	десять	*dye*·syat'
20	двадцать	*dva*·tsat'
30	тридцать	*tri*·tsat'
40	сорок	*so*·rak
50	пятьдесят	pi·*dis*·yat
60	шестьдесят	shihs·*dis*·yat
70	семьдесят	*syem*'·dis·yat

80	восемьдесят	vo·sim'·di·sit
90	девяносто	di·vi·no·sta
100	сто	sto
1000	тысяча	tih·si·cha

TRANSPORT

Public Transport

A ... ticket (to Novgorod).	Билет ... (до Новгорода).	bil·yet ... (do nov·ga·rat·a)
one-way	в один конец	v a·din kan·yets
return	туда-обратно	tu- da ob·rat·no
bus	автобус	af·to·bus
train	поезд	po·ist
tram	трамвай	tram·vai
trolleybus	троллейбус	tra·lyey·bus
first	первый	pyer·vih
last	последний	pas·lyed·ni
platform	платформа	plat·for·ma
(bus) stop	остановка	a·sta·nof·ka
ticket	билет	bil·yet
Podorozhnik (SPB travel pass)	Подорожник	Pa·da·rozh·nik
ticket office	билетная касса	bil·yet·na·ya ka·sa
timetable	расписание	ras·pi·sa·ni·ye

When does it leave?
Когда отправляется?   kag·da at·prav·lya·it·sa

How long does it take to get to ...?
Сколько времени нужно ехать до ...?   skol'·ka vrye·mi·ni nuzh·na ye·khat' da ...

Does it stop at ...?
Поезд останавливается в ...?   po·yist a·sta·nav·li·va·yit·sa v ...

Please stop here.
Остановитесь здесь, пожалуйста.   a·sta·na·vit·yes' zdyes' pa·zhal·sta

Driving & Cycling

I'd like to hire a ...	Я бы хотел/ хотела взять ... напрокат. (m/f)	ya bih kha·tyel/ kha·tye·la vzyat' ... na pra·kat
4WD	машину с полным приводом	ma·shih·nu s pol·nihm pri·vo·dam
bicycle	велосипед	vi·la·si·pyet
car	машину	ma·shih·nu
motorbike	мотоцикл	ma·ta·tsikl

KEY PATTERNS

To get by in Russian, mix and match these simple patterns with words of your choice:

When's (the next bus)?
Когда (будет следующий автобус)?   kag·da (bu·dit slye·du·yu·shi af·to·bus)

Where's (the station)?
Где (станция)?   gdye (stant·sih·ya)

Where can I (buy a padlock)?
Где можно (купить навесной замок)?   gdye mozh·na (ku·pit' na·ves·noy za·mok)

Do you have (a map)?
У вас есть (карта)?   u vas yest' (kar·ta)

I'd like (the menu).
Я бы хотел/ хотела (меню). (m/f)   ya bih khat·yel/ khat·ye·la (min·yu)

I'd like to (hire a car).
Я бы хотел/ хотела (взять машину напрокат).   ya bih khat·yel/ khat·ye·la (vzyat' ma·shih·nu na·pra·kat)

Can I (come in)?
Можно (войти)?   mozh·na (vey·ti)

Could you please (write it down)?
(напишите), пожалуйста?   (na·pi·shi·te·mne) pa·zhal·sta

Do I need (a visa)?
Мне нужна (виза)?   mne nuzh·na (vi·za)

I need (assistance).
Мне нужна (помощь).   mnye nuzh·na (po·mash)

diesel	дизельное топливо	di·zil'·na·ye to·pli·va
regular	бензин номер 93	ben·zin no·mir di·vi·no·sta tri
unleaded	очищенный бензин	a·chi·shi·nih bin·zin

Is this the road to ...?
Эта дорога ведёт в ...?   e·ta da·ro·ga vid·yot f ...

Where's a petrol station?
Где заправка?   gdye za·praf·ka

Can I park here?
Здесь можно стоять?   zdyes' mozh·na sta·yat'

I need a mechanic.
Мне нужен автомеханик.   mnye nu·zhihn af·ta·mi·kha·nik

The car has broken down.
Машина сломалась.   ma·shih·na sla·ma·las'

I have a flat tyre.
У меня лопнула шина.   u min·ya lop·nu·la shih·na

I've run out of petrol.
У меня кончился бензин.   u min·ya kon·chil·sa bin·zin

GLOSSARY

(m) indicates masculine gender, (f) feminine gender and (n) neuter gender

aeroport – airport

alleya – alley

apteka – pharmacy

avtobus – bus

avtomaticheskie kamery khranenia – left-luggage lockers

avtovokzal – bus station

babushka – grandmother

bankomat – ATM

banya – bathhouse

bolshoy/bolshaya/bolshoye (m/f/n) – big, great, grand

bulvar – boulevard

bylina – epic song

dacha – country cottage

datsan – temple

deklaratsiya – customs declaration

dom – house

duma – parliament

dvorets – palace

elektrichka – suburban train; also prigorodnye poezd

galereya – gallery

glasnost – openness; policy of public accountability developed under the leadership of Mikhail Gorbachev

gorod – city, town

kafe – cafe

kamera khranenia – left-luggage office or counter

kanal – canal

kladbische – cemetery

kolonnada – colonnade

kon – horse

korpus – building within a building

koryushki – freshwater smelt

kruglosutochno – open 24 hours

lavra – most senior grade of Russian Orthodox monastery

letny sad – summer garden

liteyny – foundry

maly/malaya/maloye (m/f/n) – small, little

marshrutka – minibus that runs along a fixed route; diminutive form of marshrutnoye taxi

Maslenitsa – akin to Mardi Gras; fete that celebrates the end of winter and kicks off Lent

matryoshka – nesting doll; set of painted wooden dolls within dolls

mekh – fur

mesto – seat

morskoy vokzal – sea port

morzh – literally walrus, but the name commonly given to ice swimmers in the Neva

most – bridge

muzey – museum

naberezhnaya – embankment

novy/novaya (m/f) – new

Novy God – New Year

ostrov – island

parilka – steam room (at a banya)

Paskha – Easter

passazhirskiy poezd – passenger train

perekhod – transfer

pereryv – break, recess

perestroika – reconstruction; policy of reconstructing the economy developed under the leadership of Mikhail Gorbachev

pereulok – lane, side street

pivnaya – beer bar

ploshchad – square

politseyskiy – police officer

politsiya – police

prigorodnye poezd – suburban train; also elektrichka

proezd – passage

prospekt – avenue

rechnoy vokzal – river port

reka – river

restoran – restaurant

Rozhdestvo – Christmas

rynok – market

ryumochnaya – equivalent of the local pub

samizdat – underground literary manuscript during the Soviet era

sanitarny den – literally 'sanitary day'; a day during the last week of every month on which establishments such as museums shut down for cleaning

shosse – highway

skory poezd – fast train; regular long-distance service

sobor – cathedral

stary/staraya/staroye (m/f/n) – old

stolovaya – cafeteria

tapochki – slippers

teatralnaya kassa – theatre kiosk; general theatre box office scattered about the city

troika – sleigh drawn by three horses

tserkov – church

ulitsa – street

vagon – carriage (on a train)

veniki – bundle of birch branches used at a banya to beat bathers to eliminate toxins and improve circulation

vokzal – station

vyshaya liga – Russia's premier football league

zal – hall

zamok – castle

MENU DECODER

bliny – pancakes блины
borsch – beetroot soup борщ
buterbrod – open-faced sandwich бутерброд

garnir – garnish, or side dish гарнир

ikra (chyornaya, krasnaya) – caviar (black, red) икра (чёрная, красная)

kartoshki – potatoes картошки
kasha – porridge каша
kefir – sour yoghurt drink кефир
khleb – bread хлеб
kvas – mildly alcoholic fermented-rye-bread drink квас

lapsha – noodle soup лапша
losos – salmon лосось

mineralnaya voda (gazirovannaya, negazirovannaya) – water (sparkling, still) минеральная вода (газированная, негазированная)

moloko – milk молоко
morozhenoye – ice cream мороженое
myaso – meat мясо

obed – lunch обед
okroshka – cold cucumber soup with a *kvas* base окрошка
ovoshchi – vegetables овощи
ovoshnoy salat – tomato and cucumber salad, literally 'vegetable salad' овошной салат

pelmeni – dumplings filled with meat or vegetables пельмени
pirog/pirogi (s/pl) – pie пирог/пироги
pivo (svetloe, tyomnoe) – beer (light, dark) пиво (светлое, тёмное)
ptitsa – poultry птица

ris – rice рис
ryba – fish рыба

salat olivier – see *stolichny salat* салат Оливье

seld pod shuboy – salad with herring, potatoes, beets and carrots, literally 'herring in a fur coat' сельдь под шубой
shashlyk (myasnoy, kuriny, rybnoy) – kebab (meat, chicken, fish) шашлык (мясной, куриный, рыбной)
shchi – cabbage soup щи
sok – juice сок
solyanka – a tasty meat soup with salty vegetables and hint of lemon солянка
stolichny salat – 'capital salad', which contains beef, potatoes and eggs in mayonnaise; also called *salat olivier* столичный салат
svekolnik – cold beet soup свекольник

tvorog – soft sweet cheese similar to ricotta творог

uzhin – dinner ужин

zakuski – appetisers закуски
zavtrak – breakfast завтрак

Behind the Scenes

SEND US YOUR FEEDBACK

We love to hear from travellers – your comments keep us on our toes and help make our books better. Our well-travelled team reads every word on what you loved or loathed about this book. Although we cannot reply individually to your submissions, we always guarantee that your feedback goes straight to the appropriate authors, in time for the next edition. Each person who sends us information is thanked in the next edition – the most useful submissions are rewarded with a selection of digital PDF chapters.

Visit **lonelyplanet.com/contact** to submit your updates and suggestions or to ask for help. Our award-winning website also features inspirational travel stories, news and discussions.

Note: We may edit, reproduce and incorporate your comments in Lonely Planet products such as guidebooks, websites and digital products, so let us know if you don't want your comments reproduced or your name acknowledged. For a copy of our privacy policy visit lonelyplanet.com/privacy.

OUR READERS

Many thanks to the travellers who used the previous edition and wrote to us with helpful hints, useful advice and interesting anecdotes:

Anna Charles, Ben Searle, Diego Tan, Iulia Tenenhaus, Lyn Simons, Mascha Nottelmann, Michael Fosberg, Nova Dudley-Gough, Paul Watters, Robyn Hilder, Sain Alizada, Sassoon Grigorian, Veronica Chorcoco

WRITER THANKS

Mara Vorhees

Many thanks to my coauthors and resident Moscow experts Marc Bennetts and Leonid Ragozin. Always a pleasure to work with colleagues so insightful and well-informed. I also received useful information from Andrei Musiano and Sasha Serbina at Garage Museum of Contemporary Art and Dmitry Elovsky at Zaryadye Project, as well as Andrey Muchnik and Marina Dedozhdy. Unlimited thanks and love to мои самые любимые – Van, Shay and Jerry – for coming along for the adventure.

Leonid Ragozin

Many thanks to my Moscow friends, too numerous to be listed here, for ideas on new places and latest developments. Separate thanks to my wife Maria Makeeva for enduring the mayhem.

ACKNOWLEDGEMENTS

Cover photograph: Hall, Komsomolskaya station, Moscow metro, Gubin Yury/Shutterstock ©

Illustration pp62-3 by Javier Zarracina

THIS BOOK

This 7th edition of Lonely Planet's *Moscow* guidebook was researched and written by Mara Vorhees and Leonid Ragozin. The previous two editions were also written by them. This guidebook was produced by the following:

Destination Editor Brana Vladisavljevic
Product Editors Anne Mason, Amanda Williamson
Senior Cartographer David Kemp
Book Designer Wibowo Rusli
Assisting Editors Janet Austin, James Bainbridge, Michelle Bennett, Emma Gibbs, Paul Harding, Jennifer Hattam, Charlotte Orr
Cartographer Valentina Kremenchutskaya
Cover Researcher Naomi Parker
Thanks to Ronan Abayawickrema, Imogen Bannister, Lauren O'Connell, Kira Tverskaya, Tony Wheeler

Index

See also separate subindexes for:
EATING P267
DRINKING & NIGHTLIFE P267
ENTERTAINMENT P268
SHOPPING P268
SPORTS & ACTIVITIES P268
SLEEPING P268

Sights 000
Map Pages **000**
Photo Pages **000**

INDEX M–P

INDEX ENTERTAINMENT

Moscow Maps

Sights

- Beach
- Bird Sanctuary
- Buddhist
- Castle/Palace
- Christian
- Confucian
- Hindu
- Islamic
- Jain
- Jewish
- Monument
- Museum/Gallery/Historic Building
- Ruin
- Shinto
- Sikh
- Taoist
- Winery/Vineyard
- Zoo/Wildlife Sanctuary
- Other Sight

Activities, Courses & Tours

- Bodysurfing
- Diving
- Canoeing/Kayaking
- Course/Tour
- Sento Hot Baths/Onsen
- Skiing
- Snorkelling
- Surfing
- Swimming/Pool
- Walking
- Windsurfing
- Other Activity

Sleeping

- Sleeping
- Camping
- Hut/Shelter

Eating

- Eating

Drinking & Nightlife

- Drinking & Nightlife
- Cafe

Entertainment

- Entertainment

Shopping

- Shopping

Information

- Bank
- Embassy/Consulate
- Hospital/Medical
- Internet
- Police
- Post Office
- Telephone
- Toilet
- Tourist Information
- Other Information

Geographic

- Beach
- Gate
- Hut/Shelter
- Lighthouse
- Lookout
- Mountain/Volcano
- Oasis
- Park
- Pass
- Picnic Area
- Waterfall

Population

- Capital (National)
- Capital (State/Province)
- City/Large Town
- Town/Village

Transport

- Airport
- Border crossing
- Bus
- Cable car/Funicular
- Cycling
- Ferry
- Metro station
- Monorail
- Parking
- Petrol station
- S-Bahn/Subway station
- Taxi
- T-bane/Tunnelbana station
- Train station/Railway
- Tram
- Tube station
- U-Bahn/Underground station
- Other Transport

Routes

- Tollway
- Freeway
- Primary
- Secondary
- Tertiary
- Lane
- Unsealed road
- Road under construction
- Plaza/Mall
- Steps
- Tunnel
- Pedestrian overpass
- Walking Tour
- Walking Tour detour
- Path/Walking Trail

Boundaries

- International
- State/Province
- Disputed
- Regional/Suburb
- Marine Park
- Cliff
- Wall

Hydrography

- River, Creek
- Intermittent River
- Canal
- Water
- Dry/Salt/Intermittent Lake
- Reef

Areas

- Airport/Runway
- Beach/Desert
- Cemetery (Christian)
- Cemetery (Other)
- Glacier
- Mudflat
- Park/Forest
- Sight (Building)
- Sportsground
- Swamp/Mangrove

Note: Not all symbols displayed above appear on the maps in this book

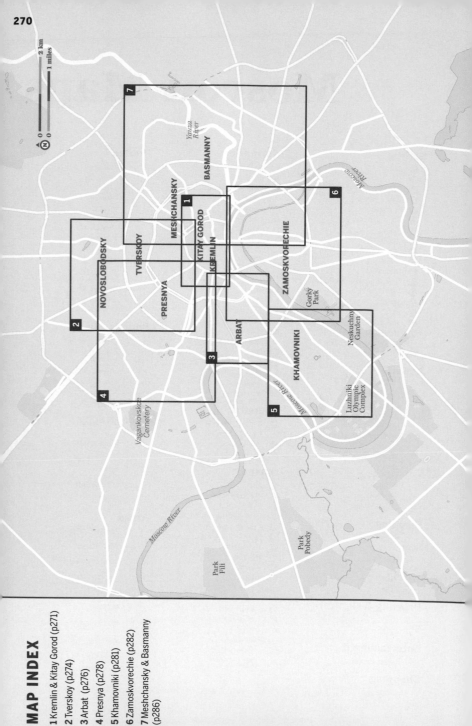

MAP INDEX

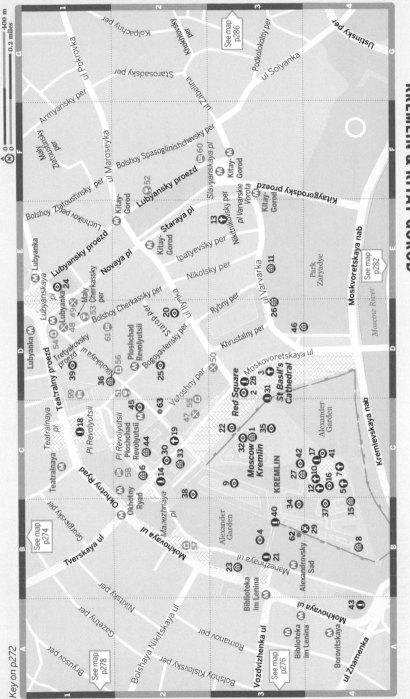

Key on p272

See map p278

See map p286

See map p282

See map p276

See map p274

400 m
0.2 miles

Ustinsky Per

Kolpachny per

Mokhovaya per

Starosadsky per

ul Pokrovka

Armyansky per

Maly Zlatoustinsky per

ul Maroseyka

Bolshoy Spasoglinishchevsky per

ul Solyanka

Podkolokolny per

ul Zabelina

Slavyanskaya pl

Kitay-Gorod

Lubyansky proezd

Bolshoy Zlatoustinsky per

Luchnikov per

Kitay-Gorod

Staraya pl

Nikitnikovsky per

pl Varvarskie Vorota

Kitay-Gorod

Kitaygorodsky proezd

Moskvoretskaya nab

Lubyanka

Lubyanskaya pl

Lubyanka

Maly Cherkassky per

Ipatyevsky per

Kitay-Gorod

Novaya pl

Nikolsky per

Moscow River

Park Zaryadye

Bolshoy Cherkassky per

ul Ilyinka

ul Varvarka

Rybny per

Khrustalny per

Teatralny proezd

Teatralnaya pl

Tretyakovsky proezd

Nikolskaya ul

Ploshchad Revolyutsii

Bogoyavlensky per

Staropansky per

Moskvoretskaya ul

St Basil's Cathedral

Red Square

Kremlevskaya nab

Teatralnaya

Pl Revolyutsii

Ploshchad Revolyutsii

Vetoshny per

Moscow Kremlin

Alexander Garden

KREMLIN

Okhotny Ryad

Okhotny Ryad

Manezhnaya pl

Manezhnaya ul

Alexander Garden

Georgievsky per

Tverskaya ul

Mokhovaya ul

Nikitsky per

Alexandrovsky Sad

Biblioteka im Lenina

Mokhovaya ul

Gazetny per

Bolshaya Nikitskaya ul

Bolshoy Kislovsky per

Romanov per

Biblioteka im Lenina

Vozdvizhenka ul

Borovitskaya

ul Znamenka

Bryusov per

KREMLIN & KITAY GOROD Map on p271

TVERSKOY Map on p274

TVERSKOY

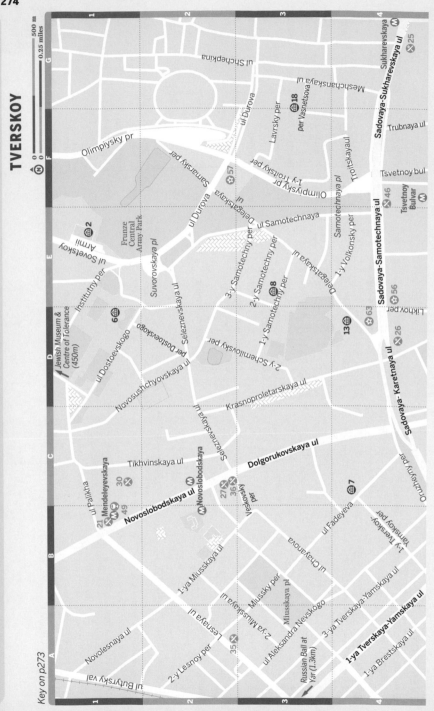

500 m
0.25 miles

ul Shchepkina

Olimpiysky pr

ul Durova

Meshchanskaya ul

Lavrsky per

per Vasnetsova

18

Sadovaya-Sukharevskaya ul

Sukharevskaya

25

Trubnaya ul

Tsvetnoy bul

57

Samarsky per

1-y Troitsky per

Olimpiysky pr

Delegatskaya ul

Troitskaya ul

Samotechnaya pl

Tsvetnoy Bulvar

46

Tsvetnoy
Bulvar

ul Durova

ul Samotechnaya

Samotechnaya ul

Sadovaya-Samotechnaya ul

ul Sovetskoy
Armii

2

Frunze
Central
Army Park

Suvorovskaya pl

3-y Samotechny per

2-y Samotechny per

8

1-y Samotechny per

1-y Volkonsky per

Samotechny per

Delegatskaya ul

56

63

Likhov per

Institutny per

Jewish Museum &
Centre of Tolerance
(450m)

ul Dostoevskogo

6

per Dostoevskogo

Seleznevskaya ul

2-y Schemilovsky per

13

26

Novosushchyovskaya ul

Krasnoproletarskaya ul

Sadovaya-Karetnaya ul

Oruzheyny per

Tikhvinskaya ul

Seleznevskaya ul

Dolgorukovskaya ul

ul Palikha

Mendeleyevskaya

30

49

21

Novoslobodskaya ul

Novoslobodskaya

27

36

Veskovsky
per

7

ul Fadeyeva

1-y Tverskoy-
Yamskoy per

1-ya Miusskaya ul

ul Chayanova

Miussky per

ul Fadeyeva

3-ya Tverskaya-Yamskaya ul

Novolesnaya ul

Lesnaya ul

2-ya Miusskaya ul

Miusskaya pl

ul Aleksandra Nevskogo

Russian Ball at
Yar (1.3km)

1-ya Tverskaya-Yamskaya ul

1-ya Brestskaya ul

35

2-y Lesnoy per

ul Butyrsky val

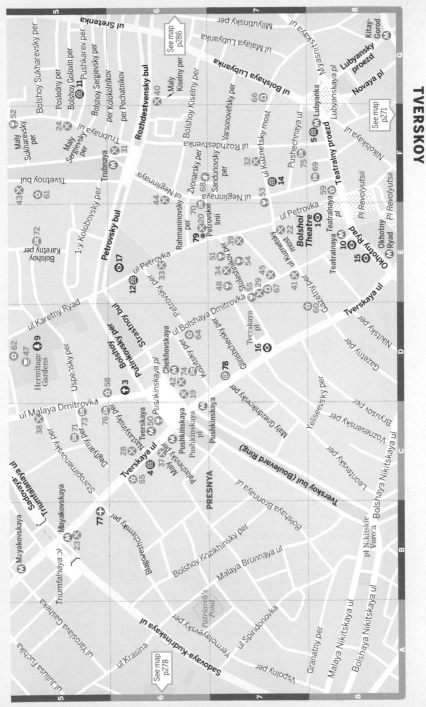

See map p286

See map p271

See map p278

Kitay-Gorod

Lubyanskiy proezd

Novaya pl

ul Sretenka

Bolshoy Sukharevsky per

Bolshoy Golovin per

Pushkarev per

Bolshoy Sergievsky per

per Pechatnikov

Posledny per

Maly Sukharevsky per

Maly Sergievsky per

ul Trubnaya

Trubnaya

Rozhdestvensky bul

Maly Kiselny per

Bolshoy Kiselny per

ul Malaya Lubyanka

Milyutinsky per

ul Bolshaya Lubyanka

ul Rozhdestvenka

Varsonovevsky per

Myasnitskaya ul

Lubyanka

Lubyanskaya ul

Pushechnaya ul

Teatralny proezd

Nikolskaya ul

Tsvetnoy bul

Petrovsky bul

ul Neglinnaya

Zvonarsky per

Sandunovsky per

ul Kuznetsky most

Rozhdestvenka

ul Neglinnaya

Rahmaninovsky per

Petrovskie linii

ul Petrovka

ul Petrovka

Petrovsky per

Bolshoy Karetny per

Bolshoy Kolobovsky per

1-y Kolobovsky per

Petrovka

ul Bolshaya Dmitrovka

Stoleshnikov per

Pl Revolyutsii

Pl Revolyutsii

Bolshoi Theatre

ul Petrovka

Teatralnaya pl

Teatralnaya pl

Okhotny Ryad

Okhotny Ryad

ul Kuznetsky most

Gazetny per

Tverskaya ul

Tverskaya ul

Tverskaya pl

Nikitsky per

Gazetny per

Glinishchevsky per

Maly Gnezdnikovsky per

Eliseevsky per

Bryusov per

Voznesensky per

Leontevsky per

pl N.Kitskie Vorota

Bolshaya Nikitskaya ul

ul Karetny Ryad

Hermitage Gardens

Uspensky per

ul Malaya Dmitrovka

Degtyarny per

Chekhovskaya

Chekhovskaya pl

Pushkinskaya pl

Putinkovsky per

Bolshoy Strastnoy bul

Strastnoy bul

Kozitsky per

Pushkinskaya

Pushkinskaya pl

Pushkinskaya

Tverskaya

Maly Palashevsky per

Tverskaya ul

Tverskaya pl

Bolshoy Palashevsky per

Starotpimvovsky per

Tverskoy bul (Boulevard Ring)

Bolshaya Bronnaya ul

PRESNYA

Mayakovskaya

Triumfalnaya ul

Sadovaya-Triumfalnaya ul

Triumfalnaya pl

ul Yarolava Gasheka

ul Krasina

Sadovaya-Kudrinskaya ul

Yermolaevsky per

Patriarch's Pond

Malaya Bronnaya ul

Bolshoy Kozikhinsky per

Malaya Bronnaya ul

ul Spiridonovka

Vspolny per

Granatny per

Malaya Nikitskaya ul

Bolshaya Nikitskaya ul

Bolshaya Nikitskaya ul

Blagoveshchensky per

ul Juliusa Fuchika

ARBAT

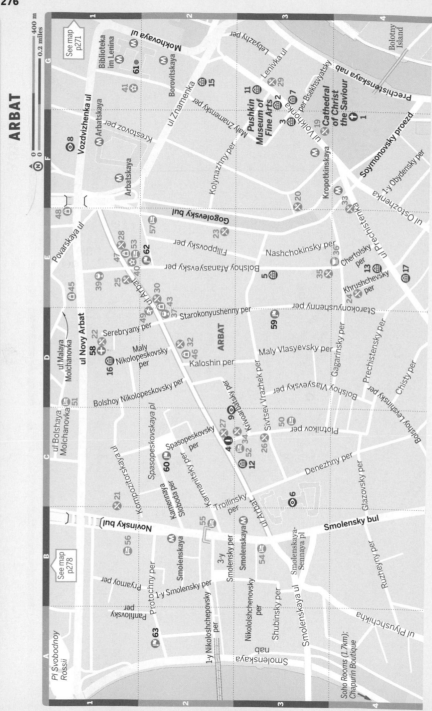

See map p271

400 m
0.2 miles

See map p278

KHAMOVNIKI

See map p281

See map p282

Moscow River

Prechistenskaya nab

Krasny Oktyabr

PRESNYA

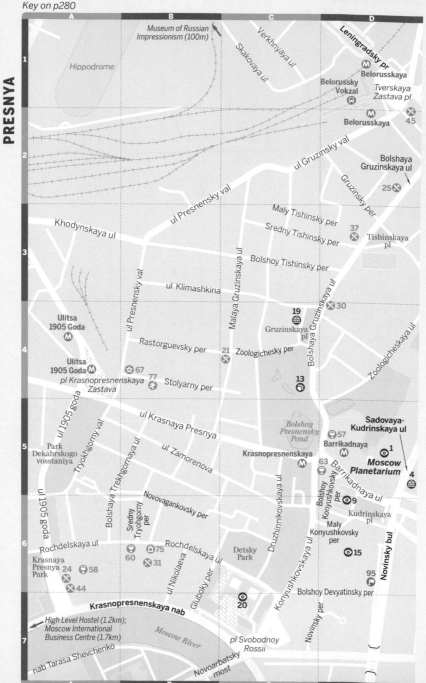

Museum of Russian
Impressionism (100m)

Leningradsky pr

Hippodrome

Skakovaya ul

Verkhnyaya ul

Belorussky
Vokzal

Belorusskaya

Tverskaya
Zastava pl

Belorusskaya

45

ul Gruzinsky val

Bolshaya
Gruzinskaya ul

Gruzinsky per

25

Khodynskaya ul

ul Presnensky val

Maly Tishinsky per

Sredny Tishinsky per

37

Tishinskaya
pl

Bolshoy Tishinsky per

ul Klimashkina

Malaya Gruzinskaya ul

Bolshaya Gruzinskaya ul

30

Ulitsa
1905 Goda

ul Presnensky val

19

Gruzinskaya
pl

Zoologicheskaya ul

Ulitsa
1905 Goda

pl Krasnopresnenskaya
Zastava

Rastorguevsky per

67

21

Zoologichesky per

77

Stolyarny per

13

ul Krasnaya Presnya

Bolshoy
Presnensky
Pond

Sadovaya-
Kudrinskaya ul

ul 1905 goda

Tryokhgorny val

Bolshaya Trekhgornaya ul

ul Zamorenova

57

Barrikadnaya

1

Moscow
Planetarium

Park
Dekabrskogo
vosstaniya

Krasnopresnenskaya

63

Barrikadnaya per

4

Novovagankovsky per

Druzhinnikovskaya ul

Bolshoy
Konyushkovsky per

9

Kudrinskaya
pl

ul 1905 goda

Sredny
Tryohgorny
per

Rochdelskaya ul

Detsky
Park

Maly
Konyushkovsky
per

15

Novinsky bul

Rochdelskaya ul

60

75

31

ul Nikolaeva

Konyushkovskaya ul

Krasnaya
Presnya
Park

24

58

44

Gluboky per

95

Bolshoy Devyatinsky per

Krasnopresnenskaya nab

20

Novinsky per

High Level Hostel (1.2km);
Moscow International
Business Centre (1.7km)

Moscow River

pl Svobodnoy
Rossii

nab Tarasa Shevchenko

Novoarbatsky
most

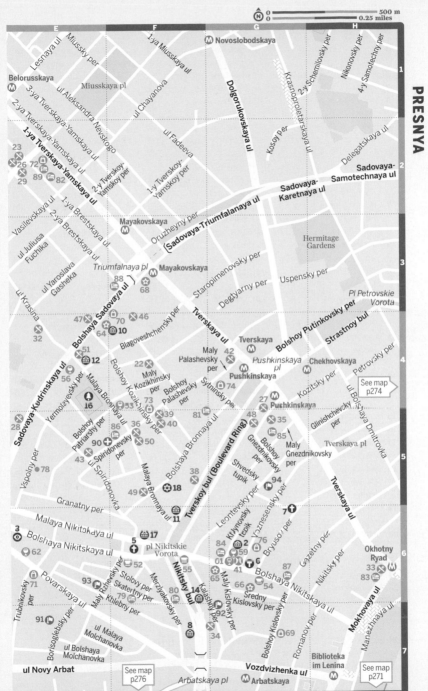

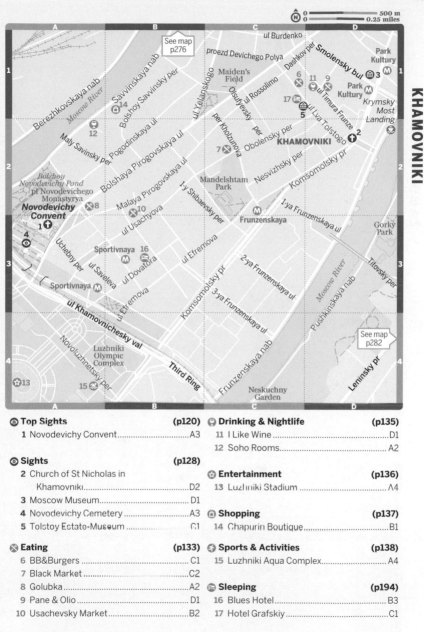

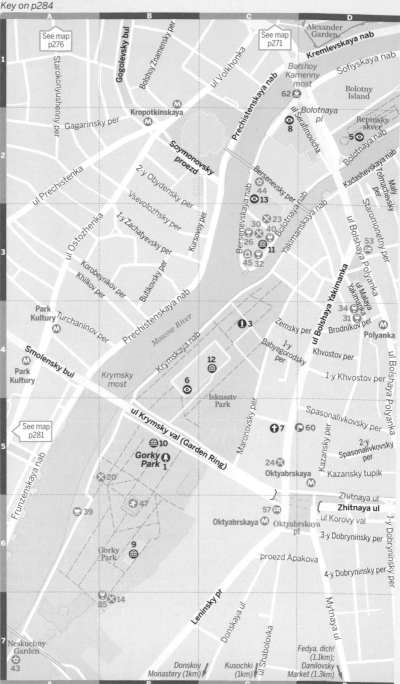

ZAMOSKVORECHIE

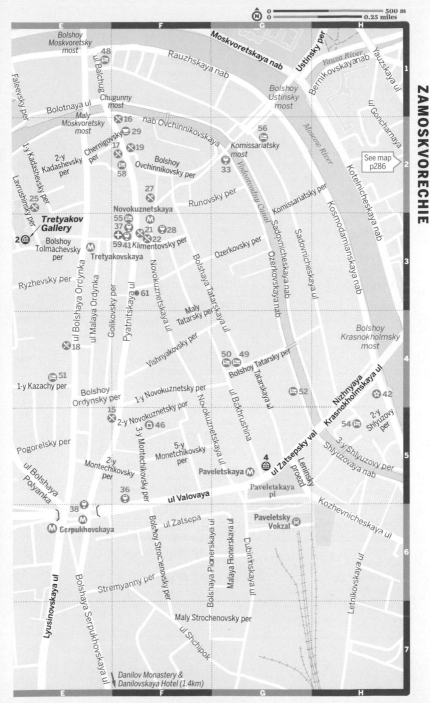

ZAMOSKVORECHIE *Map on p282*

MESHCHANSKY & BASMANNY

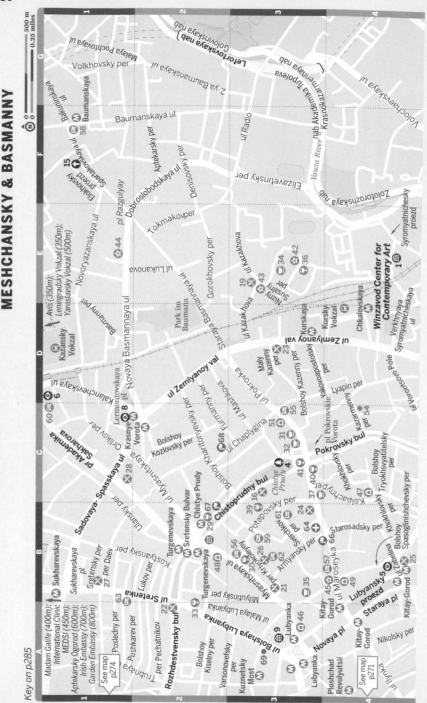

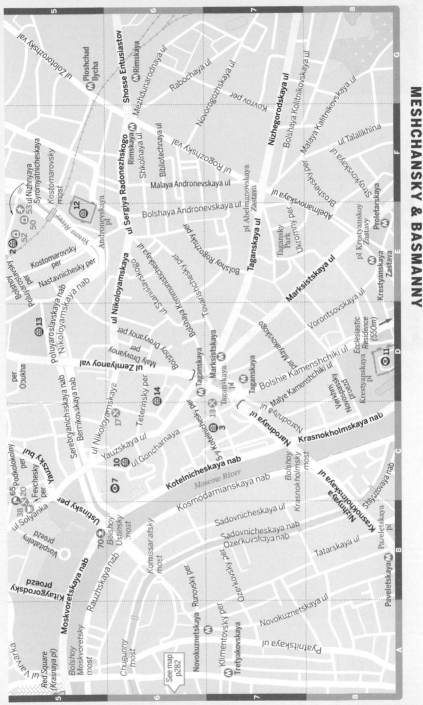

M Ploshchad Ilycha
ul Zolotorozhsky val
M Shosse Entusiastov
Shosse Entusiastov
M Rimskaya
Mezhdunarodnaya ul
Rabochaya ul
Novorogozhskaya ul
Kovrov per

Nizhegorodskaya ul
Bolshaya Kalitnikovskaya ul
Malaya Kalitnikovskaya ul
ul Talalikhina
Stroykovskaya ul
Proletarskaya
Bratievskaya per

Rimskaya M
Shkolnaya ul
ul Rogozhsky val
Bibliotechnaya ul
Malaya Andronevskaya ul
Bolshaya Andronevskaya ul
ul Sergiya Radonezhskogo

Andronevskaya pl
12

Syromyatnichesky
Kostomarovsky most
ul Nizhnyaya
53
50
52
2
Yauza River

Kostomarovsky per
Nastavnichesky per
Bolshoy Poluyaroslavsky per
poluyaroslavskaya nab

pl Abelmanovskaya
Zastava
Taganskaya ul
Taganskaya
Park
Ukromny per
Abelmanovskaya ul

Taganskaya ul
Marksistskaya ul
pl Krestyanskaya
Zastava
M Krestyanskaya
Zastava

13
ul Nikoloyamskaya
Bolshaya Kommunisticheskaya ul
ul Stanislavskogo
Bolshoy Rogozhsky per
Tatarschtchesky per

Vorontsovskaya ul
per Mayakovskogo
Ecclesiastic
Residence
(550m)

ul Zemlyanoy val
Maly Drovyanoy
per
Bolshoy Drovyanoy per
M Taganskaya
Marksistskaya
pl Taganskaya

Marksistskaya M
Taganskaya
M Taganskaya
Bolshie Kamenshchiki ul
Malye Kamenshchiki ul
Krestyanskaya
pl
Novospassky
proezd
ul Vlakhm
Novospassky
11
D

per
Oukha
Serebryanicheskaya nab
Bernikovskaya nab
ul Nikoloyamskaya
Teterinsky per
14
17
13
3
Narodnaya ul
Krasnokholmskaya nab

Yauzskaya ul
ul Goncharnaya
10
Kotelnicheskaya nab
Moscow River

Nizhnyaya
Krasnokholmskaya ul
Shlyuzovaya nab
Krasnokholmskaya nab
Paveletskaya
pl
M Paveletskaya
B

7
Kosmodamianskaya nab
Bolshoy
Krasnokholmsky
most

65
20
38
ul Solyanka
Fevchesky
per
Vospitatelny
proezd
Yauzsky bul
Podkolokolny
per
Ustinsky per

70
Bolshoy
Ustinsky
most
Komissarratsky
most
Sadovnicheskaya ul
Sadovnicheskaya nab
Ozerkovskaya nab
Tatarskaya ul

Kitaygorodsky
proezd
Moskvoretskaya nab
Rauzhskaya nab
Chugunny
most
Runovsky per
Ozerkovsky per

M Novokuznetskaya
Novokuznetskaya
Klimentovsky per
Novokuznetskaya ul
Pyatnitskaya ul

ul Varvarka
Red Square
(Krasnaya pl)
Bolshoy
Moskvoretsky
most

See map
p282

M Tretyakovskaya

Our Story

A beat-up old car, a few dollars in the pocket and a sense of adventure. In 1972 that's all Tony and Maureen Wheeler needed for the trip of a lifetime – across Europe and Asia overland to Australia. It took several months, and at the end – broke but inspired – they sat at their kitchen table writing and stapling together their first travel guide, *Across Asia on the Cheap*. Within a week they'd sold 1500 copies. Lonely Planet was born.

Today, Lonely Planet has offices in Franklin, London, Melbourne, Oakland, Dublin, Beijing and Delhi, with more than 600 staff and writers. We share Tony's belief that 'a great guidebook should do three things: inform, educate and amuse'.

Our Writers

Mara Vorhees

Kremlin & Kitay Gorod, Arbat & Khamovniki, Presnya, Day Trips

Mara has been travelling to Moscow since it was the capital of a different country, and the ambition and dynamism of this city never ceases to surprise her. The pen-wielding traveller has contributed to dozens of Lonely Planet titles, including *Russia* and *Trans-Siberian Railway*. Her stories have appeared in *Delta Sky*, *BBC Travel*, *Vancouver Sun* and *Boston Globe*, among others. Nowadays, she often travels with her seven-year-old twins (who are crazy about Kuklachev's cats). Follow their adventures at www.havetwinswilltravel.com. Mara also wrote the Plan, Understand & Survive sections of the guide.

Leonid Ragozin

Tverskoy, Zamoskvorechie, Meshchansky & Basmanny

Leonid studied beach dynamics at the Moscow State University, but for want of decent beaches in Russia, he switched to journalism and spent 12 years voyaging through different parts of the BBC, with a break for a four-year stint as a foreign correspondent for the *Russian Newsweek*. Leonid is currently a freelance journalist focusing largely on the conflict between Russia and Ukraine (both his Lonely Planet destinations), which prompted him to leave Moscow and find a new home in Rīga.

Published by Lonely Planet Global Limited
CRN 554153
7th edition – March 2018
ISBN 978 1 78657 366 7
© Lonely Planet 2018   Photographs © as indicated 2018
10 9 8 7 6 5 4 3 2 1
Printed in China

Although the authors and Lonely Planet have taken all reasonable care in preparing this book, we make no warranty about the accuracy or completeness of its content and, to the maximum extent permitted, disclaim all liability arising from its use.